Veröffentlichungen des
Instituts für Europäische Geschichte Mainz

Abteilung für Abendländische Religionsgeschichte
Herausgegeben von Irene Dingel

Band 269

A Forceful and Fruitful Verse

Genesis 1:28 in Luther's Thought and its Place
in the Wittenberg Reformation (1521–1531)

by
Brandt C. Klawitter

Vandenhoeck & Ruprecht

This publication was printed with support of MF – Norwegian School of Theology, Religion and Society and
The Leibniz Open Access Monograph Publishing Fund.

Bibliographic information published by the Deutsche Nationalbibliothek:
The Deutsche Nationalbibliothek lists this publication
in the Deutsche Nationalbibliografie;
detailed bibliographic data available online: https://dnb.de.

© 2023 by Vandenhoeck & Ruprecht, Robert-Bosch-Breite 10, 37079 Göttingen, Germany,
an imprint of the Brill-Group
(Koninklijke Brill NV, Leiden, The Netherlands; Brill USA Inc., Boston MA, USA;
Brill Asia Pte Ltd, Singapore; Brill Deutschland GmbH, Paderborn, Germany;
Brill Österreich GmbH, Vienna, Austria)
Koninklijke Brill NV incorporates the imprints Brill, Brill Nijhoff, Brill Hotei,
Brill Schöningh, Brill Fink, Brill mentis, Vandenhoeck & Ruprecht,
Böhlau, V&R unipress Wageningen Academic.

This publication is licensed under a Creative Commons Attribution – Non Commercial –
No Derivatives 4.0 International license, at https://doi.org/10.13109/9783666573507.
For a copy of this license go to https://creativecommons.org/licenses/by-nc-nd/4.0/.
Any use in cases other than those permitted by this license requires the
prior written permission from the publisher.

Cover image: Cover page of Thomas Stör's, Der Ehelich standt (Erfurt: Wolfgang Stürmer, 1524), depicts Christ joining the first man and woman in marriage. The caption reads, »Genesis 1 & 9. Be fruitful and multiply and fill the earth«. Image source: Herzog August Bibliothek Wolfenbüttel: Yv 2395.8° Helmst.

Cover design: SchwabScantechnik, Göttingen
Typesetting: le-tex publishing services, Leipzig
Printed and bound: CPI books GmbH, Birkstraße 10, D-25917 Leck
Printed in the EU.

Vandenhoeck & Ruprecht Verlage | www.vandenhoeck-ruprecht-verlage.com

ISSN: 0537-7919 (print)
ISSN: 2197-1048 (digital)

ISBN: 978-3-525-57350-1 (print)
ISBN: 978-3-666-57350-7 (digital)

Verbum »crescite« expugnat, schlehet darnider als ein donnerschlag
omnes traditiones humanas et doctrinas demoniorum.

*The word »Be fruitful« conquers and strikes down as a thunderclap
all human traditions and demonic doctrines.*

—Martin Luther

Gott vnser vater vnd vnser herre Jesus Christus,
durch die genad des heyligen Geysts,
sey mit euch, macht euch fruchtbar, auff das yhr die welt meret. Amen.

*God our Father and our Lord Jesus Christ,
through the grace of the Holy Ghost,
be with you [and] make you fruitful, so that you multiply the world. Amen.*

—Benediction from *Johannes Bugenhagen's wedding liturgy*

Contents

Preface 9

Acknowledgements 11

1. Introducing a Verse 13
   1.1 Topic, Research Question, and Literature Review 13
   1.2 Project Overview, Methodology, and Limitations 27
   1.3 Further Theoretical Considerations and Project Notes 29

2. Background: Tension, Ambiguity, and Discussion
   Surrounding a Verse.. 33
   2.1 The Historical Tension between Genesis 1:28 and Celibacy
       in the Church 34
   2.2 Liturgical Use of Genesis 1:28 41
   2.3 Natural Law, Nature, Human Will, and Reason 46
   2.4 Teleology and Anatomy in the Natural Philosophy Tradition 67

3. The Emergence of a Verse 79
   3.1 Background to the Controversy (1518–1521) 79
   3.2 New Developments in Wittenberg during Luther's Time at
       the Wartburg 94
   3.3 Developments at the Wartburg... 103
   3.4 The Appearance of Genesis 1:28 112
   3.5 Melanchthon, *affectus naturales*, and Genesis 1:28 122

4. Contesting a Verse: The Debate Surrounding Genesis 1:28
   (1522–1524) 129
   4.1 Abiding Command or No Longer in Force? (1522–1524) 129
   4.2 Luther's Thought on Genesis 1:28 as Presented in
       Vom ehelichen Leben 130
   4.3 Initial Opposition 138
   4.4 Martin Luther and the Wittenberg Defense 144
   4.5 Further Opposition to Luther 170
   4.6 Traces of Melanchthon's *Affektenlehre* in the Writings of
       Luther and His Wittenberg Colleagues on Genesis 1:28 (1522–1524) .. 173
   4.7 Excursus: Controversy in Erfurt Surrounding Genesis 1:28............... 178

5. Confessing and Conforming to a Verse – The Ongoing
   Influence of Genesis 1:28 199
   5.1 Genesis 1:28 and Wittenberg Theology 199
   5.2 The *Confessio Augustana*, the *Confutatio*, and the *Apologia* 216
   5.3 Melanchthon and the Debut of στοργαὶ φυσικαί............................. 229

6. The Future of a Verse and Concluding Thoughts 235
   6.1 A Glance Ahead: The Prowess and Limitations of a Verse 235
   6.2 Concluding Summary... 245

Appendix 251
   1. *Apologia Confessionis Augustanae* Art. 23 Comparison Table 251
   2. Works Cited 253
   3. Abbreviations 276
   4. Glossary 277
   5. Index... 278

Preface

At first glance, it may seem strange to dedicate an entire study to the role of one particular verse in the Wittenberg Reformation – a verse, suffice it to say, which is only indirectly connected to such central Reformation themes as grace, Scripture, and faith. And, while the topic of this study is not as far removed from these subjects as one might initially imagine, there is perhaps a need to explain how this study's theme was arrived upon.

The journey to this verse began with a very different question. About a decade ago, the question emerged in my mind regarding how it was that the Reformers – and Luther especially – could frown so deeply on Onan's deed (Genesis 38:8–10)? The brief writings dealing with this question had something of a self-evident nature to them – a nature which failed to explain and satisfy the contemporary mind, my own included. Yet, rather than simply decide that such statements were somehow out of touch with more central Reformation teachings, I began to wonder whether there was perhaps a world – and a worldview – which was no longer easily accessible and, for that reason, not entirely comprehensible? Thus, the idea of undertaking a reconstruction of such a worldview involving Reformation ideas about the body, sexuality, marriage, and creation began to emerge in my mind. Was it possible to put such strong statements into a frame that would somehow makes sense?

The path led down many roads – and dead ends. Questions and unsatisfying answers revealed new horizons. What about Luther and contraception? Luther and natural law (admittedly, my first foray into that topic proved futile!)? Luther and sexuality? Off weekends spent biking down to the library at Tübingen (I was stationed in Stuttgart at the time) began to lead to further sources. Yet, none of these questions – or at least my tentative answers to them – helped me to understand the worldview that I felt must exist somewhere.

It was first in reading through *Luther's Works* in the early mornings during that same period that an initial lead presented itself. In arriving at Luther's *Lectures on Genesis*, my focus began to shift to something more positive. What about Luther and procreation? A second journey through those volumes resulted in a hundred pages of typed notes. Material abounded. It was there, I thought, that I would find my answer. With the assistance of Prof. Otfried Czaika, my eventual doctoral supervisor, the contours of a PhD proposal began to take form and I was introduced to the world of Reformation scholarship. By 2016, an actual project had been approved and, now in Oslo in the doctoral program of MF – Norwegian School of Theology, I was working to systematize and contextualize the mass of material I had put together.

Things began to grind to a halt, however, as I tried to define »procreation« in Luther's thought. It seemed to be sex. It seemed to be bearing children. It seemed to be quite a bit. Even more, why was Luther even talking about this topic, even inordinately? What could possibly explain and define all of this?

Several things happened in the summer following my first year of research, however. In perusing the stacks at MF, I happened across Jeremy Cohen's book, *Be Fertile and Increase, Fill the Earth and Master It*. There was a historic tension with this verse, it turned out. Had something happened during the early years of the Reformation? It must have. Christian Witt's *Martin Luthers Reformation der Ehe* was also recommended to me around that same time. His emphasis on Genesis 1:28 seemed to fit with the very rough outlines of a picture which was beginning to form and was begging to be investigated. Then, during a wonderful research stay in Wolfenbüttel, as I began to piece together the what?, when?, and why? of Luther's initial employment of Genesis 1:28 (at least in a more recognizable Reformation form), Melanchthon's own simultaneous wrestling with natural law in the early 1520s began to play with my mind – simply because the phrase *naturales quosdam affectus* somehow defied straight-forward translation.

While the puzzle pieces did not fall together overnight, the conclusion that *Be fruitful and multiply* was, in some way, the definition and story of procreation in Luther's (and Wittenberg) thought, began to dawn on me. And, as much as I wanted to write more about Luther's *Lectures on Genesis*, it slowly occurred to me that there was a different, perhaps more fundamental, story which was really asking to be told. It was a story larger than Luther himself. It was natural law, though generally not under that title. It was the power of God's creative word. It was – and is – a cornerstone for a worldview and understanding of man's sexual nature which remains largely foreign to anything seen in our contemporary western world. Perhaps for that reason alone, if for no other, the story of this verse during the first full decade of the Reformation now asks to be told, this even as it is, indeed, now my privilege to attempt to retell it.

November 2021,
at the 500th anniversary of Luther's writing of *De votis monasticis*

Brandt Klawitter

Acknowledgements

It is only with a great measure of appreciation that I can look back on the past decade or so of inquiry, research, and writing. Thus, in the following paragraphs, I wish to acknowledge some of the many debts of gratitude which I have incurred along the journey.

To begin with, in grateful memory, I would like to acknowledge Pastor Herman Otten, not only for sparking my interest in this topic, but also for continual friendship and support throughout the years. Many thanks also to Prof. Robert Kolb for his friendly advice and encouragement, whether in spurring me to further research during my initial student days in St. Louis or since becoming reacquainted during research in Wolfenbüttel.

A particularly great debt of gratitude is owed to Prof. Otfried Czaika, without whose immediate and continual interest and enthusiasm for my topic, not to mention unwavering support throughout my doctoral work at MF, it is unlikely that I would have dared to undertake this project. Also, for sage advice and encouragement – especially at those times when the project seemed to resist all attempts at taming – I am most grateful. Many thanks are also due to Dr. Joar Haga and Prof. em. Oddvar Johan Jensen, both of whom provided me with encouragement, constructive criticism, and valuable suggestions throughout the PhD process. I have furthermore benefited from the learning and academic exchanges that took place at MF in both classes and conversations, through the ATTR research group, and more recently, to colleagues at NLA University College in Bergen.

In addition to the above-named, two institutions have provided me with superb research opportunities and academic exchanges, proving themselves vital for the progression of my research. Thus, I would like to offer thanks to the Herzog August Bibliothek in Wolfenbüttel (with its Rolf und Ursula Schneider-Stiftung) for its support and the use of its splendid library as well as to the Leibniz-Institut für Europäische Geschichte (IEG) in Mainz for support, warm collegiality, and a most delightful research stay.

This project has furthermore benefited through encouragement and constructive feedback from many others. Thus, many thanks to those who served as opponents at my defense, Prof. Dr. Irene Dingel, Prof. Sivert Angel, and Dr. Eivor Oftestad. My appreciation also to Profs. Thomas Kaufmann and Günter Frank, both of whom were kind enough to make time to hear my ideas and discuss specific sections of my work, and also to PD Dr. Christian Witt for his encouragement and for our many friendly exchanges regarding my project. Additionally, thanks to Mr. Matthew

Carver for suggestions in improving my Latin translations and Mrs. Pamela Woolery for her proofreading assistance.

In connection with publication, gratitude is, once again, owed to Prof. Dr. Irene Dingel for accepting my study for publication in the VIEG series as well as MF (and its rector, Prof. Vidar Haanes) for so willingly assisting with the financing of my dissertation's publication.

Finally, and here words are truly inadequate, this project would not have been possible without the lifelong support of my parents, the frequent assistance of my in-laws, and – most especially – my wife, Anna, for her great sacrifices of time and energy, her encouragement, love, and support. Finally, to my children, for the blessings that you are and the patience and love you have for me, you especially have given meaning to this work.

1. Introducing a Verse

וַיְבָ֣רֶךְ אֹתָם֮ אֱלֹהִים֒ וַיֹּ֨אמֶר לָהֶ֜ם
אֱלֹהִ֗ים פְּר֥וּ וּרְב֛וּ וּמִלְא֥וּ אֶת־הָאָ֖רֶץ

—Genesis 1:28a (*BHS*)

Then God blessed them, and God said to them,
»Be fruitful and multiply; fill the earth [...]«.

—Genesis 1:28a (*NKJV*)

1.1 Topic, Research Question, and Literature Review

In a relatively recent monograph dealing with Luther's teaching about marriage, Christian Witt makes the remarkable statement that the words of Genesis 1:28 (i. e. »Be fruitful and multiply and fill the earth«) play a role in Luther's understanding of marriage that is difficult to overestimate[1]. On the other hand, Jennifer Hockenbery Dragseth, in a similarly recent article dealing with the body, desire, and *sexuality*[2] in Martin Luther's thought, barely mentions procreation as relating to these topics and does not once refer to Luther's usage of Genesis 1:28[3]. The polarity and tension between these two presentations of Luther's thought on marriage and

---

1 Commenting on Luther's *Vom ehelichen Leben*, Christian Volkmar WITT, Martin Luthers Reformation der Ehe, Tübingen 2017, p. 15, makes the sweeping statement, »Die Worte Gen 1,28 [...] spielen für seine Ehevorstellung eine schwerlich zu überschätzende Rolle«.
2 This term, on account of its varied use and meaning, will be employed throughout this study with reference to sexual propensity, nature, and disposition (and such things as relate to these), as opposed to a referent for male/female distinctness. Similarly, when referring to the conjugal act, the designation »sex« will be employed, so as not to be confused with male/female sexual differentiation, or *sex* (without quotation marks).
3 Jennifer Hockenbery DRAGSETH, Martin Luther's Views on the Body, Desire, and Sexuality, in: Oxford Research Encyclopedia of Religion (2016), URL: <https://doi.org/10.1093/acrefore/9780199340378.013.354> (18 Aug 2022).

sexuality raise an interesting question: What role and significance did Genesis 1:28 have for Luther's thought and more generally in the Wittenberg Reformation[4]?

Sharpening our focus somewhat on this topic, we do well to try to ascertain the current state of the question. Here, while Reformation and Luther literature is comprised of an ever-increasing expanse of material, we note that the general area of our research has received only limited attention. On the closely-related topic of reproduction, John McKeown, with his own anti-natalist interests, aptly observes, »Little research has been done on Luther's writings with regard to the theme of human reproduction, let alone natalism in particular«[5]. This observation naturally holds true with respect to our verse as well. In fact, of direct relevance to our own study, one finds only two works with a direct focus on Genesis 1:28 which also touch on the Reformation: David Anthony Yegerlehner's dissertation[6] and Jeremy Cohen's Be Fertile and Increase, Fill the Earth and Master It. The Ancient and Medieval Career of a Biblical Text[7]. With respect to the former, we note that Yegerlehner's

---

4 Here we must briefly note that this study's usage of the term »Reformation«, unless otherwise specified or made clear through context, will be in reference to the Wittenberg Reformation and the theological thought that emanated from that movement. It will, however, at times also preserve its broader conceptual applications with reference to the momentous and wide-spread religious movements of Europe which took place during the first half of the sixteenth century, of which the Wittenberg Reformation was one important manifestation. Along the same lines, it should be noted that this study's usage of the term »Lutheran« will be used *either* to reflect the polemical, heretical designation attempted by the opponents of the early evangelicals of the Wittenberg Reformation, *or*, when not in quotations, in connection with the churches and confession that grew out of the latter half of the sixteenth century. Where it is employed in footnotes, it will occasionally reflect an author's usage of that designation. Otherwise, with respect to the period of this study, the more era-appropriate designations »evangelicals, evangelical, etc.« will be employed. Finally, we might also note that the term »Catholic«, though used somewhat sparingly in this study, is used to refer to the Roman Church prior to Trent and not in reference to the modern instantiation of the same. See Irene DINGEL, Confessional Transformations from the Wittenberg Reformation to Lutheranism, in: Lutheran Quarterly 33, 1 (2019), pp. 1–3; Heinrich HEPPE, Ursprung und Geschichte der Bezeichnungen »reformirte« und »lutherische« Kirche, Gotha 1859, pp. 1–11.

5 John McKEOWN, God's Babies. Natalism and Bible Interpretation in Modern America, Cambridge 2014, p. 81. It should not be overlooked that there is some amount of irony in this fact given that it is not from theological circles, nor in any way out of sympathy for Luther's views, that his observation arises. Merry E. WIESNER-HANKS, Christianity and Sexuality in the Early Modern World. Regulating Desire, Reforming Practice, New York 2000, p. 96, also notes this seeming absence of attention to »Luther's ideas about women, gender, or sexuality« in the English language.

6 David Anthony YEGERLEHNER, »Be Fruitful and Multiply, and Fill the Earth […]«. A History of the Interpretation of Genesis 1:28a and Related Texts in Selected Periods, Boston University Graduate School 1975.

7 Jeremy COHEN, Be Fertile and Increase, Fill the Earth and Master It. The Ancient and Medieval Career of a Biblical Text, Ithaca 1989.

doctoral thesis, written out of concern for the population debate of his era, undertakes a study of the history of Genesis 1:28a. It thus provides a historic overview of the interpretation of this verse throughout the church's history, to include a cursory treatment of the place of this verse in Luther's thought. Unfortunately, this cursory treatment of Luther's thought in connection with Genesis 1:28 deals solely with his *Lectures on Genesis* (1535–1545) and otherwise entirely ignores the use and significance of this text in the Reformation prior to these lectures[8]. Moreover, with respect to Yegerlehner's treatment of the relevant material, we note that it constitutes something of a surface-level discussion of the topic and, thus, leaves a great many stones untouched and unturned. With respect to the latter, Cohen's study takes the topic and basic contours of Yegerlehner's dissertation and provides a much more thorough – though not exhaustive – thematic treatment. Nevertheless, Cohen concludes the main portion of his study just prior to the Reformation, though pointing forward to the important role of Genesis 1:28 in the Reformation[9]. In this way, Cohen provides an exceedingly important introduction to the historic place of Genesis 1:28 and the ways in which it has been understood over time – to include the controversy and historic ambiguity surrounding this verse's interpretation.

Beyond these two directly related works, we quickly slip out into a number of other subject areas that are somewhat less directly related to our verse, the main categories dealing with the strife surrounding vows of celibacy, the marriage of priests, and early Wittenberg-related teaching on marriage, respectively. Further related topics include discussions of gender, sex, and sexuality. With respect to these primary categories, though, we already glean an indication of our verse's role and function during the Reformation, both as to its polemical use as well as its more constructive use. Nevertheless, as previously noted and as will be observed in the review that follows, no thoroughgoing consensus is found in the literature as to the importance or even the presence of this verse.

Taking a brief look at literature related to the debate surrounding monastic vows and priestly marriage, we may pose the question: what was the place and significance of Genesis 1:28 in that discussion? Beginning chronologically, we turn to Josef Sjöholm's *Luthers Åskådning i Kampen mot Klosterlifvet*[10]. In documenting the timeline and developments in Luther's struggle with monasticism, he notes – though without elaboration – the presence of Genesis 1:28 in *De votis monasticis iudicium* in the late fall of 1521[11]. Shortly thereafter, we arrive at Siegmund Baranowksi's *Luthers Lehre von der Ehe*[12]. Baranowski also notes the presence of our verse at

---

8 YEGERLEHNER, »Be Fruitful«, pp. 160–172.
9 COHEN, Be Fertile, pp. 307f.
10 Josef SJÖHOLM, Luthers Åskådning i Kampen mot Klosterlifvet, Lund 1908 (reprinted 2012).
11 Ibid., p. 130.
12 Siegmund BARANOWSKI, Luthers Lehre von der Ehe, Münster 1913.

this same juncture of the Reformation[13]. Nevertheless, he somewhat downplays its importance in deference to Luther's other concerns regarding human weakness. Already here, therefore, we have the question of the relationship between our verse and the question of human sexuality and desire.

A further survey of the literature, however, expands upon these basic findings. Stephen Buckwalter, for instance, notes the presence of our verse in this discussion, also granting it a powerful influence in Luther's thought at this juncture[14]. Namely, he points out that »Be fruitful and multiply« was, for Luther, »a divine directive (*Bestimmung*) of nature« which man might only struggle against with futility[15]. Bernd Moeller's *Wenzel Lincks Hochzeit* similarly implies the significance of Genesis 1:28 as one of the more powerful arguments Luther brought forward in *De votis monasticis* as Luther argued that monastic celibacy militated against the »command of the Creator«[16]. Christian Witt and August Franzen, respectively, also briefly comment upon the place of Genesis 1:28 in Luther's *De votis monasticis*[17]. Otherwise, Sammeli Juntunen's *Sex, Engaging Luther*, though not directly referring to our verse, makes an interesting – and relevant – observation about the role of »nature« in the developments during the autumn of 1521[18]. Similarly, Robert Grimm's *Luther et l'experience sexuelle* convincingly points to Luther's concern for the power of the human sex drive in *De votis monasticis*, yet without specific reference to Luther's deployment of Genesis 1:28 in that particular writing[19]. McKeown also notes the presence of our verse in the same writing, but his concern is primarily the question whether Luther is to be taken seriously regarding the notion that Genesis 1:28 represents a law of nature[20].

It should also be noted, on the other hand, that several significant works on this topic neither mention nor lend any significance to our verse at this juncture.

---

13 Ibid., p. 51.
14 Stephen E. Buckwalter, Die Priesterehe in Flugschriften der frühen Reformation. Quellen und Forschungen zur Reformationsgeschichte, Gütersloh 1998.
15 Ibid., p. 105.
16 Bernd Moeller, Wenzel Lincks Hochzeit. Über Sexualität, Keuschheit und Ehe in der frühen Reformation, in: Zeitschrift für Theologie und Kirche 97, 3 (2000), pp. 317–342, at p. 323, URL: <http://www.jstor.org/stable/23585758> (23 Aug 2022).
17 Witt, Reformation der Ehe, p. 204; August Franzen, Zölibat und Priesterehe in der Auseinandersetzung der Reformationszeit und der katholischen Reform des 16. Jahrhunders, Münster 1971, p. 28.
18 Sammeli Juntunen, Sex, in: Olli-Pekka Vainio (ed.), Engaging Luther. A New Theological Assessment, Eugene, OR 2010, pp. 193f., URL: <https://books.google.no/books?id=H4BJAwAAQBAJ> (19 July 2019).
19 Robert Grimm, Luther et l'experience sexuelle. Sexe, célibat, mariage chez le réformateur, Genève 1999, esp. pp. 133–165.
20 McKeown, God's Babies, p. 91.

Here we can include writings from Berhard Lohse, Otto Scheel, and, more recently, Andreas Stegmann[21].

In light of the above, while we do gain an appreciation for the fact that our verse was at least involved – somehow – in Luther's theological development and argumentation in the fall of 1521, we do not find any clarity as to its exact role and significance. Nevertheless, the connection between our verse, sexuality with its corresponding drives, and God's creative ordinance and working (perhaps including natural law) do clearly come into our purview.

We now come to the pertinent literature on Luther and the interwoven topics of marriage, sexuality, and sex/gender. Given that the literary field on these topics is expansive, it is not feasible to include an exhaustive overview of all possible literature on these topics. Nevertheless, the following overview – greatly benefiting from the helpful bibliographic compilation provided by Andreas Stegmann's *Bibliographie zur Ethik Martin Luthers*[22], it should be noted – should serve to provide reasonably solid orientation. We should, however, note that this literature review attempts to limit its focus to Luther's earlier thought on marriage (app. 1520–1530) and, for the most part, bypasses treatments of Luther's own marriage and his later thought and works. It also takes into account, though to a lesser degree, works dealing with Luther's (and Reformation) understandings of the body and sexuality.

Turning to the literature, we can begin by observing that a sampling of more classic studies on these topics offers a relatively unified picture. Werner Elert's *Morphologie des Luthertums*, for example, strongly emphasizes the purpose-oriented nature of Lutheran marriage in the first two centuries of Lutheranism with Lutheran teaching on the *Fortpflanzungszweck* remaining undeniably central in his presentation[23]. Julius Boehmer's *Luthers Ehebuch*, though primarily a compendium of Luther citations, also offers the reader a glimpse into the centrality of procreation (and Genesis 1:28) for Luther's overall thinking about marriage[24]. A similarly strong emphasis can be found in Paul Althaus's *Luthers Wort von der Ehe*, where, among other insights, he provides an important introduction to the creational foundations of marriage (including Luther's emphasis upon Genesis 1:28) and such drives as

---

21 See Bernhard LOHSE, Mönchtum und Reformation, Göttingen 1963; id., Luthers Kritik am Mönchtum, in: Evang. Theol. 20 (1960), pp. 413–432; Otto SCHEEL (ed.), Luthers Werke, Ergänzungsbände, Berlin 1905, vol. 1, pp. 201–207; Andreas STEGMANN, Luthers Auffassung vom christlichen Leben. Beiträge zur historischen Theologie, Tübingen 2014, pp. 360–396.

22 The following review of literature owes a great deal to the helpful bibliographic compilation provided by Andreas STEGMANN, Bibliographie zur Ethik Martin Luthers, in: Lutherjahrbuch 79 (2012), pp. 305–342.

23 Werner ELERT, Morphologie des Luthertums, München 1932, vol. 2, pp. 80–91, 109–114.

24 Julius BOEHMER, Luthers Ehebuch. Was Martin Luther Ehelosen, Eheleuten und Eltern zu sagen hat, Zwickau 1935.

serve its ends, in addition to briefly noting the centrality of procreation for Luther's thought[25]. Reinhold Seeberg's article, *Luthers Anschauung von dem Geschlechtsleben und der Ehe und ihre geschichtliche Stellung*, paints a similar picture[26]. Here, in a classic treatment on Luther's understanding of marriage and marital life, Seeberg outlines the contours and context of Luther's thought on these topics, giving particular attention to Luther's own emphasis on the natural elements of marriage, not the least of which is his emphasis upon the fearful power of man's natural drive. Seeberg's article thus leaves little doubt either as to the powerful force of human sexuality or as to its procreation-directed aims in Luther's thought. Oddly, perhaps, although Luther's thought on Genesis 1:28 is unquestionably the basis for much of Seeberg's work, an explicit connection between the biblical text and Luther's related thought is reserved only for the endnotes. The aforementioned notwithstanding, the impression given by older scholarship offers a relatively unified picture, even if and even though no comprehensive treatment of our topic is readily available.

Taking our survey somewhat further, however, one begins to note – in some instances, at least – something of a divergence in research interests and emphasis. In this sense, some of the research remains in line with the general contours noted above while other scholarship verges in somewhat different directions, sometimes to the neglect of our topic and verse. For example, Olavi Lähteenmäki's classic treatment of Luther's thinking in these areas, *Sexus und Ehe bei Luther*, has surprisingly little to say about procreation and Genesis 1:28[27]. Somewhat remarkably, what he does have to say about these topics is largely, though not completely, reserved for the very end of his book[28]. Otherwise, Lähteenmäki treats the human *Geschlechtstrieb* and sexuality as entities and goods, in and of themselves, and nearly entirely without connection to their procreation-related institution and purpose as understood by Luther in Genesis 1:28[29]. Thus, Lähteenmäki's depiction of marriage for Luther seems to be weighted disproportionately toward 1 Corinthians and the antidotal purpose of marriage.

Ernst Kinder's *Luthers Auffassung von der Ehe*, however, appears more along classic lines, painting Luther's teaching on marriage in several swift strokes, though without neglecting to emphasize the creational aspects of the reformer's teaching[30]. In a noteworthy observation, he comments that Luther's apparent disinterest for

---

25 Paul Althaus, Luthers Wort von der Ehe, in: Luther 24 (1953), pp. 1–10.
26 Reinhold Seeberg, Luthers Anschauung von dem Geschlechtsleben und der Ehe und ihre geschichtliche Stellung, in: Lutherjahrbuch 7 (1925), pp. 77–122.
27 Olavi Lähteenmäki, Sexus und Ehe bei Luther, Turku 1955.
28 Ibid., pp. 159f., though see also pp. 49f.
29 See, for example, ibid., pp. 32, 57–61, 66f.
30 Ernst Kinder, Luthers Auffassung von der Ehe, in: Ernst Sommerlath/Ernst-Heinz Amberg (eds.), Bekenntnis zur Kirche. Festgabe für Ernst Sommerlath, Berlin 1960, pp. 325–334.

Ephesians 5 in preference for Genesis 1, Matthew 19, and 1 Corinthians 7 was on account of its connection with the Roman sacramental view of marriage. Nevertheless, the importance of Genesis 1:28 for Luther is certainly noted by Kinder[31].

Klaus Suppan's *Die Ehelehre Martin Luthers,* perhaps on account of the author's own legal perspective and Catholic background, makes his own interesting and significant contributions to our understanding of Luther's thought on marriage[32]. First, he notes that one of the decisive shifts in Luther's thought was his rejection of canon law's prescriptions concerning marriage by which he simultaneously removed marriage from the *Erlösungsordnung* and placed it entirely within the *Schöpfungsordnung*[33]. According to Suppan, Luther's understanding of marriage is thus entirely grounded in the creational accounts of Genesis 1–2. Furthermore, Suppan rightly notes that this institution is decisive for Luther's thinking and thus the New Testament has nothing of substance to add or alter for such an established order of creation[34]. While Suppan does not deal to any great extent with a detailed history of Genesis 1:28 in his account, his insistence that the creational aspects of Luther's teaching on marriage are the constitutive element is a point that will be reflected in our own study.

Hans Hattenhauer's study, *Luthers Bedeutung für die Ehe und Familie,* is somewhat noteworthy for its general disinterest in our verse[35]. While he does note Luther's concern for the burning of the flesh and its fulfillment of procreative purposes[36], Hattenhauer otherwise takes little note of our study's overall theme and makes no explicit mention of Genesis 1:28.

Georg Kretschmar's, *Luthers Konzeption von der Ehe* finds itself squarely in the norms of Luther research with respect to the interests of this study[37]. Kretschmar, whose central interest is to discover and trace the basis for Luther's thinking regarding marital love, does not neglect to point out the creational institution of marriage and the importance of Genesis 1:28 for Luther.

---

31 Ibid., pp. 326, 328.
32 Klaus Suppan, Die Ehelehre Martin Luthers. Theologische und rechtshistorische Aspekte des reformatorischen Eheverständnisses, Salzburg 1971.
33 Ibid., pp. 20f.
34 Ibid., p. 22.
35 Hans Hattenhauer, Luthers Bedeutung für die Ehe und Familie, in: Hartmut Löwe/Claus-Jürgen Roepfe (eds.), Luther und die Folgen. Beiträge zur sozial-geschichtlichen Bedeutung der lutherischen Reformation, München 1983, pp. 86–109.
36 Ibid., p. 89.
37 Georg Kretschmar, Luthers Konzeption von der Ehe. Die Liebe im Spannungsfeld von Eros und Agape, in: Peter Manns (ed.), Martin Luther »Reformator und Vater im Glauben«, Stuttgart 1985, pp. 178–207.

Joel Harrington's, *Reordering Marriage and Society in Reformation Germany* is both informative in its contribution as well as somewhat remarkable in its silence[38]. In dealing with Luther, Harrington rightly notes the centrality of the sexual urge and its normative nature in Luther's marital thought, also making the important observation that this urge was simultaneously God-ordained and sinful. Yet, while Genesis 1:28 certainly lurks in the background here, its connection with this urge remains unstated.

Walter Tillmann's *Unkeuschheit und Werk der Liebe. Diskurse über Sexualität am Beginn der Neuzeit in Deutschland* is also noteworthy, both for its attention to Luther as well as its inattention to the role of Genesis 1:28 in the reformer's thought[39]. Briefly summarized, in this book Tillmann challenges Foucault's thesis regarding the novelty of the supposed nineteenth century deployment of discourse to create and assert power in the realm of sexuality. Tillmann notes, for example, that language for sexuality existed to a broader extent than Foucault acknowledged prior to this time[40]. In asserting this thesis, Tillmann notes the Protestant recognition of a certain goodness in sexuality. This development he attributes particularly to Luther but then further argues that Luther's tacit allowance opened the door (and indeed was itself open) to practically every possible expression and practice of sexuality, even while the Catholic antipode of the Middle Ages was viewed as having no positive understanding of sexuality whatsoever. With respect to Tillmann's understanding of Luther, it is worth noting that his work is confined largely, though not exclusively, to Luther's *Large Catechism*[41]. Furthermore, we note a couple of shortcomings in Tillmann's depiction of Luther's thought. First, his categorization of Luther's understanding of sexual sinfulness as merely pertaining to the *extra*- vs. *intra*-marital setting is rather shortsighted. Secondly, in Tillmann's effort to emphasize the goodness of sexuality in Luther's thought, the generalized category of »sex« proves prohibitive of discovering what, for Luther, is in fact positive about it. In this respect, while Tillmann does mention the procreative purpose of sexuality in Luther's thought, he fails to notice that, for Luther, it is the force of God's procreative word and command that is the operative power in sexuality (i. e. Genesis 1:28) – even as lust is ever and only a disordering of this original good word.

Appearing in the year after Tillmann's work, two further contributions also demonstrate what one might perhaps term a lack of interest and perhaps insight into the role of Genesis 1:28 in Luther's thought. Michael Beyer, in *Luthers Ehelehre*

---

38 Joel F. HARRINGTON, Reordering Marriage and Society in Reformation Germany, Cambridge et al. 1995, pp. 62–64, 67.
39 Walter TILLMANN, Unkeuschheit und Werk der Liebe. Diskurse über Sexualität am Beginn der Neuzeit in Deutschland, Berlin 1998.
40 Ibid., p. 149.
41 See ibid., especially pp. 102–127, 144–150.

bis 1525, for example, offers an examination of Luther's teaching on marriage up to 1525[42]. While Beyer certainly does make mention of Genesis 1:28 and the procreative purpose of marriage throughout the essay[43], it is somewhat odd that he seems to juxtapose Luther's repeated emphasis upon the connection of Genesis 1:28 and the effective word of God (largely overlooked in his essay) with the relatively seldom connection of this same word of God to Genesis 2[44]. Indeed, equally surprising is Beyer's summary statement, where he states that it is »not simple to discover developments in Luther's teaching on marriage in the period of time up to 1525«[45].

Robert Grimm's *Luther et l'experience sexuelle*, for its many positive contributions, also somewhat misses the normative functioning and role of Genesis 1:28, becoming mired down instead in the opaquer categories of sexuality and desire[46]. To be fair, Grimm's study offers one of the more thorough topical treatments on sexuality, celibacy, and marriage in Luther's life and teaching. Noteworthy is that Grimm – as we have also observed with other authors – rightly captures the power of sexuality and desire (i. e. »the imperialism of sex«, as Grimm calls it) in the reformer's thinking. Moreover, he correctly stresses, again and again, the creational foundation of marriage, its primary end of procreation, and thus also rightly notes the subsidiary – though not unimportant – place of affective love, sensuality, and other such matters for Luther. Nevertheless, while not failing to note the place of Genesis 1:28 in this schema, Grimm gives somewhat greater weight to Genesis 1:27 with its male/female references and seems to overlook the direct connection between the »imperialism of sex« and Luther's understanding of Genesis 1:28.

Venturing into the current millennium, Thomas Fudge's article, *Incest and Lust in Luther's Marriage* offers a look at Luther's marriage to Katherina von Bora, masterfully depicting the social and religious context of the time, and then also presents the astonishingly vitriolic responses of Luther's foes – most especially of Thomas

---

42 Michael BEYER, Luthers Ehelehre bis 1525, in: Martin TREU (ed.), Katharina von Bora. Die Lutherin. Aufsätze anlässlich ihres 500. Geburtstags, Wittenberg 1999, pp. 59–82.
43 See ibid., pp. 67–69 and endnotes.
44 Ibid., p. 72. Note that this connection of Genesis 2 with the creative and powerful word of God, so far as I can tell, is relatively rare in Luther's opus. Interestingly, such a correlation between Genesis 2 and the active power of God effecting marriage between man and woman is more commonly observed in the writings of other reformers, such as Simon Reuter, Heinrich Schratt, Jakob Strauss, and Paul Speratus. For this, see Brandt KLAWITTER, A Forceful and Fruitful Verse. Textual and Contextual Studies on Genesis 1:28 in Luther and the Wittenberg Reformation (1521–1531), Oslo 2019, pp. 178–182.
45 Cf. »nicht einfach, Entwicklungen in Luthers Ehelehre im Zeitraum bis 1525 zu entdecken«, BEYER, Luthers Ehelehre, p. 77.
46 GRIMM, Luther et l'experience sexuelle.

More in England[47]. While it is clear from Fudge's account that »Luther's lust« was a central concern in the polemical attacks of the era, what is perhaps not made entirely clear in this otherwise very informative article – though perhaps implied – is the connection of lust (i. e. sexual desire) with the words of Genesis 1:28[48].

Scott Hendrix's *Luther on Marriage* similarly leans slightly away from our verse[49]. Briefly summarized, Hendrix provides a general outline of primarily Luther's early teaching (pre-1525) on marriage as well as an overview of Luther as a married man. With respect to Luther's marital teachings, Hendrix especially emphasizes Luther's interpretation of 1 Corinthians 7[50]. As concerns Genesis 1:28, Hendrix mentions it as a foundational ordinance in Luther's understanding[51]. Noteworthy, however, is the fact that it receives no real further discussion beyond that. A second writing from Hendrix, *Masculinity and Patriarchy in Reformation Germany*, is also of relevance for our discussion[52]. Here, Hendrix outlines an overview of masculinity based on normative sources such as sermons and pamphlets produced by various early evangelical reformers, dealing with two topics he views to be central to the meaning of Reformation masculinity: namely, sexual vulnerability and sexual expression/restraint. Interestingly, in his accounting, these topics only implicitly relate to procreation. Given what will later be observed about the role of Genesis 1:28 in the writings of the reformers he observes[53], one cannot help but wonder if the category of »sexual expression« clouds a clearer understanding of what the various reformers were positively emphasizing and how this emphasis pertained to our verse.

Michael Parsons, in *Reformation Marriage*, places Luther's (and Calvin's) thought against the background of Augustine's understanding of marriage, the concept of *ordo*, and the place of sexuality and procreation within marriage[54]. Although Parsons's main interest in Luther's teaching on marriage relates to questions of hierarchy and mutual love, he nonetheless manages to rightly emphasize Luther's creational (and procreational) emphasis[55].

---

47 Thomas A. FUDGE, Incest and Lust in Luther's Marriage. Theology and Morality in Reformation Polemics, in: Sixteenth Century Journal 34, 2 (2003), pp. 319–345, URL: <https://www.jstor.org/stable/20061412> (7 May 2019).
48 Ibid., p. 326.
49 Scott HENDRIX, Luther on Marriage, in: Timothy J. WENGERT (ed.), Harvesting Martin Luther's Reflections on Theology, Ethics, and the Church, Grand Rapids 2004, pp. 169–184.
50 Ibid., p. 173.
51 Ibid., p. 174.
52 Scott HENDRIX, Masculinity and Patriarchy in Reformation Germany, in: Id. (ed.), Masculinity in the Reformation Era, Kirksville, MO 2008, pp. 71–91.
53 In this study, Luther, Bugenhagen, and Klingebeyl, but elsewhere in KLAWITTER, Forceful and Fruitful, p. 182, also Althamar.
54 Michael PARSONS, Reformation Marriage, Eugene, OR 2005.
55 See esp. ibid., pp. 142–172, and esp. p. 145 for Parsons's discussion of Genesis 1:28.

Thomas Kaufmann's *Ehetheologie im Kontext der frühen Wittenberger Reformation*, given its parameters of Luther's early writings on marriage (1520 and prior) and somewhat also his catechetical literature, understandably does little to draw attention to our verse[56]. Thus, in this otherwise very informative article, Genesis 1:28 is kept both out of view and out of the discussion. The related themes of procreation and the Reformation concern with the impossibility of containing the sexual urge are, however, given attention.

Charles Cortright's dissertation, *»Poor Maggot-Sack That I Am«. The Human Body in the Theology of Martin Luther*, is perhaps one of the more significant works we encounter amongst the secondary literature, even if its focus offers more attention to the later works of Luther's life than is the interest of this study[57]. Although Cortright is seeking to address the larger topic of »the body« in Luther's theology – and thus is not solely addressing our own concerns – his writing does indeed give much attention to the centrality of procreation in Luther's thought surrounding the body, marriage, and sexuality[58]. Indeed, Cortright's efforts to deal fairly with Luther's view of the sex drive are some of the better and more nuanced that one will come across[59], in addition to his presentation of the connection of the sex drive with procreation in Luther's thought[60]. This dissertation thus offers us a solid overview of the prominent areas into which our verse ventures and how it does so, though at the same time leaving ample room for further research.

Jane Strohl's *Luther's New View on Marriage, Sexuality and the Family*, offers a well-balanced chronological and topical overview of Luther's thought on marriage and sexual matters[61]. While the article does not dwell excessively on Genesis 1:28 and procreation, neither does it give short shrift to these topics.

Kathleen Crowther's *Adam and Eve in the Protestant Reformation* is significant for the purposes of this study for at least three reasons[62]. To begin with, not only is the focus of Crowther's project very nearly related to aspects of our own study, it also includes one of the very few direct treatments of procreation in the form of the chapter, *Gender and Generation*, though the preceding chapter, *Framing Eve*,

---

56 Thomas KAUFMANN, Ehetheologie im Kontext der frühen Wittenberger Reformation, in: Ines WEBER/Andreas HOLZEM (eds.), Ehe – Familie – Verwandtschaft. Vergesellschaftung in Religion und sozialer Lebenswelt, München 2008, pp. 285–299.
57 Charles Lloyd CORTRIGHT, »Poor Maggot-Sack That I Am«. The Human Body in the Theology of Martin Luther, Marquette University 2009, URL: <https://epublications.marquette.edu/dissertations_mu/102> (18 Aug 2022).
58 See, for example, ibid., pp. 96–101, 134–178.
59 Ibid., pp. 151–171.
60 Ibid., pp. 171–178.
61 Jane STROHL, Luther's New View on Marriage, Sexuality and the Family, in: Lutherjahrbuch 76 (2009), pp. 159–192.
62 Kathleen M. CROWTHER, Adam and Eve in the Protestant Reformation, New York 2010.

is also just as relevant for our purposes. In addition to this, discussions contained within this book help prefigure and introduce many discussions in our own study. Among such discussions, we first note Crowther's observation of the importance of Genesis 1:28/procreation in Lutheran marital writings – especially as the woman's primary role and work[63]. Secondly, Crowther's discussion of Lutheran ambivalence toward sexuality[64] provides one of the best starting points regarding the created nature of sexual desire in our own investigation of the natural affects. Finally, Crowther's concern for Lutheran treatments of anatomical literature nods toward an area of interest for this study, namely, what anatomical thinking during the Reformation might have to say about our own topic. While Crowther takes her investigation in other directions on this particular topic, the purpose-focused understanding of woman and her anatomy as depicted by Crowther nicely augments our own later discussion of Wittenberg anatomy[65].

Paul R. Henlicky's *The Redemption of the Body. Luther on Marriage*, in alignment with the greater theme of his book, discusses various possible applications related to »community« that might be derived from Luther's teaching on Genesis 1–3[66]. While his essay is not a textual and contextual study of Luther in classic form, Henlicky seems to grasp the centrality of Genesis 1:28 for Luther's marital thought and this verse's relationship with sexual desire better than perhaps most[67].

The reason for Henlicky's insight on these matters is likely, as he himself admits, because of the impetus he received from Sammeli Juntunen's work[68]. Notably, Juntunen's writing, perhaps better than any other source encountered, captures both the contours and purposes of Luther's thought on »sex«, while also rightly discerning its two-fold existence – both according to its institution and its fallen nature. Furthermore, Juntunen's explanations of such topics as »natural reason«, concupiscence and its Augustinian background, not to mention his correct criticism of Protestant streams of interpretation regarding Luther on sexuality[69], all make for a particularly commendable essay.

Likewise within the fold of more traditional Luther research, Markus Matthias's *Das Verhältnis von Ehe und Sexualität bei Luther und in der lutherischen Orthodoxie* rightly strikes the major chords of Luther's Reformation teaching on marriage, to include his stress upon both the place and purpose of sexuality in accordance with

---

63   Ibid., pp. 108–110.
64   Ibid., pp. 117–126.
65   Ibid., pp. 140–183.
66   Paul R. Henlicky, The Redemption of the Body. Luther on Marriage, in: Id., Luther and the Beloved Community. A Path for Christian Theology after Christendom, Grand Rapids 2010, pp. 179–218.
67   Ibid., pp. 202.
68   See Juntunen, Engaging Luther, esp. pp. 186–209.
69   Ibid., p. 200.

Genesis 1:28[70]. Matthias also makes brief – though not detailed – allusion to the role of the affects in this discussion[71] and captures the »liberation« experienced by adherents of the Reformation found in the freedom to marry[72].

Marjorie Elizabeth Plummer's *From Priest's Whore to Pastor's Wife. Clerical Marriage and the Process of Reform in the Early German Reformation*, is interesting inasmuch as her writing, as respects our own verse and interests, provides something of a glimpse of conclusions reasonably derived from the general state of research[73]. Here, Plummer makes mention of Genesis 1:28 on several occasions, though perhaps neglects to note the theological significance of this verse – even as she does give special treatment to the importance of the role of mother within the Reformation household[74].

Although previously mentioned, McKeown's chapter, *Martin Luther. Forerunner of Natalism?* deserves further treatment at this juncture[75]. Here, McKeown gives significant attention to Luther's view on reproduction in attempting to ascertain whether the reformer ought to be considered a forerunner of the modern natalist movement. While McKeown's discussion of Luther's writings on reproduction are wide-ranging, it comes as no surprise that Genesis 1:28 does receive mention on several occasions. Generally speaking, McKeown's concern is whether and to what extent Luther considers Genesis 1:28 to be a law of nature *and* whether Luther views multiplication to be something to be pursued limitlessly. Overall, McKeown does an admirable job in bringing significant themes to the surface and reaches a conclusion which runs generally, though not entirely, consistent with Luther's thought. Unfortunately, his chapter shows a tendency to rely overly much on contextual factors in order to limit the meaning of Luther texts as occurs, for example, with his emphasis upon a supposed relationship between the demographic slump of the late Middle Ages and Luther's view of procreation[76]. It furthermore betrays a lack of nuanced understanding of Luther's thought, perhaps as McKeown is too quick in applying observations derived from secondary literature to his exposition of Luther. The chief example of such weaknesses might be seen in his

---

70 Markus MATTHIAS, Das Verhältnis von Ehe und Sexualität bei Luther und in der lutherischen Orthodoxie, in: Wolfgang BREUEL/Christian SOBOTH (eds.), »Der Herr wird seine Herrlichkeit an uns offenbaren«. Liebe, Ehe und Sexualität im Pietismus, Wiesbaden 2011, pp. 19–50.
71 Ibid., p. 27.
72 Ibid., pp. 20, 22.
73 Marjorie Elizabeth PLUMMER, From Priest's Whore to Pastor's Wife. Clerical Marriage and the Process of Reform in the Early German Reformation, Farnham, England et al. 2012, and ead., Reforming the Family. Marriage, Gender and the Lutheran Household in Early Modern Germany, 1500–1620, Charlottesville, University of Virginia 1996.
74 With respect to the latter point, see ibid., pp. 208–239.
75 MCKEOWN, God's Babies, pp. 78–107.
76 Ibid., pp. 103–105.

discussion of the question of freedom from marriage and reproduction[77]. Here McKeown seems to let the idea of Luther as the hyperbole-prone reformer override the reformer's actual understanding of the force of Genesis 1:28[78].

Entering the last half-decade, Merry Wiesner-Hanks' article on *Martin Luther on Marriage and the Family* offers a balanced overview of Luther's teaching on marriage, not failing to note the importance of Genesis 1:28 and the procreative purpose of marriage[79]. Similarly, Christian Witt, as mentioned previously, offers a valuable presentation with *Luthers Reformation der Ehe*[80]. Witt's basic argument is that Luther's distinct teachings on justification and creation caused a shift in emphasis towards procreation and family life which separated Luther from his predecessors – to include Augustine. Of particular importance in this book is the emphasis Witt gives to the place of Genesis 1:28 and procreation in Luther's thought. As previously mentioned, others – though not all – have observed the presence and significance of our verse. Witt, however, is perhaps unique in the emphasis he gives to these matters in Luther's marital teaching and, in many ways, helps to reframe the discussion.

One final, also rather recent study deserves mention, that being Sini Mikkola's dissertation, *In Our Body the Scripture Becomes Fulfilled*, in which the author examines Luther's construction of gender and his related understanding of bodiliness[81]. As is to be expected in a work dealing with such topics, a good amount of discussion is directed towards sexuality, sexual desire, reproduction, motherhood/fatherhood, and other such related topics. While Mikkola's findings rightly deal with a great deal of relevant material for our purposes, one notes comparatively little discussion of Genesis 1:28 and its relationship, if any, to the aforementioned topics. Indeed, one wonders whether somewhat greater interest in this verse would have perhaps clarified and furthered many of her otherwise solid findings – particularly as involve the positive and negative aspects of man's affective/sexual nature, sexuality as something (divinely) implanted, the relationship between our verse and man's »unavoidable sexual drive« in general, and even Luther's shift in thought regarding celibacy.

Given the above, we conclude our literature survey with the following observations: To begin with, it seems fair to say that our verse is *generally*, though certainly not in every instance, acknowledged to be of importance – perhaps significant

---

77 Ibid., p. 93.
78 See ibid., pp. 90f., 209.
79 Merry E. Wiesner-Hanks, Martin Luther on Marriage and the Family, in: Oxford Research Encyclopedia of Religion (2016), URL: <https://doi.org/10.1093/acrefore/9780199340378.013.365> (18 Aug 2022).
80 Witt, Reformation der Ehe.
81 Sini Mikkola, »In Our Body the Scripture Becomes Fulfilled«. Gendered Bodiliness and the Making of the Gender System in Martin Luther's Anthropology (1520–1530), Helsinki 2017.

importance – for Luther's teaching on marriage and his polemic against celibacy. Its absence and lack of emphasis, to be sure, may at times be excused on account of research interests and study parameters. Nevertheless, in view of the high importance given our verse in other instances, such scholarly dissonance is notable. Should we probe this dissonance, we do certainly find a general connection between the creational words, »Be fruitful and multiply« and the concepts of procreation and reproduction. Yet, we may also note a near affinity to the idea of sexuality and, arguably, its corresponding drives. This is, however, an area clouded by ambiguity – especially regarding the boundary between created sexual nature and lustful desire for Luther. We might also note at this juncture that, though perhaps not of central importance, such areas as anatomical understanding and natural law have also been brought into our purview.

Having thus sketched out a general picture of our verse via an informed, though by no means complete, sampling of relevant secondary literature, we are now able to home in on more specific questions which will help guide our present investigation. These include:

1) When did Genesis 1:28 first emerge in Luther's thought, how was it employed, and what was its significance?
2) What was the role and significance of Genesis 1:28 in the ongoing debates surrounding monastic celibacy and priestly marriage in Luther's thought, in the Wittenberg Reformation movement?
3) What was the role and significance of Genesis 1:28 in Luther's (and that of the Wittenberg Reformation) understanding of marriage – to include matters related particularly to man's sexual drive?

With such questions and such a general overview of the literature in mind, we now turn our attention to both the structure and delineations of this project.

1.2 Project Overview, Methodology, and Limitations

As previously alluded to, Jeremy Cohen's research as to this verse's »ancient and medieval career« provides an important introduction and, indeed, *point de départ* for this project. Briefly summarizing, Cohen begins his book by offering an overview of the historic Jewish interpretation of this verse. Within this tradition, he discovers a persistent applicability of this verse, though with varying degrees of interpretation within that general understanding. Remarkably, though, as Cohen comes to the Christian tradition of the interpretation of this verse, he notes historic tension and ambiguity latent in this verse's interpretation and application. Indeed, within the Christian tradition there exists divergence of thought as to whether this verse has any remaining applicability since Christ's advent, or whether it is still, in some way, normative for mankind. Cohen thus traces out the place of our verse in the theology of the church fathers, significant developments leading into and then throughout the Middle Ages, the place of Genesis 1:28 in Christian legal thought and natural law theory, Scholastic thinking, and finally ends his study just shy of the Reformation, though pointing to the significance of »Be fruitful and multiply« once more in that context. In other words, Cohen demonstrates quite clearly a historical tension as concerns the interpretation of this verse and as relates to its continued applicability, even offering clear indication that the Reformation had a great deal more to say about this topic as it took its own place in this ancient conversation.

Before pressing forward into the Wittenberg Reformation, however, our study will begin by noting several of the background conversations significant for Genesis 1:28, both prior to and during the Reformation. Here we should be clear that our primary interest is the *thought* context of this verse's interpretation and then, to a lesser extent, the wider context of the early Reformation. Thus, we will give brief attention to the historical discourse surrounding celibacy, virginity, and marriage, giving special notice to the ancient controversy involving Jerome and Jovinian, but also note the ambiguity found in the thought of Augustine, Chrysostom, and even historic liturgical practice. Following that, we will turn our attention to important discussions stemming out of both natural law and natural philosophy, respectively.

Continuing, then, with our study proper, we ask the question, »What was the continued *career* of this verse throughout the early years of the Wittenberg Reformation?« – here understood roughly as the decade of the 1520s up until the *Confessio Augustana* and Melanchthon's *Apologia*. Thus, Chapter 3 takes on the question: When and under what circumstances did Genesis 1:28 enter the polemical discourse of the Reformation? Moreover, how was it employed and what was its significance? Here we present the argument that this verse comprised a significant and powerful argument, both complementing Luther's Gospel-centered thrusts against monastic vows and the forbiddance of priestly marriage, but also augmenting and intensifying these arguments with its own creational reverberations. We furthermore raise the question of whether Luther's fundamental shift *in favor of* marriage for those struggling with monastic vows would have had the same theological strength without the forceful support of our verse.

Chapter 4 then outlines initial sparring over Genesis 1:28 between the Wittenberg reformers and their opponents from 1522–1524. Here we observe that while Genesis 1:28 grew to serve as a sort of explicit and implicit foundation for the Wittenberg rejection of monastic vows and exuberant demand for priestly marriage, it also served as fodder for the claim that the Wittenberg theologians rejected the teachings of the church fathers and perpetuated heretical teachings. Furthermore, we also observe that the propagation of the Wittenberg understanding of Genesis 1:28 was not merely limited to Luther's activity but was fundamentally a combined effort of the Wittenberg theologians. By means of an excursus, this chapter also offers a glance at the role of Genesis 1:28 in the differing, yet related, context of reformation Erfurt.

In Chapter 5, we will then observe the transformed/transforming role of Genesis 1:28 as we proceed into the latter half of the 1520s. Here, we will be able to observe our verse no longer functioning primarily as a *destructive* force in opposition to vows and the imposed celibacy of priests. Rather, we will be able to view it as an increasingly powerful *constructive* and foundational element in the Wittenberg teaching on marriage and family. Additionally, we will mark an important transition of this verse as it is elevated from a mere presence in the personal and polemic writings of various reformers to an expression of common confession in such foundational Reformation documents as the *Confessio Augustana* and its *Apologia*.

This project then concludes, looking ahead to the ongoing work and significance of Genesis 1:28 toward the end of Luther's career and even beyond. Here we will give cursory attention to Luther's later works – especially his *Lectures on Genesis*. We will furthermore observe the continued controversy surrounding our verse – to include amongst certain advocates and allies of the Wittenberg Reformation – and note some of the limits inherent in the Wittenberg understanding of Genesis 1:28.

1.3 Further Theoretical Considerations and Project Notes

Having thus introduced our project, there are several important theoretical discussions which prove significant throughout the pages of this study. To begin with, we raise the question of whether the Reformation movement which issued forth from Wittenberg was more properly Luther's Reformation or a more collective Wittenberg Reformation in which Luther played the leading role? Can we, should we, dare we read Luther in isolation apart from the works of his colleagues, contemporaries, and confidants? What light does he shed on them, and what light do they shed on him? This study argues that an important element of »Luther's« understanding of Genesis 1:28 would be understood only with difficulty apart from Melanchthon's writings. Indeed, the larger Wittenberg context of Melanchthon, Jonas, Amsdorf, Menius, and many others brings into focus what might otherwise remain mysterious and unclear in Luther's own writings. Thus, this study will, of necessity, speak to the importance of the collective nature of the Wittenberg Reformation even as it focuses largely on the thought of Luther.

Secondly, as pertains to the interaction and relationship of text and context, we note what has perhaps been an underdeveloped contextual factor in the relevant Luther literature for understanding and discussing not only procreation (and hence our own verse), but also such topics as sex and sexuality. Namely, we will note the importance of, by our present categories, the *non-theological* disciplines of law and natural philosophy for the theological thought of Luther's day. To be fair, a good amount of attention has been given such topics with Melanchthon due to the wide-ranging scope of his writings. Thus, the interplay between law, natural philosophy, and theology has been well noted with him. Nevertheless, Luther literature often gives the impression of reading the reformer through something of *theological blinders*. That is to say, Luther is often read as if he was merely in conversation with Scripture and the church fathers and not as the encyclopedic scholar boasting some legal training, who received a top-notch education from professors of great renown, who was given the nickname *Philosophus*[82] by his earlier peers, and who remained abreast of developments within the university context in which he was active. Thus, by keeping our eyes open toward such seemingly non-theological fields of law and natural history, we will observe how these can indeed inform our understanding of Luther's context and thought for our own work, even somewhat fixing, or perhaps verifying, interpretive possibilities for reading Luther on topics related to our own.

Furthermore, as we interact with the ever-relevant question and debate regarding text and context[83], we will also do well to extend the question somewhat, inquiring whether context ought merely to be broad or should it also necessarily be deep – and if so, how deep? In this respect, we will observe that, if anything, the Reformation was *backward facing* as it took part in what we might describe as something of a series of conversations. Here, we discover that Luther and his fellow reformers were not only taking part in the contemporary conversations of the early sixteenth century; rather, they were simultaneously conversant with and taking part in a set of conversations on controversial topics that stemmed from the thought of

---

82 Günter Mühlpfordt, Das Natürliche bei Martin Luther, in: Wolfram Kaiser et al. (eds.), Medizin und Naturwissenschaften in der Wittenberger Reformationsära, Bernburg 1982, pp. 203–240, at p. 216.

83 A classic instantiation of debate regarding the interplay and relationship of text and context took place between the Reformation and Luther heavyweights Leif Grane and Heiko Oberman in the 1970s. In this discussion Grane issued a criticism of an article by Oberman and his methodology. For Grane's criticism, see Leif Grane, Lutherforschung und Geistesgeschichte. Auseinandersetzung mit Heiko A. Oberman, in: Archiv für Reformationsgeschichte 68 (1977), pp. 302–315, in which he raises the question whether the historical context surrounding the text or the actual text itself should receive primary emphasis. Grane decides heavily in favor of the latter with the following statement: »Dennoch – mit dem Rahmen zu arbeiten ist nützlich und notwendig. Doch der Rahmen […] deutet sehr gut an, daß es um *das Bild* geht« (p. 308). For Oberman's article, see Heiko Oberman, Reformation. Epoche oder Episode, in: Archiv für Reformationsgeschichte 68 (1977), pp. 56–111. Of course, the discussion of the relationship between text and context is not at all limited to the confines of Reformation scholarship. See, for example, Paul Ricœur, What Is a Text? Explanation and Understanding, in: John B. Thompson (ed.), Hermeneutics and the Human Sciences. Essays on Language, Action, and Interpretation, Cambridge et al. 1981, pp. 145–164, in which Ricœur argues that in order to establish meaning within a text, the analyzed text must be placed within a meaningful context.

the ancients – both secular and religious – and which continued through their immediate predecessors. Indeed, without a historical awareness of the outlines of these various conversations, some of what we encounter when reading Luther becomes, or perhaps remains, unintelligible[84].

There are, of course, further discussions upon which this project will serve to shed a certain amount of light. One of these that must certainly be named has to do with the spread of Reformation ideas and the importance of the Wittenberg Reformation for wider Reformation« thought. Here also our own investigation will provide its own limited insights – at least with respect to one specific Reformation meme and its presence in the city of Erfurt.

One discussion, however, about which our work will have seemingly little to say is the theory of Heinsohn and Steiger[85], that behind the legal-political opposition of witches (i. e. wise women) reaching out from *malleus maleficarum* (1486) and stretching through the witch trials of the sixteenth and seventeenth centuries, was an organized agenda targeting specifically the contraceptive knowledge and effectiveness of such wise-women/midwives. While some have criticized this theory[86], here we will merely mention that in our project (which, theoretically, would seemingly run strongly parallel to such a thesis), limited or no textual evidence gives indication that Luther's concern for Genesis 1:28 was connected with the contraceptive knowledge and practices of such witches[87]. Thus, this project rather prioritizes such historical factors (i. e. the debate over celibacy and vows) as are

---

84 In addition to the previously discussed Grane/Oberman debate, we would be remiss not to mention the seminal article of Quentin SKINNER, Meaning and Understanding in the History of Ideas, in: History and Theory 8, 1 (1969), pp. 3–53, whose concern for the interplay and proper relationship of text and context is entirely relevant for our own topic and its discussion. Noteworthy, on the one hand, is his concern for determining meaning, as it were, from below (i. e., the unique and individual usages of a concept or phrase) as opposed to from above (i. e. imported by the reader) and within an appropriate context. On the other hand, however, his caution is well taken that context is not determinative of the text. Rather, he posits it as something of a »court of appeal« capable of shining revealing light upon »mythical« and ahistorical interpretations.

85 Gunnar HEINSOHN/Otto STEIGER, Die Vernichtung der Weisen Frauen. Beiträge zur Theorie und Geschichte von Bevölkerung und Kindheit, Herbstein 1985.

86 For a brief discussion and critique of the Heinsohn-Steiger thesis, see Lyndal ROPER, Oedipus & the Devil. Witchcraft, Sexuality and Religion in Early Modern Europe, London et al. 2013, pp. 220f., or Jörg HAUSTEIN, Martin Luthers Stellung zum Zauber- und Hexenwesen, Stuttgart et al. 1990, pp. 31, 178. A much stronger criticism of the Heinsohn-Steiger theory can be found in Robert JÜTTE, Die Persistenz des Verhütungswissens in der Volkskultur. Sozial-und medizinhistorische Anmerkungen zur These von der »Vernichtung der weisen Frauen«, in: Medizinhistorisches Journal 24, 3/4 (1989), pp. 214–231, URL: <https://www.jstor.org/stable/25803986> (18 Aug 2022).

87 Sigrid BRAUNER/Robert H. BROWN, Fearless Wives and Frightened Shrews. The Construction of the Witch in Early Modern Germany, Amherst 1995, p. 134, note that »there are only two passing references to impotence induced by sorcery« in the entirety of Luther's works (see WA 10/I/1, p. 591 and

clearly related to our theme. We might further add that the topic of contraception itself does not appear to have been a major contextual factor for Luther's concern with Genesis 1:28, though Luther and his contemporaries were, unquestionably, opposed to any and all such practices[88].

Finally, before concluding our introduction, a couple of notes about transcriptions and translations in this study are in order. First, regarding transcription, every effort has been made to convey the format of the original text. Along these lines, the texts documented in the footnotes generally include original ligature from which not only the text is derived, but then also the translation (as applicable) has been made. While it is acknowledged that such a decision makes, in some cases, for a less-accessible text, such a decision also makes for a less-mediated text[89]. The decision has also been made to offer the main body of this text in English, thus offering translations of sources whenever necessary. Along these lines, already extant translations are used whenever possible. In many instances, however, no known translations were available. Thus, if not otherwise noted, translations are the author's own as are any related shortcomings they may contain.

WA 15, p. 560). Furthermore, their work argues that Luther was not particularly consistent with the concerns of *Malleus Maleficarum*, and thus not overly preoccupied with the idea of wanton witches.

88 There is some debate as to the prevalence of contraceptive knowledge (and practice) in early modern Europe. John RIDDLE, Contraception and Abortion from the Ancient World to the Renaissance, Cambridge, MA 1992, pp. 144–157, argues that it was present, albeit declining within wider society by the sixteenth century. Robert JÜTTE, Lust ohne Last. Geschichte der Empfängnisverhütung von der Antike bis zur Gegenwart, Munich 2003, pp. 87–120, similarly argues that there would have been various ways for early modern women (and men) to learn about contraceptive techniques, though he does not speculate as to their overall prevalence and practice in the sixteenth century. Nevertheless, both of these authors give the impression that the knowledge available (at least to some) could have been somewhat effective. On the other hand, Norman E. HIMES, Medical History of Contraception, New York 1970, pp. 168f., 183–185, is more circumspect regarding the possibility, not of a knowledge of contraceptive methods, but regarding their effectiveness prior to the nineteenth and twentieth centuries. Related, but somewhat less relevant, are Angus McLAREN, A History of Contraception. From Antiquity to the Present Day, Oxford et al. 1992, pp. 141–177, and Klaus BERGDOLT, Das Gewissen der Medizin. Ärztliche Moral von der Antike bis heute, München 2004, pp. 122–129.
That Luther was opposed to contraceptive practices can be clearly understood from his comments on Onan (see fn. 185) as well as the following quote from his *Lectures on Genesis* (1535–1545): »Quanta ergo malitia est humanae naturae? quam multae puellae sunt, quae impediunt conceptionem, et necant atque expellunt teneros foetus? cum generatio sit opus Dei. Ac coniuges quidem, qui honeste contrahunt et cohabitant, diversos fines, sed raro prolem spectant«. WA 43, p. 354,18–21.

89 For difficulties with the ligature and common abbreviations encountered with such texts, see esp. Adriano CAPPELLI, The Elements of Abbreviation in Medieval Latin Paleography, Lawrence, KS 1982.

2. Background: Tension, Ambiguity, and Discussion Surrounding a Verse

> Quod autem ait: *Crescite et multiplicamini, et replete terram*, necesse fuit prius plantare silvam et crescere, ut esset quod postea posset excidi. Simulque consideranda vis verbi, *replete terram*. Nuptiae terram replent, virginitas paradisum.

> *And whereas he says »Be fruitful and multiply, and replenish the earth«, it was necessary first to plant the wood and to let it grow, so that there might be an aftergrowth for cutting down. And at the same time we must bear in mind the meaning of the phrase, »replenish the earth.« Marriage replenishes the earth, virginity fills Paradise.*

> —Jerome, *Against Jovinianus*

In the following chapter, we examine several historic conversations that trace their origins back to both the ancient world and the early church and which are, furthermore, pertinent to the Reformation understanding of our verse as well as to topics closely related to its interpretation. The first conversation dates back to the time of Jerome, Ambrose, Augustine, and concerns the teachings of one Jovinian. Specifically, we will observe how his condemnation led to the subsequent association of the Jovinian heresy with its particularly strong normative understanding of our verse. Somewhat tangential to this conversation, we will note elements of ambiguity stemming from that same period, whether in the theology of Augustine and Chrysostom or in liturgical practices connected with marriage which were present already at this time. We will then undertake an investigation of the relationship between historic strains of natural law thinking and what relevance these have for such topics as procreation and Genesis 1:28. Here we will especially note developments – and latent tensions – of the Middle Ages. Finally, we will offer attention to Reformation understandings of anatomy (as gleaned from the reception of such classical thinkers as Aristotle or Galen), and what these might have to say vis-à-vis the use of the body, procreation, and our own verse.

2.1 The Historical Tension between Genesis 1:28 and Celibacy in the Church

Having made brief allusion to Jovinian in our introductory chapter – and before we encounter particularly the polemics surrounding Genesis 1:28 in subsequent chapters – it will be helpful to provide a brief overview of the historic tension and ambiguity surrounding Genesis 1:28 in the church. To begin with, then, we recall that throughout the church's history »Be fruitful and multiply« has been treated with a certain amount of ambivalence. Whereas Judaism historically has generally understood this verse both as covenantal confirmation and ongoing divine mandate, Christianity has often questioned the nature and ongoing relevance of the words contained therein, namely, »Be fruitful and multiply and fill the earth.« According to Jeremy Cohen, this likely relates both to the fact that Genesis 1:28 is not referenced in the New Testament and that early Christianity was more concerned with its formative theological debates to pay too much attention to this verse[1]. Additionally, as ascetic thought and influence gained precedence, such topics as virginity and celibacy were generally of much greater interest to early church fathers than were concerns for fertility[2]. Nevertheless, there remained a certain ambiguity and divergence of opinions surrounding this verse. On the one hand, such second century fathers as Irenaeus of Lyons and Clement of Alexandria used this verse to establish their marital theology over against condemnations of heretical Encratism (with its strong asceticism), Gnosticism, and Marcionism – all of whose tendencies despised the materiality and worldliness of marriage and sexual relations[3].

On the other hand, however, moving into the third century, the sway of Encratism grew. In the West, for example, while continuing their opposition to the previously mentioned heretical teachings, such voices as those of Cyprian and Tertullian spoke out clearly in favor of celibacy and relegated marriage and procreation to a secondary, if not sinful, status[4]. This situation was, however, even more extreme in the East. Here, such teachers as Eusebius of Ceasarea and Origen, with their

---

1 Cohen, Be Fertile, p. 221.
2 Ibid., p. 231. We might, however, note that the indifference toward Genesis 1:28 may not be as prominent as Cohen suggests. In a recent article, Allan C. Carlson, A Prophetic Witness to Creation, in: Todd Aglialoro/Stephen Phelan (eds.), Inseparable. Five Perspectives on Sex, Life, and Love in Defense of Humanae Vitae, El Cajon, CA 2018, pp. 149–178, at p. 154, argues that the early church was likely a community »open to the propagation, protection, and rearing of children«. If such was the case, it seems unlikely that Genesis 1:28 was not part of the greater spiritual context.
3 Cohen, Be Fertile, pp. 230f. For the role of heretical teachings in the context of Irenaeus and Clement of Alexandria, see David G. Hunter, Marriage, Celibacy, and Heresy in Ancient Christianity. The Jovinianist Controversy, in: Oxford Scholarship Online (May 2007), pp. 101–113, URL: <https://doi.org/10.1093/acprof:oso/9780199279784.001.0001> (18 Aug 2022).
4 Hunter, Marriage, pp. 116–122.

heavy encratistic emphasis and their decided preference for allegorical and spiritual interpretations, deprived Genesis 1:28 of any literal application and significance[5]. In fact, Cohen notes a most remarkable complaint lobbied by one fourth century Jew and recorded by a protégé of Eusebius,

> But you [Christians] do a thing which was not commanded by God, for you have received a curse and have multiplied barrenness. You have prohibited procreation, the blessings of righteous men. You do not take wives, and you do not become wives for husbands. You hate procreation, a blessing given by God[6].

Be that as it may, the events of the latter part of the fourth century deserve special attention. While one often gets the impression that the church had largely sided in favor of celibacy and virginity as the preferred modes of spiritual life by this time, the reality of the situation is somewhat more complicated. The fact is that, with the church's earlier rejection of Encratism, many in the church were still skeptical (and critical!) of its practice, viewed it as socially disruptive, and held suspicions of its past heretical associations[7]. In other words, a decision in favor of celibacy over marriage – with its corollary interpretation as to the enduring nature of Genesis 1:28 as command – had yet to be reached[8].

It is in this charged setting that perhaps the most significant historic debates surrounding marriage, celibacy, procreation, and sexuality prior to the Reformation occurred. In the late fourth century, a certain monk and teacher of the church, Jovinian, began to attack the growing emphasis upon the ascetic leanings of the church. His teachings, derived largely from Jerome's responses, can be summarized in the following main points:

1) Virgins, widows, and married women, once they have been washed in Christ, are of the same merit, if they do not differ in other works.
2) Those who have been born again in Baptism with full faith cannot be overthrown by the devil.
3) There is no difference between abstinence from food and receiving it with thanksgiving.

---

5 COHEN, Be Fertile, pp. 232–237. HUNTER, Marriage, p. 123, notes especially the influence which Origen's Encratite teachings had upon such important fourth century figures as Ambrose and Jerome, both of whom would play important roles in the Jovinianist controversy.
6 COHEN, Be Fertile, p. 234.
7 See esp. HUNTER, Marriage, Chapter 4 (pp. 131–171).
8 Ibid., pp. 164–169, notes the »state of the question« regarding Genesis 1:28 just prior to the Jovinian controversy as seen in the writings of Ambrosius and Jerome. See also COHEN, Be Fertile, pp. 244f.

4) There is one reward in the kingdom of heaven for all who have preserved their Baptism[9].

Jovinian's teachings attracted a considerable following around Rome, even among older ascetics who were compelled to marry on account of his persuasive scriptural argumentation on behalf of marriage[10]. Furthermore, Jovinian was not shy in attacking those who practiced celibacy, such as Jerome and Ambrose, and charging them with »Manichaean« heresy[11]. This was a charge which, though technically inaccurate, had its own precedent in the church's past dealings with Encratism and other heretical teachings[12]. In fact, such a charge could – with good reason – consider itself within the mainstream of earlier orthodox teachers, to say nothing of contemporaries such as the anonymous Ambrosiaster[13].

There are two points that we do well to note about the teachings of Jovinian and the events that ensued. First, Jovinian's teachings had dramatic egalitarian implications and very much threatened the higher status of monastics and church authority itself. For one thing, in emphasizing the fact that all Christians are equal before God through the waters of Baptism and that neither monastic practice nor virginity constitutes a better path to salvation, the special status and calling of monks, virgins, and widows was directly challenged. Furthermore, given the fact that one vocation was not to be preferred over another, Jovinian was also free to strongly emphasize scriptural teachings on the goodness of creation – including matters related to both food and marriage, if received in the right spirit. Along these lines, Jovinian also stressed the enduring importance of procreation and marriage[14] as well as the importance of the primordial command in both the life of the Old Testament patriarchs as well as in salvation history[15].

The second point that we might note is that, despite Jovinian's claims to orthodox opposition against heresy and correct scriptural teachings, he and his followers did not carry the day. His opponents, though for varying reasons, countered charges of heresy with their own cries of the same. Pope Siricius reacted to Jovinian's challenge of supposed contempt of marriage by some celibate priests[16]. Ambrose took offense to Jovinian's leveling of virginity and celibacy with marriage – and then particular

---

9 HUNTER, Marriage, p. 26, cited as »Jerome, Jov. 1.3 (PL 23, 224)«.
10 Ibid., p. 18.
11 Ibid., p. 20.
12 Ibid., p. 131.
13 For a discussion of the thought and teaching of Ambrosiaster – particularly in opposition to Jerome and including the former's thought on Genesis 1:28, see ibid., pp. 159–169.
14 Ibid., p. 40.
15 Ibid., pp. 33–35.
16 Ibid., p. 17.

offense at Jovinian's rejection of Mary's continued virginity *in partu*[17]. This resulted ultimately in Jovinian being condemned as a heretic at the synods at Rome and Milan in 393[18].

Yet, as serious as this was, the most forceful counter to Jovinian's writings came a year later from the pen of Jerome. In 394 he wrote *Adversus Jovinianum*, a scathing work that was likely as self-serving for Jerome as it was condemnatory of his opponent[19]. For the sake of our own study, what is important is the fact that Jerome retained his status as an orthodox teacher of the church while Jovinian has forever been recorded as a heretic. Thus, not only were Jovinian's own writings condemned, but also anyone who said or wrote things similar to what he had argued (never mind that his teachings had been within the frame of orthodox teaching *before* his condemnation) could now be immediately tagged as a heretical troublemaker. Thus, when Jerome said that marriage (i. e. Genesis 1:28) had been given to fill earth but now celibacy was given to fill heaven[20] (a phrase which will often appear in Reformation discussions), such a saying could be made on good authority. Yet, should someone argue that Christians were equal before God through Baptism or that the married state was just as holy as the celibate, one was beginning to tread on dangerous turf that could lead to the charge of Jovinianism.

Augustine, of course, did not position himself against Jovinian with the same zeal as Jerome. Nevertheless, in attempting to navigate a more moderate course, one which could both distance him from Jovinian as well as properly emphasize the value of chastity, he ended up strengthening the cause of celibacy, largely through his teaching on the inherent sinfulness of »sex« and his praise of chastity. At the same time, he created a certain amount of ambiguity over these matters through his praise of the goods of marriage[21]. Furthermore, with respect to Genesis 1:28, Augustine was rather ambiguous. At first, he was decidedly allegorical about the verse and thus hesitant in his endorsement of marriage. Later, however, he shifted to a decidedly literal approach regarding »Be fruitful and multiply«, even emphasizing *proles* (i. e. offspring) as one of the clear »goods« of marriage. Nevertheless, his own celibate life and emphasis upon unimpeded service of God clearly favored

---

17 Ibid., pp. 20–24. »*In partu*« refers in theology (usually Roman Catholic) to Mary's continued virginity even in and after Christ's birth.
18 See ibid., pp. 16f., for discussion as to the debate over this dating and arguments in favor of 393.
19 Ibid., pp. 231f.
20 Cf. »Quod autem ait: *Crescite et multiplicamini, et replete terram* (Gen. 1,28), necesse fuit prius plantare silvam et crescere, ut esset quod postea posset excidi. Simulque consideranda vis verbi, *replete terram*. Nuptiae terram replent, virginitas paradisum«. Jerome, Adversus Jovinianum, 1, 16 (PL 23, p. 246; NPNF, ser. 2, vol. 6, p. 360). A similar quotation can also be found in Jerome, Letter XXII, to Eustochium, 19 (PL 22, p. 405; NPNF, ser. 2, vol. 6, p. 29).
21 COHEN, Be Fertile, pp. 254f.

virginity and celibacy[22]. In any event, in the aftermath of the Jovinianist controversy and through the teachings of those who had opposed him, any heated discussion was largely silenced for the ensuing centuries. Nevertheless, a certain unresolved tension remained. On the one hand, there continued to exist the literal, naturalistic understanding of Genesis 1:28 as at some level constitutive of God's will for human nature (i. e. the good of *proles*). On the other hand, the privileged place of celibacy had now gained much greater prominence in Christian teaching[23].

Turning eastward, we can note a similar latent and significant tension with the distinguished church father, John Chrysostom. Similar to many of his contemporaries, Chrysostom was an outspoken advocate of celibacy and virginity. Indeed, Peter Brown notes that Chrysostom's preaching in Antioch strove to steer the city's citizens away from marriage[24] and that Chrysostom, like Jerome, viewed the world as already being fully populated[25]. Thus, at a surface level, Chrysostom would not seem to be terribly pertinent for our contextual discussion.

This would especially seem to be the case as we turn our attention to his general usage of – and the corresponding emphasis which he places upon – Genesis 1:28. Here we can note that in Chrysostom's *Homilies on Genesis* – a work with which Luther would have had some familiarity in the late 1510s[26] – that our verse receives rather sparing attention. We can note, for example, that as his Lenten series of sermons arrives at Genesis 1:28 in Homily 8, his emphasis is placed in a rather lopsided manner upon the dominion granted to mankind in creation[27]. Among other things, this dominion for Chrysostom included not merely lordship over creation, but especially the subjugation of the passions[28]. In comparison, his concern for the blessing of procreation seems rather slight given that it is merely pointed out that that was the same blessing as was given to the beasts. According to Chrysostom, »Those words, ›Increase and multiply and fill the earth‹, anyone could see are said

---

22 Ibid., pp. 245–259.
23 Helen L. Parish, Clerical Celibacy in the West, c. 1100–1700, Ashgate 2010, pp. 41f., notes that it was on the heels of the Jovinianist controversy that such phenomena as an increase in »*sacrificial* language related to the eucharist, and a sacerdotal terminology in relation to the clergy« were to be observed.
24 Peter Brown, The Body and Society, New York 1988, pp. 306f.
25 Ibid., p. 308.
26 Luther, for example, shows familiarity with Chrysostom's *Homilia in Gen.* already in his *Scholia in librum Genesios* in the late 1510s. See WA 9, p. 333,5, p. 335,38. See also fn. 62 of this work, for a note on the dating of Luther's *Scholia*.
27 PG 53, p. 84; cf. John Chrysostom, Homilies on Genesis 1–17, translated by Robert C. Hill, Washington, D.C. 1986, p. 132 (Homily 10:7).
28 Cohen, Be Fertile, p. 228; PG 53, p. 78; cf. Chrysostom, Homilies 1–17, pp. 120f. (Homily 9:7).

of the brute beasts and the reptiles alike, whereas ›Gain dominion and have control‹ are directed to the man and woman«[29].

In many ways, of course, the aforementioned should come as no surprise. After all, along with other church fathers, Chrysostom – unlike Augustine – made no room for the work of procreation prior to the Fall[30]. Indeed, the propagation of the race through intercourse is something only seemingly begrudgingly »allowed for« by the Golden-mouthed father in God's condescension and kindness, especially as offspring would have buoyed up the hope of Adam and Eve prior to an understanding of the resurrection[31].

Nevertheless, despite such seeming ambivalence towards the blessing and promise of procreation and deference for celibacy and the state of angels, there is also a latent power in both Chrysostom's understanding of Genesis 1:28 as well as his view of God's creative work. While lacking that of a compelling force, one catches a glimpse of this power as he treats Genesis 9:18 and the seemingly overwhelming odds in repopulating the earth as faced by Noah and his family following their exit from the ark. Chrysostom remarks, »Don't be surprised, dearly beloved: God it was who was managing everything, and the Creator of our nature was removing all these difficulties, and that direction of his in the words, ›Increase and multiply, and fill the earth‹, also granted them this increase«[32]. Chrysostom finds a similar parallel and working power of God at work in the multiplication of the Israelites while enslaved in Egypt[33]. As mentioned, however, for Chrysostom, this power seems to be one divinely vested in mankind. It is, for him, not one compelled and urged in man's prelapsarian state. At times, however, it does seem to show glimmers of prowess and compelling power as noted in his work *De virginitate*[34] where he likens the power of God's word in the Lord's Supper with the original divine blessing on mankind[35].

---

29 Chrysostom, Homilies 1–17, p. 134 (Homily 10:9); cf. PG 53, p. 86.
30 PG 53, p. 123; cf. Chrysostom, Homilies 1–17, p. 202 (Homily 15:14).
31 John Chrysostom, Homilies on Genesis 18–45, translated by Robert C. Hill, Washington, D.C. 1990, p. 11 (Homily 18:12–13); cf. PG 53, p. 153.
32 Chrysostom, Homilies 18–45, pp. 192f. (Homily 28:13); cf. PG 53, p. 257.
33 Chrysostom, Homilies 18–45, pp. 192f. (Homily 28:13); PG 53, p. 257.
34 »Ὅτι οὐχ ὁ γάμος αὔξει τὸ ἡμέτερον γένος. Καὶ νῦν δὲ οὐχ ἡ τοῦ γάμου δύναμις τὸ γένος συγκροτεῖ τὸ ἡμέτερον ἀλλ' ὁ τοῦ κυρίου λόγος ὁ παρὰ τὴν ἀρχὴν εἰπών· ›Αὐξάνεσθαι καὶ πληθύνεσθαι καὶ πληρώσατε τὴν γῆν‹«. De Virginitate/ΤΟΥ ΧΡΥΣΟΣΤΟΜΟΥ ΠΕΡΙ ΠΑΡΘΕΝΙΑΣ, XV/IE (PG 48, p. 544).
35 De proditione Iudae, Hom. 1, 7; cf. PG 49, pp. 380, 389f. This analogy would reappear throughout the Middle Ages in the context of discussions involving the Lord's Supper, whether by Pascase Radbert in his conflict against Ratramnus (De Corpore et Sanguine Domini, XII; CCSL, Cont. Med. XVI, pp. 77f.), by Alberic of Monte Cassino (*Adversus Berengarium Diaconum de Corpore et Sanguine Domini*; see Charles M. Radding/Francis Newton, Theology, Rhetoric, and Politics in the Eucharis-

In some ways, however, Chrysostom's treatment of creation, in general, and particularly Genesis 1:22 – as it runs parallel to Genesis 1:28 – proves informative and, perhaps, even significant. In looking at Chrysostom's *Homilies on Genesis* and how he understands God's creative work, one quickly becomes cognizant of the active working of God's powerful word in the days of creation. This is something, in addition to God's purposeful and marvelous intentionality and ordering, which receives repeated emphasis[36]. What is especially enlightening, however, is Chrysostom's connection of God's original creative word with an ongoing, continuous effectiveness into the present. For example, in speaking of God's creation of plants, Chrysostom comments, »Now the plants bring forth. It is the word of God, even unto the present«[37]. Even more clearly, however, Chrysostom states regarding the creation of the birds and sea creatures – and God's word of blessing to them (i. e. »Be fruitful and multiply«), »That word, you know, influences them right up to the present, and has spanned such an extent of time without one of those species being diminished. After all, God's blessing and the form of words, ›Increase and multiply‹, bestowed on them life and permanence«[38]. We meet a similar understanding of the ongoing »upholding« of creation by God's »word of power« (Hebrews 1:3) in Chrysostom's second homily on the book of Hebrews[39].

For our purposes it is not necessary to take this brief survey regarding Chrysostom's thought on creation and the working of God's word in creation – especially as involves the words »Be fruitful and multiply« – much further. From the above, it is evident that there is a tension to be found in the thought of Chrysostom which would allow the disparate strands, potentially, to be pulled from each other. After all, as concerned with the idea that God's word has influence up to the present and that it upholds and grants life and permanence, if this idea is transposed from the animal to the human realm, it quickly leads in a direction contradictory to Chrysostom's own ideas about human freedom. It is, in fact, not a very far leap to imagine that the ongoing influence of this creating word cannot but have its way even to the present. While we will not be able to draw a direct link from Chrysostom's thinking to Luther's own thought, it should be mentioned that Luther drew upon Chrysostom's *Homilies on Genesis* for his initial lectures on Genesis – though seemingly without effect in this particular area. Nevertheless, as pointed out by Mickey Mattox, Chrysostom played a not insignificant role – often anonymously and remaining in

---

tic Controversy, 1078–1079. Alberic of Monte Cassino Against Berengar of Tours, New York 2003, p. 138), or by Thomas Aquinas (see COHEN, Be Fertile, p. 294).
36 PG 53, pp. 41, 51, 64 (Homily 4:6, 5:11–12, 7:8–9), cf. CHRYSOSTOM, Homilies 1–17, pp. 54, 71f., 95f.
37 CHRYSOSTOM, Homilies 1–17, p. 72 (Homily 5:13); cf. PG 53, p. 52.
38 CHRYSOSTOM, Homilies 1–17, pp. 98f. (Homily 7:12); cf. PG 53, p. 66.
39 PG 63, pp. 23f.; cf. NPNF, ser. 1, vol. 14, p. 372.

the background – in Luther's later sermons on Genesis[40]. Chrysostom's homilies on Hebrews were also studied and frequently mentioned by Luther in his own lectures on that book. In this way, Chrysostom not only illustrates the tension present within earlier Christian thought, he is also important on account of Luther's own familiarity with the Golden-mouthed preacher.

Continuing into the Middle Ages, the emphasis upon the celibate life generally held sway throughout Western Christianity. This naturally required the continuance of a corresponding, non-naturalistic (at least not at the individual level), and somewhat ambiguous interpretation of Genesis 1:28. One development of significance, however, arrived with the church's appropriation of Aristotelian thought (ca. thirteenth century) and its influence upon natural law theory[41]. Whereas ideas of natural law in the Christian theological tradition had generally excluded Genesis 1:28 from any foundational and normative role[42], now »Be fruitful and multiply« came more and more to be understood as a precept of nature in the thought of such men as Albertus Magnus and Thomas Aquinas[43]. Nevertheless, with Aquinas the application of such *ius naturale* was left somewhat arbitrary in that it was explained as a communal command to be fulfilled by the community[44]. Thus, throughout the remainder of the Middle Ages and leading into the Reformation, a certain expectant ambiguity remained. On the one hand it balanced and maintained the status quo favoring the monastic orders and celibate hierarchy. On the other hand, Genesis 1:28 was poised to play a decisive role through the literal exegesis of Augustine and the growing impulse of natural law. That is simply to say: the stage was set for the controversy that would emerge surrounding this verse in the sixteenth century.

2.2 Liturgical Use of Genesis 1:28

An interesting topic which runs somewhat adjacent to our discussion thus far involves liturgical practice and, more specifically, ecclesial involvement and blessing of marriages. To this point, we have observed a general ambivalence towards, and even devaluation of, our verse in the early church. We noted, as it were, a decisive shift in trajectory in the late fourth century, particularly to be observed in the polemics of Jerome against Jovinian. Nevertheless, we also have observed that there were elements of tension present in some significant – and subsequently

---

40 Mickey MATTOX, Defender of the Holy Matriarchs, Boston 2003, pp. 23, 127 (and fns. 56, 58), and 193. See also the many further references available in Mattox's index (p. 313).
41 COHEN, Be Fertile, p. 289.
42 Ibid., pp. 274f.
43 Ibid., pp. 289–292.
44 Ibid., p. 291.

influential – characters of this time, notably such post-Nicene fathers as Augustine and Chrysostom.

These tensions within the thought of Augustine and Chrysostom notwithstanding, is it the case that all remnants of competing early theologies of marriage vis-à-vis virginity were simply erased from the life of the church? Is there nothing further to be said about the more elevated view of marriage and sexuality – that espoused by the likes of Jovinian, the Ambrosiaster, or Helvidius[45] – and its concomitant exaltation of our verse? Significantly for our own purposes is that there appears to be at least one such trace of such a competing theology which continues in the realm of liturgical practice and understanding. This is nothing other than the association of Genesis 1:28 with the nuptial blessing. Although the significance of such a residual element may be questioned, its presence alone gave witness to something far different than an idealized idea of virginity and celibacy. Moreover, in the survey that follows, we will see that not only did such a practice linger, but that it even came to reverberate more strongly, and least in some regions, through the span of centuries leading out of the early church and approaching the Reformation. We thus turn our attention to Christian nuptial rites and their incorporation of Genesis 1:28.

It has been suggested that some sort of priestly nuptial blessing was in use already in the first centuries of the church's history – *perhaps* in the east as early as Clement of Alexandria[46] and, subsequently, with Basil of Caesarea and Gregory of Nazianzus[47]. In the west, however, though Tertullian perhaps refers to such a practice[48], it is only in the later fourth century in the environs around Rome that such a practice can be concretely attested[49]. Here, we encounter the unknown

---

45 On Helvidius, see David G. HUNTER, Helvidius, Jovinian, and the Virginity of Mary in Late Fourth-Century Rome, in: Journal of Early Christian Studies 1, 1 (1993), pp. 47–71, at pp. 48–50. Additionally, id., »On the Sin of Adam and Eve«. A Little-Known Defense of Marriage and Childbearing by Ambrosiaster, in: The Harvard Theological Review 82, 3 (1989), pp. 283–299, at p. 289, URL: <http://www.jstor.org/stable/1510079> (21 May 2021), argues that Jerome's *The Perpetual Virginity of Blessed Mary – Against Helvidius* (see NPNF, ser. 2, vol. 6, p. 344/PL 23, p. 203) was responding to Helvidius's use of Genesis 1:28.

46 Kenneth STEVENSON, Nuptial Blessing. A Study of Christian Marriage Rites, New York 1983, pp. 13–20, argues for the idea that there is some sort of a Christian marriage liturgy present in the first three centuries of the church's history – though others, such as Korbinian RITZER, Formen, Riten und religiöses Brauchtum der Eheschliessung in den christlichen Kirchen des ersten Jahrtausends, Münster 1981, pp. 52–69, shy somewhat away from this idea due to lack of concrete evidence. Ibid., pp. 68f., does, however, point to the possibility of a pre-Constantinian nuptial blessing based on artwork found at the Catacomb of Priscilla.

47 STEVENSON, Nuptial Blessing, pp. 21–23; RITZER, Formen, p. 47.

48 David G. HUNTER (ed./tr.), Marriage in the Early Church, Eugene, OR 2001, p. 27.

49 STEVENSON, Nuptial Blessing, p. 26.

figure of Ambrosiaster and his *Quæstiones veteris et novi testament* 127, *De peccato Adæ et Evæ*[50]. In a discussion that runs counter to the then-contemporary and ever-increasing emphasis on virginity and celibacy, Ambrosiaster turns to Genesis 1:22/28 and points to its use as a nuptial blessing. He writes,

> And that these words signify nothing else, the facts themselves attest. For all created things have multiplied and improved upon the earth at God's command. For nothing could grow in a manner other than as the will and blessing of God decreed to the seeds. Therefore, how could something, which receives its increase with God's blessing and favor, be said to have come into being wrongly or not to be allowed? The tradition of this thing has remained in the synagogue and now is celebrated in the church. The result is that God's creature is joined under the blessing of God, and not by arrogant presumption, since the form has been given by the Maker himself[51].

Two points can be taken from this. First, a general correspondence can be observed – whether as particular blessing or as petition for blessing[52] – between God's word of blessing in creation and that which took place in the marital blessing offered by clergy, a role that seemed to be emerging, or is at least first attested in the West – around that time[53]. Second, such an act reflected a *de facto* understanding of marriage's original and actual blessing which ran rather counter to the emerging preeminence given to celibacy and virginity. Thus, reflected in the act of blessing itself, whether through explicit usage of Genesis 1:28 or through such indirect echoes of the blessing of offspring as later often came to the fore in reference to Tobit[54], one might argue that the idea of the blessing of procreation (and thus, Genesis 1:28)

---

50 Thomas FISCH/David G. HUNTER, Echoes of the Early Roman Nuptial Blessing. Ambrosiaster, De Peccato Adæ et Evæ, in: Ecclesia Orans 11, 2 (1994), pp. 225–244, at p. 226,: <http://search.ebscohost.com/login.aspx?direct=true&db=lsdah&AN=ATLAiBCA170327000129&site=ehost-live> (11 Oct 2021).
51 Ibid., pp. 229f.; cf. CSEL 50, p. 400. It should be noted that the blessing mentioned by Ambrosiaster was to be given only in first marriages as it was viewed that a second marriage lacked the same glory. See ibid., p. 230. See also HUNTER, Sin of Adam and Eve, pp. 287f.
52 See the discussion of these different but related understandings in Philip L. REYNOLDS, Marriage in the Western Church. The Christianization of Marriage during the Patristic and Early Medieval Periods, Leiden 1994, pp. 366–375.
53 FISCH/HUNTER, Echoes, p. 231.
54 Admittedly, references to Tobit – following in Jerome's wake – were of interest to medieval moralists due to the book's references to marital continence. Nevertheless, blessings based on this writing still referred to the blessing of seeing »one's children's children«, cf. Tobit 9:10–12. See REYNOLDS, Marriage, pp. 334–337, 372f.

had a practical function which was rather more positive than contemporaneous and ensuing theological developments may have otherwise indicated[55].

For our purposes, it is not necessary to provide a comprehensive study of the link between Genesis 1:28 and marital liturgies throughout the Middle Ages. What is helpful, however, is to simply show that this connection between Genesis 1:28 and practical, liturgical life did not simply vanish in the coming centuries. Instead, depending on time and location, our verse could serve a noticeable, if not prominent, role in church life. While prayers for blessing and fertility were a mainstay in most historic western liturgical rites (Gregorian, Gelasian, Leonine)[56] and these, conservatively speaking, at least indirectly alluded to the continued role of the primordial blessing, from time to time throughout the Middle Ages we see the *ipsissima verba* of our verse find a liturgical use.

We see, for example, a reference from Isadore of Seville (c. 560–636) to our verse and, simultaneously, to that which takes place with the nuptial blessing in the church[57]. Pope Nicholas I, in his letter to the Bulgarians from the year 866, also gives reference to the priestly nuptial blessing in connection with Genesis 1:28[58]. Interestingly, in a matter which Nicholas was also involved – i. e. the divorce of Lothar II and Theutberga[59] – the presence of our verse in relation to the nuptial blessing also appears from the pen of Hincmar of Reims. Ritzer notes that in *De Divortio Lotharii et Tetbergae*, Hincmar derives the right of the clergy to pronounce a divorce from the same right which the clergy exercised in blessing or consecrating a marriage[60]. This is grounded in Genesis 1:28, as can clearly be seen from Hincmar's words:

---

55 Ibid., pp. 362–366, offers a historic overview of the ecclesial use of a nuptial blessing and also connects the idea of blessing in this context back to the original blessing of Genesis 1:28.
56 See ibid., pp. 374–383. The Leonine form, dating back to the mid-seventh century, does not directly reference our verse, and yet is full of allusion to both Genesis 1–2 and Tobit (pp. 375–378). The Gelasian form, dating to the first half of the eighth century, is likewise rich in allusion to Genesis and the blessing originally bestowed upon Adam and Eve – though without direct citation (pp. 378f.). In the Gregorian Sacramentary, dating to around 780, one perceives an emphasis upon 1 Corinthians 7, Ephesians 5, and John 2 – but not explicitly Genesis 1:28. There is, however, a concern for blessing and progeny, which, no doubt, must be linked to 1:28. Ibid., pp. 379f., notes the Gregorian version of the *Pater mundi condito*, which, in part states, »O God, through whom the woman was joined to the man and who ordained this covenant in the beginning, and gave with it a blessing that alone neither the punishment of original sin nor the judgment of the flood could take away [...]«. See also STEVENSON, Nuptial Blessing, pp. 35–43, for his treatment of these liturgical forms.
57 RITZER, Formen, p. 356; STEVENSON, Nuptial Blessing, pp. 53f.
58 RITZER, Formen, p. 344; STEVENSON, Nuptial Blessing, p. 44; REYNOLDS, Marriage, p. 373.
59 REYNOLDS, Marriage, p. 232. See also RITZER, Formen, p. 173, who notes that Nicholas I inquired as to whether Lothar had previously received the priestly blessing with his mistress, Waldrada, prior to being joined to Theutberga.
60 See RITZER, Formen, p. 285, esp. fn. 500. Reynolds also deals extensively with the marital theology of Hincmar of Reims.

And therefore both the deputies (*vicarii*) of Christ and the successors of the apostles [bishops] established these laws, and we howsoever presiding over the Church of God in their place, insert them here, so that the blessing which the Lord first gave to Adam and his wife in paradise, saying »Increase and multiply« [Genesis 1:28], which given once is to this day and to the end not denied not only to the faithful but also to infidels, may be given individually by the mouths of the priests to the faithful and the devout, as a holy mystery – which Christ brought through His presence to the wedding where He made water into wine[61].

Interestingly, we might here note that such liturgical use – to whatever extent it existed – would easily place our verse in common parlance. This, of course, raises the question as to whether the popular references to *Crescite et multiplicamini*, such as were associated with medieval magical practices[62] or as are found in Chaucer[63], may acknowledge the presence of these words in more general liturgical usage?

Whatever the case may be, it is interesting to note that as we approach the Reformation era, the priestly nuptial blessing had not disappeared. In fact, in some regions and liturgies, its usage is quite pronounced. We note, for example, that our verse enjoyed at least a minimal recognition in fifteenth century France, appearing, as it did, in the Lyon Agenda of 1498[64]. Somewhat closer in proximity to Wittenberg, one notes that our verse was also reflected in one of the blessings contained in the Meissen Agenda of 1512[65]. Thus, while perhaps not particularly prevalent in the medieval church, Bugenhagen and Luther's later incorporations of

---

61 Rachel STONE/Charles WEST, The Divorce of King Lothar and Queen Theutberga. Hincmar of Rheims's De Divortio, Manchester 2016, p. 134; cf. PL 125, p. 653. Hincmar elsewhere writes of this same ritual blessing in a letter to the king, *De coercendo et exstirpando raptu viduarum, puellarum ac sanctimonialium*, where he states, »Nam et in exordio mundi ad propagationem generis humani masculum et feminam Deus fecit, eosque sua benediction conjunxit dicens: *Crescite et multiplicamini* (Gen. 1:28)«. »[…] Cujus rei imitatione etiam sancta Ecclesia antiquitus solemniter et venerabiliter custodivit, eos qui in illa velut in paradiso Dei conjugio copulandi essent, divina benedictione et missarum celebratione conungens«. Ibid., p. 1020.
62 COHEN, Be Fertile, p. 271; cf. Oswald COCKAYNE (ed.), Leechdoms, Wortcunning, and Starcraft of Early England, London 1864, vol. 1, pp. 399, 404f. Here are referenced several charms and spells of medieval England (prior to the Norman Conquest of 1066) which make use of *Crescite*.
63 Famously, in the prologue to *The Wyves Tale of Bathe*, Chaucer (c. 1343–1400) has his concupiscent character citing God's command to be fruitful and multiply as justification for her lascivious living. See also COHEN, Be Fertile, pp. 271f., 301–305.
64 At the completion of the nuptial Mass in Lyon, the priest was to say, »Ite in nomine Domini; crescite et multiplicamini et replete terram, et fructus vester maneat«. Jean-Baptiste MOLIN/Protais MUTEMBE, Le rituel du mariage en France du XIIe au XVIe siècle, Paris 1974, p. 316 (Ordo XVIII); cf. STEVENSON, Nuptial Blessing, pp. 76, 225, n. 39.
65 Ibid., pp. 90, 228, n. 20; cf. Albert SCHÖNFELDER, Sammlung gottesdienstlicher Bücher aus dem deutschen Mittelalter, Paderborn 1904, vol. 1, pp. 26f.

Genesis 1:28 into marital liturgies and blessings were not entirely unprecedented. Indeed, while the sources they may have relied upon are not easily identifiable, their later employment of our verse falls within the wider spectrum of ancient and medieval liturgical practice[66].

2.3 Natural Law, Nature, Human Will, and Reason

We now turn our attention toward the long history of natural law thought and debate in which the reformers also participated. To be fair, this is a somewhat complicated topic due to terminological fluidity and the presence of multiple historical, theological, and philosophical layers. In point of fact, if approaching this topic from the vantage point of Luther scholarship on natural law, one might well arrive at the conclusion that the topic of natural law is of little relevance for our study[67]. Nevertheless, if the topic is approached from the broader vantage point of

---

66 For more on the liturgical use of Genesis 1:28 in the Reformation, see Chapter 5. See also Appendix 2 of KLAWITTER, Forceful and Fruitful, pp. 291–296.

67 A thorough, though not exhaustive, investigation of this matter shows that the contours of »natural law« in Luther's thought – as treated by scholarship – have been defined by the terminological usage of Luther, though not according to the historic expanse of the historic debates (even as he would have recognized it). For example, one finds in Hermann Wolfgang BEYER, Luther und das Recht, München 1935, p. 24, a telling subheading and quotation. Beyer states, »Der Begriff des ›Naturrechts‹ ist mißverständlich. Denn Recht gibt es nur unter den Menschen«. A quote from Luther's *Tischreden* then follows (here citing directly from WA Tr 1, nr. 581, pp. 267f. and not from Beyer's translation): »Iureconsulti non proprie definiunt ius naturae, quod hominibus et bestiis commune est, quia necesse est in iure naturali distingui hominem tanquam dominum a ceteris bestiis, et est ei tribuendum aliquid excellentius. Rectius igitur loquerentur, si dicerent aliud ius naturae brutale, aliud rationale. Secundo ius non est apud bestiam, sed tantum in homine, ergo non proprie vocant ius naturae. Quia ius est, quod debet fieri. Quinque et tria non debent esse octo, sed sunt octo. Sic improprie dicitur ius naturae in bestia, quod se defendit; defendere enim fit sua sponte, et est ipsa natura. Res igitur est in bestia, et non ius, quod tantum existit in homine. Gignere et alere sunt facta, res, et non iura. In omni iure mus das debet sein. Zur sau darff man nit sagen, das si essen sol, sed sie thuts ungeheissen. Iureconsulti igitur proprie non habent ius naturale, sed tantum ius gentium, quod profluit ex ratione humana«. Clearly, Luther is addressing the age-old debate, even if he uses terminology other than that of natural law.

Given the above state of Luther scholarship, if one is familiar with the fact that Romans Catholic traditions of natural law thought do, in fact, give thorough treatment to matters of sexuality as a part of natural law and the natural order of things – here see, for example, Humanae vitae, sections 4 and 11; cf. Pope (Papst) PAUL VI., Über die Geburtenregelung. Rundschreiben »Humanae vitae« »Vom menschlichen Leben«, Leutesdorf am Rhein 1968, pp. 10, 18, one will quickly be surprised to discover that Luther scholarship tends to be bogged down with discussions of the Ten Commandments, the Golden Rule, and other seemingly abstract principles. It might even lead to the conclusion that Lutheran ethics have nothing concrete to say on the topic (at least from this perspective). Be that as

the history of natural law, it becomes clear that historical discussions surrounding natural law comprise an important backdrop for our own investigation – even if and even though they largely emerged in Reformation discussions under slightly different categories.

Historic Background

We begin our discussion of this topic, therefore, by noting that the concept of natural law has historically contained various divergent strands. The predominate strand, both in classical times as well as in pre-Reformation scholasticism, involved reason's recognition of the natural moral order of things. Thus, the fundamental strain of natural law generally discussed pertains to reason's understanding of morality in such maxims as the Golden Rule, the Ten Commandments, or *lex charitatis*. In fact, for the most part, when reformers such as Luther and Melanchthon discuss natural law, they are in dialogue with this understanding of natural law.

---

it may, the point here is not to say that previous studies are incorrect in their findings. According to Luther's understanding of what is properly to be included under natural law (see above), their findings are appropriate. Nevertheless, the point can be maintained that these studies have not given proper attention to the full expanse of the historic natural law landscape and how and under which topics the »leftovers« were appropriated into Luther's thought.

In making the above conclusions as to the »state of the question« on this matter in Luther scholarship, the sources listed below offer the following general picture:

1 As noted above by Beyer, several other sources note Luther's (as well as his Wittenberg colleagues') rejection of the Ulpianic (i. e. naturalistic) definition of natural law. Franz Xaver ARNOLD, Zur Frage des Naturrechts bei Martin Luther, München 1936, pp. 110f.; Rudolf HERMANN, Studien zur Theologie Luthers und des Luthertums. Gesammelte und nachgelassene Werke, edited by Horst BEINTKER, Göttingen 1981, vol. 2, p. 98, though he refers only to the *jurists*; and Richard NÜRNBERGER, Die lex naturae als Problem der vita christiana bei Luther, in: Archiv für Reformationsgeschichte 37, 1 (1938), pp. 1–12, at p. 3, can be included in this grouping. Franz LAU, »Äußerliche Ordnung« und »Weltlich Ding« in Luthers Theologie, Göttingen 1933, notes that a study of Luther's usage of *Ordnung* terminology ends up nearer to commonly held understandings of natural law, although Lau is clear as to Luther's own usage of the term (see esp. pp. 115–160). John T. McNEILL, Natural Law in the Thought of Luther, in: Church History 10, 3 (1941), pp. 211–227, at p. 224, esp. fn. 45, URL: <https://doi.org/10.2307/3160251> (23 Aug 2022), cites Arnold's writing and then also notes that »the Lutheran jurist John Oldendorp rejected Ulpian's views that ›ius naturale est quod natura omnia animalia docuit‹ as an abuse of the word ›ius‹, and agrees with Cicero: in the brutes there is no *ratio* hence there is no *ius*«. Thomas D. PEARSON, Luther's Pragmatic Appropriation of the Natural Law Tradition, in: Roland Cap EHLKE/Robert C. BAKER (eds.), Natural Law. A Lutheran Reappraisal, St. Louis 2011, pp. 39–64, at pp. 41–44, notes the various strands and complex history of natural law prior to Luther – including the Ulpianic tradition. One might, however, question whether his assessment of Luther's understanding of »nature as implanted by God« (pp. 61f.) has not somehow missed the connection between the Ulpianic tradition of natural law and Luther's use of »nature« in this case.

In the history of natural law, however, there is a second important strain of thought that originated out of the Stoic tradition[68], was propagated via Cicero, brought into the Roman legal tradition, and thus manifested itself in certain schools

---

2 Other sources with their divergent focuses, though providing their own insights to Luther's thought, do not mention this rejection of Ulpian's definition of natural law, much less offer any extensive treatment of Luther's interaction with this historic strain of natural law. Here we include Johannes HECKEL, Lex Charitatis. Eine juristische Untersuchung über das Recht in der Theologie Martin Luthers, Köln 1973; Martin SCHLOEMANN, Natürliches und gepredigtes Gesetz bei Luther, Berlin 1961; Knut ALFSVÅG, Natural Theology and Natural Law in Martin Luther, in: Oxford Research Encyclopedia of Religion (2016), URL: <https://doi.org/10.1093/acrefore/9780199340378.013.368> (18 Aug 2022); Gifford GROBIEN, A Lutheran Understanding of Natural Law in the Three Estates, in: Concordia Theological Quarterly 73 (2009), pp. 211–229, URL: <http://www.ctsfw.net/media/pdfs/GrobienALutheranUnderstandingOfNaturalLaw.pdf> (18 Aug 2022); Gary SIMPSON, »Written on Their Hearts«. Thinking with Luther about Scripture, Natural Law, and the Moral Life, in: Word and World 30, 4 (2010), pp. 419–428, URL: <https://wordandworld.luthersem.edu/content/pdfs/30-4_Paul/30-4_simpson.pdf> (18 Aug 2022); Charles J. DARYL, Protestants and Natural Law, in: First Things Dec (2006), pp. 33–38, URL: <https://www.proquest.com/openview/60fd7bd86fb8eba72ae01b750345ea75/1?pq-origsite=gscholar&cbl=45949> (23 Aug 2022); Klaus Detlev SCHULZ, Two Kinds of Righteousness and Moral Philosophy. Confessio Augustana XVIII, Philipp Melanchthon, and Martin Luther, in: Concordia Theological Quarterly 73 (2009), pp. 17–40, URL: <http://www.ctsfw.net/media/pdfs/SchulzTwoKindsofRighteosnessAndMoralPhilosophy.pdf> (18 Aug 2022); George W. FORELL, Luther's Conception of Natural Orders, in: Word and World Supplement Series 2 (1994), pp. 66–82; Herbert OLSSON, Schöpfung, Vernunft und Gesetz in Luthers Theologie, Uppsala 1971; Eckehart STÖVE, Natürliches Recht und Heilige Schrift. Zu einem vergessenen Aspekt in Martin Luthers Hermeneutik, in: Irene DINGEL et al. (eds.), Reformation und Recht, FS G. Seebaß, Gütersloh 2002, pp. 11–25; Antti RAUNIO, Divine and Natural Law in Luther and Melanchthon, in: Virpi MÄKINEN (ed.), Lutheran Reformation and the Law, Boston 2006, pp. 21–62; Antti RAUNIO, Summe des christlichen Lebens, Mainz 2001; LÄHTEENMÄKI, Sexus, pp. 142–150. One further work of interest is A[ndries] RAATH, Moral-jural Reflections on the Right to Marital Dignity and the »Nursery of Human Society«. Interpreting Luther's Views on Conjugal Rights and Benevolent Love, in: Koers – Bulletin for Christian Scholarship 73, 3 (2008), pp. 411–443, URL: <https://doi.org/10.4102/koers.v73i3.168> (18 Aug 2022). This essay places Luther's thought regarding marriage and sexuality on the moral philosophical framework of Cicero and thus seeks to demonstrate how Luther's thought on these matters can be viewed as consistent with certain classic traditions of natural law understanding.

68 Felix FLÜCKIGER, Geschichte des Naturrechtes, Zürich 1954, vol. 1, p. 203. It should be noted that throughout our review of this strain of thought, we will largely follow Felix Flückiger's most helpful and thorough historic introduction to the history of natural law up through Aquinas as well as Rudolf WEIGAND, Die Naturrechtslehre der Legisten und Dekretisten von Irnerius bis Accursius und von Gratian bis Johannes Teutonicus, München 1967, who offers a complementary and detailed treatment of the natural law thought of the lawyers and decretalists in roughly the twelfth and thirteenth centuries. A further work of utmost relevance for this topic is Michael Bertram CROWE, The Changing Profile of the Natural Law, The Hague 1977.

of thought all the way into the Middle Ages[69]. This strain of legal thought is characterized less by reason's ability to make moral determinations than by reason's recognition of the universal arrangement of nature/creation and the moral responsibility to live according to that ordering[70]. We will benefit from a closer examination of this strain of natural law thinking in that it lays the context for a certain amount of the discussion which we will encounter throughout our study.

Beginning with Stoic thought, Felix Flückiger notes its fusion of divine wisdom with the *lex naturae*. Thus, classic Stoic thought embraced not merely the idea of a divine fatalism but also fully embraced the ideal of living according to the creative ordering of the *Logos* through the pantheistic notion of a shared participation of the *Logos* present in man[71]. This becomes then especially noteworthy in that the Stoics understood the *Logos's lex naturae* as ordering and working the creature's natural drives toward self-preservation, whether in finding food or through procreation[72].

---

69 Weigand does a masterful job of tracing out these various strains of thought and of highlighting the presence (or lack thereof) of the Ulpianic definition throughout his study.
70 FLÜCKIGER, Geschichte, pp. 203f.
71 *Logos (lat. from grk. λόγος)*, in Stoic philosophy, refers to the universal governing principle/wisdom; in Christian theology it refers to the eternal Son of the Father (Jn 1:1).
While Luther shares neither in the fatalism of the Stoics nor their pantheistic understanding of creation, it will be clearly recognized that there are distinct points of similarity between Stoic thought on the *Logos*, its *Nomos* (reason and *lex naturae* in one), and creation with Luther's own understanding of the creative Word. The following quote from FLÜCKIGER, Geschichte, pp. 196f., is insightful: »Gottes Vernunft ist der Logos. Und so wie Gott in der ganzen Natur tätig ist, muß auch der Logos überall wirksam sein[…]«.
»In Gott gibt es keinen Zufall. Alles, was die göttliche Vernunft wirkt, ist zweckmäßig in Hinsicht auf die Vollkommenheit des Weltganzen. Zufolge dieser Zweckmäßigkeit – die jede Möglichkeit ausschließt, daß etwas auch anders geschehen könnte – kann der Logos auch als Weltgesetz oder Naturgesetz bezeichnet werden. Alle Dinge werden durch dieses Gesetz gelenkt und determiniert. Auch das scheinbar Zufällige unterliegt in Wahrheit einer Zwangsläufigkeit, die dem Betrachter bloß nicht erkennbar ist. Der Nomos, das Weltgesetz, ist also göttliche Vernunft und Naturordnung (lex naturae) in einem: Er bewegt die Gestirne, läßt die Pflanzen wachsen, er wirkt als Naturtrieb in der belebten Natur und heißt die Tiere Nahrung suchen und sich fortpflanzen, er bewirkt aber auch die Handlungen der Menschen, er ist überall und ewig, denn die Einheit und Unvergänglichkeit Gottes bedingt auch die Einheit und Unvergänglichkeit des Gesetzes in allem«. On the importance and strength of this fusion of the divine law and nature, see also ibid., pp. 224f.
72 Ibid., p. 197. FLÜCKIGER, Geschichte, p. 203, also observes that according to Stoic thought, »Jedem Lebewesen wohnt von Natur der Trieb inne, ›daß es sich, sein Leben und seinen Körper zu erhalten versucht, indem es meidet, was schädlich scheint, hingegen alles aufsucht und beschafft, was zum Leben notwendig ist, wie Nahrung und Unterkunft. Ferner ist allen Lebewesen der Trieb zur geschlechtlichen Vereinigung zum Zweck der Fortpflanzung gemeinsam, sowie eine gewisse Fürsorge für die Nachkommen‹. Selbsterhaltungstrieb und Paarungstrieb sind also wirkliche Seinsordnung. Das Naturgesetz ist eine Macht, welche die Dinge antreibt und in bestimmter Richtung lenkt. Aber aus dem Vorhandensein dieser naturgesetzlichen Triebe folgt dann auch ein ›Recht‹ auf Geschlechtsgemeinschaft«.

It is noteworthy that Flückiger, in making the foregoing observations, cites Cicero's *De officiis* as representative of Stoic thought on this matter. For our purposes, the mention of Cicero – and particularly this writing – is significant in that both of these were held in high esteem by Luther and Melanchthon[73]. Quoting from Cicero:

> First of all, Nature has endowed every species of living creature with the instinct of self-preservation, of avoiding what seems likely to cause injury to life or limb, and of procuring and providing everything needful for life – food, shelter, and the like. A common property of all creatures is also the reproductive instinct (the purpose of which is the propagation of the species) and also a certain amount of concern for their offspring[74].

Indeed, according to Cicero, the parts of the body themselves indicate this procreative purpose of nature, especially in combination with the natural love »Nature« provides between parents and their offspring. Along these lines, Cicero writes in *De finibus*,

> Again, it is held by the Stoics to be important to understand that nature creates in parents an affection for their children; and parental affection is the source to which we trace the origin of the association of the human race in communities. This cannot but be clear in the first place from the conformation of the body and its members, which by themselves are enough to show that nature's scheme included the procreation of offspring. Yet it could not be consistent that nature should at once intend offspring to be born and make no provision for that offspring when born to be loved and cherished. Even in the lower animals nature's operation can be clearly discerned; when we observe the labour that they spend on bearing and rearing their young, we seem to be listening to the actual voice of

---

73 Melanchthon produced several annotated versions of *De officiis* with the first appearing in 1525: Marcus Tullius Cicero/Philipp Melanchthon, OFFICIA CIERONIS, CVM SCHOLIIS PHIL.MELAN. QVAE possint esse uice prolixi commentarij. Nam pleriq; loci quos hactenus nemo attigit, hic enarrantur, Hagenau 1525 (VD16 C 3180). Additionally, Luther's appreciation for Cicero has long been noted. See, for example, Carl P.E. Springer, Cicero in Heaven. The Roman Rhetor and Luther's Reformation, Leiden 2018. See also Anne Eusterschulte, Zur Rezeption von »de officiis« bei Philipp Melanchthon und im Kreis seiner Schüler, in: Ead./Günter Frank (eds.), Cicero in der frühen Neuzeit, Stuttgart-Bad Cannstatt 2018, pp. 323–362, for an account of the importance to Cicero generally, but particularly the writing *De officiis* as a basic text for non-theological Reformation ideals.
74 Marcus Tullius Cicero, De Officiis, translated by Walter Miller, Cambridge et al. 1975, (Cicero in Twenty-Eight Volumes 21), bk. 1:4 (p. 13); cf. »Principio generi animantium omni est a natura tributum, ut se, vitam corpusque tueatur, decline tea, quae nocitura videantur, omniaque, quae sint ad vivendum necessaria, anquirat et paret, ut pastum, ut latibula, ut alia generis eiusdem. Commune item animantium omnium est coniunctionis adpetitus procreandi causa et cura quaedam eorum, quae procreata sint«. Ibid., p. 12.

nature. Hence as it is manifest that it is natural for us to shrink from pain, so it is clear that we derive from nature herself the impulse to love those to whom we have given birth[75].

Particularly noteworthy in the above citation is the fact that in the Stoic tradition (especially as exemplified by Cicero), such understandings of *natural affection* – particularly for and then between children and their parents – and also of the self-evident, procreation-directed nature of the body and its members, serve as component elements. While Cicero is not the only source from which the reformers may have derived the natural language which they employed in their argumentation, it certainly is worth highlighting that precisely these arguments will be observed again and again in our study. At the very minimum, however, we may observe that Cicero (and the Stoic tradition he represents) ought to be considered as a part of the conversation being carried on during the Reformation, both on account of the reformers' familiarity with the famed Roman, but also on account of their appreciation for him.

Before moving further with this strain of natural law thinking and its possible reception by the reformers, we do well to highlight a latent tension present within this ideation. Flückiger notes that although the Stoics recognized the natural drive toward procreation, the question of the relationship between desires and this drive was something of a conflicted matter. For example, a purer Stoic tradition downplayed and disparaged the role of the affects, likening them to something of a sickness or weakness. Along those lines, he notes a difference between Aristotle's understanding of the affects and that espoused by the Stoics. Whereas Aristotle placed the affects under the rule of reason, thus assuming them to be inherently good albeit disordered, the Stoics had no use for desire, as such, and strove toward an unaffected state[76]. It is of more than passing interest that Cicero displayed a more mediating view, even expressing some conflict with the stricter expressions of Stoicism on this matter[77]. At any rate, the place of urges and the desires that

---

75 Marcus Tullius CICERO, De Finibus Bonorum et Malorum, translated by H. Rackham, Cambridge et al. 1971 (Cicero in Twenty-Eight Volumes 17), bk. 3:19 (pp. 281, 283), cf. »Pertinere autem ad rem arbitrantur intelligi natura fieri, ut liberi a parentibus amentur; a quo initio profectam communem humani generis societatem persequimur. Quod primum intelligi debet figura membrisque corporum, quae ipsa declarant, procreandi a natura habitam esse rationem. Neque vero haec inter se congruere possent ut natura et procreari vellet et diligi procreatos non curaret. Atque etiam in bestiis vis naturae perspici potest; quarum in fetu et in educatione laborem cum cernimus, naturae ipsius vocem videmu audire. Quare ut perspicuum est natura nos a dolore abhorrere, sic apparet a natura ipsa ut eos genuerimus amemus impelli«. Ibid., pp. 280, 282.
76 FLÜCKIGER, Geschichte, pp. 209–213.
77 In comparing Cicero's thought with that of more strict Stoicism, ibid., pp. 236f., observes, »Entsprechend diesem bekannten doppelten Ansatz wird das ›Naturgemäße‹ bald vom Standpunkt der materialen Wertethik, bald vom Nützlichkeitsprinzip aus begründet, wobei allerdings der letztere

accompany them remained somewhat conflicted amongst the Stoic tradition and its followers.

Aside from familiarity with the writings of Cicero and other classical thinkers, Luther and the reformers would have also had contact with this strain of natural law thought via the Roman Law tradition codified some two centuries after Cicero. Of particular importance to this tradition were the writings of the legal commentator, Domitius Ulpianus (170–223 A.D.), who appropriated a modified version of Stoic thought into the Roman Law tradition. Along these lines, Ulpian emphasized especially the compulsory nature of procreation as expressed through its corresponding drives[78]. Moreover, it is certainly fair to bring up Luther in connection with Ulpian's appropriation of this topic in that Johannes Heckel observes Luther to have interacted with Ulpian's definition of this aspect of natural law. Here Luther rejected Ulpian's usage of the term »law« for anything having to do with animals, though admittedly he did not reject the compulsory nature expressed therewith by Ulpian[79].

Various scholars have also observed the influence of Stoic thought on early Christian thinkers. Coincidentally, we note that in those where this seems to be the strongest (e. g. Clement of Alexandria) we also find a higher valuation of Genesis 1:28[80]. Nevertheless, for our own study, the influence of this natural law tradition seems somewhat less significant in that those aspects concerned with the normative nature of the natural procreative drive were generally downplayed by theologians

---

    Gesichtspunkt vorwiegt. In der Schrift vom ›höchsten Gut und Übel‹ polemisiert Cicero sogar ausdrücklich gegen den strengen Ethizismus jener Stoiker, welche nur die Tugend als Gut anerkennen und daher selbst die ersten naturgemäßen Dinge, d. h. die angeborenen Triebe, als nicht dem Naturgesetz entsprechend ablehnen«.

78 »Auch für Ulpian ist das ius gentium ein gemeinsames Recht der Völker und daher zu unterscheiden vom ius civile. Ebenso muß es aber auch unterschieden werden vom Naturrecht, das ein Recht ist, welches für die ganze belebte Natur Geltung hat, für die Tiere nicht anders als für die ganze belebte Natur Geltung hat, für die Tiere nicht anders als für die Menschen. Dieses Recht gründet sich auf die vitalen Naturtriebe, die sich in der ganzen Natur auswirken, wie z. B. der Geschlechtstrieb. Im Wesentlichen scheint für Ulpian nur die natürliche Fortpflanzung, und was durch diese bedingt ist, zum Naturrecht zu gehören. Die vitale Natur ist hier wirklich zum Prinzip gemacht; es handelt sich um eine Ordnung des Seins, eine Gesetzmäßigkeit, der die Natur zwangsläufig folgt […]«.

»Das Naturgesetz ist für ihn der Naturtrieb, das Recht der Natur demnach das Recht, nach diesem Triebe zu leben und ihm zu folgen. Wenn in diesem Zusammenhang auch die Ehe genannt wird, so darf hierbei nicht schon an die Einehe im kirchlichen Sinn gedacht werden; eine solche Auslegung verbietet schon der betonte Hinweis, daß dieses Recht auch den Tieren bekannt sei. Es wird nur festgestellt, daß der natürliche Trieb der Fortpflanzung allen Lebewesen mitgegeben ist und daß sich in diesem Trieb das Naturgesetz kundgibt«. Ibid., p. 269. See also WEIGAND, Naturrechtslehre, pp. 12–14.

79 HECKEL, Lex Charitatis, p. 115, fn. 592.
80 COHEN, Be Fertile, p. 231.

on account of the prevalent and ever-increasing association of concupiscence with sexual desire. The growing emphasis placed upon virginity and celibacy naturally only exacerbated this situation. This might be said for such luminaries as both Ambrose and Augustine, the latter's Neoplatonist contribution to natural law thought notwithstanding[81].

Returning, however, to the progression of natural law thinking that would have likely influenced the reformers on the topic of procreation, it seems that the legal-philosophical tradition would have served as the central purveyor. In this respect, an important ideological leap occurred in Christian legal thought as principles of Roman Law were gradually fused into the Christian legal tradition. Naturally, this also involved the natural law thought of Ulpian, to include his emphasis on procreation as a sort of natural law also in force within the animal world. In fact, despite the church's theological ambiguity and uncertainty as pertained to procreation, Christian legal thought at the beginning of the Middle Ages generally embodied a strong emphasis upon procreation with its respective drives[82].

Canon Law's Struggle with Ulpian[83]

As we approach the developments of the High Middle Ages, it is of benefit to sketch out the contours of some of the major themes and events shaping church life in

---

81 FLÜCKIGER, Geschichte, p. 252, notes that it is from Plotin's Neoplatonic vision of a hierarchic order that the well-developed systems of Thomas Aquinas and others eventually emanated. An important intermediate development, however, was that of Augustine. He, most notably, contributed the idea that also the postlapsarian state of nature, given its corruption but not essential loss, could still reflect the natural ordering established by God in creation. For the influence of Neoplatonism on Augustine and his resultant contribution to the development of natural law thought, see ibid., pp. 377–387.

82 WEIGAND, Naturrechtslehre, p. 62. Weigand notes, amongst other changes, the following developments at the beginning of the Middle Ages: »In Form eines kurzen Überblickes über die gesamte legistische Entwicklung soll noch bemerkt werden: Am Anfang der mittelalterlichen Rechtswissenschaft stand für längere Zeit ein doppelter Naturrechtsbegriff: das nach *Ulpians* Definition Mensch und Tier gemeinsame Naturrecht (wenn Naturrecht ohne Zusatz gebraucht wird, ist fast immer dieses ›Recht‹ gemeint, das für die Legisten eindeutig im Vordergrund steht!), und das nur den Menschen eigene rationale Naturrecht, das mit dem ›Völkerrecht‹, wenigstens zum Teil, identisch ist«. Representatives of this time period and school of thought would not have been totally unknown in Wittenberg. For example, as noted in Sachiko KUSUKAWA, A Wittenberg University Library Catalogue of 1536, Cambridge 1995, p. 101, Portius Azo's *Summa Azonis* (Venice 1498) was part of the University of Wittenberg's library. WEIGAND, Naturrechtslehre, pp. 51–56, also offers discussion concerning Azo.

83 This section (up to »The Turn away from Ulpian«) is, in part, an adaptation taken from a portion of Brandt KLAWITTER, Where Laws, Sexes, and Bodies Converge. Discussions of Sex and Gender in Church and Natural Law (ca. 1140–1234), in: Zeitschrift für Kirchengeschichte 132, 1 (2021), pp. 16–32.

the Christian West in and around the twelfth and thirteenth centuries. One of the most prominent features stemming out of the eleventh century and into the twelfth century has to do with the consolidation of papal power relative to the power of the state. This was, however, part of a larger movement of church reform which was aimed, generally, at the renewal and betterment of the church under the unquestioned authority of the pope[84]. In addition to questions of simony and lay investiture, a further significant element of reform was also the question of clerical celibacy, a matter that found its official resolution particularly in the Second Lateran Council (1139) and further legal codification in canon law developments only slightly later[85].

Here it is of significance that a major instrument in this reform movement and its associated consolidation of papal power was the collection and employment of canon law. Church law or canon law had been in existence since earliest Christian memory and, as the church grew, became legalized, and then institutionalized, church law also grew in significance and scope[86]. Nevertheless, church law in the eleventh century remained a scattered and disorganized hodge-podge and was thus a rather ineffective tool for applying ecclesiastical/papal policy for a church that had become political in nature. To become effective, therefore, it needed to be compiled, systematized, and consolidated. Several eleventh century efforts already tended in this direction. An early example of this was Bishop Burchard of Worms (d. 1025), whose *Decretum* of 1012 with its 1785 canons in twenty books signified an important step in this direction[87]. Three significant collections, attributed to Bishop Ivo of Chartres, also appeared near the end of the century and introduced developments in methodology and organization[88]. Nevertheless, despite growing focus upon canon law throughout the eleventh century and into the twelfth, the desired effectiveness and ability to apply and implement ecclesial/papal judgments in the Christian West was still less than desired[89].

---

84 For a helpful overview of the events of this era, see, for example, Carl A. VOLZ, The Medieval Church. From the Dawn of the Middle Ages to the Eve of the Reformation, Nashville 1997, chapters 4 and 5 [cf. pp. 73–117].
85 James A. BRUNDAGE, Law, Sex, and Christian Society in Medieval Europe, Chicago 1987, p. 220.
86 Id., The Medieval Origins of the Legal Profession. Canonists, Civilians, and Courts, Chicago/London 2008, pp. 39–45, traces out the expansion and unwieldiness of canon law already in the waning days of the western Christianized Roman Empire and, pp. 63–68, details its growth throughout the early Middle Ages.
87 Ibid., p. 67, notes that Burchard's *Decretum* was composed for teaching purposes, though elsewhere he mentions the *Decretum* as part of the larger church reform movement of the eleventh century. See BRUNDAGE, Law, Sex, and Christian Society, pp. 180f.
88 Id., The Medieval Origins, pp. 94–96.
89 See id., Law, Sex, and Christian Society, pp. 180–182.

All of this changed as we work our way into the twelfth century. Carried along by the renewal particularly of civil (i. e. Roman) law centered in Bologna – which, significantly for this study, accompanied the reemergence of the Justinian Code and especially the *Digests*[90] – church law was catapulted to new political-ecclesial[91] heights by the compilation, systematization, and reconciliation of existing materials by one Gratian[92]. Beginning in perhaps 1125 and extending through the 1140s, several compilations of canon law material were produced, culminating with *Concordia discordantium canonum* (reconciliation of discordant canons or ecclesial rules), otherwise known as Gratian's *Decreta* and later officially as the *Decretum*[93]. It was, for all intents and purposes, a summary of church law from the first 1100 years and the authoritative basis for ecclesial jurisprudence throughout

---

90 Id., The Medieval Origins, pp. 80–94, traces out the revival of the study of Roman Law in Bologna and, to a lesser extent, elsewhere in Western Europe. As noted by Adam Vetulani, Gratien et le Droit Romain, in: Revue Historique de Droit Français et étranger Quatrième Série 24 (1946), pp. 11–48, at p. 11, URL: <www.jstor.org/stable/43844212> (25 May 2020), and Stephan Kuttner, Gratian and the Schools of Law, 1140–1234, London/New York ²2018, p. 48, URL: <https://doi.org/10.4324/9781351058957> (18 Aug 2022). The Digests played a more significant role for Gratian than did the Institutes.

91 Regarding the growing importance of church law for the twelfth century western church, see Kenneth Pennington/Wolfgang P. Müller, The Decretists. The Italian School, in: William Hartmann/Kenneth Pennington (eds.), The History of Medieval Canon Law in the Classical Period, 1140–1234. From Gratian to the Decretals of Pope Gregory IX, Washington, D.C. 2008, pp. 121–173, at pp. 126f., URL: <http://search.ebscohost.com/login.aspx?direct=true&db=nlebk&AN=360295&site=ehost-live> (23 April 2020). Moreover, in connection with the political-ecclesial nature of church reform, Walter Ullmann, Medieval Papalism. The Political Theories of Medieval Canonists, New York 2010 (first published 1948), makes the powerful argument that, corresponding with the papal claims amounting to universal sovereignty, canon law represented the legal arm, and thus enactment, of that universal claim. It claimed for itself the status of divine, natural, and universal law and was, therefore, not merely limited to scriptural proof texts and quotations from church fathers. Rather, it amalgamated within its volumes classical philosophy and Roman legal thought, even as it incorporated and transformed ancient ideas about natural law for service in the church reform movement, which was, in many respects, tantamount to the consolidation of papal power. At any rate, its claim to universality rested heavily upon its ability to claim itself as an expression of universal law – that is divine and natural law. Brundage, The Medieval Origins, pp. 78f., offers an overview of further, more recent, instantiations – and counters – to such argumentation, particularly to that of Harold Berman, Law and Revolution. The Formation of the Western Legal Tradition, Cambridge et al. 1983.

92 Brundage, Law, Sex, and Christian Society, p. 229.

93 For dating, see Peter Landau, Gratian and the Decretum Gratiani, in: Hartmann/Pennington (eds.), History of Medieval Canon Law, pp. 22–54, at pp. 24f., URL: <http://search.ebscohost.com/login.aspx?direct=true&db=nlebk&AN=360295&site=ehost-live> (23 Apr 2020). See also Brundage, The Medieval Origins, pp. 102f., for his discussion of the development of the *Decretum*. Regarding the naming of Gratian's work and its unofficial status, see Landau, Gratian and the Decretum, pp. 22f.

the remainder of the Middle Ages – the fact that it never officially received papal authorization notwithstanding[94].

We might further note that what was especially important for Gratian's work was not simply that he compiled so much material under various topics. Rather, it was especially his scholastic method of presentation which proved especially helpful[95]. His manner was to present various normative texts and to these, where seeming contradictions emerged, he would add his own attempted reconciliations, or *dicta*. In many ways, this synthesis would be influential for not only scholastic thought, but also the basis upon which canon law could become a more unified and effective legal instrument[96].

Gratian's *Decretum* thus quickly became the standard text from which those who taught canon law worked. Needless to say, these decretists, while using Gratian's work as their basis, did not always limit themselves to his solutions. Rather, his text served as a basis for their own legal speculations, discussion, and debate – much of which eventually made its way into marginal notes and then later appeared in semi-authoritative collections such as Johannes Teutonicus's *Glossa ordinaria* [cir. 1215][97]. The central corpus of canon law was also largely defined during this period. It was based on Gratian's *Decretum* and then stretched to include particularly Raymond de Peñafort's compilation of primarily papal decretals, *Liber extra*, which was given official sanction by Pope Gregory IX in 1234[98].

Yet what did these developments mean for topics related to marriage and celibacy and to what extent was Ulpian's understanding of natural law present in these discussions? We can begin with the observation that these topics were indeed important points of ecclesial discussion during this formative era in the history of canon law. Practical concerns derived from the church's newfound legal authority – also in the realms involving marriage and sexuality – required this[99]. Thus, the manner in which canon lawyers defined their terms was not of mere pastoral or theological concern, but also had real-world, legal ramifications which would be of significance in untangling such thorny issues as who could legally marry and what constituted a lawful marriage, not to mention such questions as the significance and proper function of the sexual relationship for and within marriage. In hashing out such matters, definitions of natural law played their own important role.

---

94 BRUNDAGE, The Medieval Origins, p. 75.
95 See LANDAU, Gratian and the Decretum, p. 42, or BRUNDAGE, The Medieval Origins, pp. 97f.
96 LANDAU, Gratian and the Decretum, p. 22.
97 CROWE, Changing Profile, p. 109.
98 VOLZ, The Medieval Church, p. 95, among others notes this. Kriston R. RENNIE, Medieval Canon Law, Leeds 2018, Digital Edition, p. 7, URL: <https://doi.org/10.1515/9781942401698> (23 Aug 2022), refers to this as the »›Classical Period‹ of canonical history«.
99 BRUNDAGE, Law, Sex, and Christian Society, p. 223.

Where, then, did Gratian find himself in this historic discussion of natural law? Taking his point of departure from his own contemporary, Hugo of St. Victor (d. 1141), Gratian argues that natural law is tantamount to the Golden Rule[100]. Somewhat confusing the matter, however, is that he then subsumes the former conception under the remark: »natural law is that which is contained in the law and the gospel«[101]. Continuing on, he connects natural law with divine law[102] before finally also tacking on Isadore of Seville's modified definition of Ulpian[103]. With so many different conceptions thus attached to Gratian's notion of natural law, it nearly goes without saying that there was more than ample room within which able legal minds would be able to tinker. Such ambiguity would also serve to cloud, rather than clarify, the precise relationship between natural law, marriage, and sexuality.

It therefore comes as no surprise that the heirs of Gratian's *Decretum*, the glossators and decretists, presented a wide array of interpretational possibilities for natural law – a development that is perhaps further compounded by something of a »cross-fertilization« which took place between canon and civil lawyers throughout the mid-twelfth[104] and on into the beginning of the thirteenth centuries[105]. This meeting of the legal minds, accordingly, would have urged interaction between civil law's understanding of Ulpian and church law's Isadorian counterpart as had been utilized by Gratian.

The outcome of the aforementioned makes for lively and variegated interpretations. Rufinus, for example, identifies natural law with the moral law's *implanted urge* towards good and away from evil[106]. Ulpian, in an inverted fashion, is here to be recognized, along with elements of reason and Rufinus's own independent thought. Following Simon of Bisignano's lead, ideas involving the conscience, *synderesis*, came into the mix in the Bolognese school of the later twelfth century[107]. The

---

100 WEIGAND, Naturrechtslehre, pp. 132f.
101 »Ius naturae est, quod in lege et evangelio continetur, quo quisque iubetur alii facere, quod sibi vult fieri, et prohibetur alii inferre, quod sibi nolit fieri […]«. GRATIAN, Decretum Magistri Gratiani, CIC(L), D. 1. WEIGAND, Zur Problematik des Naturrechts. Inhalt, Erkennbarkeit, Veränderlichkeit, Dispensierbarkeit, in: Id., Liebe und Ehe im Mittelalter, Goldbach 1998, pp. 217*–241*, at p. 241, notes that this usage makes Scripture a significant source for natural law teaching.
102 GRATIAN, D. 1, c. 1.
103 Ibid., D. 1, c. 7. Isadore of Seville (ca. 560–636) had somewhat conflated the traditional Roman Law understanding (Ulpian) with the notion that natural law is the *ius gentium* or law of the nations. See CROWE, Changing Profile, pp. 69f.
104 BRUNDAGE, The Medieval Origins, p. 75.
105 Kenneth PENNINGTON, The Decretalists 1190 to 1234, in: HARTMANN/PENNINGTON (eds.), History of Medieval Canon Law, pp. 211–245, at p. 227, URL: <http://search.ebscohost.com/login.aspx?direct=true&db=nlebk&AN=360295&site=ehost-live> (23 April 2020).
106 WEIGAND, Naturrechtslehre, pp. 144ff.
107 Ibid., pp. 173ff.

Anglo-Norman School of approximately the same era brought in ideas of the objective ordering of nature[108]. Along these lines, an exact and shared understanding of natural law is hardly to be found among Gratian's heirs given that natural law definitions discussed during this era freely include (or omit) everything from the Golden Rule, the Law and the Gospel, the teachings of Scripture[109], or that which is shared with the animals (Ulpian). Any or nearly all of these elements could be included, expanded upon, or omitted – all of which served to complicate the exact relationship between natural law, marriage, and sexuality[110].

As concerns this study's interests, however, it is important to focus on the fate of Ulpian's definition. This is especially the case given that it was Ulpian's definition which, historically, had been used to legally ground the relationship between the sexes. As for Ulpian's definition, it was usually understood as that which nature teaches the animals. Given the Latin, however, it could also be understood as that which is taught to the animals by nature. Michael Crowe notes the following regarding this point:

> In his *Summa Institutionum*, when he discusses Ulpian's definition of the natural law, Placentinus makes an interesting suggestion. The meanings for the phrase *quod natura omnia animalia docuit* will depend upon the parsing of the *quod*. Taken as an accusative (as it usually is) and the word *natura* as nominative, the sense is that nature has taught all animals natural law. But, if the cases are reversed and *quod* becomes nominative, then the sense is that natural law is the nature that has taught all animals, namely by instinct[111].

A first possibility for incorporating, albeit subverting, Ulpian was to connect the »urge/instinct« presented in his definition as a working of reason which thus grounds marriage. While such an appropriation of Ulpian is clearly suspect as relates to his traditional understanding, it had the advantage of keeping natural

---

108 This seems to be particularly a phenomenon of the Anglo-Norman School near the end of the 12th century. See ibid., pp. 196ff.
109 On the relationship between the teachings of Scripture and natural law, see Jean PORTER, Natural & Divine Law. Reclaiming the Tradition for Christian Ethics, Grand Rapids 1999, esp. pp. 129–146, and id., Natural Law as a Scriptural Concept. Theological Reflections on a Medieval Theme, in: Theology Today (Jan 2002), pp. 226–243, URL: <https://doi.org/10.1177/004057360205900205> (23 Aug 2022).
110 For the variety found during this period, see esp. WEIGAND, Naturrechtslehre, pp. 140–259. Especially noteworthy are perhaps the interpretational possibilities found in the Anglo-Norman school (pp. 196–215).
111 CROWE, Changing Profile, p. 90. See also Philip L. REYNOLDS, How Marriage Became One of the Sacraments. The Sacramental Theology of Marriage from Its Medieval Origins to the Council of Trent, Cambridge 2016, pp. 451–454, and Robert GREENE, Instinct of Nature. Natural Law, Synderesis, and the Moral Sense, in: Journal of the History of Ideas 58, 2 (1997), pp. 173–198.

law distinct and free from such a physical act as could also include fornication[112]. Another attempt to avoid physical (and possibly sinful) implications of natural law – while simultaneously grounding marriage – sees natural law as effecting »the comingling of souls and not of bodies«[113]. Still others granted Ulpian limited room, seeing his definition as establishing marriage, all while requiring the addition of something more specifically human, such as proper mores and ordering[114]. God, also, given the fact that He could be identified with the »highest Nature«, might be thought of as establishing the natural foundation for marriage simply in speaking the words »Be fruitful and multiply«[115]. Such definitions all rather subjugated, avoided, or minimalized a more traditional understanding of Ulpian.

Another approach for relating natural law, marriage, and sexual expression was to identify the former as that which grounded the latter within the confines of marriage. Such argumentation began with a notion of a rational understanding of natural law, identified this with the divine law, and concluded that natural law thus could not establish anything less than rightly ordered sexual relations *within* marriage[116]. A similar attempt to deal with problematic implications of such physical connotations of marriage was to limit the Ulpianic understanding of natural law to a role as the *initiator*, as it were, of human sexuality. This point of departure was then placed under the necessary guidance of human reason, thus alleviating problematic implications which might have resulted from giving too much credence to Ulpian. In this way, one could argue that the marital/sexual basis provided by natural law was *both* to be identified in man's animal and rational nature[117].

---

[112] This was Simon of Bisignano's concern. See WEIGAND, Naturrechtslehre, pp. 285f.

[113] The natural law grounding of marriage, according to the gloss apparatus »*Ecce vicit leo*« is termed as follows: »[…] hic intelligitur de animorum coniunctione et non corporum; coniunctio enim corporum sepius est fornication et sic peccatum et sic esse non potest de iure naturali […]«. Ibid., p. 287.

[114] Rufin, influential for both the Bolognese and Anglo-Norman schools, commented: »Coniunctio maris et femine est de iure nature; ne vero isto bono passim et precipitanter homines sicut bestie uterentur, lex huiusmodi naturalis nodificata est per ordinem discreti et honesti moris, scilicet ut non nisi tales persone et sub tanta celebritate coniugii iungerentur. Ecce iam liquet quod iuri naturali ab extra adauctum sit, scilicet modus et ordo morum«. Ibid., pp. 287f.

[115] According to Odo of Dover: »Quod hic dicitur coniunctioni (!) viri et femine instinctu habetur natura, non constitutione hominum (intelligendum est) quantum ad originem; Dei namque constitutione, que summa natura est, coniunctio uiri et femine facta est ipso dicente: Crescite et multiplicamini«, ibid., p. 288.

[116] Such argumentation corresponds with that of Egidius, *Summa »Reverentia«*, and *Summa »Et est sciendum«*. See ibid., pp. 289f.

[117] Thus Huguccio: »Michi tamen videtur quod intelligatur de coniunctione carnali matrimoniali, non formicaria, cum ex iure naturali peccatum non possit esse; et hoc est coniunctio de iure naturali quod dicitur instinctus nature et de eo quod dicitur ratio; mouetur enim homo quodam naturali appetite sensualitatis ut carnaliter commisceatur femine et statim succedi ratio dictans homini ut

The various attempts of the canonists, however, were not limited to the relatively benign definitions related above. Some canonists took Ulpian at face value as referring to what man and animal *physically* have in common – even to such an extent that they did not blush to say that it was the very sexual act which accords with natural law (so long as its natural form and use is maintained)[118]. Avoiding any possible ambiguity on this point, one glossator pointed out that the natural law foundation of marriage refers to the joining of the male and female seed[119]. While this was recognized as being potentially problematic – as would have been the case in connection with potential fornication, adultery, polygamy, and incest – such an approach was not exclusive and thus could be combined with further aspects of natural law, whether reason or Scripture, thus sidestepping dangerous implications[120].

One further effort to appropriate a stronger understanding of the Ulpianic definition also deserves our attention. This conception did not relate the form of the act to natural law, but rather the sexual urge/drive held in common with the animals[121]. Positive with this view was that it did not associate various sinful sexual acts with natural law. Yet, in giving sanction to the inclination of one sex towards the opposite and identifying this with natural law, the boundary between nature, concupiscence, and sin was quickly blurred. One attempt to thwart this issue was to claim that the urge was natural and initial in a sense, but it must still be under the charge and dominion of the will[122]. One might similarly caution, as did a further French canonist, that anything over and above such an initial urge is a venial sin at

---

    non commisceatur nisi uxori et modo legitimo, scilicet causa sobolis uel causa reddendi debitum; nam alia commixtio siue cum uxore siue cum alia non est de aliquo iure naturali, set contra illud«. Ibid., p. 291. Weigand commends in connection with Huguccio, »Er vertritt also weder das rein legistische Verständnis (jeder Geschlechtsverkehr entspricht dem Naturrecht, d. h. der Naturanlage) noch das rein kanonistische (die Ehe als Rechtsverhältnis, als Verbindung der Herzen ist gemeint), sondern versucht beide harmonisch zu verbinden: Entsprechend dem sinnenhaften Naturrecht […] ist der Geschlechtsakt gemeint, in Übereinstimmung mit dem Vernunftrecht aber nur der erlaubte Geschlechtsakt«. Ibid., p. 292.
118 Ibid., p. 294, indicates that this view was associated with the Anglo-Norman school.
119 A glossator of the *Summa Parisiensis* comments on Gratian, D. 1 c. 7, »v. viri et femine coniunctio: Id est seminis uiri et femine coniunctio«. Ibid., p. 293. Emphasis in original.
120 Ibid., pp. 293–298, indicates how various canonists struggled to incorporate a more traditional understanding of Ulpian while not thereby allowing for sin in the process.
121 Ibid., pp. 299–306, demonstrates that this conception is found almost entirely in the French school starting around 1200.
122 The French *Summa Duacensis'* comments on D. 1 c. 7: »Addit lex ›quam matrimonium appellamus‹ insti. de iure natur. in principio. Set queritur de quo iure naturali sit matrimonium. Et sciendum, quia appetere coitum est de iure concreto quod quidem corruptum fuit ex peccato Ade ut fiat cum pruritu carnis et inobedientia membrorum quod est pena. Vtrum etiam sit peccatum dubitant theologi. Et credo quod non secundum quod distinguitur inter motus primos et primoprimos. Illud etiam planum est quia ipsum appetere nec in precepto nec in prohibitione nec in demonstratione

minimum[123]. In such a way, reason or the »inspired law [*ius inspiratum*]« still had the upper hand.

It was, of course, the theologically acceptable course of action to hold Ulpian within contemporary theological limits. Demonstrating independence of thought, however, we find at least one source that certainly strayed outside of the norms. Namely, we find one French decretist in the commentary *Animal est substantia*, who claims that the appetite towards the joining of the sexes is devoid of sin – this on account of procreation[124]. This author maintained not only that procreation was a divine good, but that that which leads to procreation is itself a divinely given urge and creation which is not to be unnaturally impinged upon. Perhaps especially remarkable for this time period, the author then marches on and argues that no one should be prohibited from marriage – not even clergy! To do otherwise might incur the sin against nature[125]. Notably, the author makes such comments *after* the third Lateran Council's condemnation of clerical marriage and sins against nature and would presumably have realized the unorthodoxy of his own view[126]. For our purposes, however, this lonely French decretist nicely demonstrates the latent explosiveness contained within the Ulpianic definition of natural law, even

---

     est, quia ius concretum ista non habet. Statim atem nato appetite suscipit illud ius inspiratum; unde homini dictum est dominaberis appetitus tui«. Ibid., pp. 300f.
123 Commenting on D. 1 c. 7, the French »*Ecce vicit leo*« states, »Vel aliter potest dici quod conuenit etiam brutis animalibus ut scilicet uocetur coniunctio non coniunctio animorum uel corporum, set potius appetitus coniungendi quo primo mouemur, quid est communis nobis et brutis, nec in illis est peccatum nec in nobis, quia est primo primus motus qui non est peccatum ut dixit magister Symon de tornato, set secondo primus est ueniale«. Ibid., pp. 301f.
124 *Animal est substantia*, in commenting on D. 1 c. 7, states, »Id est appetitus coniungendi in uiro et femina est de iure naturali, non uero coniunctio, potius est iuris quam effectus. Vnde exempla hic supposita potius sunt su(m)pta in effectu iuris quam in ipso iure. Et nota quod cum hic appetitus forte de iure naturali inspecta prima natura hominis, in homine hic appetitus nec est nec fuit peccatum. Nam hic est et fuit tantum causa sobolis procreandum cuius signum est cohitus in brutis que choire non solent nisi ut concipiant et suum genus restaurent«. Ibid., pp. 302–333. Note that Wiegand includes two differing versions of this text. They are, however, substantially in agreement.
125 »Et nota quod hodie licet choire non solum causa sobolis, set causa uitande fornicationem infra di.xiii. Nerui et hinc sumitur ratio illius decretalis quam habemus extra de cohab. clericorum et mulierum c. Clerici, ubi dicitur quod episcopi non debent cogere sacerdotes ut abiurent focarias, nam hoc esset contra ius naturale«. Ibid., p. 303.
126 Ibid., pp. 304f., mentions that the decretist in question is most probably aware of his own aberrant views and is actually twisting the natural language of Canon 11 [i. e. »Quicumque autem in incontinentia illa, quae contra naturam est […]« Mansi 22, col. 224] against the canon's own intent. WEIGAND, Naturrechtslehre, p. 305, notes: »Die eben besprochene Stelle ist die einzige, welche in den Schriften der Dekretisten gefunden wurde, die ausdrücklich von einem naturrechtlichen Anspruch auf die Ehe redet, also von einem subjektiven, natürlichen Recht auf Ehe bzw. auf geschlechtliche Verbindung«.

unwittingly prefiguring a spark which would later more fully ignite in the tinder of the Reformation.

The Turn away from Ulpian

Turning now away from canon law and towards the Scholastic period of the high and later Middle Ages, we note a shift in trajectory and a nearly complete separation of *nature* (i. e. the Ulpianic heritage) from what came to be understood as natural law. Luis Tomás Scherz notes a dramatic shift in this regard during the life of the influential Thomas Aquinas (1225–1274). Scherz notes that whereas Aquinas's earlier works leaned upon that best-known expositor of the Roman legal tradition, by the time Aquinas's natural law thought had matured, Ulpian was nowhere to be found and natural law had become the sole prerogative of human reason[127]. Perhaps even more interesting, however, are the developments which then occurred in the relationship between human inclinations/appetites and reason as a result of this development. Namely, with nature's deemphasis as a source and norm for natural law, and reason's simultaneous emphasis, human drives and instincts were no longer normative, neither for natural law nor within theological anthropology[128].

This is, of course, not to deny Genesis 1:28 any role in the natural law thinking of Thomas Aquinas. As Cohen notes, »Thomas Aquinas likewise maintained that ›be

---

127 Luis Tomás Scherz, Das Naturgesetz bei Thomas von Aquin und die tentatio stoicorum. Heutige Auffassungen eines umstrittenen Begriffs, Tübingen 2006, p. 43, writes, in commenting upon Thomas's *Summa*, »Hier ist nicht mehr von einem Unterschied zwischen *finis primarius* und *secundarius* die Rede, weil die Natur zunächst nicht als das, was die Menschen mit den Tieren gemeinsam haben, gesehen wird, sondern primär als das, was die Vernunft diktiert«. See also Wolfgang Kluxen, Lex naturalis bei Thomas von Aquin, Wiesbaden 2001, pp. 34–36, as he notes the constitutive importance for reason in Thomas's understanding of natural law and also the relative silence with respect to the normativity of procreation therein (pp. 41f.). Crowe, Changing Profile, pp. 142–155, shows Aquinas still interacting with Ulpian, though struggling with the question of whether and in what manner he ought to be included in the natural law.
128 Scherz, Das Naturgesetz, pp. 51–53, 55. »Weil die natürlichen Neigungen nicht normativ sind, darf man nicht die Idee eines Sollens a priori mit ihnen verbinden. Den Vorrang hat immer die Vernunft, weil nur sie die *Hervorbringung* der Gesetze realisieren kann, die wesentlich zum Gesetzbegriff gehört […] Anders gesagt: Die Vernunft *befiehlt* kraft eines vorausgehenden Strebensaktes, und dieser ist es, dem das *wirksam Bewegen* zu verdanken ist. Das bedeutet eine große Distanz zur stoischen Lehre von den natürlichen Neigungen« (p. 53). See also Scherz's note on Thomas's view of the affective life and its relationship with reason (pp. 169, 172). It is worthwhile noting, however, that the exact relationship between reason and the will in Thomas's thought is thus somewhat problematized, as noted by D.J. O'Connor, Aquinas and Natural Law, London 1969, pp. 54–56. This weakness is perhaps what was targeted by the later Scholastic thinkers in their further emphasis and thought in connection with the human will.

fertile and increase‹ is a precept of natural law, ›for in it is ordained the act of generation by which nature is preserved and multiplied‹«[129]. Nevertheless, Aquinas's view of procreation as a natural law precept was derived from the value placed upon the preservation of the species and not from what might be understood of human urges and inclinations. Furthermore, it is noteworthy that Aquinas understood this precept to apply to the human race as a whole, though not necessarily to individuals[130]. In this way Aquinas's natural law understanding left ample room, unsurprisingly, for those who would instead offer their time and energies to contemplation of the divine and other similar spiritual pursuits.

While it is debated how familiar the thought of Thomas Aquinas was to the reformers[131], and particularly Luther[132], it is fair to note that a similar shift also took place in schools of thought somewhat closer to the reformers. Here it is important for us to take into account the relationship between natural law, reason, and various aspects of the human will in the Scholastic teachings of Duns Scotus (d. 1308), William of Occam (d. 1347), and particularly Gabriel Biel (d. 1495). Of particular interest will be their respective understandings of the connection between the *appetitus sensitivus*, the *appetitus rationalis*, the will, human reason, and bodily needs (*appetitus naturalis*)[133].

To begin with, then, we note that on account of Aquinas's emphasis upon both reason and the established rational order (cf. *lex aeterna*), a response began to emerge. Duns Scotus countered the teachings of Aquinas through his own emphasis upon the interrelationship between the divine will and creation[134]. A corollary

---

129 COHEN, Be Fertile, p. 290. Quotations cited by Cohen as »Thomas Aquinas, *Quaestiones quodlibetales* 7.7.I, ed. Raymundus Spiazzi (Torino 1956), p. 150«.
130 COHEN, Be Fertile, p. 291.
131 Denis R. JANZ, Luther on Thomas Aquinas. The Angelic Doctor in the Thought of the Reformer, Stuttgart 1989, pp. 111–113, points out that such reformers as Karlstadt, Melanchthon, and Calvin had a relatively weak understanding of Thomas, while Luther fared somewhat better, though still paled in comparison to Thomist, scholastically trained theologians such as Cajetan.
132 According to ibid., pp. 96f. and 111–113, the general (though not completely universal) judgment on this question with respect to Luther is that his knowledge of Aquinas was limited, at best. Janz, however, argues convincingly that Luther did indeed possess a certain familiarity with Aquinas, whether mediated (esp. through the writings of Biel) or more directly as was the case with such works as *Summa Theologiae* (at least in part), *Summa Contra Gentiles*, *De Angelis*, and perhaps further works as well. For this, see ibid., Chapter IV (cf. pp. 96–113).
133 The various appetites were thought to correspond with the three aspects of the human souls and their desires (i. e. the nutritive, sensitive, and rational souls) according to Aristotle's thought. Thus, at the level of the nutritive soul, the desires correspond with such basic desires as hunger, thirst, sleep, elimination, and – some would argue – procreation. The sensitive soul thus relates to sensitive, irascible, or concupiscent desires (as opposed to those of reason). The rational soul is concerned with the rational will (sometimes free will).
134 Günter STRATENWERTH, Die Naturrechtslehre des Johannes Duns Scotus, Göttingen 1951, pp. 5–7.

to this was his corresponding emphasis upon the human will. In other words, with respect to his teachings on man, will was given priority over reason. This is not to say that the will acts apart from reason. Indeed, Scotus held that the will *follows* reason. Nevertheless, the will, inasmuch as it is constituted by man's love, is also that which opens up reason's eyes toward the object of its desire and is thus the decisive factor[135]. Together, however, these both were given priority over man's lower animal nature, which includes man's *appetitus sensitivus* (i. e. his sensual or sensory appetites and desires)[136]. These sensitive appetites included man's concupiscent desires, which, if not rightly ordered according to the highest love, comprise a corrupt perversion of the will. Nevertheless, given that sexual desire (i. e. the procreative drive) was categorized essentially as a sensitive appetite and *not* a necessity of nature, it no longer received true normative value at the individual level. Instead, it was placed under the rule and domain of will and reason. In other words, although the separation of the Ulpianic strain of natural law from Scholastic thought by no means necessitated the devaluation of man's procreative drive, the reality is that in these streams of thought man's procreative drive was assumed to be within the purview of free will[137]. Indeed, for Scotus, natural law was granted a

---

135 Ibid., pp. 9–12.
136 Ibid., pp. 8, 19.
137 »Der Mensch ist gegenüber seiner Natur nicht nur insofern frei, als er die Möglichkeit hat, die natürlichen Neigungen zu beherrschen, ihnen frei zuzustimmen oder sie zu unterdrücken – dies war schließlich, wenn man von dem Streben zur beatitudo absieht, auch die Auffassung des Aquinaten –, sondern die Natur ist für den Menschen nicht Norm und Maßstab seines Handelns«. Ibid., p. 73. We might furthermore note that Stratenwerth sees in Aquinas more openness toward physical nature as a source for reason's understanding of the created order and thus natural law. See also ibid., p. 79.
Somewhat later Stratenwerth observes Scotus's view of marriage and the procreative act as relates to natural law. Most striking is the lack of any language that deals with any sort of corresponding »drive«, »urge«, or »compulsion«. Rather, it is addressed as a neutral matter properly and reasonably ordered within marriage (pp. 96–98). That is to say, the conversation regarding natural law (with corresponding emphasis upon that »taught by nature to all animals«) has moved a great distance within just a century. Indeed, according to Stratenwerth, Scotus seems unwilling to even take into account the natural familial bonds in grounding his own derivative relationship between natural law and the family (p. 99).
It should also be noted that Jean Porter offers an alternative interpretation of this apparent separation or disappearance of the Ulpianic definition and understanding of natural law from the more theological realms. For Porter, this disappearance is not necessarily a rejection of Ulpian's understanding, but rather the recognition that it is not an appropriate starting point for the theological (as opposed to the civil) consideration of natural law. See, PORTER, Natural & Divine Law, esp. pp. 130f. Whatever merits her arguments may have, this section's own thesis is based on the combination both of this disappearance as well as the simultaneous emphasis upon the primacy of reason and will in Scholastic thought and thus argues that there was likely more than simply a professional distinction being made.

very narrow jurisdiction in that it was understood to deal only properly with the relationship between God and man and then secondarily with other matters[138] – to the exclusion of formerly important elements of natural law thought[139].

As we continue forward with Occam and Biel, we can note, despite their differences with Scotus regarding theories of knowledge and perception (i. e. realism vs. nominalism), that with respect to our topic their thought presents itself to us along the lines of variations on a theme. For example, we can briefly observe that Occam's voluntarism was so pronounced that for him the will not only exerted dominion over all human faculties, but also (perhaps) tended to undermine any viable conception of natural law[140].

Turning to Biel, despite the oft-posited claim that he was clearly on the voluntarist side of the debate, Heiko Oberman offers arguments that Biel held a more

---

138 STRATENWERTH, Naturrechtslehre, p. 94.
139 Antonie Vos, The Scotian Notion of Natural Law, in: Vivarium 38, 2 (2000), pp. 197–221, at pp. 211–213, URL: <https://doi.org/10.1163/156853400753621725> (23 Aug 2022), builds a strong case that Scotus's use of terminology underlying natural law cannot be reconciled with the created, natural order of things. He writes, »Basically a truth is naturally (naturaliter) true, because it is true in terms of the intrinsic nature or structure of the proposition involved. Thus the meanings of ›natura‹ and ›naturalis‹ have to be elucidated in a logical-analytical way and not in terms of an absolutistic and unpersonal concept of nature derived from cosmology«. Ibid., p. 213.
140 We note that with Occam one observes the same fundamental structure as concerns the will over and above the affective and appetitive life of man. For example, Girard J. ETZKORN, Ockham's View of the Human Passions in the Light of his Philosophical Anthropology, in: Wilhelm VOSSENKUHL/Rolf SCHÖNBERGER (eds.), Die Gegenwart Ockhams, Weinheim 1990, p. 274, notes that »for Ockham, the intellective soul, as the more noble and higher entity, has a domain which includes the passions and must deal with them in the moral order«. Elsewhere Etzkorn states, »Here it is instructive to turn to his [Ockham's] moral theory in order to discern the role of the rational appetite. In the normal course of events the will's moral task is to moderate the passions, taking ›moderation‹ in the classical Aristotelean sense. Hence, sooner or later in normal human beings, and consequent upon the assessment of right reason or prudence, the will makes free decisions with regard to the passions, and to the extent that the will is operative with regard to these passions, they may be called acts of the rational appetite as well«. Ibid., p. 273.
CROWE, Changing Profile, p. 202, mentions a prevailing view of the role of the will in Occam's thought even more when he records, »Ockham, more than Scotus, took the voluntarism of the Franciscan tradition to its ultimate consequences. Man is free, even to will or not his own happiness; he is free even in the face of the judgment of his own intellect«. Crowe proceeds to note that such extreme voluntarism and its subsequent deemphasis of reason would serve to undermine the very foundations of natural law. See, however, Heiko OBERMAN, The Harvest of Medieval Theology. Gabriel Biel and Late Medieval Nominalism, Cambridge 1963, pp. 91–93, who somewhat – but only somewhat – mollifies such overly strong claims. See also Wilhelm ERNST, Gott und Mensch am Vorabend der Reformation, Leipzig 1972, pp. 200f., regarding a further tempering of any claim to an unnuanced understanding of voluntarism. For a helpful comparison between the natural law thought of Aquinas and Occam, see RAUNIO, Divine and Natural Law, pp. 26–33.

conciliatory view between reason and the will[141]. Whatever the case, for Biel, man is free with respect to his will and reason. Moreover, this remained man's prerogative also after the loss of *iustitia originalis* (original righteousness), even if and even though this freedom was now somewhat tempered by the encroachment of the sensitive and natural appetites[142]. Thus, it is now only with difficulty that virtue and *habitus* might maintain the hegemony of the upper faculties[143]. The point to be observed here is that, for Biel, the will (accompanied by reason) likewise had primacy in areas both spiritual and physical. Thus, it should come as no surprise that Biel also understands Genesis 1:28 as a divine imperative of natural law, but – like Aquinas – on the basis of the good of the furtherance of the species and with the acknowledgment that it is a command applicable to the race at large, whereby some may be exempted from this duty[144].

In concluding this section, we do well to simply highlight once more the fact that this wider natural law discourse forms a heretofore largely neglected background which is of significance not only for natural law thought during the Reformation but particularly for our own study of Genesis 1:28[145]. While it is easy to overlook

---

141 OBERMAN, Harvest, pp. 64f. This conciliatory interpretation of Biel is also reflected by John FAR-THING, Thomas Aquinas and Gabriel Biel. Interpretations of St. Thomas Aquinas in German Nominalism on the Eve of the Reformation, Durham 1988, as he shows Biel's mediation, though not always acceptance, of the writings of Aquinas. See also Leif GRANE, Contra Gabrielem. Luthers Auseinandersetzung mit Gabriel Biel in der Disputatio Contra Scholasticam Theologiam 1517, Gyldendal 1962, pp. 51f., and ERNST, Gott und Mensch, p. 197.

142 GRANE, Contra Gabrielem, p. 82. See also LW 34, p. 155, fn. 6, as regards the relationship between original righteousness and man's pure natural gifts.

143 ERNST, Gott und Mensch, pp. 279–283.

144 »Sed ›sciendum quod duplex est praeceptum legis naturae‹: quoddam ordinatur ad tollendum defectum singularis personae vel spiritualem, sicut praecepta de actibus virtutum, vel corporalem, ut illud Gen. 2: ›De omni ligno paradisi comedes‹; aliud vero, quod ordinatur ad tollendum defectum specie, sicut illud Gen. 3: ›Crescite et multiplicamini‹, quo praecipitur actus generationis«, quo species humana conservatur. Inter haec duo praecepta hoc interest: Nam ad praeceptum legis naturae primi generis quilibet tenetur, ad praeceptum vero secundi generis (›quod ordinatur ad defectum speciei tollendum) non quilibet tenetur singulariter‹, sed tota communitas hominum tenetur, ut aliqui ex ea huic officio vacent«. Gabriel BIEL, Collectorium circa quattuor libros Sententiarum, edited by Hans RÜCKERT and Wilfridus WERBECK, Tübingen 1977, vol. 4/2, pp. 453,46–54 (d. 16, q. 4, S).

145 As noted previously, comparatively little attention has been given to this specific topic, something which, to the best of my own knowledge, is particularly the case with Luther. Melanchthon fares slightly better, given the fact that scholarship related to him is generally accustomed to dealing with wider fields of thought. Perhaps for that reason, as well as the fact that the philosophical terminology is somewhat more apparent with Melanchthon, he has received somewhat more attention on this topic. Regarding Melanchthon, see Merio SCATTOLA, Das Naturrecht vor dem Naturrecht. Zur Geschichte des »ius naturae« im 16. Jahrhundert, Tübingen 1999, esp. p. 49, whose work is helpful not only on account of his treatment of Melanchthon's natural law thinking, but

this reality from our own historic vantage point, the fact of the matter is that the Reformation discourse, both implicitly and also explicitly, takes part in this debate. In fact, one of the important threads we will follow and occasionally comment upon throughout our study – i. e. the place of *affectus naturales/στοργη φυσικη* in the discourse of Luther and particularly Melanchthon – is nothing other than a way of participating (and taking sides!) in this historic and even ancient discussion. Additionally, the repeated presence of terms such as *inclinatio, appetitus, insitus*, and any number of other terms, not to mention their German equivalents, serve as continual reminders and likely references to this very discussion. Furthermore, Luther's own repeated references to Genesis 1:28 as *nature* (along with Melanchthon's telling comment that the desires toward self-preservation are not properly natural law) should not in any way be construed as a devaluation of what they are saying, even if they are not comfortable referring to such procreative drives and urges as »natural law«.

2.4 Teleology and Anatomy in the Natural Philosophy Tradition

Shifting our attention now to a similar cross-disciplinary conversation – though perhaps not as much discussion – within medieval and early-modern thought, we come to subject areas that are today commonly held to be under the purview of medicine and the sciences, but which previously enjoyed a more integrated existence with the study of theology. Namely, here it is necessary for us to discuss natural philosophy and the anatomical understanding held by the Wittenberg reformers. How did they view the body and what did *their* contemporary understanding of medicine, anatomy, and such other »scientific« subjects say about their understanding of man with respect to our topic?

To begin with, it is important for us to note that the study of the body was not a sub-section within the scientific subject of biology some five hundred years ago. Rather, it was part of the larger field of natural philosophy. As Andrew Cunningham notes, »Natural Philosophy was the branch of academic study concerned with

---

also because of its historical overview of the topic. Other works that touch on this topic include Lars KLINNERT, Verheißung und Verantwortung. Die Entwicklung der Naturrechtslehre Philipp Melanchthons zwischen 1521 und 1535, in: Kerygma u. Dogma 50 (2004), pp. 25–56, and Wilhelm MAURER, Der junge Melanchthon zwischen Humanismus und Reformation, Göttingen 1967, vol. 2, esp. pp. 288–296. Slightly less relevant, though still informative, is Clemens BAUER, Melanchthons Naturrechtslehre, in: Archiv für Reformationsgeschichte 42 (1951), pp. 64–91.

nature« and is not to be confused with what is today classified as science[146]. Instead, the study of natural philosophy was the study of nature as God's creation. Thus, natural philosophy was in many respects secondarily focused on studying the works of God with the primary goal of better understanding *God* through these works[147].

Along these lines, natural philosophy existed in the universities and focused on the natural world as expressed through several works of Aristotle, notably: *Physics, On the Heavens (De caelo), On Generation and Corruption (De generatione et corruption), On the Soul (De anima),* and *Meteorology*[148]. Thus, it is possible to see that the subject matter focused on a wide expanse of topics mediated through the Aristotelian corpus. Furthermore, it is important to note that the teaching of natural philosophy occurred at either/both the bachelor level or/and the master's level of the university education, something that was also the case in Wittenberg[149]. In other words, one cannot simply assume that only the »scientifically-minded« of the age were educated in natural philosophy. Rather, all of those completing university studies, including those who proceeded on to studies in law, medicine, or theology, shared a relatively common background in the natural thought of

---

146 Andrew Cunningham, The Anatomical Renaissance. The Resurrection of the Anatomical Projects of the Ancients, London/New York 1997, pp. 52f., URL: <https://books.google.no/books?id=sBqoDQAAQBAJ&printsec=frontcover&hl=no#v=onepage&q&f=false> (18 Aug 2022).

147 Ibid., p. 53. It should be noted that Cunningham's claim as to the nature and purpose of natural philosophy is the subject of academic debate, particularly challenged by Edward Grant. Grant counters that natural philosophy was much akin to modern science in that many of the Scholastics who conducted such studies were concerned primarily about nature as nature and that modern-day scientists cannot be said to be unconcerned about God. See Edward Grant, The Nature of Natural Philosophy in the Late Middle Ages, Washington, D.C. 2010, pp. 91–95, URL: <https://doi.org/10.2307/j.ctt284vbb> (23 Aug 2022). While there are certainly points to be taken from Grant's argumentation, when it comes to the thought of the reformers, Cunningham's arguments certainly seem to better align with the evidence presented in this study. Vivian Nutton, Wittenberg Anatomy, in: Ole Peter Grell/Andrew Cunningham (eds.), Medicine and the Reformation, New York 2001, pp. 11–32, URL: <https://books.google.no/books?id=9sN5133IBjYC&printsec=frontcover&hl=no#v=onepage&q&f=false> (18 Aug 2022), also argues strongly in favor of the Cunningham thesis within the Reformation context.

148 Grant, Natural Philosophy, p. 97.

149 James H. Overfield, Humanism and Scholasticism in Late Medieval Germany, Princeton 1984, p. 41. The University of Wittenberg, founded in 1502, required *Physics, De caelo et mundo, De generatione et corruption, De anima, Metaphysics, Ethics,* and *Parva naturalia* for their master's students under the direction of Johann von Staupitz (p. 212). An updated translation and commentary on *De anima* was introduced in 1509 (p. 214). For the Wittenberg curriculum and the place of natural philosophy within it prior to Reformation developments, see also Sachiko Kusukawa, The Transformation of Natural Philosophy, Cambridge 1995, pp. 7–26.

Aristotle[150]. In point of fact, as Grant notes, during the medieval era, the foremost scientific minds were also the foremost theologians[151].

Furthermore, as Cunningham observes, anatomy existed as a subtheme of natural philosophy already from around the mid-1200s[152]. Typically, topics of anatomy were dealt with in connection with Aristotle's *De anima* (*On the Soul*) in that Aristotle viewed observation of the body and its activities as the only means whereby one might know anything of the soul[153]. In such a setting the study of the human body combined with matters physical, psychological, and spiritual. We might therefore conclude that anatomy, by virtue of its position within the natural philosophical canon, was very much a spiritual study[154].

There is, however, a further element of anatomy within its natural philosophical setting to which we must also give attention. Namely, the prevailing discourses on the human body, those with which the reformers would have been familiar, would have availed them of the notion of a *telos*-oriented body[155]. In other words, in the thought of Aristotle and other authorities of antiquity (Plato, Cicero, and Galen), the body and its respective parts were understood with reference to their functions, i. e. the purpose(s) for which it and they exist. While it is beyond the

---

150 GRANT, Natural Philosophy, p. 96.
151 Ibid., p. 39.
152 CUNNINGHAM, Anatomical Renaissance, p. 53. See also Sander BOER, The Science of the Soul. The Commentary Tradition on Aristotle's De Anima, c. 1260 – c. 1360, Leuven 2013, pp. 15–18, for the introduction of *De anima* in Western Europe.
153 CUNNINGHAM, Anatomical Renaissance, pp. 30f. Note that the soul, for Aristotle, was more along the lines of a life principle as opposed to the corresponding Christian understanding of the same, though there was a certain element of ambiguity in Aristotle's writing. See Mariska LEUNISSEN, Explanation and Teleology in Aristotle's Science of Nature, Cambridge 2010, p. 51, URL: <https://doi.org/10.1017/CBO9780511762499> (18 Aug 2022), also BOER, Science, pp. 18–23.
154 »As a part of Natural Philosophy, anatomy too was therefore also about God. It was also of course relevant to the study of medicine, as conducted in and out of universities […] But even as studied for medicine, anatomy never ceased to be centrally about God. Anatomy was not a study which was primarily of value to medicine, and also about God. It was the other way about: it was primarily about God, and also of value to medicine. Thus at no time in the period from c. 1250 to the nineteenth century was anatomy a matter of so-many discrete ›facts‹ which had to be learnt or memorized. The teaching of anatomy certainly had the conveying of certain discrete information (as we might care to call it) as one of its goals, but the teaching of anatomy – even when conducted in a medical faculty – was centrally about God because it was about God's creation«. CUNNINGHAM, Anatomical Renaissance, p. 53.
For the varying subjects (in our modern categories) treated along with and arising out of the historic commentaries on Aristotle's *De anima*, see Fernando VIDAL, The Sciences of the Soul. The Early Modern Origins of Psychology, Chicago 2011, p. 25, URL: <https://books.google.no/books?id=4SS0fcbm3xMC&printsec=frontcover#v=onepage&q&f=false> (23 Aug 2022). See also BOER, Science, pp. 1–4.
155 »*telos*« (cf. grk. τέλος) – goal, end.

scope of this study to trace out the thought of all possible relevant influences here, we will offer brief attention to the presence of such teleological thinking in the writings of Aristotle and Galen, due to their importance in the anatomical and medicinal studies[156].

As mentioned above, Aristotle and Galen were the two main points of departure for the reformers when it came to the academic and philosophical discussions of the soul and its corresponding body. Aristotle was the main starting point for the discussions surrounding natural philosophy and Galen was the preeminent authority in the world of anatomy and medicine. The differences in the thought of these two giants notwithstanding, both of these men imparted to their readers a *telos*-focused understanding of the body and its respective members. This is seen very clearly in Aristotle, for example, in such works as *De anima*, *De partibus animalium*, and *De generatione animalium*[157]. Time and again in these works he concerns himself not merely with the material and form of bodies and their members, but also their functions and the corresponding purpose for which these exist

---

156 Regarding other likely natural philosophical influences on the Wittenberg reformers, we have previously noted Cicero's *telos*-oriented understanding of the human body and mankind. In connection with Plato's teleological understanding of the body, see CUNNINGHAM, Anatomical Renaissance, pp. 27f. Perhaps somewhat exceptional with respect to the teleological understanding of human anatomy are the anatomical writings of the elder Plinius. MÜHLPFORDT, Medizin, pp. 222–224, emphasizes Luther's preference for Beroaldo's edition of Pliny's *Naturalis historia* over the natural philosophical writings of Aristotle. Nevertheless, at least in the anatomical writings of Pliny (i. e. bk. 7 of *Naturalis historia*), a teleological understanding of the human body seems to be lacking. Thus, the likelihood that Pliny served as a source for Luther or Melanchthon's understanding of the body seems relatively low. Here see PLINY, Natural History in Ten Volumes, translated by H. Rackham, Cambridge et al. 1969, vol. 2. Nevertheless, we might also note that Pliny was not entirely without such causal thinking in other areas, as observed by Arthur Stanley PEASE, Caeli Enarrant, in: Harvard Theological Review 34, 3 (1941), pp. 163–200, at p. 187, URL: <https://doi.org/10.1017/S0017816000022537> (23 Aug 2022).

157 For Aristotle's *De anima*, see ARISTOTLE, On the Soul, translated by W.S. Hett, Cambridge et al. 1975, (Aristotle in Twenty-Three Volumes 8), For *De partibus animalium*, see ARISTOTLE, Parts of Animals, translated by A.L. Peck, Cambridge et al. 1983, (Aristotle in Twenty-Three Volumes 12). For *De generatione animalium*, see ARISTOTLE, Generation of Animals, translated by A.L. Peck, Harvard et al. 1979, (Aristotle in Twenty-Three Volumes 13). CUNNINGHAM, Anatomical Renaissance, pp. 32–35, offers general discussion as pertains to Aristotle's teleological understanding of anatomy.

With respect to the teleological focus of Aristotle's biological thought, it is interesting to note that this remains of interest within academic discussion to the present. See, for example, Mariska LEUNISSEN/Allan GOTTHELF, What's Teleology Got To Do With It? A Reinterpretation of Aristotle's »Generation of Animals« V, in: Phronesis 55, 4 (2010), pp. 325–356, URL: <https://www.jstor.org/stable/41057449> (5 Dec 2018); Karen M. NIELSEN, The Private Parts of Animals. Aristotle on the Teleology of Sexual Difference, in: Phronesis 53, 4/5 (2008), pp. 373–405; and LEUNISSEN, Explanation and Teleology.

as evidenced by their placement and observable use. Within this broader emphasis, it is most interesting for us to note the overarching importance Aristotle gives to reproduction as the normal goal of life on the level of the nutritive soul[158] and his understanding of the functionality of parts in serving the sustainment of life and its further generation[159]. Nevertheless, we must also observe that with Aristotle, the *telos* toward which bodies and their members are focused is internal in its nature. That is to say, it is not expressive of an external or divine will and ordering, but rather, is the expression of the fulfillment of the soul/life principle's own purpose of growth, self-maturation, and reproduction[160].

In briefly looking at the thought of Galen, we note a very similar emphasis upon the *telos*-oriented human body. Like Aristotle, Galen's reentry into the thought of Western Europe began well into the Middle Ages. In the case of Galen, this occurred around 1000 A.D., from which point his writings defined official medicine well into the seventeenth century[161]. What is especially noteworthy about the writings of Galen is that, while he stands in discourse with the Greek tradition of Plato and Aristotle with their teleological understandings of the body (though perhaps especially with Plato's emphasis on design), he is also particularly reacting against those in the ancient world who held that the world (and thus the body) were the products of randomness and chance. He is furthermore responding to the school of a certain Erasistratus who, in his view, had failed to properly emphasize the significance of the »uses« of the parts[162]. Galen's thought, perhaps because of his inclination toward Plato, also particularly emphasized an understanding of the human body as the best possible product and evidence of design, thus making Galen the preeminent advocate for design and purpose, even over Aristotle[163]. Of further significance is that, despite advocating an internal- and not an externally-focused

---

158 ARISTOTLE, On the Soul, bk. 2:4 (pp. 84–87). Note that for Aristotle, the nutritive/reproductive soul and its functions were held in common with all life and were the natural purpose and function of all non-mutilated and properly functioning beings.
159 Note, for example, in ARISTOTLE, Parts of Animals, bk. 3:10 (pp. 278f.), Aristotle's attention to the purpose of the lesser (i. e. nutritive) regions of the body and Aristotle's discussion of the reproductive processes and their parts in id., Generation of Animals, bk. 1:2 (pp. 10–15).
160 Mark J. SCHIEFSKY, Galen's Teleology and Functional Explanation, edited by D. Sedly, Oxford 2007, p. 26.
161 CUNNINGHAM, Anatomical Renaissance, pp. 39f. For the latter point, see also Roger FRENCH, Medicine Before Science. The Rational and Learned Doctor from the Middle Ages to the Enlightenment, Cambridge 2003, p. 178.
162 CUNNINGHAM, Anatomical Renaissance, pp. 42–46. For further discussion of Galen's reliance upon and appropriation of various Greek sources, see R.J. HANKINSON, Galen's Anatomy of the Soul, in: Phronesis 36, 2 (1991), pp. 198–208.
163 SCHIEFSKY, Galen's Teleology, p. 24.

teleology[164], Galen leaned heavily upon the idea that design and corresponding function were the result of the Craftsman's (i. e. Demiurge's) intelligence[165]. He thus developed a strain of anatomical-teleological thought, which, along with the writings of Plato and Aristotle, would lend itself remarkably well to later Christian appropriation[166]. The extent of such appropriation prior the Reformation need not concern us here. Nevertheless, considering that this *teleological orientation* did, in fact, permeate the reformers' understanding of the human body and its members – though understood as *extrinsic* to nature![167] –, it is fitting for us now to turn our attention more closely toward Wittenberg and the place of anatomy and natural philosophy there.

As previously mentioned, the reformers would have been steeped in the natural philosophical thought of Aristotle during their university education. While Melanchthon is best known for his expertise and contributions to this field, Luther was himself also very well versed in this area. Günter Mühlpfordt convincingly demonstrates, in fact, that Luther's knowledge of this field was quite expansive. Not only was Luther thoroughly familiar with Aristotle's natural philosophical thought, but he was also knowledgeable enough with it that at the end of the 1510s and early 1520s he was advocating a wholesale rejection of Aristotle in this area. Notably, however, he did leave the Stagirite's teachings on medicine, anatomy, and related topics to the judgment of those competent in these areas[168]. That is to say, while Aristotle was generally rejected, he maintained a certain authority in the area of medicine – at least for the time being. Thus, it is perhaps not overly shocking that Aristotle's views regarding conception continued to show up in Luther's writings –

---

164 Ibid., pp. 26f. Note that Davide CELLAMARE, Anatomy and the Body in Renaissance Protestant Psychology, in: Early Science and Medicine 19, 4 (2014), pp. 341–364, at p. 350, URL: <https://doi.org/10.1163/15733823-00194p03> (18 Aug 2022), notes Galen as having an external teleological orientation.
165 SCHIEFSKY, Galen's Teleology, pp. 24–29.
166 CUNNINGHAM, Anatomical Renaissance, pp. 207f. See also PEASE, Caeli Enarrant, esp. pp. 189–198, for a helpful treatment of the teleological argument in the ancient world (to include its appropriation and use amongst some of the church fathers).
167 CELLAMARE, Anatomy and the Body, p. 350. What is meant by »extrinsic« in the case of Melanchthon is that the *telos* has not been established by the creature itself. Rather, it has been established by the Creator. This is, of course, also certainly the case for Luther.
168 MÜHLPFORDT, Medizin, pp. 216–218. See also Richard TOELLNER, Die medizinischen Fakultäten unter dem Einfluß der Reformation, in: August BUCK (ed.), Renaissance – Reformation. Gegensätze und Gemeinsamkeiten, Wiesbaden 1984, pp. 287–297, at pp. 293f., who points out the apparent contradiction of eliminating while simultaneously maintaining the theoretical basis for medicine at that time.

even in the mid-1530s[169]. We might further note that Luther had a thorough familiarity with Pliny's *Naturalis historia*[170] and, as regards medical knowledge, seems to show at least some familiarity with Galen's theories on at least one occasion[171]. One suspects, however, on account of the university setting and Luther's interactions with Melanchthon, that this would have been more than a passing knowledge – the point here being that Luther was not merely a theologian according to our contemporary conception of the term. There was a reason why his fellow students in Erfurt nicknamed him *Philosophus* and we, therefore, would do wrong to assume that Luther either had little familiarity with the various academic discussions of his day, or that he was reticent in employing them in support of his theological arguments.

Similar and further observations might be made regarding Melanchthon. In fact, Melanchthon, with his encyclopedic interests and learning, became almost certainly the leading Reformation voice in natural philosophy – to include matters related to medicine and anatomy[172]. For example, in 1519, simultaneous to Luther's and

---

169 Luther remarks, for example, in his *Lectures on Genesis* (1535–1545), »An enim non absurdum iudicabis hominem, qui in aeternum victurus est, nasci quasi ex una guttula seminis in lumbis patris?«. WA 42, p. 64,13–14.
170 MÜHLPFORDT, Medizin, pp. 222–224. TOELLNER, Renaissance – Reformation, p. 294, notes the limited appropriation of Pliny in Wittenberg in the early 1520s – and that coexisting with the supposedly rejected Aristotelian teaching on physics.
171 In Luther's later Genesis Lectures, he seems to refer to Galen's two-seed theory on at least one occasion (WA 42, p. 34,33–34), though on other occasions he seems to have Aristotle's theory in mind.
172 In addition to works cited throughout this section, further relevant sources on Melanchthon, anatomy, and medicine include Wolfgang U. ECKART, Philipp Melanchthon und die Medizin, in: Stefan RHEIN/Günter FRANK (eds.), Melanchthon und die Naturwissenschaften seiner Zeit, Sigmaringen 1998, pp. 183–202; Jürgen HELM, Galen-Rezeption im 16. Jahrhundert am Beispiel Philipp Melanchthons, in: Europäische Geschichte Online (EGO) (2010), published by the Leibniz Institute for European History (IEG), URL: <http://www.ieg-ego.eu/helmj-2010-de> (17 Dec 2018); Jürgen HELM, Religion and Medicine. Anatomical Education at Wittenberg and Ingolstadt, in: Id./Annette WINKELMANN (eds.), Religious Confessions and the Sciences in the Sixteenth Century, Leiden 2001, pp. 51–68; Hans-Theodor KOCH, Melanchthon und die Vesal-Rezeption in Wittenberg, in: RHEIN et al. (eds.), Melanchthon und die Naturwissenschaften, pp. 203–218; Volkhard WELS, Melanchthons Anthropologie zwischen Theologie, Medizin und Astrologie, in: Kaspar von GREYERZ et al. (eds.), Religion und Naturwissenschaften im 16. und 17. Jahrhundert, Gütersloh 2010, pp. 51–85. See also the following very helpful introductory essays: Sandra BIHLMAIER, Naturphilosophie, in: Günter FRANK (ed.), Philipp Melanchthon. Der Reformator zwischen Glauben und Wissen. Ein Handbuch, Göttingen 2017, pp. 469–482; Sandra BIHLMAIER, Anthropologie, in: Ibid., pp. 483–494; Jürgen HELM, Medizin, in: Ibid., pp. 507–513.
The following are more generally related to the topics of medicine/anatomy in the Early Modern Era: Gerhard BAADER, Die Antikerezeption in der Entwicklung der medizinischen Wissenschaft während der Renaissance, in: Rudolf SCHMITZ/Gundolf KEIL (eds.), Humanismus und Medizin, Weinheim 1984, pp. 51–66; Ole Peter GRELL, Medicine and Religion in Sixteenth-Century Europe, in: Peter ELMER (ed.), The Healing Arts. Health, Disease and Society in Europe 1500–1800,

his own rejection of Aristotle, we observe Melanchthon's recommendation of the works of Galen and Hippocrates in a letter to Spalatin[173]. Melanchthon's interest and concern for medicinal and anatomical knowledge can be further noted in his lectures on these themes throughout his career. For example, as early as 1518 we note Melanchthon's dedicatory speech on Hippocrates's *Parva Hippocratis Tabula* at the arrival of the newly called medical professor, Peter Burckhard[174]. Moreover, he remained abreast of developments in medicine throughout his career. Notably, in 1525 he had received the most up-to-date Galen edition[175]. Around 1533, we find Melanchthon already beginning work on a commentary on Aristotle's *De anima* in which he was seeking to utilize the best available sources in his efforts to assemble a work that was not merely about the soul but just as much about the human body, anatomy, and theology[176].

The point, once again here as with Luther, is simply that the reformers were both well-read in and knowledgeable of the contemporary natural philosophical (and even anatomical) thought of their day. Moreover, the theological importance of these topics did not somehow slip past the attention of the reformers. If anything, natural philosophy – and particularly anatomy – carried a significance that was very closely related to theology itself. Along these lines, Vivian Nutton argues that the importance of anatomy in Wittenberg extended well beyond mere natural knowledge. The study of anatomy offered evidence of a purposeful designer. It

---

Manchester 2004, pp. 84–107; Erik A. HEINRICHS, Plague, Print, and the Reformation. The German Reform of Healing, 1473–1573, London 2018; Sachiko KUSUKAWA, Medicine in Western Europe in 1500, in: ELMER (ed.), The Healing Arts, pp. 1–26; Sachiko KUSUKAWA, The Medical Renaissance of the Sixteenth Century. Vesalius, Medical Humanism and Bloodletting, in: Ibid., pp. 58–83.

173   MBW T1, pp. 109f.; cf. CR 1, col. 74f.
174   Ralf-Dieter HOFHEINZ, Philipp Melanchthon und die Medizin im Spiegel seiner akademischen Reden, Herbolzheim 2001, p. 19. More generally, Hofheinz documents Melanchthon's interest in medicine, as evidenced by his academic speeches, throughout his book.
175   Ibid., p. 11.
176   See KUSUKAWA, Transformation, pp. 83–85, regarding Melanchthon's preparations for his work on *De anima*, and particularly his concern for the works of Galen. See also HOFHEINZ, Medizin im Spiegel, pp. 12–15. For further information on Melanchthon, Commentarius de anima, Wittenberg 1540 (VD16 M 2749), see CELLAMARE, Anatomy and the Body, pp. 341–353; Jürgen HELM, Die »Spiritus« in der medizinischen Tradition und in Melanchthons »Liber de anima«, in: RHEIN/FRANK (eds.), Melanchthon und die Naturwissenschaften, pp. 219–237; Sascha SALATOWSKY, Die aristotelische Psychologie bei Luther und Melanchthon. De Anima. Rezeption der aristotelischen Psychologie im 16. und 17. Jahrhundert, Amsterdam 2006, esp. pp. 69–75, 91–99, 101–106, 112–128, URL: <https://books.google.no/books?id=EY06AAAAQBAJ&printsec=frontcover#v=onepage&q&f=false> (23 Aug 2022); and KUSUKAWA, Transformation, pp. 85–114.
      According to HOFHEINZ, Medizin im Spiegel, pp. 17f., a subsequent edition of *De anima*, complete with knowledge gleaned from the innovative approach and work of Vesal's *Fabrica* (1543), appeared in 1552 and experienced frequent republication.

argued against the atheistic and Epicurean atomistic theories and their teachings that man is the result of chance[177]. Furthermore, for the reformers, there was a connection between knowledge of anatomy and human morality, whether in providing opportunity for reflection on the fragility of human life or for other theological and moral insights[178].

Given the above, it should not surprise us that the anatomical understandings of the reformers – and particularly the associated teleological conception of the body – are to be found in the discussion of Genesis 1:28 and procreation throughout the sources observed in this study. We will observe anatomical references with Luther from very nearly the beginning of our study with *Vom ehelichen Leben* (1522)[179] – along with other relatively early polemic and pastoral writings[180] – clear through the 1530s and 40s as we glance ahead toward Luther's *Lectures on Genesis*[181]. The correlation between physical anatomy with its divinely-given function and purpose is furthermore readily apparent not only with Melanchthon [182] but also will be observed in the argumentation of Justus Jonas[183]. Where such argumentation does occur, there is both an appeal to the self-evident purposes of the body and its members, as well as the implied or explicitly-made conclusion that such divinely-given purpose corresponds with a proper (and improper) use[184]. Most commonly, this is simply that man and woman are made for marriage and procreation and

---

177 Nutton, Medicine and the Reformation, pp. 18–20. See also Sachiko Kusukawa, The Natural Philosophy of Melanchthon and His Followers, in: École Française de Rome (ed.), Sciences et religions de Copernic à Galilée, (1540–1610), Rome 1999, pp. 443–453, at pp. 445f., URL: <http://digital.casalini.it/10.1400/36916> (18 Aug 2022).
178 Nutton, Medicine and the Reformation, p. 20.
179 WA 10/II, p. 276,25.
180 See, for example, Wider den falsch genannten geistlichen Stand (WA 10/2, p. 156,1–22), Ursach und Antwort (WA 11, p. 398,1–20), An die Herren deutschs Ordens (WA 12, p. 242,8–18), and a letter to three nuns (WA Br 3, p. 327,21–34). Note that in both this and the following footnote, many of the references correspond with – or were discovered through – those provided in Cortright, Poor Maggot-Sack, pp. 171–178.
181 For example, WA 42, p. 76,13–18, pp. 125,33–126,4, p. 644,39–42; WA 43, p. 344,15–20, p. 627,37–40, pp. 673,37–674,6.
182 Melanchthon's entire anatomical treatment in *Commentarius de anima* offers a display, par excellence, of his teleological understanding of human anatomy. In connection with the ethical use of the body, we might simply note that he bemoans the misuse of the seed which was created solely for the purpose of procreation. See Melanchthon, Commentarius de anima, 72r. Regarding the members and their purposes, see also ibid., 21r–21v (on the testes), 69r–71r (the matrix), 196v (on the appetites created for the purpose of procreation).
183 Justus Jonas, Adversvs Iohannem Fabrum Constantien[sem] Vicarium, scortationis patronum, pro coniugio sacerdotali, Iusti Ionae defensio, Wittenberg 1523 (VD16 J 871), C1v.
184 It is important to point out that the self-evident nature of man, woman, and their anatomy does not have to be understood at the level of a highly complex academic discussion. Such arguments could readily be made at the »common sense« level – as Luther did in the *Large Catechism* (BSELK,

not for celibacy and virginity. Nevertheless, we might also assume that it is such a teleological understanding of the body, the use of its parts, and their divinely-given purposes, which – at least in part – underlies Luther's understanding and condemnation of, for example, the Onan incident[185].

The anatomical and natural philosophical writings of the classical authors are not merely important to the proper understanding of our topic on account of their teleological understanding of the human body, however. They also contribute to the discussions surrounding nature, the affects, and the appetites – topics that are constantly at play behind the scenes in our discussion of Genesis 1:28.

Turning now to this discussion, we make the following brief observations. First, we note that the relationship of the soul and body, along with such appetites and desires as correspond with these, is very much an item of concern in the natural philosophical and anatomical writings of Aristotle and Galen. Aristotle's *De anima* spends ample time discussing the various souls (nutritive, sensitive, and rational), their respective organs and functions, and what can be said about affects, appetites, and desires as relate to these divisions[186]. Galen, likewise, is concerned with the delineation between soul and nature and what is proper to each. As Cunningham observes,

> Growth, nutrition (and generation too, as Galen later makes clear) are activities performed by *Nature*: they are simply the work of Nature. (Galen then argues in this work [i. e. *On the Natural Faculties*] that they can each be understood as a sequence of *faculties* – faculties of attraction, retention, assimilation and expulsion of nourishment – both in animals and plants)[187].

The point of this observation is that when Luther, Melanchthon, and the other authors concerned in our study make comments with respect to nature, affects, appetites, or inclinations, they are taking part in conversations that are intertwined in age-old philosophical, theological, legal, and anatomical discussions. As a brief illustration, when Luther says,

---

p. 1002) – while still corresponding with the natural philosophical context in which the reformers lived.
185 See WA 14, pp. 471,29–472, 9; WA 24, pp. 621,27–622,13, pp. 622,36–623,15; WA 44, pp. 316,35–317,8.
186 Here see Aristotle, On the Soul, bks. 2, 3. See also id., Parts of Animals, bk. 2:10, 3:14 (pp. 172f., 288f.), where Aristotle talks about the innateness of ingestion and discharge for all animals – something which Luther will repeatedly include in his list of natural functions (along with procreation).
187 Cunningham, Anatomical Renaissance, pp. 42f.

Second, the pope has as little power to command this as he has to forbid eating, drinking, the natural movement of the bowels, or growing fat. Therefore, no one is bound to keep it [...][188],

Or:

For this word which God speaks, »Be fruitful and multiply«, is not a command. It is more than a command, namely, a divine ordinance [*werck*] which it is not our prerogative to hinder or ignore. Rather, it is just as necessary as the fact that I am a man, and more necessary than sleeping and waking, eating and drinking, and emptying the bowels and bladder. It is a nature and disposition just as innate as the organs involved in it [...] And wherever men try to resist this, it remains irresistible nonetheless and goes its way through fornication, adultery, and secret sins, for this is a matter of nature and not of choice[189],

we ought not think that Luther is *merely* taking part in a scriptural, theological discussion. Rather, he is likely *also* tapping into a rich discourse of the classical, ecclesiastical, and academic world. Whether he is thinking about Aristotle, Galen, Cicero, someone else, or a combination of these writers is perhaps impossible to rightly say. Nevertheless, we can be sure that these allusions to ancient conversations would not have fallen on deaf ears. Indeed, they would have almost certainly been understood as referring to such ancient and ongoing discussions.

Having now offered some general and significant observations regarding the natural philosophical background of the reformers along with their teleological understanding of the human body and its members, we now are able to comment upon the importance of this subject area for our study and in the wider research areas of Reformation understandings of such topics as marriage and sex. Here we note that both our current discussion as well as the previous discussion on nature (natural

---

188 LW 44, p. 178, cf. »Zum andern/das der Bapst solchs nit [35] macht hat zupietten/als wenig als er macht hat zovorpieten essen/trincken [36] und den naturlichenn auszgang/odder feyst werdenn/ drumb ists niemandt [37] schuldig zuhaltenn [...]«. Cited from Thomas KAUFMANN, An den christlichen Adel deutscher Nation von des christlichen Standes Besserung, Kommentare zu Schriften Luthers, Tübingen 2014, p. 317 (cf. WA 6, p. 442).
189 LW 45, p. 18, cf. »Denn diß wort, da got spricht: ›Wachsset und mehret euch‹, ist nicht eyn gepot ßondern mehr den eyn gepott, nemlich eyn gottlich werck, das nicht bey uns stehet tzuverhyndern odder noch tzulaßen, ßondern ist eben alßo nott, alß das ich eyn manß bild sey, und nöttiger denn essen und trinken, fegen und außwerffen, schlaffen und wachen. Es ist eyn eyngepflantzte natur und artt eben ßo wol als die glidmaß, die datzu gehören. Drumb gleych wie got niemandt gepeut, das er man sey oder weyb, ßondern schaffet, das sie ßo mussen seyn, Alßo gepeutt er auch nicht, sich mehren, ßondern schafft, das sie sich mussen mehren. Und wo man das wil weren, das ists dennoch ungeweret und gehet doch durch hurerey, ehebruch und stummen sund seynen weg, denn es ist natur und nicht wilkore hierynnen«. WA 10/II, p. 276,21–31.

law) perform important fixing functions that help facilitate a proper understanding of the worldview of the reformers. That is simply to say, the reformers worked within a realm of presuppositions regarding the body and its divinely-given functions and purposes that circumscribe the extent to which »Reformation« views of these topics may be understood. Divorced from such a wider worldview, theological concepts might be taken out of their own context and float more freely – perhaps even taking on meanings that would have been unthinkable to the reformers[190]. Yet, when these topics are better situated in their proper context, they are both more accurately understood and become less of a waxen nose[191].

---

190 What is meant with the above remarks might be briefly illustrated with Dragseth, Martin Luther's View on the Body, Desire, and Sexuality. In this article Dragseth argues that Martin Luther's views on the body, desire, and sexuality are to be understood, not through philosophy, but through the incarnation and the Gospel (pp. 4f.). Furthermore, Dragseth argues that, for Luther, whereas it is sin that »makes desire or appetite perverse« (p. 11), it is »only faith in God's justifying grace« which »can justify the desire of the lover« (p. 12). While the outlines of the above argument are generally correct (aside perhaps from turning Christ's incarnation and the Gospel into an epistemological principle), the conclusions Dragseth draws from the Gospel – in Luther's name – are unfortunately far-wide of his own clearly-defined views on these topics. Indeed, in arguing that it is the »incarnation and justification« that is the foundation for understanding the body, desire, and sexuality, Dragseth not only ignores the wider body of thought in Luther's *Lectures on Genesis* (one of her oft-cited sources), but also leaves undefined what was quite obviously established in Luther's mind, whether through his understanding of Scripture's teaching, or – as is relevant here – his understanding of nature and anatomy. In short, Dragseth has ignored Luther's own context and wider thought and thus reached an open-ended, nebulous, and untenable conclusion.

191 Aside from the work of such scholars as Cunningham, Kusukawa, and Nutton, seemingly meager attention seems to have been given to the relationship between the teleological-anatomical orientation of the reformers and what this would have meant for their understandings of sex, sexuality, and marriage. Such standard works on these topics as Merry E. Wiesner-Hanks, Women and Gender in Early Modern Europe, New York 2008; ead., Christianity and Sexuality; and Susan C. Karant-Nunn/Merry E. Wiesner-Hanks, Luther on Women. A Sourcebook, Cambridge 2003, while dealing with a vast array of material, take little or no note of this. In his valuable treatment on Luther and the body, Cortright does give attention to this by offering several relevant citations (see Cortright, Poor Maggot-Sack, pp. 42 [quoting Aquinas], 153, 171–178) and even notes on one occasion Luther's focus on »purpose«, ibid., p. 171. He does not, however, delve into the natural philosophical background underlying this understanding and its relationship with Reformation understandings of the body.

3. The Emergence of a Verse

> Hac ratione docebis nos omnes coelibatum vovere et postea orare, ne sit impossibilis, ac per hoc illud statutum naturae »Crescite et multiplicamini« coges deum mutato suo verbo, quo creavit omnia, revocare.

> *By this kind of reasoning you will teach us all first to vow celibacy and then afterward pray that it prove not to be impossible. Moreover, by the same reasoning, you are trying to compel God to revoke his word, that divine commandment of nature by which he created all things, »Increase and multiply«.*

> —Martin Luther, *De votis monasticis iudicium*

3.1 Background to the Controversy (1518–1521)

Jeremy Cohen concludes his study of our verse by looking ahead to the sixteenth and seventeenth centuries[1]. Here he notes the important polemic role it played during the time of the Reformation and beyond. He observes, for example, that already in 1522 in *Vom ehelichen Leben* Luther was placing striking emphasis upon Genesis 1:28, both in his understanding of marriage and in his polemic aimed at Catholic teaching and practice[2]. Certainly, this was the case later in Luther's career, too. A mere cursory reading of Luther's *Lectures on Genesis* demonstrates that the topic of procreation, to include numerous references to Genesis 1:28, takes up an inordinately large amount of Luther's attention. Yet, if we venture back to *Scholia in librum Genesios* (1518–1521) and compare these earlier notes with Luther's later works, we make the striking discovery that the primordial blessing, »Be fruitful and multiply«, was of comparatively little concern for Luther prior to 1521[3]. It simply did not play the same role; neither was it thought of in the same way. We therefore must ask the question, what happened during these brief years to cause Luther to

---

1 Cohen, Be Fertile, pp. 306ff.
2 Ibid., pp. 307f.
3 In *Scholia in librum Genesios*, see WA 9, p. 330,26, pp. 346,33–347,1, p. 347,42, p. 348,6.

give such attention to this verse? Moreover, when and under what circumstances did Luther first start to teach and write about this verse in powerful polemic fashion?

In undertaking such an investigation, it is helpful to outline some methodological considerations as well as the approach we will take in answering our guiding questions. To begin with, the investigation we are undertaking here is an attempt to isolate the first polemical appearance of Genesis 1:28 in Luther's writings within the backdrop of correspondence and relevant contemporary writings. Thus, even in locating and identifying the shift in Luther's thought – very plausibly, one might argue – it is also done with a certain tentativeness. After all, it is always possible that there exists, or perhaps used to exist, some note, manuscript, letter, *Flugschrift*, or other additional source which contains the actual emergence of our verse within reformation controversy, this despite all attempts to best reconstruct the available data[4].

Having qualified our investigation in such a way, however, the following method would seem to constitute a reasonable approach to the questions at hand: First, through the historical information present in the *Weimar Ausgabe*, we can identify with a good degree of certainty when and under what circumstances Luther first made use of the verse in question in addition to the circumstances and concerns of the time. Access to the era's *Flugschriften*, both through online databases[5] as well as printed collections[6] also make it possible to attain something of an overview of the significant writings of the era, their content, and their concerns. Finally, secondary literature on the debate over the marriage of priests and monastic vows – here especially Stephen Buckwalter, Waldemar Kawerau, Ulrich Bubenheimer, Marjorie Plummer, Heinz-Meinolf Stamm, and others[7] – proves invaluable in reconstructing

---

4 Otfried Czaika, A Vast and Unfamiliar Field. Swedish Hymnals and Hymnal-Printing in the 16th Century, in: Maria Schoildt et al. (eds.), Celebrating Lutheran Music. Scholarly Perspectives at the Quincentenary, Uppsala 2019, pp. 125–138, refers to this discussion on lost books and their impact on the historical canon. This topic is elsewhere treated by Andrew Pettegree, The Legion of the Lost. Recovering the Lost Books of Early Modern Europe, in: Flavia Bruni/Andrew Pettegree (eds.), Lost Books. Reconstructing the Print World of Pre-industrial Europe, Leiden 2016, pp. 1–27. One particular missing letter of Melanchthon that could prove most significant (should it ever be found) is a letter dating from September 1521 in which the issue of the impossibility of keeping the vow of chastity was apparently discussed. See Maurer, Der junge Melanchthon, p. 304, for reference to this.
5 Verzeichnis der im deutschen Sprachbereich erschienenen Drucke des 16. Jahrhunderts (VD 16): <https://www.bsb-muenchen.de/sammlungen/historische-drucke/recherche/vd-16/>.
6 Adolf Laube/Ulman Weiss, Flugschriften gegen die Reformation (1518–1524), Berlin 1997.
7 Buckwalter, Priesterehe; Waldemar Kawerau, Die Reformation und die Ehe. Ein Beitrag zur Kulturgeschichte des sechzehnten Jahrhunderts, Halle 1892; Ulrich Bubenheimer, Streit um das Bischofsamt in der Wittenberger Reformation 1521/1522, in: Zeitschrift der Savigny-Stiftung für Rechtsgeschichte (1987), pp. 155–209; Plummer, Clerical Marriage; Heinz-Meinolf Stamm, Luthers Stellung zum Ordensleben, Wiesbaden 1980; Sjöholm, Luthers Åskådning; Grimm, Luther et l'experience sexuelle; Lohse, Luthers Kritik; id., Mönchtum und Reformation.

the timeline of events and circumstances leading to the appearance of Genesis 1:28 in Luther's writings, a development, we might note, that would later play such a significant role in both his – and the evangelical – polemic against vows of celibacy along with his understanding of marriage and human sexuality.

One final methodological note is in order before we embark on the investigation itself. This chapter will concern itself not merely with the existence or absence of Genesis 1:28 in various texts but will also give attention to the contours of the ongoing arguments surrounding the topics of priestly marriage and monastic vows. This is important in that theological arguments tend to function as more or less integrous systems. Noting this, it comes as no surprise that a shift in one element of a system can lead to significant readjustment in many related areas[8]. Thus, it will be important for us to observe how the various elements of the systems of argument in these debates tended to function. Such observations can also give indications as to the presence or absence of our own verse in these debates of the early Wittenberg Reformation.

Erasmus and Albrecht von Eyb

Having said so much by way of introduction, it is helpful to ask the question, what was the status of the debate surrounding priestly marriage and celibacy in the late

---

[8] Examples abound with respect to this observation, though an obvious one from Reformation times can be observed with the many second- and third-order effects resulting from Luther's insights into Scripture's teaching on sin and, consequently, grace. The monastic vocation and the entire ecclesiastical system all reverberated from the impact of redefining teaching on this single point as is most evident from such a writing as Luther's *De Captivitate Babylonica Ecclesiae* (WA 6, pp. 497–573).

In connection with the redefinition of sin, and particularly original sin, Wilhelm Braun, Die Bedeutung der Concupiscenz in Luthers Leben und Lehre, Berlin 1908, traces out the intensification of Luther's understanding of original sin, i. e. concupiscence, as well as the background from which Luther's understanding emerged. Interestingly, this was not only significant for Luther's understanding of grace, but this helped to set the stage for a renewed consideration of sexuality. After all, given the fact that concupiscence had formerly been identified with the desires of the *flesh*, Luther's redefinition of such desires as residing in the human will (p. 171) not only intensified Luther's conception of sin, but also freed up aspects of man's sexual nature to be understood in the positive light of God's good creation.

A further point of importance related to the systemic nature of theology and this study can be seen in the historic relationship between priestly celibacy and the priest's function in the Mass. Here we can note that a positive correlation between these two elements developed throughout church history and also waxed (and waned) in accordance with the prevailing understanding of celibacy vis-à-vis the marriage of priests. For example, Parish, Clerical Celibacy, p. 6, notes – even as she traces out both the broad and the narrow theological landscape with which the question of priestly celibacy relates – that it was especially after the eleventh century's enforcement of the celibacy of priests that an increased emphasis upon »cultic purity« grew.

1510s? Did Genesis 1:28 play any role whatsoever at this time? In answering such questions, we certainly can note that these topics, though perhaps not so much this verse, were items of discussion. A significant example of exactly this point can be observed with the Louvain printing of Desiderius Erasmus's *Encomium matrimonii* in March of 1518[9]. Although the work was ostensibly a piece of rhetorical amusement, in its roughly twenty-five pages it managed to touch on some very serious marriage matters[10]. These included brief discussions of what would come to be elements of confessional division in the ensuing years. Most interestingly for the sake of this study, Erasmus's fictive counselor speaks with highest regard for marriage, particularly in contrast to the unfruitful and unfriendly life of the celibate[11]. He even goes so far as to equate the work of marriage – and procreation – as normative for the human constitution and basic humanity[12], a work of

---

9 BUCKWALTER, Priesterehe, p. 49, notes that in the following months of 1518, print shops in Cologne and Strasbourg began printing this work in German-speaking areas, thus speaking to the relative importance of this work – at least in the Latin-speaking portions of the community. Interestingly, Michael MESSING, Fatal Discord. Erasmus, Luther, and the Fight for the Western Mind, New York 2018 (Kindle ed.), p. 219, notes that Erasmus had composed this work some twenty years earlier and that it was on account of this work, along with two others, he would be condemned by the theological faculty in Paris in 1525. See ibid., p. 545.
One question that arises with regard to the discussion of Erasmus's *Encomium matrimonii* and Reformation-era discussions involving the marriage of priests, celibacy, and other related matters, is whether and to what extent Erasmus influenced the various reformers. Thomas Kaufmann gives brief attention to this question in KAUFMANN, Ehetheologie, pp. 286f. Here he points out that up to the time of the Reformation no one had addressed such questions to the extent with which Erasmus had addressed them. Furthermore, Kaufmann argues that although one should not overestimate the extent to which Erasmus influenced the non-Latin-speaking public, his influence within the academic world was considerable.
Yet to what extent was Erasmus known in Wittenberg? While it is difficult to give an entirely satisfactory answer to the question of whether Erasmus's book was in Wittenberg already by 1518–1521, we can note that in KUSUKAWA, Wittenberg Library Catalogue, p. 64, Erasmus's *Encomium matrimonii* is listed as part of the university collection at that later date.

10 BUCKWALTER, Priesterehe, p. 49. In this, as in other matters, it is nearly impossible to truly pin Erasmus down to a single position. In fact, depending on the audience, Erasmus can be found to favor chastity more highly than he did marriage. See, for example, Albert HYMA, Erasmus and the Sacrament of Marriage, in: Archiv für Reformatorischegeschichte 48 (1957), pp. 145–164, at p. 159. Thus, all that might really be said is that Erasmus, if anything, helped fuel a certain openness of thought. In point of fact, Antje FLÜCHTER, Der Zölibat zwischen Devianz und Norm. Kirchenpolitik und Gemeindealltag in den Herzogtümern Jülich und Berg im 16. und 17. Jahrhundert, Köln et al. 2006, pp. 66–73, argues that for Erasmus, such human freedom which allowed one to choose between a lesser (marriage) and a greater good (celibacy) was the decisive factor – though his ideal was actually that of celibacy (pp. 68, 70f.).

11 Desiderius ERASMUS, Encomium Matrimonii, Strasbourg 1518 (VD16 E 2813), a2ᵛ.

12 »Quid æquius, quam id reddere posteris, quod ipsi a maioribus accepimus. Quid inconsyderatius q̃ id sanctimoniæ studio, perinde ut prophanum fugere, quod deus ipse totius sanctimoniæ fons

the Creator, and an abiding command[13]. While in 1518 such topics were not yet the subject of confessional wrangling, in four short years these exact points would work their way into the heart of discussions surrounding celibacy, the marriage of priests, and monastic vows, ultimately even comprising aspects of what would become a distinctively evangelical understanding of marriage and procreation. In the meantime, however, neither the theme of procreation nor its *locus classicus,* »Be fruitful and multiply«, would be a central component of the discussions that were to take place.

We would, however, be remiss if we were to overlook the ongoing importance of the works of Albrecht von Eyb (1420-1475) in the early sixteenth century. Von Eyb was a theologian, lawyer, and an early German humanist, who had spent significant periods of his life studying in Italy[14]. Significantly, he wrote several Latin and German works treating the topics of women and marriage[15]. His exposition of these themes is notable both for its artful expression of the ideals of humanism as well as his untypically positive regard for these topics, most especially for women[16]. His most famous work, *Ob ainem sey zu nehmen ain Eelich weib,* expressed these concerns and enjoyed numerous reprintings, at least two of these being in Augsburg in the 1510s[17].

---

ac parens sanctissimum haberi voluit? Quid inhumanius quam hominem ab humanæ conditionis legibus abhorrere? Quid ingratius, quam id negare minoribus, quod ipse nisi a maioribus accepisses nec esses quidem qui negare posses?«. Ibid., a2^v.

13 »Idem ille post diluuium mortaliũ generi reconciliatus hanc primam legem prouulgasse legitur, nõ ut celibatũ amplecterētur, *sed ut crescerent, ut multiplicarētur, ut terram implerent.* At quo pacto, nisi coniugio darent operam? Et ne hic uel Mosaicæ legis libertatem, uel tempestatis illius necessitatem causemur. Quid illud in Evangelicis quoq; literis repetitum comprobatumq; Christi suffragium? propter hoc, inquit, relinquet homo patrem & matrem & adhærebit uxori suæ. Quid parentum pietate sanctius? At huic tamen coniugalis præfertur fides. Quo authore? Nempe deo, quo tempore? non Iudaismi tantum, sed Christianismi quoq;«. Ibid., a3^r; emphasis added.

14 For a brief but helpful biography of Albrecht von Eyb, see Maja EIB, Der Humanismus und sein Einfluss auf das Eheverständnis im 15. Jahrhundert. Eine philosophisch-moraltheologische Untersuchung unter besonderer Berücksichtigung des frühhumanistischen Gedankenguts Albrechts von Eyb, Münster 2001, pp. 48-66.

15 Ibid., pp. 73-78.

16 Ibid., p. 78.

17 VD16 shows two printings in Augsburg during these years: 1511 (VD16 V 4749), 1517 (VD16 V 4743). Working from Albrecht von EYB, Ob ainem sey zu nemen ain Eelich weib, Augsburg 1517, it is worth noting that while von Eyb offers typical emphasis to the God-intended work of procreation (Eiii^r, Fi^r-Fi^v, Giii^r [cf. chapt. *Das lob der Ee*]), he also includes a section on the purposefulness of the body and all its members (Ei^v-Fi^r) which he largely situates between comments on mankind's intended purpose of filling the earth. In this section he does not mention sexual organs, and yet the placement of this section and the emphasis upon the purposefulness of each and every part of man is striking. In this fashion it offers an implicit argument that is comparable to some of the explicit argumentation which would appear in the 1520s regarding the self-evident purpose

More important than the longstanding popularity enjoyed by *Ob ainem sey zu nehmen ain Eelich weib* is the work, *Von dem Eelichen Standt Ain schöne leer[...]*, which, while it contained a portion of von Eyb's book (i. e. *Das lob der Ee*), also contained other sections of anonymous authorship[18]. *Von dem Eelichen Standt* enjoyed no less than five editions between 1511–1520[19]. For our purposes it is important given its application of Genesis 1:28 as part of the institution of marriage[20] as well as its insistence that the teachings of Scripture are to be placed above the teachings of the church fathers regarding monastic orders and celibacy[21]. While it can only be speculated whether this document was known amongst Wittenberg circles, it is interesting to observe the emphasis our verse received at this time – even above the teachings of the church fathers and apart from historic streams of thought on the topic.

---

of sex and the reproductive members. Furthermore, the ordering in which von Eyb speaks of the various bodily members offers a certain resonance with Luther's explanation of the First Article of the Creed as he lists the various members of the body, reason, and senses.

For more on von Eyb's influence upon fifteenth century marital thought, see HARRINGTON, Re-ordering Marriage, pp. 59f., in which Harrington views the heritage of von Eyb (and others) as more properly embraced by the reformers rather than their Catholic opponents. On the other hand, Joseph Anthony HILLER, Albrecht von Eyb, Medieval Moralist, Washington, D.C. 1939, pp. 112–156, seeks to frame von Eyb entirely as a humanist writer well within the confines of the Catholic moralist tradition.

18 Albrecht CLASSEN, Der Liebes- und Ehediskurs vom hohen Mittelalter bis zum frühen 17. Jahrhundert, Münster 2005, pp. 115f., attributes this work to an anonymous author. The first portion of this work which we have examined is clearly a well-known section of von Eyb's *Ob ainem sey [...]*. What is unclear, however, is where or from whom the remainder of the book originates.

19 Albrecht von EYB, Von dem Eelichen Standt. Ain schöne leer wie sich ain Eeman halten, un[d] sein Eefrauwen underweisen unnd zyehen soll. Auch widerumb die fraw gegen irem mann. Dardurch sy hye erlang[e]n gut und eer und ewyge fröd, Augsburg ca. 1520. This book was first printed in Augsburg ca. 1511/1512 (VD16 V 2461) but then reprinted in several editions (1512: VD16 ZV 31503, 1513: VD16 V 2462, and then in two unique printings in 1520: VD16 V 2463, 2464).

20 »Des ersten hat gott d[er] almächtig gebraucht des ampts ains rechten waren vatters. Hat wölln dz menschlich geschlecht ewig zů sein/unnd hat des ersten erschaffen den mañ nach seiner götlichen byldung. Darnach die frauwen nach gestaldt des mannes/das also seyn sollten zway geschlecht/mañ und frauwen/die sich mitt ainannder möchten vermischen/kynder zůgeberen/und das erdtrich mittmenig der menschen zů erfullñ/das dañ geschehen soll in figur der hayligen Ee. Unnd hatt darnach gott der vatter sölliche Ee selbst auff gestetzt/geordnet unnd angefanngen im lustigen/wunnreichen Paradeyß und zů der zeit der unschold«. Von EYB, Von dem Eelichen Standt, Ai^v (citing from VD16 V 2464).

21 »Wañ gott hatt die Ee beschaffen/do er sprach. Crescite. Ir solt wachssen uñ soltt euch meeren. Aber Bernhardus/Augustinus/Benedictus/Dominicus/die haben die örden beschaffen und gestifft. Darumb ist das gebott gottes grösser dañ der leerer«. Ibid., Aii^v.

Early Wittenberg Discussions on the Marriage of Priests, Monastic Celibacy, and the Presence/Absence of Genesis 1:28 (1518 through early 1521)

Turning our attention now more toward Luther and Wittenberg events, we note that discussion of the topics of marriage and chastity were not long in coming once the wheels of reform began to turn in earnest. Since the advent of the printing press in Europe, pamphlets and other publications had taken up and satirized the institutions of marriage and celibacy due to rampant sexual promiscuity[22]. It is no surprise, then, that the topics of married life, priestly celibacy, and monastic vows were also soon receiving attention in Wittenberg[23]. On Luther's part, this was not a discussion into which he readily entered. However, when several unauthorized copies of his *Sermon von dem ehelichen Stand* appeared in print in January of 1519, Luther felt compelled to take up the subject of marriage in a publication later that spring[24]. In speaking to the topic of marriage, however, Luther remained in line with medieval views in understanding marriage as a sacrament and by continuing to maintain a high regard for celibacy. Nevertheless, already in this early writing, two themes that would eventually connect with the development of Luther's thought on procreation appeared. Namely, Luther emphasized both marriage's foundation in God's creation as well as the general impossibility of celibate chastity (barring a special dispensation from God)[25]. This notwithstanding, this sermon contains neither discussion of Genesis 1:28 nor its continued normativity for human life.

Along these lines, one may fairly maintain that Genesis 1:28 did not hold any sort of notable position, let alone dominance, in the period from 1518 through the first half of 1521 in the polemic surrounding priestly marriage and monastic celibacy. In fact, while Luther shows great willingness to allow for the marriage of priests and a growing discomfort with and inclination towards the rejection of monasticism, his rationale during this time cannot be said to include our verse. Instead, arguments for the possibility of priestly marriage allude to the ongoing custom of the Greek church[26] as well as the marital practice of priests[27] and patri-

---

22 HARRINGTON, Reordering Marriage, p. 25.
23 BUCKWALTER, Priesterehe, pp. 79ff., provides a brief overview of the early discussions (beginning mid-1520) surrounding priestly marriage in Wittenberg.
24 Ibid., p. 60.
25 Ibid., p. 61. It should be noted that the claim of impossibility was a common refrain both prior to and during the Reformation, as is seen again and again in contemporary writings. BRUNDAGE, Law, Sex, and Christian Society, pp. 536–539, offers a less than glowing depiction of clerical morals during the outgoing centuries of the Middle Ages.
26 WA 6, p. 147,27–36. See also BUCKWALTER, Priesterehe, pp. 61f.
27 WA 6, p. 307,26–29. See also BUCKWALTER, Priesterehe, pp. 62–64.

archs[28] in the Old Testament. Luther also draws arguments from the New Testament and his understanding of the Gospel, whether in complaining about the church's usurpation of divine authority (cf. Matthew 19:6)[29], as demonstrated in his concern for Christian freedom and captive consciences[30], or, perhaps most strikingly, in drawing the conclusion that the Roman Church and its pope match the description of the doctrine of demons offered in 1 Timothy 4:1–3[31]. Indeed, the closest Luther comes to the realm of Genesis 1:28 (other than his *Scholia in librum Genesios*, see below) is when he alludes, as he does in *Von dem Papsttum zu Rom* (May 1520), to the fact that forbidding marriage is against God, law, reason, and nature[32], or – more significantly perhaps – in his *An den christlichen Adel deutscher Nation*. Given the content of the latter, not to mention the reaction it elicited, a closer examination of that writing is now in order.

In *An den christlichen Adel deutscher Nation* (June 1520)[33], written to address the emperor and the German nobility, Luther proposes a Christian council and suggests topics such a council might address. For our purposes, in several places in this writing, Luther addresses matters related to priestly marriage (as well as vows and celibacy). Aside from proposing that the many abuses of chastity in Rome be corrected through proper marriage[34], Luther's treatment of celibacy and vows occurs beginning with point twelve. Here, Luther makes the case that the Christian church should promote as good works those works which actually are commanded by God. Here he explicitly praises the works of marriage while criticizing and condemning monastic orders, pilgrimages, and other works of human invention[35]. Luther then proposes that monastic life should be made free of binding vows as

---

28 »Es muge keyner gott dienen, der ehlich ist, so doch Abraham und vil heyligen ehlich gewesen, Und gott die ehe selbst eyngesetzt, ausweyfell. Also steygt der Endchrist aber ubir gott«. WA 7, p. 175,1–4.
29 WA 6, pp. 553,22–555,31.
30 WA 6, pp. 558,8–559,19.
31 WA 6, pp. 307,34–308,7.
32 »Ja warumb vorpeut der Babst der gantzen priesterschafft den ehelichen standt, nit allein widder die figur [des obersten Priesters], sondern auch widder got, widder recht, widder vernunfft und natur [...]«. WA 6, p. 307,29–31.
33 D. Ernst Kohlmeyer, Die Entstehung der Schrift Luthers An den christlichen Adel deutscher Nation, Gütersloh 1922, pp. 31f., offers a generally helpful guide to the influences and development of this writing. Unfortunately, minimal attention is given to the question of Luther's thought on the marriage of priests and the question of monastic celibacy. Walter Keller, Zölibat und Priesterehe als reformatorische Anliegen auf dem Reichstag zu Augsburg 1530, in: Würzburger Diözesangeschichtsblätter 58 (1996), pp. 153–170, at pp. 153f., speaks to the historical and ecclesiastical significance of this writing, particularly when considered alongside *Von der Freiheit eines Christenmenschen* and *De captivitate Babylonica ecclesiae*.
34 WA 6, pp. 425,30–426,2.
35 WA 6, p. 437,1–30.

such a life was originally practiced in the Christian church[36]. Most concerning for Luther is the fact that although chastity is vowed (without any command of Christ), it is seldom kept and many souls become enslaved by sin and impurity[37]. Continuing, Luther argues that, according to 1 Timothy 3:2 and Titus 1:6, priests should be allowed to marry[38]. The forbiddance of marriage is nothing other than the teaching of the devil (1 Timothy 4:1–3)[39]. Moreover, if a pastor and his woman are living together faithfully, then they may consider themselves as married before God even if the church and government deny their marriage[40].

It is the next point, however, that proves interesting for our purposes. Luther continues by pointing out that his advice is with good reason. A pastor as a man cannot be without a woman. For the pope to forbid this is tantamount to forbidding that fire and straw should be placed together without either smoke or fire. Continuing, »[…] the pope has as little power to command this as he has to forbid eating, drinking, the natural movement of the bowels, or growing fat. Therefore, no one is bound to keep it, but the pope is responsible for all the sins which are committed against this ordinance […]«[41]. Although Luther has somewhat more to say about priestly marriage and vows in this writing, it is the prior point that deserves highlight.

Thomas Kaufmann comments on this section that the listing of these natural functions involves a sort of hyperbolic inflation as one proceeds from one function to the other[42]. Perhaps, however, there is something more to this list of natural functions than a mere rhetorical device? In light of the fact that similar lists are repeated time and again in Reformation literature and in view of the strong response Luther's comment elicited from Thomas Murner (see below), we might suggest that this listing of natural functions ventures into understood areas of legal/theological/philosophical discussions regarding natural law and natural philosophy. Such discussions need not be made explicit, of course, but would certainly be clearly discernable to an educated reader such as Murner. Thus, we might hypothesize that this line of thought links to a commonly understood argument, perhaps even involving Genesis 1:28. If this is the case, this could have been clearly recognizable

---

36 WA 6, pp. 439,33–440,7.
37 WA 6, p. 440,8–14.
38 WA 6, pp. 440,15–441,2.
39 WA 6, p. 441,3–10.
40 WA 6, p. 442,10–24.
41 LW 44, p. 178, cf. »Zum andern, das der Bapst solchs nit macht hat zupietten, als wenig als er macht hat zuvorpieten essen, trincken und den naturlichenn auszgang, odder feyst werdenn, drumb ists niemandt schuldig zuhaltenn, unnd der Bapst schuldig ist aller sund, die dawider geschehen […]«. WA 6, p. 442,34–38.
42 KAUFMANN, An den christlichen Adel, p. 318.

to Murner, although it would be difficult to recognize from our contemporary vantage point[43].

Directly in line with this hypothesis, Melachthon's *Capita* (1520) is quite nearly contemporaneous with Luther's writing. Prior to Melanchthon's first edition of *Loci Communes* in 1521, a work which will be considered in conjunction with Luther's time at the Wartburg below, Melanchthon had worked on previous drafts of this systematic-theological work. Interestingly, in his *Capita* of 1520, while discussing *Naturrecht* Melanchthon mentions nine basic topics pertaining to natural law. Four of these topics are directly relevant to marriage and procreation[44]. While these themes do not seem to have demonstrably impacted the discussions prior to late 1521, it is notable how strongly such themes of created order and natural law are expressed already in 1520 by Melanchthon. It should furthermore be noted that Genesis 1:22, i. e. »Be fruitful and multiply«, is regarded by Melanchthon as a precept of the divine law[45].

As previously alluded to, more remarkable – and perhaps unexpected – than Melanchthon's deliberations on natural law, was Thomas Murner's response to Luther's *An den christlichen Adel deutscher Nation*. Appearing in December 1520[46], Murner's response, *An den Großmechtigsten vn[d] Durchlüchtigste[n] adel tütscher nation*[47], addresses both Luther and the German nobility in the same *Flugschrift*. One by one, Murner takes on Luther's arguments, pointing out the errors he observed, appealing to the reasonableness and Christian sensibility of the nobility so that they would not listen to Luther's arguments, and generally defending the claims of the pope and the Roman church (while also claiming fairmindedness toward Luther's more reasonable arguments). Significantly for this writing is the

---

43 An example of such thought that might perhaps be »hanging in the air« of the time would be something like the excerpt from the anonymous canonical text, *Dinstinctio, Lex naturalis*: »The natural law of the first division [that is, the natural law that we share with other animals] consists in: *Precepts*: that each animal should unite bodily with another, male and female. This law directs, ›do not kill‹, but it does not direct, ›do not commit adultery‹, although it does direct, ›do no injury‹. *Prohibitions*: That animals should not unite contrary to nature, male with male [...] ›Increase and multiply‹ is a precept of nature and of the natural law [...] Also, this law prescribes, ›love thy neighbor‹«. Translation from the text in Weigand, no. 361 found in PORTER, Natural & Divine Law, p. 81. See also this study's previous treatment of our topic's natural law/canon law background.

44 »Primus ordo./Prima lex. Deus colendus est./2. Vita Tuenda et propaganda./Tertia Gignendum est./Quarta Iungenda sunt connubia./Quinta Genitum serunandum est«. CR 21, col. 25f., emphasis added; cf. Horst Georg PÖHLMANN (ed.), LOCI COMMUNES 1521. Lateinisch und Deutsch, Gütersloh 1993, pp. 103f.

45 CR 21, col. 27f.

46 WA 7, p. 615.

47 Thomas MURNER, An den Großmechtigsten vñ Durchlüchtigstē adel tütscher nation das sye den christlichen glauben beschirmen/wyder den zerst[oe]rer des glaubēs christi/Martinū luther einē [v]fierer der einfeltigē christē, Strasbourg 1520 (VD16 M 7020).

attention Murner gives to addressing Luther's arguments about the marriage of priests, monastic vows, and other themes related to marriage. While many arguments are not unique for the time, Murner's attention to Luther's arguments from creation and nature require further attention[48].

Beginning just past the middle of the writing, Murner mentions Luther's claim that it would be better for priests to have wives than to shamelessly maintain concubines, though he shies from entering into that particular discussion. Yet, Luther's claim that the pope does not have authority to command or require vows about priestly chastity any more than he may forbid eating, drinking, or bodily elimination, raises strong criticism from Murner. In particular, Murner argues that God would never have spoken against unchaste living in Scripture if it were no different than eating, drinking, and other natural functions. Furthermore, Luther's claim that marriage is in the same natural realm as eating and drinking is nothing less than an affront to the saints of the past who struggled so nobly against fornication and other sins – all while Luther says these cannot be avoided[49]. Moreover, Luther's claim that vows of chastity should be avoided for the vast majority of people is really no different than if he were to give permission to steal (simply because it cannot be avoided)[50]. Murner then turns to Luther's claim that the papacy has disregarded Christ's words in Matthew 19 (i. e. that man must not separate what God has joined together). Here Luther is to be criticized for applying this text to man and woman in general, instead of merely to those already married[51]. After continuing on to address fasting and other such regulations, Murner comes back once again to the topic of marriage, being particularly incensed by Luther's complaint that the pope forbids the marital estate and lords it over God's command. To this, Murner retorts that marriage is never commanded by God. It is rather a matter of free will. Genesis, with its word to »Be fruitful and multiply«, is irrelevant in this argument as these words are not a command. Therefore, it is not a sin if one does not reproduce. Nevertheless, fruitfulness is not something in man's control. Sin, however, is[52].

Here it is clear that Murner is particularly concerned about those natural law and *Schöpfungsordnung* (i. e. order of creation) aspects of Luther's argumentation.

---

48 Murner's treatment of these themes is found almost entirely in the section from ibid., Giii^v–Hii^r. There is further mention of the forbidden degrees of marriage on Jii^v.
49 Ibid., Giiii^r.
50 Ibid., Giiii^v.
51 Ibid., Hi^r.
52 »*Auch kan ich das nit fürgo*: das du sagest/der bapst verbiet den eelichen stand/und des müß gotz gebot und[er]gon/und d[er] eelich stand. Darzů sag ich/das zů heuraten oder zů d[er] ee greiffen niendert geboten ist von got/sunder in freiē willen stand/uñ wa du das harfür zühest/in dem bůch der geschöpff wachsen/und mere eüch, etc. Das ist kein gebot/dan wa einer nicht wüchβe/so thet er wider das gebot/wa es ein gebot were/und sündet. Nun ist aber wachsen in unserm gewalt nit/aber die sünden sein in unserm gewalt«. Ibid., Hii^r; italicized text as heading in original.

As Genesis 1:22 and 1:28 are not expressly mentioned in Luther's *An den deutschen Adel*, it is somewhat unclear why Murner ends up addressing these verses and attributing this argument to Luther. Nevertheless, this does comprise a very clear reference to this theme and thus the first notable entry of this verse into the controversy of this period. Moreover, the general lines of the interpretive argument are here clearly drawn. Luther is cited as claiming Genesis 1:28 to be an ongoing command of creation, whereas Murner argues that »Be fruitful and multiply« rather belongs to the realm of free will and human judgment[53].

Shifting more towards the question of monastic vows during this period, Luther's central argumentation centers more around concern for Gospel freedom, the vow of Baptism, and the authority of Scripture over any authority assumed by the church. The main outlines are best observed in *De captivitate Babylonica ecclesiae praeludium*, a writing which appeared in October of 1520.

Regarding this work, whereas Luther had previously struck at »three walls« that upheld and maintained papal authority and ecclesiastical abuse in *An den christlichen Adel deutscher Nation*, in *De captivitate Babylonica ecclesiae* Luther takes on the abuses of the church which enslaved souls and through which the Gospel and teachings of Scripture were held captive by human inventions. One by one in this writing, Luther goes through the seven sacraments of Rome, both in pointing out the abuses of those rightly considered to be sacraments or in critiquing those that have been made into sacraments solely by the presumed authority of the church.

In connection with vows and the marriage of priests, Luther deals with these themes in both the section on Baptism as well as in a specific section on marriage. Concerning Baptism, Luther points out that the vow of Baptism is more binding and

---

53 WA has no reference to Genesis 1:28 in *An den deutschen Adel*. We might speculate that Murner either introduced this verse of his own accord, or else that he was actually responding to another unidentified source. A second significant response to *An den deutschen Adel* was Hieronymus EMSER, WId[er] das vnchristenliche buch Martini Luters Augustiners, an den Tewtschen Adel außgangen, Leipzig 1521 (VD16 E 1137), Lii^v, Mi^v–Mii^r, responds to Luther's arguments from creation, yet without any mention of »Be fruitful and multiply« as part of the discussion. It is noteworthy that Emser is also concerned precisely about free will when he writes, »Czum andern das Luter sagt der bapst hab es nith macht tzu vorbieten/als wenig als essen/trincken/unnd den naturlichen außgang/das ist ein stinckende gleichnis und Luter hie gar ein grober lerer/Dann er machet kein underschidt under den dingen die an unserm freyen willen hangen als keuscheit/gehorsam/und alle ander tugeten/und den dingen darzu uns die not dringet/dy weder gehorsam gebot noch gesetz erleydē kann/Darumb so will ich dis stinckend argument faren lassen/dann ich oben gnugsam beweißt das es nith aleyn des bapstes sonder ouch der gantzen christenlichen kirchen gebot ist/wer nu dem gewalt d[er] kirchen widerstehet/der widerstehet ouch der ordnung gotes wie sant Pauel spricht Ro. xiii.«. Ibid., Mi^v–ii^r.

Similarly, Augustin von ALVELDT, Von dem ehelichen Stand wider Brudern Martin Luther, Leipzig 1521 (VD16 A 2108), though responding both to Luther's *An den deutschen Adel* as well as *De Captivitate Babylonica*, fails to show concern for Genesis 1:28.

authoritative than any vow of human invention, warning that such vows of human invention destroy the Christian freedom contained in the vow of Baptism[54]. Moreover, vows that lack the clear affirmation of Scripture should not be undertaken[55]. Additionally, the works of the baptized, regardless of their seeming importance, are acceptable and pleasing to God. Thus, the work of the common man or woman (e. g. the work of the housewife) is not to be denigrated[56]. Finally, Luther questions the pope's authority to dissolve a vow and observes that the pope's power is nothing greater than that possessed by any Christian[57]. In other words, with respect to vows, Luther's two main concerns seem to be the freedom of the Gospel and the authority of God's word over and above any authority assumed by the church. It is along these lines that Luther presents his criticism of monastic vows.

In dealing with the topic of marriage, Luther's main concerns are the fact that marriage is not properly shown to be a sacrament in Scripture[58], the church's usurpation of divine authority in wrongly separating what God has joined together (cf. Matthew 19:6)[59], and concern for Christian freedom as well as captive consciences[60]. It might be noted that, while Luther clearly bases his arguments on God's institution of marriage, Scripture's teaching, the Gospel, and Christian freedom, the purpose or good of marriage (or sexuality) does not seem to comprise any part of his argumentation in this writing, either with respect to vows or to marriage.

One final and somewhat indirectly related subject ought to be mentioned in relation to this writing. At first glance, developments in Luther's thought regarding the Mass seem somewhat distant from our own topic. Indeed, there is no *direct* relationship between the two. Nevertheless, the fact that Luther took what can only be regarded as a revolutionary step against the priestly sacrifice of the Mass and, instead, insisted upon and emphasized Christ's words of institution, along with faith, as that which is decisive in the sacrament, should not be underestimated[61]. After all, with this move, Luther accomplished something fundamentally decisive which perhaps initially went unnoticed. In arguing that it was not the priest who was decisive in the sacrament, but rather Christ's institution, one of the strong arguments that had both defended and concretized priestly celibacy was undone. If priests were no longer theologically required to maintain ritual purity on account of their sacrificial role in the Mass, then the weight of the theological system was

---

54 WA 6, pp. 538,26–539,10.
55 WA 6, p. 540,4–10.
56 WA 6, p. 541,1–17.
57 WA 6, p. 541,19–32.
58 WA 6, pp. 550,21–553,21.
59 WA 6, pp. 553,22–555,31.
60 WA 6, pp. 558,8–559,19.
61 WA 6, pp. 512–526.

now no longer prohibitive of the possibility that Genesis 1:27–28 normed human life and the role of marriage within it. Thus, while these developments were, in and of themselves, merely realizations of previous theological shifts which had taken place, they were simultaneously important steppingstones toward the unshackling of Genesis 1:28 and a differing view of human nature.

Before concluding this section, we do well to also mention Luther's *Scholia in librum Genesios* (1518–1521). Assuming that these notes do indeed date from this period, they can offer us perhaps some tentative insight into Luther's earlier understanding of our verse[62]. »Be fruitful and multiply« is itself referenced some three times in the *Scholia*. The first appearance is found in a marginal note mentioning the medieval theologian, Rupertus Tuitensis, and his work, *Opus originale [...] Tuiciensis de Victoria verbi dei*. Luther's citation refers to Rupertus's writing on the early chapters of Genesis[63]. Interestingly, within the referenced section of *Victoria verbi dei*, one finds a mixed understanding of procreation. Folia 17–20 deal largely with the negative side of procreation after the fall, including Cain, the issues surrounding the sons of God and the daughters of men, and then also the Flood. Nevertheless, the conclusion of the section, coinciding with God's blessing of Noah

---

[62] It should be noted that there is some argument as to the proper dating of these notes. Mickey Leland MATTOX, Defender of the Most Holy Matriarchs. Martin Luther's Interpretation of the Women of Genesis in the Enarrationes in Genesin, 1535–1545, Leiden et al. 2003, pp. 261f., includes a section on the basic debate surrounding this text in which he presents the various views held by prominent Luther scholars and seems to favor the later date. His overview of the situation can be summarized as follows: The basic question of importance with respect to these *Scholia* is whether they originate from a date sometime around 1518–1521 or whether they more properly belong to Luther's *Declamationes* of 1523–1524. While the likes of E. Thiele (editor of the *Scholia* for the WA), Heinrich Bornkamm, Peter Meinhold, and Kurt Aland have all set forth arguments for various dates within the earlier time frame, already in the late nineteenth century Paul Tschackert argued that the *Scholia* belonged to the later period. More recently, Tibor GALLUS, »Der Nachkomme der Frau« (Gen 3,15) in der altlutheranischen Schriftauslegung, Klagenfurt 1964, argued that developments in Luther's understanding and translation of Genesis 3:15 with respect to the translation of the seed of the woman (*ipse* as faithful to the Hebrew vs. *ipsa* as faithful to the Vulgate) force the argument strongly toward the later dating.

We might also note that Wilhelm MAURER, Der junge Melanchthon, pp. 114–116, and, more recently, Sabine HIEBSCH, Figura ecclesiae. Lea und Rachel in Luthers Genesispredigten, Münster 2002, p. 30, have addressed this debate and argue for the earlier date and against the latter. This study takes the position that the *Scholia* have their origin in the earlier period, also on account of developments in Luther's thought regarding Genesis 1:28.

[63] In the *Scholia*, Genesis 1:28 appears in one marginal note which reads, »Poliander quer am Rande zu Z. 1–13: Primae benedictioni ›Crescite et multiplicamini‹ &c. respondebit Ultima illa ›Venite benedicti patris mei‹ &c. Vide Tuicensem De Victoria verbi li. 2° ca. 17 et 18° in fine«. WA 9, p. 330,26–28. Of significance with this note is that it directs the reader back to Rupertus Tuitensis's *Opus originale[...]Tuiciensis de Victoria verbi dei*, which was first written in the eleventh century, but reprinted as recent as the late fifteenth century, likely in Augsburg in 1487.

and his sons, places special emphasis upon the decree (*propositi*) to »Be fruitful and multiply«, even including – perhaps significantly for our study – all of the saints in these words[64].

Further appearances in Luther's *Scholia* are associated with the repetition of the words »Be fruitful and multiply« to Noah and his family. In these latter appearances, however, Luther is commenting on God's goodness to man, both in His promises and His blessing, and does not inquire into the verse's ongoing relevance[65].

For our purposes, we may note that there is no evidence in the *Scholia* that Luther understood these verses as a command directly operative upon all of humanity (with only a few divinely granted exceptions). Neither do the *Scholia* offer evidence that Luther saw sexuality and fertility in humanity as derived from and contingent upon these words. Be that as it may, these words do offer evidence that Luther was already giving careful consideration to this text. Even more, it could very well be that in Ruperto we find a certain inspiration for an element of Luther's later understanding of Genesis 1:28, that all humanity is contained in these words[66].

Taking a slightly wider view of the landscape during this period, our findings thus far seem fitting. After all, in reviewing Adolf Laube's volumes on the *Flugschriften* of (and against) the early Reformation, as well as the relevant literature mentioned for this period in both Buckwalter's *Die Priesterehe* and Elizabeth Plummer's *From Priest's Whore to Pastor's Wife*, the weight of evidence leads to the conclusion that the authors of this period were more concerned with themes such as the abuses of papal power, the weakness and inability of (particularly) men to keep their vows of celibacy, and the biblical arguments surrounding these issues[67]. This

---

64 The citation in question reads as follows: »Trina verborum eorundes repetitio: magna est propositi dei confirmatio quod proposuit in verbo suo sciēs & presciens atqʒ predestinatos habēs omnes sanctos atqʒ electos suos quos nasci volebat sibi de genere humano: quantis meritis crescere quanto numero multiplicari haberent extunc usqʒ in finem seculi quanto & congregatis illis ad dexieram suam dicet ipsum verbum incarnatū ihesus christus victor propositi (Math. XXV) Venite benedicti patris mei possidete regnum quod vobis paratum est a constitutione mundi«. RUPERTUS, Opus originale Ruperti abbatis Tuiciensis de Victoria verbi dei in tredecim libros diuisum, Augsburg 1487 (BSB-Ink R-286 – GW M39213), Liber III, xx^v.

65 WA 9, pp. 346,33–347,1, p. 347,42, p. 348,6.

66 See WA 42, pp. 57,34–58,10.

67 Sources here include Ulrich BOSSLER, Ain schoner Dialogus oder gesprech des Appostolicums Angelica vñ anderer Specerey der Apotecken Antreffen Doctor Marti. Lutthers leer vnd sein anhang, Augsburg 1521 (VD16 B 6782); Martin BUCER, Ain schoener dialog[us] Vñ gespresch zwischen aim Pfarrer vnd aim Schulthayß betreffend allen übel Stand der gaystlichen. Vnd boeß handlūg der weltlichen. Alles mit geytzigkayt beladen. [et]c., Augsburg 1521 (VD16 B 8911); Johann EBERLIN VON GÜNZBURG, Ein vermanung aller christe[n] das sie sich erbarme[n] vber die klosterfrawe[n] […]; Der. III. bu[n]dtgnosz, Basel 1521 (VD16 E 100); Ulrich von HUTTEN, Gespräch büchlin. Feber das erst. Feber das Ander. Wadiscus oder die Römische dreyfaltigkeit (etc.), Strasbourg 1521 (VD16 H 6342); Johann ROEMER, Eyn schöner Dialogus von den vier grösten bechwernüß

notwithstanding, it must also be admitted that the potentially explosive nature of Genesis 1:28, though apparently only recognized by Murner, does seem to lurk somewhat in the background of the writings of this period – whether in the natural law tradition cited by Melanchthon and alluded to by Luther or perhaps via Luther's wrestlings with various works of theology, be they in the writings of the church fathers such as Chrysostom (as noted previously) or the more recent deliberations of Rupertus.

3.2 New Developments in Wittenberg during Luther's Time at the Wartburg

1521 was a landmark year in the development of the Reformation for any number of reasons, not the least of which included Luther's appearance before Emperor Charles V at Worms, his subsequent exile at the Wartburg, translational efforts on the German New Testament, and – more closely related to our theme – developments in thought with respect to monastic vows and the marriage of priests. Regarding the marriage of priests, it was in 1521 that the first priests boldly stepped away from celibacy and embraced marriage. This was done largely with the enthusiastic support of leadership in Wittenberg, though some hesitance by Luther. Even more, it was during 1521, and in the midst of the discussions about monastic vows, that the significance of Genesis 1:28 as divine imperative and *Schöpfungsordnung* really emerged into the foreground of Reformation thought. Karlstadt led the way in this, Melanchthon and others played their own lesser roles in the developments, but it was Luther who made the decisive step in formulating a new and powerful understanding of this verse.

Luther's shift in approach and argumentation on the themes of vows and celibacy, as will be shown, almost certainly took place during the span from September through November 1521 during his time at the Wartburg[68]. These developments

---

eins jeglichen Pfarrers, Strasbourg 1521 (VD16 R 2783); Hans SCHWALB, Beclagung aines Leyens, genant Hanns schwalb über vil mißbreüch Christliches lebens vnd darin[n] begriffen kürtzlich von Johannes Hußsen: Im Jar MDXXI, Augsburg 1521 (VD16 S 4582).
One note of interest from these sources: EBERLIN VON GÜNZBURG, Ein vermanung aller christen, Ai^r–Aii^r, speaks most directly to the issue of unstoppable and unquenchable human desires which, apart from marriage (strongly urged also for those who have previously taken vows), are unable to be controlled and inevitably express themselves in sinful ways when trapped by the vows of the cloister. Nevertheless, Eberlin does not connect these desires with Genesis 1:28 as would later decisively occur with Luther and his Wittenberg cohorts.

68 It has long been noted that Luther's treatment of marriage and related topics underwent a shift around 1521. LÄHTEENMÄKI, Sexus, p. 24, mentions this as taking place sometime after 1520 and understands this development to result especially from Luther's reinterpretation of original sin (p. 28), though it should be noted that he fails to give much attention to the specific historic situation

in thought set off an immediate change in the contours of Luther's teaching on marriage, vows, and celibacy. Perhaps more importantly, such developments also triggered continued debate, not to mention a hardening of interpretations – both for the Wittenberg reformers and their opponents – with respect to Genesis 1:28. The following section, therefore, seeks to trace these developments, their timeline, impetus, and initial expression as it reviews the literature, correspondence, and events stretching from May of 1521 into the early months of 1522.

The Marriage of Priests and Karlstadt's Writings

In May of 1521, Luther by this time having been whisked away to the Wartburg, the discussion of priestly marriage moved decisively from theoretical consideration to lived reality. In that month Bartholomäus Bernhardi, Heinrich Fuchs, and Balthasar Zeiger, all former students of Wittenberg, celebrated their marriages and provocatively crossed the line that had been drawn by church and state ever since the Second Lateran Council in 1139[69]. It was the occasion of Berhardi's wedding, specifically, that led to a series of publications by Andreas Karlstadt. Two of these writings, *Super coelibatu, monachatu et viduitate* and *Von Gelübden Unterrichtung*, especially seem to have triggered, or perhaps rather reflected, further developments regarding the question of Genesis 1:28 in the debates about monastic vows and the marriage of priests[70].

---

and its corresponding developments and pastoral concerns. SJÖHOLM, Luthers Åskådning, p. 27, argues that a break with monastic tradition occurred in 1520 but that it was only completed in 1521. Erich VOGELSANG, Das Deutsche in Luthers Christentum, in: Lutherjahrbuch 16 (1934), pp. 92ff., at p. 93, also observes that Luther's theology seemed to experience a shift during his time at the Wartburg, for the first time returning to the natural ordering of life and away from the unnatural spiritual and allegorical interpretations of his monastic years. More recently, Witt has argued that Luther's theology of marriage crystalized by 1522, having already undergone a decisive break with the predominant Augustinian influence that marked his earlier writings. Regarding the historical, and not merely the theological, situation, BARANOWSKI, Luthers Lehre, pp. 30–34, 50–52, brings the discussion the furthest in noting the Wittenberg concern for the impossibility of vows during this decisive time. See also KAWERAU, Die Reformation und die Ehe, pp. 12–18, for a similar description of the historical context connected with priestly marriage and the question of vows as was discussed in Wittenberg.

69 BUCKWALTER, Priesterehe, pp. 79f. For an extended treatment of the marriages of these men and the varying events that followed, see BUBENHEIMER, Streit, pp. 162–198, and also Dorothea McEWAN, Das Wirken des Vorarlberger Reformators Bartholomäus Bernhardi, Dornbirn 1986, pp. 15–37. For a brief overview of the historical development, enforcement, and logic of priestly celibacy, see FLÜCHTER, Der Zolibat, pp. 49–57.

70 BUCKWALTER, Priesterehe, pp. 81f., hypothesizes that Karlstadt was already occupied with the question of priestly marriage and monastic vows in the spring of 1521 and thus argues that the

The initial writing occasioned by the nuptials was a series of seven theses, or *Axiomata*[71], as they were called, which was made public in Wittenberg through disputation near the final week in June[72]. In these brief theses, Karlstadt argues against youth taking vows and then commands that those who are to become priests should first marry. He then continues by asserting that those priests who strongly burn may marry, even though they sin in breaking their vows. Nevertheless, it is a worse sin to vow chastity and not keep it than to take a wife. Furthermore, priests may promise chastity only in as far as human weakness allows. Finally, bishops should urge priests with concubines to marry. Although the theses are brief, Karlstadt's understanding of them, and their connection with Genesis 1:28, is expounded upon in *Super coelibatu, monachatu et viduitate*, which appeared in print in August[73].

Super coelibatu, as noted, functions as a commentary on Karlstadt's *Axiomata* and provides a plethora of arguments which served to intensify the attack against monastic vows on the Wittenberg front – an act that would also serve to provoke Luther's further reflection and later involvement. Taking a closer look at Karlstadt's argumentation, we note that his introduction presents two particularly noteworthy claims. First, Karlstadt strongly attributes imposed celibacy to the greed of the papacy[74]. He also dramatically increases the gravity of secret sexual sins through his interpretation of Leviticus 20 and his assertion that such sins are nothing less than offering one's seed to Moloch[75]. This argument about wasting seed is further supported through Karlstadt's reference to Genesis 38 in the introduction[76]. Such argumentation supports his assertion that breaking a vow of celibacy is of lesser significance than being guilty of such sexual sins.

The main portion of *Super coelibatu*, however, concerns itself with the role of widows (cf. 1 Timothy 5), who should be allowed to serve in such capacity, and who should serve in other capacities (i. e. as wives and mothers). Of note here is that Karlstadt emphasizes that younger women (under sixty) are not to take on the vow of widowhood. This he equates with the vow of celibacy required in his own day. Instead, the younger women are to marry[77].

---

events of May 1521 and the marriages that took place gave him specific occasion to publicly set forth his thought on these topics.

71 Andreas KARLSTADT, Super Coelibatu, Monachatu Et Viduitate Axiomata Perpensa Wittembergae, (Schirlenz) Wittenberg 1521 (VD16 B 6126).
72 BUCKWALTER, Priesterehe, p. 82, notes that there is some amount of controversy as to the exact date of disputation, though he argues for 21 June 1521 as the date of presentation.
73 Dedication dated 29 June 1521, appeared in print in August of that year (ibid.).
74 KARLSTADT, Super Coelibatu, ai^v. See also BUCKWALTER, Priesterehe, pp. 84f.
75 KARLSTADT, Super Coelibatu, aii^v. See also BUCKWALTER, Priesterehe, pp. 85f.
76 KARLSTADT, Super Coelibatu, aiii^r.
77 Ibid., aiiii^r–bi^r.

Relevant for this investigation is the fact that it is in this context Karlstadt inserts Genesis 1:28. After speaking to Paul's command that only the women above sixty should be taken in as true widows, Karlstadt comes back to Paul's words for the younger widows, that they should marry and tend to family matters. After all, it is with good reason that sterility is detested as was also the case with the holy women in the Scriptures. For the Lord is not joking when He speaks and commands (also to each individual), »Be fruitful and multiply«[78]. Karlstadt also goes on to give careful attention to 1 Corinthians 7, and while he does not discount the possibility of celibate devotion to God, he does understand Paul to view celibate chastity as a rare gift[79]. Furthermore, in opposition to the church's rulings allowing for youth to take vows, Karlstadt does not want anyone less than sixty years of age to be allowed to take the vow of chastity[80].

While already the introduction and discussion of the first thesis covers the majority of the themes and arguments, it is worth noting that on two further occasions Karlstadt refers to both the duties and good of marriage, including that of bringing forth children and instructing them in the word of God[81]. Thus, it is clear that with this writing Genesis 1:28 has already very much entered into the discussion. Nevertheless, as will be discussed below, the fundamental importance and polemical weight of this verse still had yet to be set forth, even if some of the decisive elements of this verse had now been presented.

A further, roughly contemporaneous work of Karlstadt, *Von Gelübden Unterrichtung*[82], had its dedication on the Feast of St. John the Baptist[83]. Although also dealing with the matter of vows, it is noteworthy that its concerns vary slightly from

---

78 Karlstadt writes, »Repudiatas se sciant iuniores annis sexaginta a professione viduitatis, contracturas matrimonia & dispensationi reifamiliaris dedendas. Neque absque causa, sterilitatem detestātur. Sara. Rebecka. Rachel. atque deinde Lia. Anna & reliquæ sanctæ mulieres. *Neque ioco tot locis loquitur precepitque dominus. Crescite & multiplicamini. Item, Cresce & multiplicare*«. Ibid., bi^r; emphasis added.

79 Ibid., bii^r.

80 Ibid., biii^v–ci^r. See also BUCKWALTER, Priesterehe, pp. 88f.

81 Karlstadt writes, »Postremo in hac itidē re delectus vitæ, opertūque est adhibēdus quoniā oportet bonis meliora anteponere. At melius est dispensare rē domesticā & familiam verbum dei docere, quā frigida precum murmura in fanis canere […]«. KARLSTADT, Super Coelibatu, ci^r.
 Near the end of *Super coelibatu* he writes, »Sus est, religiosi minus peccant ducēdo vxores, quā paciēdo carnis incendiū. Probatur etiam Quia multa bona proficiscuntur ex matrimonio. Ex incendio carnis quae bona veniūt. Matrimoniū propagate liberos, fidei verbo efformat, homines auget, terrā excolit & charitati & fidei & aliis inuigilat. coelibatus persæpe filios necavit desertas terras fecit«. Ibid., ciiii^r.

82 Andreas KARLSTADT, Von gelubden vnterrichtung Andres Bo. von Carolstadt Doctor: Außlegung, des xxx. capitel Numeri, wilches von gelubden redet […], Wittenberg 1521 (VD16 B 6245). See BUCKWALTER, Priesterehe, pp. 92f., for a general discussion of this work.

83 Dedicated 24 June 1521, this work only appeared in print in November of that year (ibid., p. 83).

those of *Super coelibatu*. Whereas *Super coelibatu* was concerned primarily with the marriage of priests and the proper age for vows, *Von Gelübden* directly addressed the issue of monastic vows and their permissibility[84]. As noted by Buckwalter, the creative workings of God and the corresponding attributes of the creature are emphasized throughout this work[85]. This is apparent most especially in one of the main arguments of the writing, that chastity – when it is given – can only be a divine work and not an achievement of man. Thus, if it is something offered by man, it is useless and displeasing to God as it does not come from God and faith[86]. Moreover, Karlstadt questioned whether vows should be kept which are discovered to be displeasing to God? His answer: »Should I give God what He does not want?«[87].

A second central argument, also present in *Super coelibatu*, involves the age of discretion for vows, i. e. sixty years[88]. He claims that the vow of celibacy is really nothing other than a vow that one will be neither chaste nor pious because it militates against human nature[89]. Moreover, throughout the second half of the work, Karlstadt interweaves 1 Timothy 5 with Numbers 30, giving particular attention to the question of who had authority to make a vow and how one was released from such a vow[90]. In placing emphasis on the authority of the man in matters concerning vows, Karlstadt goes on to turn the question back at those who were to be devoted to Christ, asking if they have asked their *Man* (i. e. Christ) as to the permissibility of their vows? Clearly not, he concludes, for marriage and its works are more pleasing to God than unwanted vows[91].

In the final section of this writing, and most important for our investigation, Karlstadt discusses the relationship between men and women[92]. He affirms the literal meaning of authority and headship presented in Numbers 30 as well as by Paul, while also criticizing the *siemann* woman and *mannin* man who would confuse these roles[93]. In continuing with his emphasis on creational arguments, Karlstadt then addresses the work and command of marriage, a work for which and with which the woman was created to help. He points out that God gave humanity the

---

84 Ibid., p. 92.
85 Ibid., p. 93.
86 KARLSTADT, Von gelubden, Ciii^v–Ciiii^r.
87 »Item alßo must ich gott/das geben das er nit haben wil?«. Ibid., Diii^r.
88 Ibid., Ei^r–Eiii^r.
89 Ibid., Eiii^r.
90 Ibid., Fiiii^v ff.
91 Ibid., Gii^r–Giiii^r.
92 Ibid., Hi^r ff.
93 Ibid., Hiii^v. The terms *mannin/siemann* are derogatory titles making use of masc.-feminine word combinations. They thus refer to a womanly man (who is weak and does not exercise proper rule of the house) and a manly woman (who lords it over her husband).

command that its members should »Be fruitful and multiply«, thus commanding the conjugal act and the procreation of children. Such should not be confused with the perverse Grubenheimer[94]. Rather, He said that each should have his own wife and beget children. The monks and nuns have, however, forcefully separated themselves from this command, divine ordinance, and help. They thus give more heed to the institution and forbiddance of the Antichrist than to the divine ordinance[95].

Additionally, he points to the praise of offspring and fertility which is found amongst the saintly matriarchs of the Old and New Testaments and argues that the nuns have forgotten that purpose for which they were created to help. They despise the command to multiply and laugh off the production of children. They thereby discard what is godly and, moreover, fulfill that which is devilish[96]. Shortly later, in concluding this writing, he exhorts parents to take their children out of the cloisters, let them marry and serve God in that way so that they may be parents and help their children toward salvation.

In summary, we note that Karlstadt had by this point developed his thought on Genesis 1:28 and its meaning in very significant ways. He clearly viewed it as a divine command to humanity and one that is preferable to God over and above humanly devised works and vows. While Karlstadt had not yet developed his thought to the point of a universally applicable natural law embodied and empowered by God's command to »Be fruitful and multiply«, with his understanding of vows and his presentation of Genesis 1:28, he had largely set the stage for the development in thought that would take place in a few short months.

Karlstadt additionally produced two additional works that same summer involving priestly marriage and celibacy, namely, a series of sixty-six theses[97] and a defense of the now-married Bernhardi[98]. While neither of these works adopt

---

94 Grubenheimer refers to »eine adamitische Sekte in Böhmen, 1501 endeckt, die die Kirche und Sakramente verachtete, sich nachts in Höhlen traf und sexuellen Libertinismus trieb«. LAUBE/WEISS, Flugschriften, p. 414, fn. 40.
95 »Gott gab auch den menschē ein gebott. sagende. Ihr solt wachssen/uñ euch gemeren. Gott hat vermuschung des ebeths/uñ samelung der kinder geboten. Nit wie gesagt ist vō den unsuttigē grubēheymer. Sonder dz iglicher man mit seiner efrawē sich befliß ekinder zuzewgē [...] Von disez gebot/gotlicher ordnung/uñ hilff. habē sich monich uñ noñen gewaltiglich abgesondert. uñ achtē vil mer Endchristische einsetzung uñ verbot/dan gotliche ordenung«. KARLSTADT, Von gelubden, Hiiii^r.
96 »Aber unser Noñen vergessen yrer hilff. datzu sie geschaft. Verachten das gebott der gemerung/ Verlachen kinder tzucht/verwerffen das gotlich uñ mer ist/uñ volbrengē das teuffelisch«. Ibid., Hiiii^v.
97 Martin Luther et al., Lutheri, Melanch., Carolostadii etc. propositiones, Wittembergae viva voce tractatae, in hocque, pleraeque, aeditae ab auctoribus, ut vel nos absentes cum ipsius agamus, vel certe ut veritatis, et seductionum admoneantur boni [...], Basil 1522 (VD16 L 7642). Disputed near the end of July in Wittenberg, appeared in print in August 1522, see BUCKWALTER, Priesterehe, p. 83.
98 Andreas KARLSTADT, Contra Papisticas leges sacerdotibus prohibentes matrimonium apologia pastoris Cemergensis [...], Basel 1521 (VD16 B 6100); id., An Maidenbergers etrzbischof.

argumentation involving Genesis 1:28, procreation, or such related themes, it is of note that the latter work, *Apologia pastoris Cembergensis*, does concern itself with the problem of sinful desires and views marriage as the necessary cure, even should it require the breaking of one's vow of celibacy[99].

Melanchthon's *Loci Communes* (1521)

Between the spring and fall of 1521, in response to a discerned need to clearly formulate the biblical basis for the beliefs of the reformers in a more systematic way, Philipp Melanchthon began to write his influential *Loci Communes*[100]. This work proposed to treat the major theological topics related to God and creation under some twenty-three separate headings. For the purposes of this study, of particular importance with this work is Melanchthon's writing in his section, *De lege*, and particularly what he wrote about the natural law. We note here that Melanchthon was somewhat torn about the concept of natural law. Due to his understanding of the depravity of human reason, he questioned whether humanity could ever come to any certain conclusions in this area[101]. On the other hand, Melanchthon had no problem acknowledging Paul's teaching that there was, in fact, a *legem naturae* as spoken of in Romans 2[102].

In an interesting turn, however, although in 1520 Melanchthon clearly included such topics as self-preservation and procreation under the auspices of natural law[103] in Melanchthon's 1521 *Loci*, he shifted their status toward a seemingly different realm. Under the title of natural law, he now sought to treat merely those topics

---

herforderung uber Eelichs stantzhandel aines ersamen pristers Bernhardj leyppfarres Kemberger kirche[n] enschuldigung und antwurt, Colmar 1521[?] (VD16 ZV 2155). The *Apologia* was written already in July but sent to Archbishop Albrecht of Mainz on 9 August (Buckwalter, Priesterehe, p. 94). There has been some historic discussion as to whether Melanchthon or Karlstadt was the author of the *Apologia*. The question was resolved finally when a formerly overlooked letter of Justus Jonas settled the matter in favor of Karlstadt. Nevertheless, the question of attribution of authorship can be somewhat misleading considering that there is little doubt that both Melanchthon and Karlstadt were indeed discussing these matters in the Wittenberg context in the summer of 1521. See Richard Wetzel, Melanchthon und Karlstadt im Spiegel von Melanchthons Briefwechsel, in: Sigrid Looss/Markus Matthias (eds.), Andreas Bodenstein von Karlstadt (1486–1541). Ein Theologe der frühen Reformation, Wittenberg 1998, pp. 159–222, at pp. 161–163.

99 See Buckwalter, Priesterehe, pp. 94–96, and Plummer, Clerical Marriage, pp. 64f., for further discussion of Karlstadt's *Apologia*, its context, and its content.
100 Philipp Melanchthon, Loci Commvnes Rervm Theologicarvm Sev Hypotyposes Theologicae, Wittenberg 1521 (VD16 M 3585). For ease of reference, citations will be given from Pöhlmann.
101 Pöhlmann, Loci Communes 1521, 3:6, 12 (pp. 100–103).
102 Ibid., 3:7 (pp. 100f.).
103 See ibid., pp. 103–105, fn. 266.

related to the worship of God and pertaining to human relationships[104]. Those aspects of natural life held in common with the animal world, such as to protect and reproduce life or to procreate offspring, were now excluded from his treatment of natural law and rolled up under the phrase »certain natural affections« (*naturales quosdam affectus*)[105].

This raises an important question. First, we must ask how Melanchthon understood and, even more importantly, defined this new category. Did he use *naturales quosdam affectus* in the negative sense of lower or ignoble passions and emotions which must be rightly ordered and held in check, or did he understand this phrase in a more positive sense which reflected such natural urges, drives, and desires as essentially God-given and good? That is to say, was Melanchthon talking about nature proper or a distortion of nature?

While a more thorough answer to this question will be offered throughout the course of this work[106], a few observations are in order. First, it must be conceded from the general context that Melanchthon does not seem to have in mind the more negative understanding of *affectus* which takes place in his discussion of sin[107]. Wilhelm Maurer makes the point that Melanchthon does indeed separate the higher affections from the lower bodily affections and that when Melanchthon speaks pejoratively about the affections, his concentration is on the higher ones of the soul and not those of the body. Maurer also adds that the human will is *incapable* of opposing the affections (whether higher or lower)[108]. Thus, we can reasonably conclude from the context of 3:15 that Melanchthon is not attempting in any way to condemn specifically *naturales quosdam affectus*, even if elsewhere affections have a clearly negative connotation. Moreover, inasmuch as Melanchthon

---

104 Ibid., 3:17–45 (pp. 104–111).
105 »Omitto autem ea, quae cum brutis communia habemus, vitam tueri gignereque et aluid ex sese procreare, quae in ius naturae referunt iurisconsulti, ego naturales quosdam affectus animantibus communiter insitos voco«. Ibid., 3:15 (p. 102).
106 See esp. pp. 87–91, 128–131, 172–176, 184.
107 Ibid., pp. 44f., fn. 83, includes a discussion of Melanchthon's *Affektenlehre*. Here Pöhlmann discusses the spiritual nature of the natural affections, though giving no real attention to the natural affections as discussed in *Loci* 3:15. MAURER, Der junge Melanchthon, pp. 244–261, includes a more in-depth exposition of Melanchthon's *Affektenlehre* in which he shows this teaching to be a central and important theme of the *Loci*. Unfortunately for the purposes of this study, he gives little attention to Melanchthon's usage of *naturales quosdam affectus* either in his discussion of *Affektenlehre* (p. 248) or in his treatment of *Leges naturales* (pp. 288–296).
108 »›Die Erkenntnis ist Sklavin des Willens‹ (9,21f.); der Wille mit seinen Affekten ist der Tyrann, der den Menschen völlig beherrscht (9,24ff.). Melanchthon konzentriert dabei seine Affektenlehre ausdrücklich auf die höheren Affekte, die die seelischen Regungen wie Liebe, Haß, Hoffnung, Furcht, Traurigkeit, Zorn und was aus ihnen entspringt, hervorbringen; von den niederen, die die körperlichen Triebe bewegen, redet er nicht weiter. Keinem dieser Affekte hat der menschliche Wille etwas entgegenzusetzen (16,3ff.)«. MAURER, Der junge Melanchthon, p. 245.

previously listed such natural affection as belonging to natural law, and thus as something given a high positive value and normative nature, there is every reason to believe that in this text Melanchthon is simply describing realities of nature or creation as they exist[109].

The following possibility thus lends itself to our understanding Melanchthon's shift in numbering from his previous *Capita* of 1520: Whereas Melanchthon's section on *lex naturae* dealt with those things about God and human relationships which reason has some understanding of and may therefore regulate accordingly, in 3:15 Melanchthon is actually emphasizing the created, implanted (*insitus*) drives of human and animal life against which man is in no position to contend[110]. They are simply to be acknowledged and lived out in their proper ordering. In other words, by removing the *Capita*'s sections dealing with procreation, marriage, and the raising of offspring from his treatment of *lex naturae* (perhaps on account of the general ambiguity and tentativeness of natural law), the reality emerges that Melanchthon has actually raised these components to a higher level and that an important distinction is actually being made between nature and natural law[111]. This shift, though perhaps not decisive, allowed for the possibility that already by late summer of 1521, the seeds of Luther's developing thought would come into place – partially through Melanchthon's pen[112]. Nevertheless, the synthesis of these various ideas that would go on to form a further decisive argument against monastic vows (and subsequently a part of the foundation for Luther's understanding of marriage),

---

109 While Maurer does not comment directly on Melanchthon's usage of *naturales quosdam affectus*, Maurer does suggest that the changed numbering on natural law (*Capita* vs. *Loci*) is not to be taken as removing the withdrawn topics entirely from natural law, but as simply including them under the other topics. In this case, items 2–6 of the *Capita* would be grouped under point two of Melanchthon's *Loci* (3:18: »Quia nascimur in quandam vitae societatem, nemo laedendus est«. PÖHLMANN, Loci Communes 1521, p. 104). Whatever the proper interpretation may be, Maurer's interpretation also gives credence to the argument that *naturales quosdam affectus* is not to be understood in the same way as Melanchthon's treatment of the affects elsewhere.

110 MAURER, Der junge Melanchthon, pp. 245f., 305.

111 My hypothesis here is that this development corresponds with, and perhaps influences, a development in Luther's thought that can first be observed in *Judgment on Monastic Vows* and then even more clearly in *Vom ehelichen Leben* in Luther's understanding and explanation of Genesis 1:28. In these writings, and then subsequently throughout the remainder of Luther's career, the couching of God's creative word with natural legal and philosophical categories expresses a most powerful and even unique understanding of the human procreative urge.

112 LÄHTEENMÄKI, Sexus, p. 32, notes the argument of Josef Sjöholm that Melanchthon's *Loci Communes* were indeed decisive in Luther's arguments in *De votis monasticis*, particularly as concerns the question of whether or not one was free to vow celibacy. SJÖHOLM, Luthers Åskådning, pp. 31–35, indeed notes the correlation between Melanchthon's *Loci Communes* and Luther's developing thought. Nevertheless, he does not note the potential correlation between Melanchthon's shift in thought on nature/natural law and the ensuing shift in Luther's thought.

had not yet taken place at this time. That would only come to pass in the following months and in a location far removed from university life in Wittenberg, namely in Luther's isolated existence at the Wartburg.

3.3 Developments at the Wartburg

In turning our attention now to Luther and developments at the Wartburg Castle, there are many questions which will require our attention. What did he know? When did he know it? Which materials were sent to him from Wittenberg? In the following section we will therefore attempt to develop the timeline of events as well as the available resources permit. Although it will not be possible to establish a cut-and-dried argument as to exactly when and how the developments in Luther's thought on Genesis 1:28 took place, the evidence will allow us to set forth a reasonable, and even very plausible, explanation for that which was to follow.

Luther's Correspondence and the Debate about Monastic Vows

On the evening of 4 May 1521, during the return trip from Worms, Luther was taken »captive« in an apparent kidnapping in the Thuringian forest outside of Eisenach. The months that followed were both trying and very productive for Luther, though he certainly initially struggled in adjusting to his relatively sparse contact with the outside world and his initial lack of books and other theological resources (excepting a Greek and Hebrew copy of the Scriptures). Nevertheless, already by mid-May the first letters were arriving and being sent[113] and, as the weeks and months dragged on, a steady exchange of letters and resources emerged – channeled through and managed by Georg Spalatin, secretary to Elector Frederick the Wise. In this way, Luther was able to somewhat stay abreast of developments and discussions in Wittenberg. He was also able to help guide, encourage, and advise from a distance. Perhaps most important among the exchanges of correspondence which took place during these months was that of his friend, advisor, and understudy, Philipp Melanchthon: the twenty-four-year-old apparent leader of the Wittenberg Reformation movement in Luther's absence. It is primarily from Luther's correspondence with Melanchthon, in addition to details gleaned from other correspondence and writings, that a timeline of events can be reconstructed.

With respect to the theme of monastic vows, we have already observed that the discussions were initiated by the slightly different, but still related, controversy

---

113 Heinrich BORNKAMM/Karin BORNKAMM, Luther in Mid-Career, 1521–1530, Philadelphia 1983, p. 2, note that the first letter Luther received arrived from Spalatin around 12 May.

involving the marriage of priests which occurred contemporaneous to Luther's stay at the Wartburg. The first of these marriages, that of Bartholomäus Berhardi, was announced to Luther sometime in mid or late May so that already on 26 May he was expressing his wonder – and concern – for the new groom[114]. As discussions of priestly marriage picked up in Wittenberg shortly thereafter, they were not content to remain with that topic. By June, as we noted above, they had already spilled over into the topic of monastic vows[115]. Luther was also gradually drawn into the debates. Near the end of July, Melanchthon directed the first two sheets of Karlstadt's *Super coelibatu*, via Spalatin, to his exiled friend[116].

A short time later, on 1 August, Luther responded to Melanchthon. The response gives evidence of Luther's reaction to Karlstadt's thought. It also offers insight into the state of the question in Luther's mind at the time[117]. In this letter Luther makes a distinction between the matters of priestly marriage and monastic vows and defends the marriage of priests as a matter of freedom and as something sanctioned by Scripture (1 Timothy 4:1ff.). On the other hand, a freely-taken vow was an entirely different matter for Luther, even if the vow of celibacy was of human invention. Luther had no trouble with the idea of releasing those who had taken vows before reaching maturity from such vows. Yet, for all others a clear word from Scripture must be found. Here Luther expresses his discontent with Karlstadt's solution based on the status of widows in 1 Timothy 5:9, 11. Luther argues that such an interpretation cannot be maintained and simply invites criticism and, more importantly, peril of conscience. Secondly, Karlstadt's argument that a sin might be committed for the sake of avoiding a greater sin is entirely unacceptable for Luther. If such logic were consistently employed, then all moral laws might be abolished for the sake of human weakness and urges[118]. Nevertheless, Luther confesses that he also wishes that monks and nuns might be freed from the entrapment of their vows.

---

114 WA Br 2, p. 346,30–32.
115 It should be noted that this was not the first time the subject of monastic vows had been mentioned. Already in 1520 in *An den christlichen Adel* Luther had broached the subject. For a more extensive analysis of Luther's previous thought on monastic vows, see STAMM, Luthers Stellung, pp. 11–37.
116 WETZEL, Melanchthon und Karlstadt, p. 163.
117 WA Br 2, pp. 370–373. See also WETZEL, Melanchthon und Karlstadt, pp. 163f.
118 For this section, particularly with respect to the question of »burning« and the impossibility of man controlling his sexual drive, see also MAURER, Der junge Melanchthon, pp. 304–306. Note that my reconstruction of the situation differs in overall interpretation from that of Maurer. Of particular note is that, although he correctly notes Luther's *initial* rejection of Melanchthon's argument based on insurmountable sexual urges (p. 304), Maurer does not seem to pick up on the importance of Melanchthon's argument in light of Luther's forthcoming *De votis monasticis iudicium* in November. Thus, the arrow of influence arguably flows just as much from Melanchthon to Luther on this question as it does from Luther to Melanchthon as Maurer asserts.

Two days later Luther wrote Melanchthon once again to continue his discussion on the theme of monastic vows[119]. While Luther's exact source for his information about Karlstadt's arguments in the letter written 1 August is somewhat unclear, by 3 August Luther announces that he has read two quartos from *Super coelibatu*[120]. From these, Luther criticizes Karlstadt's exegesis of Leviticus 18 and his comparison of Moloch offerings with the wasting of the male's seed[121]. Furthermore, Karlstadt's comparison of the *molles/Weichlinge*[122] with Onan's misdeed displeases Luther. Luther also critically revisits Karlstadt's treatment of 1 Timothy 5 with its instructions for widows and shows that it cannot be understood as analogous to the monastic situation. Nevertheless, Luther once again commends Karlstadt's cause and efforts, even as unsatisfactory as they have proven to be. What is needed with this subject, according to Luther, are not unclear and dark passages of Scripture, but light and clarity. Furthermore, Luther disapproves of Karlstadt's appropriation of the Old Testament law for dislodging vows. Once again, it is not clear that these passages really address the situation and thus they cannot be pressed to provide freedom to the conscience. With respect to 1 Corinthians 7, Luther notes that Paul has left marriage as a matter of freedom. Thus, any vow regarding chastity is dangerous and likely inspired by Satan. Furthermore, Luther sees vows as generally standing in opposition to the Christian's freedom and thus sincerely desires a solution to this issue, even saying that there must be a clearer answer at hand and admitting that he cannot imagine that Christ would tolerate such oppressive customs. After expressing his desire to discuss this issue with Melanchthon in person, Luther then continues to discuss questions of age and the binding nature of vows. Yet, for all his concern about these things, he admits that he fails to find a clear word from God and that human reason does not offer a solution[123]. Luther closes his discussion of vows in this section with the prayer that the Lord Jesus would give instruction and deliverance in these matters.

---

119 WA Br 2, pp. 373–377. See also Wetzel, Melanchthon und Karlstadt, p. 164.
120 Which two quartos did Luther receive? Stamm, Luthers Stellung, p. 43 (based on an assumption taken from WA Br 2, p. 373), mentions that Luther received the first two quartos. WA 8, p. 315 also states that it was the first two quartos. Thus, we are probably correct in assuming that Luther would have been aware of Karlstadt's inclusion of Genesis 1:28 (given that this verse is dealt with in those quartos) sometime around the beginning of August in 1521.
121 In *Von den guten Werken* (1520) Luther had previously compared Moloch sacrifices with parents who raise their children merely to care for the things of this world. WA 6, p. 252,19–26.
122 These are derogatory terms referring to effeminacy (i. e. softness) or those practicing any number of sexual sins.
123 Note that in *De votis monasticis iudicium* Luther would take exactly such an argument based on human reason into account, combining it powerfully with an argument from Scripture, thus seemingly answering this objection for himself in a very powerful way. See relevant section below.

Two further letters follow in August to Spalatin in which the matter of monastic vows is discussed. The first, dated 6 August[124], finds Luther (citing the two quartos of *Super coelibatu*) opposed to the idea of the marriage of monks and nuns and complains that now Karlstadt wants to let them marry. Yet, Luther says that he will not allow this and sums up Karlstadt's writing as being neither gifted nor learned enough to rightly handle the matter, even though he views him to be otherwise learned.

The second letter to Spalatin, dated 15 August[125], takes up the matter in somewhat greater detail. Here, Luther once again wishes that Karlstadt would treat the question of monastic vows with appropriate passages of Scripture. The manner with which he has taken on the task, Luther fears, will only lead to ill gossip for the reform-minded (here Luther mentions specifically Karlstadt's »giving one's seed to Moloch« interpretation). Would it not have been better for Karlstadt to simply address the matters of *mollitiem/Weichlichkeit* with St. Paul's writings? Karlstadt's reference to 1 Timothy 5 will likely also bring criticism. Nevertheless, Luther reiterates that it is a very important matter that Karlstadt has undertaken and Luther wishes simply that he had gone about it in a better manner. The question of monastic vows needs clarity and the best arguments. This is especially the case considering that even in instances where the reformers do rightly apply Scripture, they encounter enough difficulty from their opponents. It is not necessary to make their cause a laughing matter through the misappropriation of Scripture. Luther's greater concern, however, is whether those many monks and nuns who follow Karlstadt's advice were being sent out of the cloistered life merely to later discover in their conscience that they had no real scriptural basis for leaving. As much as Luther would like to present the necessary solid arguments against monastic vows, he does not believe he is yet ready to do so.

After nearly four weeks with no further mention of the subject from Luther, on 9 September Luther wrote to Melanchthon to once again discuss the topic[126]. The letter begins with Luther announcing that he is very pleased with Melanchthon's instructional book (*Loci Communes*) and bids him to simply proceed on with this work[127]. Luther then expresses his wish to be able to speak in person with

---

124 WA Br 2, pp. 377–379.
125 WA Br 2, pp. 379–382.
126 WA Br 2, pp. 382–387.
127 Stamm, Luthers Stellung, p. 41, states that by the end of August/beginning of September, Luther has already received the first five leaves of *Loci*. By 9 September, Luther has the sixth. For our purposes it is worth noting that the section on natural law was found on the fifth sheet. Thus, it is not incorrect to assume that Luther had at least read that section and would have been aware of Melanchthon's argumentation on that topic. Melanchthon's treatment of monastic vows comes later in the section on the law in which natural law is also treated. See also WA 8, pp. 316f.

Melanchthon and suggests the possibility of being able to meet secretly at some point. Proceeding to the matter of vows, Luther brings up Melanchthon's argument that a vow might be broken if a person is incapable of keeping it on account of sin[128]. Yet, argues Luther, if this is the case, one would have to admit that God's commands might also be abrogated. Furthermore, does it make a difference if the vow has not been forced, but taken of one's own volition? If that would be the case, however, God's law would govern such vows in that He has commanded, »Keep what you vow«. For Luther, here Melanchthon has followed reason instead of Scripture, and he advises his friend to remain with the latter instead of the former. No, if vows are to be lifted, the root of the problem must be done away with rather than its results. Luther then brings up Melanchthon's arguments about Christian freedom. Luther agrees that the captivity arising from vows is foreign to the Gospel and against the proper captivity of the Spirit, yet the problem he is concerned with is that of the vow itself. The fact that God's law speaks to vows actually confirms vows as the Gospel does not abrogate the Law. Along those lines, Luther argues that vows might even be confirmed through the Gospel. Continuing on, Luther says that he is not entirely pleased with what he had written to Melanchthon previously, excepting his comments on 1 Timothy 5. Thus, he will give an update on how far he has now progressed with the topic[129]. Luther then turns to the heart of the matter as he sees it. Taking up the subject of circumcision in Galatians, Luther points out the issue was not in the act, per se, but rather in the reason for the act. Considering that circumcision was performed as an act of service or merit to God, its motivation was very much the same as the monastic vow. Why does Paul dispense with it, then? Because Paul understood it as entrapping consciences in works and thereby opposing the mercy of Christ. Along these same lines, the

---

128 This corresponds with Karlstadt's argumentation in his *Super Coelibatu*. There is further evidence that the »Wittenberg circle« had already been concerned about the difficulty/impossibility of keeping vows of chastity already in the summer of 1520. In light of a letter arising from Wittenberg circles and written to Carthusians (attributed by Bretschneider to Melanchthon [CR 1, col. 192–200] – which, however, most likely originated from one of his students at that time, a certain Oswald Ülin), we observe a certain concern shown for the command given in 1 Corinthians 7, namely, *Melius est nubere quam uri* (CR 1, col. 196).

It should be further noted that Ülin's letter was later printed under Melanchthon's name as *De Tribus Votis* in 1523 (VD16 M 3213) in addition to a German translation of the same in 1524 (VD16 M 3215). That the letter can be generally taken as indicative of Wittenberg thought ca. 1520 is shown by the author's reference to the *optimum et doctissimum praeceptorem nostrum Lutherum* (CR 1, col. 200). Otto CLEMEN (ed.), Supplementa Melanchthoniana. Werke Philipp Melanchthons die im Corpus Reformatorum vermisst werden, Leipzig 1926, Abt. 6/1, p. 107, thus argues that it likely contained a fair representation of Melanchthon's thought at the time. For more information on authorship and background as well as a reconstruction of the history of this writing, see ibid., pp. 105–108.

129 See Luther's Theses on Monastic Vows (below).

monastic vow might rightly also be cursed and those who have taken it, based on the hope of merit or spiritual gain, should therefore be freed from their vows which are entirely godless and against the Gospel. Therefore, in Luther's opinion, this would be almost the entirety of those who have taken vows. If all of the monks and nuns would have been aware that their vows were of no merit before God, how many would have actually taken vows? In fact, those undertaking vows for such purposes are vowing God nothing other than godlessness and idolatry. Such vows must certainly be done away with. Yet should they be entirely lifted or should new vows in the spirit of freedom be made? And how could this be done? A vow, such as that made by Manasseh in which he vowed his son to the idol Moloch, was certainly against God's will and, had he realized the evil of it, he would not have done such a thing. Indeed, any such vow made for the sake of merit is a vow made to the lie and idol of one's own heart. Luther fears that such was the case, as God permitted, with his own vow. Therefore, as with the Galatians, one must not merely counsel but command that the vow be trampled on due to its godlessness and blasphemy. Those whom such a vow was forced upon in their youth must most certainly be released from their vows. In other cases, the vow must be a matter of conscience based on what one's motivation for taking the vow was. After reflecting on his own vow and the words of his father at the time (»God grant that this isn't a deception of the devil!«), Luther says he is content with this basis for abrogating vows, or at least releasing those who will and letting others take their vows in a free and evangelical spirit. Nevertheless, Luther is somewhat skeptical that anyone would make such a vow based on evangelical motivations. Luther then refers to the theses he is including with this letter. If published, he wants them dedicated to the congregation in Wittenberg, and he believes that his argumentation in them will be able to stand up to the light of day. As for the matter of the widows (1 Timothy 5), Luther considers that to be a dark passage. Whatever vows they might have taken would have been different as they had the light of the Gospel at that time as opposed to the situation of the Germans in his own time. Luther then goes on to briefly address the vows of poverty and obedience, the sin against the Holy Spirit, and the »burning« of desire which Melanchthon thought was so important[130]. The latter is downplayed by Luther as nothing unmanageable, citing 2 Corinthians 11:29 –

---

[130] According to an observation of John Schofield, Philipp Melanchthon and the English Reformation, Burlington 2006, p. 20, we get the idea that Melanchthon also resonated with this concern given that »weakness of flesh« was also a consideration in agreeing to Luther's recommendation of a wife for the young humanist. Schofield writes, »But Cupid waits on no man, not even Homer or Virgil, St Paul or Augustine, and Philip soon fell for Katherine's charms, confiding to a friend that she had ›the virtues and qualities that only the immortal gods could bestow‹. ›The flesh is weak‹, he admitted to another, and he yielded to Luther's matchmaking. They were married on the 25 November 1520«.

to which he adds that it will be difficult to prove anything more strongly on this matter[131]. Luther then mentions that he wants to give more consideration to the subject of blasphemy before finally closing this letter.

On the same day, Luther also penned a letter to Nicholaus von Amsdorf[132]. He begins by saying that he is sending his theses on vows, which, whenever they come out, will be new and frightening for their opponents (even if they are not entirely new). Luther then mentions that Philipp agrees with Amsdorf as to the possibility of lifting a vow on account of its impossibility[133]. Luther says that he has not dealt with this point, whatever might be made of it, but that he also does not believe it to be a safe argument capable of supporting one's conscience. Instead, Luther says he has dealt with the root factor of monastic vows, and that will provide a better foundation for the liberation from vows, namely, on the basis of godlessness and for the cause of blessedness. Luther then mentions that he will send more theses on the general topic of vows later. Otherwise, Luther is displeased with Karlstadt and, although he could easily oppose him, hesitates to do so for the sake of their opponents who would certainly use that to their own advantage. After briefly addressing several other topics, Luther concludes the letter.

Luther's Theses on Monastic Vows

Having heard mention of Luther's theses in his letters to Melanchthon and Amsdorf, respectively, we will now turn our attention to his two sets of theses.

---

131 This is a very important point. There is some dialogue going on between Luther and Melanchthon about »burning«. Could it be that Melanchthon is arguing that it is a reflection of *affectus naturales* and thus not merely sinful human passions, but actually a reflection of God's good creation that man has now opposed through vows? WETZEL, Melanchthon und Karlstadt, p. 165, notes that the letter from Melanchthon which Luther seems to be answering in his 9 September letter is missing. See also MAURER, Der junge Melanchthon, p. 304, for reference to this.

132 WA Br 2, pp. 390f.

133 It seems that at some level this was a personal concern for at least one member of the Wittenberg circle. In a letter dated later that fall (8 Nov.), Justus Jonas wrote to Johann Lang requesting that the latter pray for him as he has been stirred up by some »tentatio carnis« and now questions whether perhaps the Lord would summon him to take a wife. Although he admits that he has not previously known the passions of the flesh, he also admits that he is only restraining himself with great effort, lest he be carried off with the fury of adultery (*impetus scortationis*). Thus, these matters being discussed were certainly also very personal and pastoral matters for at least some of the reformers. Here, see Gustav KAWERAU, Der Briefwechsel des Justus Jonas, 2 volumes, Hildesheim 1964, vol. 1, p. 77. We also might somewhat humorously note that it is only thanks to the fact that Johann Lang neither followed the instructions nor heeded the will of his friend (namely, »concerpe literas et perde, servari nolunt«), that we know anything of this situation.

The first set of 139 theses, *Ivdicivm Martini Lvtheri de Votis*[134], sent simultaneously with the 9 September letters, begins with and develops the theme of acting on the basis of faith as opposed to works. In these theses, Luther notes that faith looks forward to the promises of God whereas false faith looks back at one's own works. Such a false faith, as he shows the vast majority of monastic vows to consist of, is actually a type of idolatry and nothing less than a vow made in service to Satan. Furthermore, everything Paul said about the Law must also be said about vows. If vows are made seeking merit from God, they also ought to be abolished. Anyone who recognizes his own vows as such idolatrous vows ought to leave the monastery or else take a new vow in the proper spirit (which is not contrary to faith). If one were to view his vow rightly, he would view it as Paul did his own righteousness. Monasteries could be used for a good purpose, yet their general spirit strives against Christian maturity and the freedom of the Gospel. Even more, the lack of right faith in the monasteries combined with their moral situation argues that such vows can be nothing other than the work of Satan. In short, either monasteries must rightly serve faith or they must be destroyed. Vows and the monastic life are not neutral apart from the presence of faith. Certainly, such things are evidence of the last times spoken of by Paul and Christ.

The second set of 141 theses, *An liceat perpetuum vovere votum*[135], likely sent only days after Luther announced them to Amsdorf on 9 September, takes a slightly different approach. Whereas the first set of theses focused on the dichotomy of faith versus works, the second set of theses focuses on the hierarchy of Christian commitments, with the Christian's commitment to his Lord and the freedom found in his baptismal vow being emphasized throughout. Luther argues that this freedom is a divine right and gift of God which must be maintained for the service of all and is bound solely to the word of grace. No one has the authority to change or subjugate this freedom of the Christian. Therefore, a vow may only be made insofar as it does not impinge upon this freedom. When it comes to conflicting goods and considering what is better, it must be remembered that best of all is the freedom of faith, and one dare not denigrate this freedom on account of something of lesser value. If vows are kept on account of their binding nature, and not in freedom on account of some good, then they are useless. When it comes to works (to include vows), it is wrong to prescribe how they must be. Instead, it is better to exalt faith as Paul does in Scripture. Furthermore, one must not build up servitude where God has granted freedom; neither should one tear down bonds (Luther mentions those of family and friendship in these theses) where God has established them. Moreover, what Scripture neither commands nor counsels, one must flee. Finally,

---

134 WA 8, pp. 323–329.
135 WA 8, pp. 330–335.

the vows spoken of by Moses were of a different nature and thus have nothing to say to this theme. Luther concludes, then, that free vows are not to be condemned and may be observed temporarily or perpetually.

Section Summary and Observations

At this point it will be helpful to briefly summarize and highlight several points of significance observed above. First, we have noted Luther's general displeasure with Karlstadt's approach to the problem of vows, both exegetically and the fact that it leaves consciences without a firm scriptural foundation should they act upon Karlstadt's advice. With respect to exegetical issues, Luther puts no stock in Karlstadt's central arguments from Numbers 30 and 1 Timothy 5, and neither does he find the references to Genesis 38 and the Moloch offerings satisfactory. Interestingly, however, Karlstadt's usage of Genesis 1:28, with which Luther was almost certainly familiar, draws neither criticism nor comment.

Second, we have observed that Luther's central arguments, somewhat in harmony with Melanchthon's concern for Christian freedom as expressed in his *Loci*, were strictly composed out of concern for the Gospel, the exclusive merit of Christ, the baptismal vow, and the Christian freedom found in these. Luther therefore identified these issues as the true root concern which must be addressed with respect to monastic vows. Further developments in Wittenberg throughout the fall of 1521 would show Luther's line of argumentation to be decisive and the general, but not sole, defense for his break with the monastic tradition.

A final note is to be made concerning what we might term »unfinished business«. For our purposes, it is worth noting (and emphasizing!) that the Wittenberg contingent believed the impossibility of the vow of celibacy to be an important point in this debate. This is clearly shown in Karlstadt's theses and writings. Amsdorf and Melanchthon were also concerned about this matter. Melanchthon, in a letter which has never been located, also addressed the matter of burning desires, which one might also conclude had something to do with this issue of the impossibility of maintaining (chastely) a vow of celibacy. One might perhaps question whether Melanchthon was already beginning to see this problem as corresponding, in some way, with his understanding of the natural affections as expressed in his 1521 *Loci Communes*. Regardless, during this period Luther does not give any credence to such arguments, though he does admit to not having completely thought through them. Nevertheless, within the next month and a half, an ingenious solution and answer to this problem, one combining these disparate elements and strengthening the reform movement's stance against monastic vows, will emerge – from Luther's own pen.

3.4 The Appearance of Genesis 1:28

The reception of Luther's two sets of theses caused no small stir in Wittenberg. By 8 October, the first prints had been completed and were being sent out of Wittenberg[136]. With respect to the effects these theses had in Wittenberg, the commentary in the *Weimarer Ausgabe* records an account preserved by Melanchthon. He recalled being at table with the Pomeranian noble Peter Swaven and Johannes Bugenhagen when Luther's letter with the theses on monastic vows arrived. After reading them, both Bugenhagen and Melanchthon were certain that the theses marked the beginning of true change both in public opinion and for freedom of the monks[137]. Other effects were to be observed a short time later both in the decisions made by the Augustinian monks in Wittenberg as well as through changes made in Melanchthon's *Loci*[138].

The next benchmark in the development of our theme appeared on 17 November of the same year, though it was already predicted in a 1 November letter from Luther to Nic Gerbel[139]. In this letter Luther announces that the edition of the New Testament which he received some months earlier from Gerbal has now born many children and is once again expecting. This time it would be a son who would strike the papists, sophists, religionists, and Herodists with an iron scepter. Moreover, as Luther considers the monastic state, he remarks that the estate of marriage appears to him a virtual paradise instituted by God in comparison with the abomination of monastic life. On 11 November, Luther makes a similar announcement to Spalatin regarding his forthcoming work on monastic vows and that he has decided to further attack such vows for the sake of rescuing youth from the hell of impure

---

136 WA 8, p. 317.
137 »Über die Wirkung dieser Thesen auf den Kreis der Theologen Wittenbergs hat uns Melanchthon ein werthvolle Erinnerung aufbewahrt. Kostgänger an einem Tisch waren damals der pommersche Edelmann Peter Swaven und der vor nicht langer Zeit nach Wittenberg gezogene Joh. Bugenhagen. Als sie beim Mittagsmahle waren, traf Luthers Brief mit den Thesen ein. Bugenhagen nahm sie, las sie einmal und noch einmal mit gespannter Aufmerksamkeit durch; dann nach längerem Nachsinnen brach er in die Worte aus: ›Haec res mutationem publici status efficiet: doctrina ante has propositiones tradita non mutasset publicum statum.‹ Melanchthon setzt hinzu: ›Haec sunt initia liberationis Monachorum vere recitata‹«. WA 8, p. 317.
    The excitement over the decisive nature of these theses appears to relate to the Gospel- and Baptism-related articles of Luther's theses. Nevertheless, Juntunen, Engaging Luther, p. 194, indicates – if I have read him correctly – that the shift may have had to do with the reformer's thinking on the matter of *impossibility*. While this would fit exceedingly well with the thesis presented in this chapter, my own reading of the related texts and literature concurs with the general interpretation of this discussion and not Juntunen's.
138 WA 8, pp. 317f.
139 The letter can be found in WA Br 2, pp. 396–398. See also WA 8, p. 564.

celibacy[140]. With this Luther points forward to his work on monastic vows which would appear in a matter of days.

Luther's Judgment on Monastic Vows

On 21 November 1521, Luther attached his dedicatory letter to a further writing against monastic vows: *De votis monasticis iudicium*[141]. Luther's major concern in penning this writing was for the consciences of those trapped under the tyranny of their vows. He wrote, therefore, not in order to absolve all vows but rather to discuss which vows ought to be kept and which absolved. Following a touching dedicatory letter to his father, one that relives the painful interactions between father and son at the time Luther entered the monastery[142], the writing itself is divided up into five main sections. In these sections, Luther argues that monastic vows are against (1) God's Word, (2) faith, (3) evangelical freedom, (4) God's commands, and (5) human reason[143].

Versus God's Word[144] – Briefly summarized, in the first section Luther charges that monastic vows are in no way based on God's Word and that they in fact run contrary to it. The New Testament plainly teaches that all things over and above Christ are to be rejected as He is the way, the truth, and the life. Thus, any vows claiming more than Christ, which indeed monastic vows claim, militate against Christ and are therefore godless. If anything vowed is godless, it must not only be absolved, it must not be fulfilled. Moreover, vows are made not out of faith, but out of false faith. This false faith looks to counsels and commands as the Gospel. Yet, such a claim shows that the Gospel is not even understood. Moreover, the monastic life confuses commands and counsels. The commands of Christ it attempts to make optional while the counsels of Scripture are made into commands. Can anyone imagine, though, that God is pleased when His words are changed around in such manner? Vows must therefore be an invention of Satan. In fact, the monk is actually vowing God that he will not live according to the Gospel but according to his own rules.

---

140 The letter can be found in WA Br 2, pp. 402–404. See also WA 8, p. 564.
141 WA 8, pp. 573ff.
142 WA 8, pp. 573–576.
143 For discussions of this writing, see STAMM, Luthers Stellung, pp. 49–56, and LOHSE, Mönchtum und Reformation, pp. 363–370. GRIMM, Luther et l'experience sexuelle, pp. 135–212, is also primarily devoted to Luther's argumentation within this work. Grimm makes the observation that »chastity« appears as Luther's primary concern throughout this work, both through the reformer's reference to Augustine's *Confessions* in the introduction (p. 147) as well as by evidence of the sheer weight of the references discussing chastity (p. 148).
144 WA 8, pp. 578–591.

Versus Faith[145] – In the second section, Luther charges that vows are not to be maintained as they oppose the Gospel. As the monastic vow does not proceed from faith, it is nothing other than sin. After all, it is faith that receives the forgiveness of sins and lifts God's wrath. Thus, were a monk to be poor, chaste, and obedient but lack faith, he would still be damned. Paul thundered against relying on works instead of faith, yet this is nevertheless the reason why so many become monks: they trust in their works. Even if there were no other reason to absolve monastic vows, the fact that they have denied Christ and faith is enough. Thus, unless a man repents from such a false belief in works, his vow is actually not to be a Christian. No, to exalt such a vow is to deny Christ, Baptism, and Christian freedom.

Versus Evangelical Freedom[146] – The third section argues that vows should be absolved as they are against evangelical freedom. Here Luther says that a vow can only be maintained insofar as it does not offend faith. Yet here, it can only be maintained if done in a spirit of evangelical freedom. This spirit is only found when one trusts completely in Christ and does not place his hope in any human work. Works are not, however, to be abandoned. They are to be performed in the appropriate spirit of faith. Those who take vows seek righteousness through works, yet this is to be condemned as it seeks something outside of Christ. The monks, moreover, take consciences captive in that they take something that belongs to evangelical freedom and they turn it into a strict command. Additionally, Luther, as in other places, suggests what a vow taken in Christian freedom might consist of. It is also of note in this section that Luther is already defending himself from the accusation of renewing the Jovinian heresy[147].

Versus God's Commands[148] – In the fourth section, Luther turns his attention to the commandments of God and the monastic infractions of these. The monasteries teach the monk not to love and care for those whom God has given him to love and care for. They teach that obedience should not be rendered to any neighbor in need other than those to whom it is permitted. These and such other infractions militate against the love required by God's commandments.

Versus Human Reason[149] – For the purposes of this study, section five is of special importance. In this section Luther argues that monastic vows are against human reason, and here he takes up the special concern that had arisen in Wittenberg amongst Melanchthon and Amsdorf, one which Karlstadt had also argued. Namely, here Luther addresses the question of whether a vow that proves to be impossible must be kept. It is also here that Genesis 1:28 first truly comes into the debate in a

---

145 WA 8, pp. 591–604.
146 WA 8, pp. 605–617.
147 WA 8, p. 611,7–31.
148 WA 8, pp. 617–629.
149 WA 8, pp. 629–666.

form that will remain recognizable throughout the remainder of Luther's career and also for the Lutheran Reformation[150].

Beginning in this section, Luther states that he will now turn his attention to vows in light of natural reason. He proceeds then by outlining the capabilities of natural reason, namely, that it is not capable of affirming anything positive[151], but is very clear in pointing out the errors when nature is opposed. For example, reason does not know what God is, but certainly knows what God is not. And, while reason does not know what is pleasing to God (i. e. faith), it certainly knows what is not pleasing (murder, disobedience, etc.). Indeed, how can heavenly truth not fight against that which earthly truth also opposes[152]? With that in mind, Luther shows not only that monastic vows are against the Gospel, the Law, and all of Scripture, but against reason itself. Human reason itself proves that any vow is null and void which shows itself to be humanly impossible[153]. He then brings in the example of a vowed pilgrimage which is interrupted by death, poverty, sickness, or the like. When such external factors interrupt, in spite of the will and intention of the one having made the vow, the vow is absolved. In that way, Luther shows every vow to be conditional, given that a vow is only valid in the possibility of its fulfillment. Furthermore, if such a condition applies to one vow, Luther asks, does it not apply to all vows?

Yet, how does this relate to the matter of celibacy? If one has vowed celibacy and then experiences that this vow cannot be maintained, what hinders him from departing the monastery and marrying? Does this reality not also dictate that the vow is absolved just as sickness absolves the vowed pilgrimage? Even divine commandments make exception for impossibility. Peter would certainly have been excused from preaching and doing works of love while he was in prison. Paul was excused from traveling to Rome when he was hindered, or similarly when he was prevented from traveling to Bithynia. Even the martyrs in the prisons must be judged

---

150 BARANOWSKI, Luthers Lehre, pp. 33, 50–52, observes that Luther addresses precisely this concern of Melanchthon in this section of *De votis monasticis iudicium*. Moreover, Baranowski also notes the appearance of Genesis 1:28 at this juncture (p. 51), though he interprets Luther's allowance for the »impossibility« of a vow as having more to do with the weakness of sinful man and slightly less to do with the force of God's creation. SJÖHOLM, Luthers Åskådning, p. 130, also notes the presence of the verse at this junction, but without comment. The rest of the literature, to include both Lohse's and Grimm's rather lengthy discussions of celibacy, respectively, seems to overlook the importance of this verse on this occasion.
151 Cf. Melanchthon's doubts about natural law in *Loci Communes*. See PÖHLMANN, Loci Communes 1521, 3:6, 12 (pp. 100–103).
152 WA 8, pp. 629,23–630,1.
153 »Votum, etiam si per omnia pium et rectum fuerit, tamen si impossibile factum fuerit, desinit esse votum nec amplius etiam apud deum potest ligare«. WA 8, p. 630,4–6.

as godless if impossibility does not allow for exceptions[154]. Continuing, Luther argues that the opponents will say that God crowns or completes what we are not able to accomplish ourselves. The problem with this, however, is the vow addresses both the will and the work. Thus, the vow always must allow for impossibility. This is what happens with the vow of chastity, where the will desires its fulfillment but the works cannot follow, not even with fasting, prayer, and the like, on account of the weakness of the flesh – all of this even against one's will. Indeed, in such a case the fleshly desires overpower the will and lead to impure discharges – whether awake or asleep, even when otherwise one might have controlled himself[155].

Continuing, Luther raises a series of rhetorical questions as to whether impossible vows might merely be resolved by asking for grace through prayer, or for the fulfillment of what is humanly unthinkable. If that were clearly the case, why did Peter not simply pray that he not be put in prison or Paul simply ask God that his travels to Rome not be hindered? The martyrs, too, might have simply asked God that their works of love would not be hindered by prison. Luther then asks if serious matters ought to be played with in such a manner[156]. He then makes the following accusation:

> By this kind of reasoning you will teach us all first to vow celibacy and then afterward pray that it prove not to be impossible. Moreover, by the same reasoning, you are trying to compel God to revoke his word, that divine commandment of nature by which he created all things, »Increase and multiply« [Genesis 1:28]. All this is absurd and puerile. Each one is left to see from his own experience whether this law, or rather, the privilege of increasing and multiplying, is quite settled and established, or whether he has the power to change things[157].

Offering up a possible counterargument in the name of his opponent, Luther then continues. Namely, he takes up the argument that impossibility is not the same thing for the Christian as for the non-Christian. After all, the will of the saints is powerful and nothing inward can stand in the way of their will, though outward circumstances may indeed do this. Thus, the Christian may be hindered by external

---

154 WA 8, p. 630,4–26.
155 WA 8, pp. 630,27–631,3.
156 WA 8, p. 630,4–11.
157 LW 44, p. 339, cf. »Hac ratione docebis nos omnes coelibatum vovere et postea orare, ne sit impossibilis, ac per hoc illud statutum naturae ›Crescite et multiplicamini‹ coges deum mutato suo verbo, quo creavit omnia, revocare. Stulta et puerilia sunt ista. Experientia sua cuique est relicta, ut videat, an in ipso praevaleat lex illa crescendi et multiplicandi, vel potius privilegium eiusdem legis«. WA 8, p. 631,11–16.

factors, but not by his own flesh. Thus, as the hypothetical argument goes, Luther's case would not hold[158].

Luther answers, however: just because something may or may not be in one's power does not lead to the conclusion that it ought to be done. One might, for example, pluck out one's eyes, cut off body parts, or even drown himself. And even should he do such, would he have truly shown that his »inner tyrants« are more under control than his »outward tyrants«? The truth is that one might indeed win over an outward tyrant, but no words or efforts will ever pacify the inward ones. Paul proves this both in Romans 7:19 and in Galatians 5:17[159]. Therefore, Luther recommends that a man (who wills to be celibate rather than married and yet is unable to keep his vow) be freed from his vow rather than that he be hindered by an unconquerable sickness and a tyrant which will not be tamed. Moreover, Luther asks, how much more furious is the disease and how much more dreadful the tyrant in our members than any other bodily disease[160]?

The above summary demonstrates for us how Luther finally dealt with the concern of Melanchthon, Amsdorf, and Karlstadt regarding the impossibility of keeping one's vow of celibacy. While Luther's arguments in this section are in no way his main attack against monastic vows, he does develop a case – seemingly at the urging of his Wittenberg colleagues – for the opposition of reason to monastic vows. More importantly for this study, the section presents us with Luther's first usage of Genesis 1:28 as it came to be understood by the reformers. Of particular note is that, while he does not in any way attempt to free man's drives from their sinful qualities, he also acknowledges that the essence of those urges is not merely sin. In referring to Genesis 1:28 and the divine mandate to »Be fruitful and multiply«, Luther inserts creational elements into this argument and shows that opposition to marriage and the natural order is actually also opposition to the divine word of creation. Considering that Luther is speaking about celibates, the law and word of God that they are to discern for themselves clearly has to do with the impulses and desires with which they struggle. It is therefore at least plausible to find some sort of identification of these impulses (efficacious through God's command to »Be fruitful and multiply«) with Melanchthon's *naturales quosdam affectus*. Indeed, this seems to be what has happened as will be repeatedly demonstrated in subsequent sections of this work[161].

We should also observe at this juncture Luther's understanding of the ongoing effectivity of the original creative word of God (Genesis 1). This understanding is

---

158 WA 8, p. 631,17–25.
159 WA 8, pp. 631,25–632,2.
160 WA 8, p. 632,1–5.
161 For further discussions of the relationship between Genesis 1:28 and *naturales quosdam affectus*, see sections 3.5, 4.6, and 5.3 of this work.

clearly observed in Luther's rhetorical question as to whether God has revoked His divine word of creation as well as his point that human experience can certainly discern whether this law is still applicable in human creatures and their members or not[162]. Indeed, we might note that for Luther, this application of Genesis 1 to the active and ongoing creative work of God's word in human procreation and sexuality appears to originate even with the original speaking of »Be fruitful and multiply«. One possible explanation for this development might be found in Luther's ongoing reflection on John 1:3 and Hebrews 1:2–3, particularly through his work on the *Kirchenpostille*[163]. For our present purposes, it is enough to note the emergence of Luther's teaching regarding the direct applicability of Genesis 1:28 for man's ongoing existence, as this becomes a foundational and recurrent element of Luther's teaching on this verse.

In working on *De votis monasticis iudicium*, Luther has thus synthesized disparate elements into a new – and exceedingly powerful – argument against monastic vows. The impossibility of maintaining vows of celibacy is therefore not merely due to sinful desires and a depraved will. It also follows directly from God's divine ordering of nature and the working of His creative word (to include divinely created desires and urges), and thus is opposed only with grave consequences.

Evangelium am Tage der heiligen drei Könige (Wartburgpostille)

Further evidence of these new developments in Luther's thought is also presented in the final sermon of the *Weihnachtpostille* (*Evangelium am Tage der heiligen*

---

162 WA 8, p. 631,11–16.
163 Sometime during the late summer or early fall of 1521 Luther most likely wrote the Christmas sermon on John 1:1–14. While he does not explicitly mention Genesis 1:28 in this sermon, his reflections on John 1:3, Ps. 33:6, Heb. 1:3 (WA 10/I/1, pp. 185,12–186,8, 210,18–211,9) are certainly not unrelated to this development – even if Luther's emphasis in this sermon is on Christ's divinity as opposed to His creative activity. For the connection between John 1 and Genesis 1 in Luther's thought, we refer to Albrecht BEUTEL, In dem Anfang war das Wort. Studien zu Luthers Sprachverständnis, Tübingen 1991, pp. 69–86, who also notes that this idea of the ongoing and efficacious creative word of God is already to be found during the 1510s in Luther's work with such psalms as Psalm 33 and 104 (p. 81).

There is, of course, a further possibility meriting consideration. Throughout Christian history, there is a long-standing association of Genesis 1:28 with the efficaciousness of Christ's words regarding the Lord's Supper. This stems from Chrysostom, appeared again in the tenth century with the eucharistic controversy of that era, and was also duly noted by Aquinas. Here see COHEN, Be Fertile, p. 294, fn. 76, p. 307, fn. 6; and Charles RADDING/Francis NEWTON, Theology, Rhetoric, and Politics in the Eucharistic Controversy, 1078–1079. Alberic of Monte Cassino Against Berengar of Tours, New York 2003, pp. 138f. Along these lines, it is a question worthy of further consideration whether perhaps Luther visited this historic association (i. e. of the efficacy of Genesis 1:28 and the Lord's Supper) back upon Genesis 1:28 itself.

drei Könige)[164]. While the dating of this postille is somewhat difficult, considering that it was composed during a five-month period (10 June – 19 November 1521), evidence does point to the conclusion that Luther wrote these sermons in chronological order starting with the Christmas sermons and working toward Epiphany[165]. Thus, it is quite possible that Luther was working on his sermon for Epiphany at approximately the same time he was composing *De votis monasticis iudicium*[166]. For the purposes of this study, we note that a very similar line of thought exists in Luther's sermon as we have previously observed in *De votis monasticis*. This correspondence thus increases the strength of the argument that Luther did indeed develop these two works with similar concerns in mind and perhaps even simultaneously.

The relevant section of this sermon, in which Luther has traced the journey of the Magi to Bethlehem, comes as they begin to return to their homeland and are warned in their sleep not to return to Herod[167]. This passage gives Luther occasion to discuss the problem of tempting God. More specifically, he raises the question of when exactly one's efforts should cease and a matter be given over to God in faith and prayer. This is essentially the same question addressed in *De votis monasticis iudicium*. There Luther discusses whether one ought to keep an impossible vow when its fulfillment would only tempt God by militating against His word and work.

Luther begins the discussion by posing the question: Why, if God would have most certainly protected the young child Jesus from Herod, was it necessary for the Magi to avoid Herod on their return journey? Luther answers this question by asserting that everything possible ought to be done through creaturely means. One ought not to despise such things in the name of faith. The farmer cannot simply avoid work and say, »I shall trust in God and let grow what will grow«. For what purpose are God's creatures if they are not used? In Genesis 1 God created and ordered all creatures with their works, including how man ought to make use of them and work. God will never recall this arrangement and make an exception of anyone[168].

---

164 WA 10/I/1, pp. 555–728. The related text is Matthew 2:1–12.
165 See WA 10/I/2, pp. XLVI–LIV.
166 STAMM, Luthers Stellung, pp. 56f., also interprets the evidence in this manner. SCHEEL, Ergänzungsbände, p. 203, places the composition of this sermon prior to *De votis monasticis iudicium*.
167 WA 10/I/1, pp. 615f.
168 »Das it darumb geschehen, das wyr lernen sollen, nitt gott vorsuchen; was man kan fuglicher weyß und durch mittel der creatur außrichten, soll man nit vorachten und sprechen: ia, ich will gott glewben, es wirtt wol geschehen. Als wenn du nit erbeytten wolltist und sagen: ich will gott glewben, es wirtt dennoch woll wachßen, was da wachßen soll. Was solten die creatur, wenn du yhr nit brauchen woltist? Geñ. 1. hatt er geschaffen und vorordnet alle creatur mit yhrn wercken, und wie der mensch derselben brauchen soll und erbeytten, das wirtt er nymmer widderuffen und dyr eyn eygenß machenn«. WA 10/I/1, p. 615,14–22.

Here, in addition to what has already been observed, we note the emphasis Luther places on God's creative work. Unless otherwise made clear by God, one should not expect that God will change that which He has instituted in creation. In the above section Luther is referring to man's vocation of work and his rule over creation. Yet, shortly later, Luther turns his attention toward the other portion of Genesis 1:28, namely, »Be fruitful and multiply«.

Continuing, then, Luther clarifies the problem. When ought faith to take over exclusively and human efforts be left behind, if one is to avoid tempting God? Luther's answer: One should not go beyond God's word as faith cannot be without this word. God refers to His word in the Scriptures in various ways, thereby giving witness to its priority. He has also established this word through works which testify to it. Luther then reiterates that, short of having God's word on a matter, one ought to continue, use his strength, his goods, his friend, and everything that God has given him. That is, he is to remain in the order which God established in Genesis 1. After all, God has not given this without purpose; neither will He simply change His created order on account of any individual so that wine turns into water or bread turns into stone. Rather, as God has created, so ought things be allowed to remain and be utilized, unless or until God compels something different with His word[169].

It is clearly to be observed in this section that Luther's argument assumes that the natural order of Genesis 1 is to be observed and respected until and unless God gives a clear word to the contrary. In other words, such things as work, marriage and family, and other natural orders remain in effect. Here, perhaps even more clearly than in *De votis monasticis*, we see the abiding power and norm of the created order in Luther's thought – something, as we have observed previously, which is not to be found so clearly in earlier periods.

Karlstadt's Super Coelibatu, A Second Wittenberg Printing

In light of the shift in Luther's thought observed in the foregoing material, we will conclude this section by returning to Andreas Karlstadt's *Super Coelibatu*. Sometime late in the year 1521, a revised edition of this work was printed in Wittenberg by Johann Rhau-Grunenberg. Whereas the initial edition was printed in August 1521 and gave only brief attention to Genesis 1:28, this revised printing significantly

---

[169] »Wo du nu nit hast gottis wortt, da solltu ymer forttfarn und brauchen deyner krefft, deyniß guts, deyner freund und allis, was dyr gott geben hatt, und also bleyben ynn der ordnung, die Geñ. 1. ist eyngesetʒt; denn er hatt dyrß nit umbsonst geben, wirtt umb deynen willen nitt machen, das weyn wasser werd unnd brod steyn werd, sondern wie er eyn iglichs geschaffen hatt, so soltu es lassen und seyn brauchen, biß das er dich ʒwing mit wortt odder wercken anders ʒu brauchen«. WA 10/I/1, p. 616,11–17.

expanded not only Karlstadt's treatment of the first axiom but particularly his treatment of Genesis 1:28[170]. Furthermore, the increased emphasis upon Genesis 1:28 in Karlstadt's Rhau-Grunenberg edition coincides with Luther's appropriation of Genesis 1:28 during the fall of 1521. This development further strengthens the case that a significant shift in thought took place in Wittenberg circles during the fall of 1521, even though Karlstadt does not reflect Luther's understanding of Genesis 1:28 in certain important aspects. For example, Karlstadt makes no mention of the ongoing creative working of the word nor does his thought reflect any notion of Melanchthon's natural affections. Nevertheless, the growing significant emphasis upon this verse speaks for itself. The following figure highlights the difference in emphasis placed upon this verse in the two editions:

Karlstadt, Andreas. *Super coelibatu, monachatu et viduitate axiomata perpensa Wittembergae.*
Wittenberg: Nickel Schirlentz, August 1521.

And not without cause do they detest the barrenness of Sarah, Rebecca, Rachel, then also Leah, Hannah, and the rest of the saintly women. (Gen. 16, Gen. 25, Gen. 29, 1 Kgs. [Sam.] 1, Lev. 26)

    Neither in jest does the Lord in so many places speak and command: »[You pl.] Increase and multiply«; likewise, »[You sg.] Increase and multiply.« (Gen. 1, 8, 9) They are the daughters of Abraham, whose seed ought to be as the stars of heaven and the sand of the sea, the number of which they will in no way reach by widowhood. Accordingly, they should marry, for widows will not be able (in opposition to the authority of the Scriptures) to please God. Finally, I do not desire to keep hidden from the »vestal virgins«, [i. e.] unmarried nuns, the fact that the administration of domestic business is a good work commended by the Scriptures and far surpasses those perpetual prayers which they mutter in *their* sacred temple. For as Christ says, »When you pray, do not desire to speak much, as the heathen do[171]«.

Karlstadt, Andreas. *Super coelibatu, monachatu et viduitate axiomata[...]*
Wittenberg: Joh. Rhau-Grunenberg, late 1521.

The duty of women is to be partners, to be helpers of men, to improve solitude, to cause the world to be planted with children for us.

    Neither in jest nor in vain does Scripture in so many places command as well as say with these words: »Increase and multiply and fill the earth.« This command, as it is the first one, and repeated so often, therefore ought to be fulfilled with greater inclination of the will and eagerness. So likewise we ought to follow it as constantly as possible.

    And indeed, the repetition and reiteration of a word is accustomed, by repetition, to demand and to be forceful, as it were a persistent request. Therefore, I do not weary of the labor of bringing in several passages of Scripture for this. We have this command in Genesis 1, 8, 9, and in other places. Neither do I wish to hide from you that the Lord repeated this command to one person. Accordingly, the Lord said to Jacob: »Increase and multiply«. In short, we see in

---

170 Buckwalter, Priesterehe, pp. 91f.
171 »Neque absque causa, sterilitatem detestātur. Sara. Rebecka. Rachel. Atque deinde Lia. Anna &reliquae santae mulieres. Neque ioco tot locis loquitur precepitque dominus. *Crescite & multiplicamini.* Item, *Cresce & multiplicare.* Filie sunt Abrahæ, cuius semen esse oprotet sicut coeli stellas, & maris arenam, quorum numerum haud quaquam consequentur viduitate, itaque nubant, non enim quibunt uiduæ (contra scripturarum authoritatem) deo conplacere. Postremo nolo virgines uestales,

this saying that this blessing of fruitfulness belonged to the blessed. For they wished Rebecca well, saying: »May you increase into thousands of thousands«. And not only did the Lord set forth that command, but also He has sent forth His Spirit, giving witness that multiplying is by His giving and not by human ability, saying: »I will make you to increase exceedingly«. Behold He acts mercifully, and He even provides for what He has lawfully demanded. And not only on the godly, but also on others and on the sons of the maidservant has He bestowed so great a benefit. For indeed, to Ishmael He promises and delivers the same mercy which He had pledged to the maidservant of Abraham, saying: »I will bless him, and I will increase and multiply him greatly«. Now who does not hold that those whom the Lord has made suitable for marriage are to be exhorted unto marriage?

Accordingly, they have both the command and the strength given by the Lord, for who can deny that this is a command? Moreover, who does not see that the Lord has created wives to be partners, that each with his own wife might fill the earth? The nuns and monks would respond, »Are horses and mares, which the desire of the flesh inflames outside of marriage, exempted from this commandment?« Will they now explain whether their bond to God or to the Pope is stronger? Yet truly, when they are pulled in different directions by both bonds, to whose commands will they chiefly adhere? You who maintain vestal oaths, *will you cling* to your conventicles? likewise, to your saints? Therefore, being broken by human fear, you break the divine commandment and worship the pope's witch. I now rightly ask whether this is *really* an offense against God, when we are to yield much more to the Lord God? You are first bound to God, *but* then through ignorance you are bound to the pontifical chasm. Crawl out of the pit of the pope, I beg you! Look to the serene heaven of God, cultivate the earth, and thus preserve mankind, making due intercessions for men. In this way you will be obedient to the highest, best, and greatest Pope, and happier.

Finally, I do not want that which pertains to the point of this argument to escape your notice, that nothing from the word of God will fall, and, no words of God will be able to pass away void. Heaven and earth will pass away; the words of God will not pass away. The external form of the world, which the philosophers falsely claim is eternal, will decay, *yet* not even the smallest part of the word of God will perish. For everyone knows that God promised seed to Abraham in great number, saying: »Look to heaven and count the stars, if you are able«, and added, »Thus will your seed be«. Therefore, it is necessary that the seed of Abraham be as the stars of the heaven, the sand of the sea, and the dust of the earth. It is necessary that the sons of the promise and of eternal life be innumerable. Such a number, furthermore, will in no way be attained by celibacy. Therefore, if your spirit leads you into marriage, be married to women, having banished the fear of faithlessness, vows, and oaths *of celibacy*. When would there be a finer pontifical web than that which could introduce fear of such great deeds? [172]

3.5 Melanchthon, *affectus naturales*, and Genesis 1:28

Running as a recurrent leitmotif throughout our investigation is the thought of Luther's co-reformer, Philipp Melanchthon, and particularly his natural legal and philosophical thought. For the most part, the contributions stand rather quietly in the background, as we have surmised is the case regarding Melanchthon's teaching on natural affects and Luther's initial polemic employment of Genesis 1:28. At other times, as we will observe later with Melanchthon's στοργὴ φυσικὴ in the Augsburg Confession's *Apologia*, his unique contributions and expression of Wittenberg

---

monachas viduas celare, dispensationem rei domesticæ bonum opus esse, a scripturis cōmendatum, & antecellere multis nominibus preculas illas perpetuas, quas mussant in sacra æde, Sic enim ait Christus Cum oratis, nolite multū loqui, sicut Ethnici faciunt«. KARLSTADT, Super Coelibatu, bi[r]; emphasis added.

thought on Genesis 1:28 assume center stage. Whatever the case, though, we find Melanchthon's teaching on the natural affects never far removed from our own topic. In the following, we thus seek to outline the contours of Melanchthon's teaching regarding these natural affects and their relevance for our own investigation of Luther's thought on Genesis 1:28.

Toward such ends, both here and in subsequent chapters, attention will be given to the development of Melanchthon's thought. The following pages will thus undertake a general introduction to Melanchthon's early *Affektenlehre* leading up to *Loci Communes* (1521). A second section (concluding Chapter 4) will attempt to identify the possible influence of Melanchthon's teachings concerning the natural affects (especially about procreation) in Luther's thought as well as that of other Wittenberg contemporaries, focusing especially on relevant writings of the first half of the 1520s. A third section (concluding Chapter 5) will then extend our treatment of Melanchthon's understanding of the natural affects into the later 1520s with his writing of *In Ethica Aristotelis Commentarius Philipp. Meanchtho[n]* (1529) and then further into his *Apologia Confessionis Augustanae* (1531).

Loci Communes (1521)

Melanchthon's conception of the affects (i. e. the movements, urgings, and passions arising from the heart) following his arrival in Wittenberg underwent a noteworthy transformation. Under Luther's influence and Melanchthon's own personal study of Romans, the rough outlines of what would later coalesce as his mature thought regarding the affects began to emerge[173]. Whereas the predominate Scholastic-Aristotelian understanding of the affects had conceived of these internal movements as being, in some way, under the control and in the domain of human regulation, now the affects began to be understood as thoroughly under the domination of sin and thoroughly corrupted in their entirety[174]. At the same time, whereas much of philosophical and religious teaching had striven for man's conquest over (and thus the extinction of) all affects, Melanchthon, on the basis of Romans[175], also

---

173 Hartmut O. Günther, Die Entwicklung der Willenslehre Melanchthons in der Auseinandersetzung mit Luther und Erasmus, Erlangen 1963, pp. 11–28, URL: <https://books.google.no/books?id=j_5NAQAAIAAJ&printsec=frontcover&hl=no#v=onepage&q&f=false> (18 Aug 2022). Bengt Hägglund, De Homine. Människouppfattningen i Äldre Luthersk Tradition, Lund 1959, pp. 181–214, also includes a relevant discussion on Melanchthon's *Affektenlehre* and serves as a resource throughout this introductory section. Unfortunately, these and other treatments of Melanchthon and the affects tend to focus most of their attention on the relationship between the affects and will as concerns spiritual matters and little or none on the place of the natural affects.
174 Günther, Entwicklung, pp. 22, 24, 34–37.
175 Romans 1:31 indirectly praises natural affects via its condemnation of those lacking such natural love.

had gained an understanding of the rightful place of the affects in God's ordering of creation[176]. Needless to say – and this must be underscored! – the conclusion of this development is that the significance of the affects was dramatically elevated. Melanchthon arrived at the understanding that life is played out under the auspices of the affects[177]. Life is lived in and through the affects, whether under the steering of the flesh or that of the Spirit[178].

This notion of the hierarchy of the affects over themselves and – in contrast to the Stoic, Augustinian, and Scholastic understanding of affects – over reason, is already fully visible by the time we arrive at Melanchthon's *Loci Communes* (1521), most especially in the significance of original sin and man's fallen condition as concerns man's affective nature. For our purposes, however, what is most interesting in Melanchthon's understanding of the affects is that which he presents in his treatment of law (*De lege*). Here, as previously noted, Melanchthon offers a distinction with regard to his discussion of the affects that dare not be overlooked. In introducing his thought on natural law and pointing out its correspondence and impression upon the human mind, Melanchthon bluntly states that he does not care if such thoughts liken Aristotle's thought[179]. Then, continuing, Melanchthon writes, »But I will pass over what we have in common with the animals, such as the birth and care of life and procreation. These things the lawyers classify under the law of nature, but I identify them as natural affections inborn in all living creatures«[180].

---

176 Ibid., p. 24.
177 Ibid., p. 28: »Bei Melanchthon steht neben der wertenden auch eine rein phänomenologische Betrachtungsweise. ›Omnium animantium vita affectus est,‹ heißt es in der Institutio. Affekt ist ein Strukturprinzip für das gesamte ›beseelte Leben‹. Es wird von hier aus klar, inwiefern die Affekte dem Entscheidungsvermögen vorgegeben sind. Gilt die Gleichung zwischen vita und affectus, die Melanchthon aufstellt, dann kann es Entscheidungen nur im Bereich der Affekte geben«. See also Maurer, Der junge Melanchthon, pp. 387f.
178 Günther, Entwicklung, pp. 22–24, 28.
179 Pöhlmann, Loci Communes 1521, pp. 92f. In that Melanchthon has named Aristotle in the near context of this quote and in light of Melanchthon's later treatment of *affectus*/στοργην φυσικην in connection with Aristotle's *Nicomachean Ethics*, it seems likely that *Nicomachean Ethics, II & III*, inform Melanchthon's writing here. This is especially the case considering the fact that in those portions of *Nicomachean Ethics* Aristotle discusses those affects held in common with the beasts. Melanchthon, however, seems to distinguish himself from the Stagirite in that he classifies the natural affections, not as matters of choice but as natural necessities. In this regard, the near contextual mention of Cicero in *Loci Communes*, is perhaps significant, especially given Melanchthon's relative dependence upon Stoic teaching in this same section. See ibid., p. 102, fn. 263. With regard to Melanchthon's generally negative view of Aristotle at this time, note Nicole Kuropka, Philip Melanchthon and Aristotle, in: Irene Dingel et al. (eds.), Philip Melanchthon. Theologian in Classroom, Confession, and Controversy, Göttingen 2012, pp. 19–28, at pp. 19–21.
180 Philipp Melanchthon, Commonplaces. Loci Communes 1521, translated by Christian Preus, Saint Louis 2014, p. 63, cf. »Omitto autem ea, quae cum brutis communia habemus, vitam tueri

Unfortunately, when it comes to this particular distinction of these »lower passions«, inadequate notice has generally been paid. For example, while Maurer offers extensive treatment to the importance of the affects in the young Melanchthon's thought – and particularly in his 1521 *Loci Communes* – the lower affects so closely related to the protection and furtherance of life receive comparatively little mention. In fact, the closest Maurer comes to offering direct commentary on these affects and whatever Melanchthon may have understood them to be is in his treatment of *De hominis viribus adeoque de libero arbitrio* early on in *Loci Communes*[181]. Somewhat more helpful, though still somewhat lacking with regard to the lower affects, is Maurer's discussion of Melanchthon's thought on natural law. Here, Maurer notes the shift made by Melanchthon between the nine-fold listed description of natural law contained in the *Capita* (1520) and the three-fold division as outlined by Melanchthon in the *Loci Communes* of 1521[182].

Most significantly in this section, what Maurer does do is argue for the continuity of thought, and the hierarchy of natural law, contained in both the *Capita* as well as the *Loci Communes*. He notes that natural law, for Melanchthon, consists of both a higher and lower order[183]. This ordering is a result of man's fall into sin and reflects the protection of and subservience to the greater by and through the lower. Maurer writes,

---

gignereque et aliud ex sese procreare, quae in ius naturae referunt iurisconsulti, ego naturales quosdam affectus animantibus communiter insitos voco«. PÖHLMANN, Loci Communes 1521, 3:15 (p. 102).

181 MAURER, Der junge Melanchthon, p. 245, observes, »So kann der Anschein erweckt werden, für Melanchthon bestehe der Mensch nur aus Leib und Seele, ja er sei, da die leibliche Sphäre für ihn theologisch nichts bedeutet, nichts anderes als ein willensgeladenes Seelenwesen. ›Die Erkenntnis ist Sklavin des Willens‹; der Wille mit seinen Affekten ist der Tyrann, der den Menschen völlig beherrscht. Melanchthon konzentriert dabei seine Affektlehre ausdrücklich auf die höheren Affekte, die die seelischen Regungen wie Liebe, Haß, Hoffnung, Furcht, Traurigkeit, Zorn und was aus ihnen entspringt, hervorbringen; von den niederen, die die körperlichen Triebe bewegen, redet er nicht weiter« (references to *Loci* from Stupperich's *Studienausgabe* ommitted in citation).
Karl-Heinz zur MÜHLEN, Melanchthons Auffassung vom Affekt in den »Loci communes« von 1521, in: Id., Reformatorische Prägungen. Studien zur Theologie Martin Luthers und zur Reformationszeit, edited by Athina Lexutt and Volkmar Ortmann, Göttingen 2011, pp. 84 -95, at pp. 84–93, also focuses on the spiritual nature of the affects in Melanchthon's *Loci* and does not bring our own topic of concern into the discussion.

182 MAURER, Der junge Melanchthon, pp. 291–294. Noteworthy here is the fact that Maurer notes Melanchthon's shift away from the biologically-based Stoic definition of natural law toward a reason-based Aristotelian understanding of the same – though this is observed in reference to Melanchthon's discussion of property. As outlined in the previous chapter, such a shift applies to Melanchthon's shift in thinking regarding whether or not procreation and natural affects ought to be included as properly belonging to the jurisdiction of natural law.

183 The correspondence between the discussion of natural law and its categories in both *Capita* and *Loci Communes* can be seen as follows.

There are thus for Melanchthon two basic forms of natural law, one higher and one lower. This is a consequence of sinful desire, though desire is not evil, per se. It [natural law] reveals itself much more in the higher order and counteracts sin. Because life is to be protected and preserved and no one may be harmed, desire is to be bridled, possessions must be rightly distributed, commerce and dealings regulated, the trespasser of the law must be punished. The disruption lies in man, not in natural law itself. This remains unchangeably just and good[184].

Thus, assuming Maurer's argument about the ordering of Melanchthon's thought on natural law, it seems certain that Melanchthon is concerned not merely with the protection of life in his discussion of his second category[185], but also – implicitly – with the furtherance of life. Taking this line of thought one step further, we then turn back to the preceding paragraph in *Loci Communes* where Melanchthon speaks about procreation and the furtherance of life and ask the question: what does Melanchthon mean in designating those things in common with the beasts as »certain natural affects« (*naturales quosdam affectus*)?

Capita (1520)	*Loci Communes* (1521)
1 Das Gebot, Gott zu verehren,	1 Deus colendus est.
2 Das Leben zu schützen,	2 Quia nascimur in quondam vitae societatem, nemo laedendus est.
3 Zu zeugen,	
4 Die Ehe einzugehen,	
5 Die Nachkommenschaft zu erhalten,	
6 Niemanden zu verletzen,	
7 Das allen Gehörende gemeinsam zu gebrauchen bzw. es zu verteilen,	
8 Zum Güteraustausch auf verträglicher Basis Handel zu treiben,	3 Poscit humana societas, ut omnibus rebus communiter utamur.
9 Unrecht zu bestrafen.	

Pöhlmann, Loci Communes 1521, p. 103, fn. 266; cf. CR 21, col. 25f.   Pöhlmann, Loci Communes 1521, p. 104.

184 Cf. »Es gibt also für Melanchthon zwei Grundformen des Naturrechts, eine höhere und eine niedere. Diese ist eine Folge sündhafter Begehrlichkeit; sie ist aber nicht schlechthin böse. Es entfaltet sich vielmehr in ihr die höhere Ordnung und wirkt der Sünde entgegen: Weil das Leben geschützt und erhalten werden muß und niemand verletzt werden darf, muß die Begehrlichkeit gezügelt werden. Der Besitz muß gerecht verteilt, Handel und Wandel geregelt, der Übertreter der Gesetze gestraft werden. Der Bruch liegt in den Menschen, nicht im Naturrecht an sich; dieses bleibt unveränderlich recht und gut«. Maurer, Der junge Melanchthon, p. 291.

185 »Quia nascimur in quandam vitae societatem, nemo laedendus est«. Pöhlmann, Loci Communes 1521, 2:18 (p. 104). See also further discussion of this second category in Maurer, Der junge Melanchthon, pp. 291–294.

Certainly, in answer to this question (if we are to avoid the risk of an anachronistic reading of this text), we are somewhat limited in what might be asserted. Nevertheless, the above-mentioned structure of the text suggests a more positive view and affirmation of this category of affects. One further clue also recommends the possibility that these affects, though certainly distorted and disordered by the curse of sin, are not to be wholly categorized in the general discussion of the affects otherwise present in Melanchthon's *Loci*[186]. Namely, Melanchthon's use of the term *insitus* implies that he is not talking about man's depraved desires but about man's God-given, innate disposition and impulses, however distorted and impotent they may be in view of the fall[187]. The term *naturalis*, of course, might be understood either to point to man's own depravity or, in accord with our current argument, as corresponding with God's creation and order – the latter being much more fitting in this case.

We also do well to note a further implication which arises out of this section of the *Loci* at this point. In light of the import and power Melanchthon had given to the affects ever since his *Lucubratiuncula* and *Institutio*[188], the strength of *naturales quosdam affectus* dare not be underestimated. Along these lines, it seems that in somewhat neglecting this category of affects, Maurer is perhaps led to overlook important developments in the late summer and fall of 1521 with respect to the topic of monastic vows. In Maurer's treatment of Melanchthon's thought on monastic vows, he rightly notes Melanchthon's concern for the impossibility of the vow. Nevertheless, although he rightly notes Luther's minimization of this argument in September 1521, the fact remains that Luther's thinking on the matter was not yet conclusive[189]. Indeed, Maurer seems to overlook the fact that Luther actually does respond to just this concern in the November writing of *De votis monasticis iudicium* – in which Luther first introduces a powerful new argument that seems to include aspects of man's innate nature. Thus, as we have argued elsewhere, it seems likely that Melanchthon's *naturales quosdam affectus* (and his concern about the impossibility of the vow) played a role in the development of Luther's thought on Genesis 1:28. Indeed, included in Luther's notion of the effective working of

---

186 For example, under the heading *Vis peccati et fructus* of *Loci Communes*, Melanchthon flatly asserts, »Peccatum est affectus contra legem dei«. PÖHLMANN, Loci Communes 1521, 2:118. Nevertheless, earlier in *Loci Communes* Melanchthon, 1:11 (pp. 28f.), had already distinguished between the affects seated in the body and held in common with the animal world (the lower affects) and those that are more properly located in the human will.
187 Note that Melanchthon's use of *insitos* can refer to an aspect of sin. See ibid., 2:111 (pp. 90f.), though it is generally descriptive of God's creation. See ibid., 3:13 (pp. 102f.), 4:8 (pp. 162f.).
188 Adolf SPERL, Melanchthon zwischen Humanismus und Reformation, München 1959, pp. 100–104. See also CR 21, col. 17f., 52f.
189 MAURER, Der junge Melanchthon, p. 304. Cf. WA Br 2, pp. 382–387 and a similar remark made to Amsdorf on the same date. See WA Br 2, pp. 390f.

that divine word seems to be nothing other than these same natural affects. As we will discuss later, the companionship of this portion of Melanchthon's *Affektenlehre* with Genesis 1:28 would go on to become a fixed facet of the Wittenberg argument against vows of celibacy and in support of its teaching on the nature of man and marriage.

4. Contesting a Verse: The Debate Surrounding Genesis 1:28 (1522–1524)

> Drumb gleych wie got niemandt gepeut, das er man sey oder weyb, ßondern schaffet, das sie ßo mussen seyn, Alßo gepeutt er auch nicht, sich mehren, ßondern schafft, das sie sich mussen mehren.

> *Therefore, just as God does not command anyone to be a man or a woman but creates them the way they have to be, so he does not command them to multiply but creates them so that they have to multiply.*
>
> —Martin Luther, *Vom ehelichen Leben*

4.1 Abiding Command or No Longer in Force? (1522–1524)

In the previous chapter we noted the initial emergence of Genesis 1:28 in the dialogue and debate in both Luther's thought and in the early Reformation movement in Wittenberg. In this chapter, we will look at the years that followed and note the increasing role this verse played, both as expressed by Wittenberg reformers as well as observed in ongoing polemics. This will be observed particularly in connection to the questions of priestly marriage and monastic vows. In all of this, we will be faced with the question that both the reformers and their opponents wrestled over. Namely, were the words of Genesis 1:28, »Be fruitful and multiply and fill the earth«, an abiding ordinance and command of the Creator, or had they been abrogated with Christ's coming in favor of chastity and virginity? Was man free from these words or freed to live within and in accordance with them?

By means of a survey of the pertinent writings of Luther, relevant Wittenberg contemporaries, and their opponents, we will thus seek to ascertain the positive shape and content not only of Luther's thought in connection with Genesis 1:28 but also the contours of theological debate. In order to establish the former, we will give particular attention to Luther's *Vom ehelichen Leben*. To attain an overview of the latter, we will explore opposition to Luther's teaching from such opponents as Johann Faber, Thomas Murner, Johann Cochlaeus, and Johann Dietenberger. We will then also further observe the debate through the year 1524, thus helping to confirm and clarify the contours of the relevant topics and debates surrounding our verse.

4.2 Luther's Thought on Genesis 1:28 as Presented in *Vom ehelichen Leben*

We begin our investigation, then, with Luther's sermon, *Vom ehelichen Leben*. Following the appearance of Genesis 1:28 in *De votis monasticis iudicium* in November 1521 – and in the *Wartburgpostille* at approximately the same time – the next work in which Luther builds on »Be fruitful and multiply« appears in this sermon which was perhaps written in August 1522 and likely printed the following month[1]. The context leading to this treatment of marriage seems to have been a plethora of marital themes, not least of which were issues arising from concerns pertaining to canon law, parental authority, general disdain and disregard for marriage and women, the ongoing debates surrounding monastic vows and the marriage of priests, and questions involving divorce[2].

---

1 WA 10/II, pp. 267f. It should be noted that there are trace appearances of this theme to be found in the intervening months. For example, HENDRIX, Masculinity, p. 174, notes Luther's *Vom ehelichen Leben* is based, at least in part, on a sermon or sermons preached in April/May 1522. Additionally, in *Wider den falsch genannten geistlichen Stand des Papsts und der Bischöfe*, a writing dating to perhaps July 1522 (WA 10/II, p. 95), Luther makes the following comment as part of his polemic against the spiritual orders (i. e. monasticism): »Aber nu thustu alßo umb deyns elenden guttis willen, stossistu sie dem teuffell ynn den rachen on yhren willen. Was folget den darauß? Höre tzů. Ich hab meyn tag kein Nonne beycht gehöret. Aber ich wills doch treffen nach der heutigen schrifft, wie es mit yhn gehe, unnd weyß, ich will nicht liegen. Eyn dyrne, wo nicht die hohe, seltzame gnade da ist, kan sie eyns manß eben ßo wenig geratten alß essen, trincken, schlaffen unnd andere naturliche notturfft. Widderumb auch alßo eyn man kan eyns weybs nicht geratten. Ursach ist die: Es ist eben ßo tieff eyngepflantzt der natur, kinder tzeugen alß essen und trincken. Darumb hatt gott dem leyb die gelide, oddern, fluss und alles, was datzu dienet, geben und eyngesetzt. Wer nu dißem weren will unnd nicht lassen gehen, wie natur wil unnd muß. Was thutt der anders, den er will weren, das natur nicht natur sey, das fewr nicht brenne, wasser nicht netze, der mensch nicht esse noch trincke noch schlaff?«. WA 10/II, p. 156,10–22. Given the manner that Luther speaks about Genesis 1:28 in other writings, it is almost certain that he had this verse in mind as he wrote about human nature and its disposition toward procreation.

See also Luther's comments in his Advent Postille (WA 10/I/2, pp. 144,18–145,15). There, although no mention is made of Genesis 1:28, Luther does mention Jerome, Ambrose, and Augustine with their emphasis upon virginity and chastity over marriage. Note also Luther's emphasis that the married and unmarried callings are both valued equally by God (WA 10/I/2, p. 143,3–22). This sermon probably dates to the winter/late winter of 1522 (WA 10/I/2, pp. LIVff.) and would have been printed in April 1522 (WA 10/I/2, p. LXII).

2 For more on the context of this writing see WA 10/II, pp. 267f.; Martin BRECHT, Martin Luther. Ordnung und Abgrenzung der Reformation 1521–1532, Berlin 1981, pp. 95f.

Thematically, this sermon is one of the most significant as concerns Luther's thought on marriage. Christian Witt, for example, in *Luthers Reformation der Ehe*, places Luther's *Vom ehelichen Leben* in a place of central importance. It marks, he argues, the completion of a break away from Luther's inherited medieval Augustinian understanding of marriage and establishes a baseline, though not the finalized form in every detail, for his marital theology throughout the remainder of his career[3]. One of the decisive aspects of this break, as argued by Witt, is that it applied important aspects of Luther's thought – related both to his understanding of creation and justification – to the question of marriage. With respect to Luther's understanding of creation, Genesis 1:28 forms a sort of backbone to his new view of marriage, its influence running throughout nearly the entirety of the sermon. In this manner, it serves as an essential element of Luther's break with his Augustinian heritage as concerns marital thought[4]. Witt further argues, as previously noted, that it would be difficult to overestimate the importance of Genesis 1:28 for Luther's understanding of marriage[5]. That is to say, in *Vom ehelichen Leben*, Genesis 1:28 is no longer merely an element of polemical argumentation as it was in *De votis monasticis iudicium*. Rather, for the first time, Luther expounds upon its positive teachings and its fundamental importance both to his thought on marriage as well as to his understanding of human nature itself. The following offers a synopsis and analysis of this sermon with particular attention given to Luther's understanding and application of Genesis 1:28.

Vom ehelichen Leben is divided into three sections. The first section deals with who is to marry, for what purpose(s) they are to marry, and whether there are

---

3 WITT, Reformation der Ehe, pp. 296f.
4 Augustine held that »Be fruitful and multiply« was no longer of imperative force following the appearance of Christ. Rather, it was now the *lesser* of two goods when compared with chastity or virginity. For this see AUGUSTINE, De bona coniugali (CSEL 41, pp. 187–231), and WITT, Reformation der Ehe, pp. 47–53, with his discussion of this aspect of Augustine's thought.
5 Ibid. Similarly, BUCKWALTER, Priesterehe, p. 109, comments, »Die knappe Schrift gliedert sich in drei Teile. Im ersten, der davon handelt, ›welche person mügen mit eynander tzur ehe greyffen‹, betont Luther so deutlich wie selten zuvor die Verankerung der Ehe im Schöpfungswillen Gottes«. Here he refers explicitly to Luther's use of Genesis 1:28. See also BARANOWSKI, Luthers Lehre, pp. 56–58, for the emphasis he notes respecting Genesis 1:28 in this text.
It is interesting to note that some of the literature seems to fundamentally overlook the force of Luther's understanding of Genesis 1:28 in this text. For example, HENDRIX, Masculinity, p. 174, notes in his discussion of »Luther on Marriage«, »Luther establishes marriage as a divinely willed ordinance on the basis of Genesis 1:26–28, which describes how God created human beings male and female and bid them be fruitful and multiply«. Such a description of Luther's thought seems perhaps less than adequate when compared with the actual force with which Luther writes. It also leads to his questionable conclusion that Luther's emphasis upon children and »confinement« of women to the domestic sphere was merely a reflection of sixteenth century patriarchal culture (p. 184).

any exceptions to this. We note that from the very beginning, Luther brings Genesis 1:27–28 into the discussion. He uses Genesis 1:27 to establish the »who« of marriage (namely, male and female) as an inalterable arrangement of the Creator which bears the designation of »very good« (Genesis 1:31). Luther then proceeds to discuss the purpose of this two-fold sex, namely, procreation. The basis for this is derived from Genesis 1:28 and the words »Be fruitful and multiply«. After introducing this and noting that it is the inflexible and unchangeable ordering for creation that the man and woman should and must come together for the purpose of procreating[6], Luther continues in the following paragraph,

> For this word which God speaks, »Be fruitful and multiply«, is not a command. It is more than a command, namely, a divine ordinance [*werck*] which it is not our prerogative to hinder or ignore. Rather, it is just as necessary as the fact that I am a man, and more necessary than sleeping and waking, eating and drinking, and emptying the bowels and bladder. It is a nature and disposition just as innate as the organs involved in it. Therefore, just as God does not command anyone to be a man or a woman but creates them the way they have to be, so he does not command them to multiply but creates them so that they have to multiply. And wherever men try to resist this, it remains irresistible nonetheless and goes its way through fornication, adultery, and secret sins, for this is a matter of nature and not of choice[7].

With this explanation of »Be fruitful and multiply«, we now gain deeper insight into Luther's understanding of Genesis 1:28. Whereas in *De votis monasticis iudicium* he refers to this blessing as law (*lex*), divine statute of nature (*statutum divinum naturae*), and word (*verbum*)[8], and while in his sermon for Epiphany he refers to Genesis 1:28 as an instituted ordinance (*eyngesetzte ordnung*)[9], he now adds divine work (*gottlich werck*), implanted nature and disposition (*eyngepflantste natur und art*), more than a command (*mehr den eyn gepott*), a necessary nat-

---

6 »[…] man und weyb sollen und müssen zusammen, das sie sich mehren«. WA 10/II, p. 276,11.
7 LW 45, p. 18, cf. »Denn diß wort, da got spricht: ›Wachsset und mehret euch‹, ist nicht eyn gepot ßondern mehr den eyn gepott, nemlich eyn gottlich werck, das nicht bey uns stehet tzuverhyndern odder noch tzulaßen, ßondern ist eben alßo nott, alß das ich eyn manß bild sey, und nöttiger denn essen und trinken, fegen und außwerffen, schlaffen und wachen. Es ist eyn eyngepflantzte natur und artt eben ßo wol als die glidmaß, die datzu gehören. Drumb gleych wie got niemandt gepeut, das er man sey oder weyb, ßondern schaffet, das sie ßo mussen seyn, Alßo gepeutt er auch nicht, sich mehren, ßondern schafft, das sie sich mussen mehren. Und wo man das wil weren, das ists dennoch ungeweret und gehet doch durch hurerey, ehebruch und stummen sund seynen weg, denn es ist natur und nicht wilkore hierynnen«. WA 10/II, p. 276,21–31.
8 WA 8, p. 631,11–16.
9 WA 10/I/1, p. 616,13.

ural thing (*ein nöttig naturlich ding*)[10], creature of God (*gottis geschöpffe*)[11], and ordinance (*ordnung*)[12].

Yet what is meant with the use of such terminology and what is Luther's conception of »Be fruitful and multiply«? To this we note that, for Luther, »Be fruitful and multiply« is not in any way limited to mere words on a page of the Bible. This divine utterance establishes, determines, directs, compels, and governs creation from its inception until Christ returns – with exceptions belonging solely to those clearly given exemption from this ordinance. This word, therefore, not only establishes the sexes and their members, not to mention their desires and drives, but it also enables them with the capacity to procreate and be used as the God-ordained means by which new life is to be created. That is to say, the gift of being able to produce new life does not belong to the creature itself, it is an added gift given to the creature. While every aspect of this is affected and tarnished by sin, this word remains normative and effective, expressing itself through the daily furtherance of life, the continuance of coupling and marriage, the nurturing of the young, and via every other related element. These, we might say, are all visible and experienced manifestations of this constitutive word of God. Therefore, this word – »Be fruitful and multiply« – serves as the effective basis of Luther's marital theology. It establishes the purpose of marriage (i. e. offspring), creates the necessary drives and component parts which serve such ends, and imbues creation with the divinely given capacity to reproduce itself.

With the aforementioned understanding of Genesis 1:28 serving as the established basis for marriage and procreation, Luther then proceeds to discuss who is to be exempted from this ordinance. In discussing the exceptions given by Christ in Matthew 19, Luther returns again and again to the created norm effected by »Be fruitful and multiply«. Here, although this writing is primarily speaking to the topic of marriage, the topic (and debate) surrounding monastic vows and celibacy naturally appears. Luther writes,

> Apart from these three groups, let no man presume to be without a spouse. And whoever does not fall within one of these three categories should not consider anything except the estate of marriage. Otherwise it is simply impossible for you to remain righteous. For the Word of God which created you and said, »Be fruitful and multiply«, abides and rules within you; you can by no means ignore it, or you will be bound to commit heinous sins without end.

---

10 WA 10/II, p. 276,21–26. With »eyngepflantste natur und art« it should be noted that Luther is very near the semantic realm of »affectus quosdam naturales« as used by Melanchthon in his *Loci* with respect to procreation and other dispositions and drives in common with the animal realm.
11 WA 10/II, p. 277,25.
12 WA 10/II, p. 301,30.

Don't let yourself be fooled on this score, even if you should make ten oaths, vows, covenants, and adamantine or ironclad pledges. For as you cannot solemnly promise that you will not be a man or a woman (and if you should make such a promise it would be foolishness and of no avail since you cannot make yourself something other than what you are), so you cannot promise that you will not produce seed or multiply, unless you belong to one of the three categories mentioned above. And should you make such a promise, it too would be foolishness and of no avail, for to produce seed and to multiply is a matter of God's ordinance [*geschöpffe*], not your power [...]

Therefore, priests, monks, and nuns are duty-bound to forsake their vows whenever they find that God's ordinance to produce seed and to multiply is powerful and strong within them. They have no power by any authority, law, command, or vow to hinder this which God has created within them. If they do hinder it, however, you may be sure that they will not remain pure but inevitably besmirch themselves with secret sins or fornication. For they are simply incapable of resisting the word and ordinance of God within them. Matters will take their course as God has ordained[13].

After applying this foundational text to the topic of monastic vows and required celibacy, Luther then takes a closer look at the three exceptions enumerated by

---

13 LW 45, pp. 18f., cf. »Uber diße dreyerley vermeße sich keyn mensch on ehlich gemalh tzu seyn. Und wer sich nicht befindet ynn dißer dreyer tzal, der dencke nur tzum ehlichen leben, denn da wirt nicht anders auß, du bleybst nicht frum, das ist unmuglich, ßondern das wortt gottis, das sich geschaffen hatt und gesagt: Wachß und mehre dich, das bleybt und regirt ynn dyr, und kanst yhm dich mit nichte nemen, odder wirst grewliche sund on auffhören thun müssen«.
»Und da widder soll dich nicht yrren, ob du tzehen eyd, gelubd, bund und eyttel eyßen oder Adamanten pflicht gethan hettist. Denn als wenig du kanst geloben, das du keyn manß odder weybs bilde seyn woltist, und ob du es gelobist, ßo were es eyn narrheyt und gulte nichts, denn du kanst dich nicht anders machen, Alßo wenig kanstu auch geloben, das du dich nicht samen odder mehren wolltist, wo du dich nicht ynn der dreyer tzal eyne findist. Und ob du es gelobtist, ßo were es auch eyn narheytt unnd gullte nichts, denn samen und dich mehren ist gottis geschöpffe und nicht deyner macht [...]«.
»Alßo, das Pfaffen, Munch und Nonnen schuldig sind yhr gelubd tzulassen, wo sie sich finden, das gottis geschöpffe, sich tzu samen und tzu mehren ynn yhn krefftig und tuchtig ist und keyn macht haben, durch eynigen gewallt, gesetz, gepott, gelubd, solche gottis geschöpffe an yhn selbst hyndern. Hyndern sie es aber, ßo sey du gewiß, das sie nicht reyn bleyben und mit stummen sunden oder hurerey sich besuddeln müssen. Denn sie vermügen gotis wort und geschöpff an yhn nicht weren, es gehet, wie es gott gemacht hatt«. WA 10/II, p. 277,5–18, 21–28.
Luther also offers his advice in this section on the case where particularly the husband proves to be impotent when the marriage takes place and is, therefore, unable to consummate the marriage. In such circumstances, Luther's advice has proved to be most controversial. Nevertheless, it underscores his emphasis on the »outward, bodily« nature of marriage (LW 45, p. 25) and is in accord with his emphasis on the fundamental drive and purpose(s) of marriage.

Christ. In mentioning the first category, those eunuchs who have been exempted from birth, Luther simply remarks that

> [...] these we need not take into account, for God has himself exempted them and so formed them that the blessing of being able to multiply has not come to them. The injunction, »Be fruitful and multiply«, does not apply to them; just as when God creates a person crippled or blind, that person is not obligated to walk or see, because he cannot[14].

Concerning the second category of those exempted from marriage, namely those who have been made eunuchs by violence, Luther remarks once again that this group has been set outside of the natural ordinance and concludes his brief discussion by stating, »Let us pass them by also; for they too are set apart from the natural ordinance to ›Be fruitful and multiply‹, though only by an act of violence«[15]. Similarly, with the third category of those exempted from marriage, Luther notes that although they are capable of marriage, like Jeremiah they have been exempted by a special work of God's grace, one powerful enough that »›Be fruitful and multiply‹, has no place in him«[16].

Skipping over Luther's treatment of the impediments for marriage[17], we can deal with the second section of *Vom ehelichen Leben* in summary fashion. Here, we simply note that although Luther is largely speaking of matters not directly related to our theme, continuity of thought regarding Genesis 1:28 can also be observed in this section. To begin with, the first ground for divorce is based on marital fraud in the form of impotence or natural deficiencies. A similar case for divorce is established by refusal to pay the conjugal debt. Obviously, both of these instances can be connected with »Be fruitful and multiply« as well as to the second, post-lapsarian purpose for marriage (as an antidote against sinful lust)[18].

---

14 LW 45, pp. 19f., cf. »Diße laß man faren, die hatt gott selber außtzogen und alßo geschaffen, das der segen nicht uber sie komen ist, das sie sich mehren künden, die gehet das wortt nichts an ›Wachsset und mehret euch.‹ Gleych als wenn gott yemand lam oder blind schaffet, die sind frey, das sie nicht gehen noch sehen künden«. WA 10/II, p. 278,5–9.
15 LW 45, p. 21, cf. »Nu die lassen wyr auch faren, die sind auch auß dem naturlichen orden, tzu wachssen und mehren, gesetzt, wie wol mit gewalt und nur mit der thatt«. WA 10/II, p. 279,12–14.
16 LW 45, p. 21, cf. »›Wachsset und mehret euch‹ keyne stadt an yhm hab«. WA 10/II, p. 279,23.
17 In critiquing the church's teaching on impediments to marriage, it should be noted that Luther reaffirms his opposition to vows (and thus such vows serving as a legitimate impediment to marriage) as well as his teaching that abiding impotence from the outset of marriage should be regarded, *de facto*, as no marriage. Both of these instances simply underscore Luther's teaching on Genesis 1:28. See WA 10/II, pp. 284,21–28, 287,3–6.
18 Interestingly, up to this point in *Vom ehelichen Leben*, Luther has neither provided any substantial treatment on this matter nor established it as a fundamental purpose for marriage, though his

136 | Contesting a Verse

The final section of *Vom ehelichen Leben* is also only indirectly related to our theme. In this section, Luther largely takes on those who, on the basis of flawed reason, pagan philosophers, and bitter experience, despise women, marriage, and the work of marriage. This Luther views as a sort of blasphemy of the Word of God and a despising of His works. In other words, Luther's aim in this section is that his audience would observe marriage, woman, and procreation as the work and word of God that they are. It almost goes without saying that this is derived from his understanding of Genesis 1:28 (along with passages such as Genesis 1:31, 2:18, and Proverbs 18:22). Luther then goes on to argue that through the right recognition of God's works (through His word), the difficulties of marriage may be borne, and its blessings rightly recognized[19].

Luther then offers more explicit attention to the power and work of Genesis 1:28 as he draws this sermon to a close. In speaking of the problem of immorality and God's wrath over such sins, Luther writes,

> It is certainly a fact that he who refuses to marry must fall into immorality. How could it be otherwise, since God has created man and woman to produce seed and to multiply? Why should one not forestall immorality by means of marriage? For if special grace does not exempt a person, his nature must and will compel him to produce seed and to multiply. If this does not occur within marriage, how else can it occur except in fornication or secret sins? But, they say, suppose I am neither married nor immoral, and force myself to remain continent? Do you not hear that restraint is impossible without the special grace? For God's word does not admit of restraint; neither does it lie when it says, »Be fruitful and multiply« [Genesis 1:28]. You can neither escape nor restrain yourself from being fruitful and multiplying; it is God's ordinance and takes its course[20].

Luther then notes that physicians warn against restraining »this natural function« (*diſer natur werck*)[21] and that those who are barren often experience poorer

---

references to 1 Corinthians 7 in the second section clearly allude to this intention for marriage. This is first expressly mentioned in the third section. See WA 10/II, p. 292,8–22.

19 See WA 10/II, p. 298,9–30.
20 LW 45, p. 45, cf. »Freylich ists war, das der buben muß, der nicht ehlich wirt, wie sollts anders tzu gehen? syntemal got man und weyb, sich zu besamen und zu mehren, geschaffen hatt. Warumb kompt man aber der buberey nicht zuvor mit der ehe? Denn wo ßonderlich gnad nicht außtzeucht, da will und muß die natur sich samen und mehren. Geschichts nicht ynn der ehe, wo solls anders den ynn hurerey odder erger sunden geschehen? Wie denn, sprechen sie, wenn ich widder ehlich noch bubisch wurd und hielt mich mit gewalt? Horistu nicht, das ungehallten ist, on die sonder gnad? Denn gottis wortt lesst nicht hallten, leugt auch nicht, da er spricht: ›Wachßet und mehret euch‹, das wachßen unnd mehren kanstu wider wehren noch hallten, es ist gottis werck und gehet seynen weg«. WA 10/II, pp. 300,23–301,4.
21 LW 45, p. 45, cf. WA 10/II, p. 301,6.

health[22]. It is in this context that he makes a much-maligned comment about women who »ultimately bear themselves out« (*tzu letzt todt tragen*)[23] through childbirth. Nevertheless, as horrible as such a comment sounds, it might also be defended as consistent with Luther's thought regarding the purpose of marriage and woman's creation, as he also says that »this is the purpose for which they exist« (*sie sind drumb da*)[24]. Furthermore, it forms a sort of female counterpart to the demands and risks required of males in defending, governing, or even preaching, albeit in a manner that is somewhat difficult to compare. This does seem to be the track in which Luther is thinking, however, as he continues in the next paragraph:

> But the greatest good in married life, that which makes all suffering and labor worth while, is that God grants offspring and commands that they be brought up to worship and serve him. In all the world this is the noblest and most precious work, because to God there can be nothing dearer than the salvation of souls. Now since we are all duty bound to suffer death, if need be, that we might bring a single soul to God, you can see how rich the estate of marriage is in good works[25].

From there Luther continues to discuss how parents are apostles, bishops, and priests to their children inasmuch as it is they themselves who teach their children the Gospel. In this manner, Luther continues, marriage is *better* in the sight of God than celibacy, even if celibacy encompasses fewer troubles. Finally, Luther turns his attention to the question of how the children he is advocating will be fed. Here he points to Matthew 6:25, 33 and Psalm 37:25 (among other references to Scripture) and then, once more, returns to Genesis 1. This time, he points out the ordering with which God created all things. Namely, God created the world and all its provisions for the support of man, only later creating man and woman. Therefore, if a man finds that he is not fit for celibacy, let him marry. If it is sooner, so much the better. As far as supporting the family is concerned, Luther, having previously spoken of the importance of work, simply says, »Let God worry about

---

22 WA 10/II, pp. 11–13.
23 LW 45, p. 46, cf. WA 10/II, p. 301,13–15. Note that BOEHMER, Luthers Ehebuch, p. 57*, attempts to excuse Luther's statement regarding this matter. I am, however, not so much convinced that Luther was *merely* reflecting the medical wisdom of his day as much as he was emphasizing his teaching on Genesis 1:28.
24 LW 45, p. 46, cf. WA 10/II, p. 301,13–15.
25 LW 45, p. 46, cf. »Das aller best aber ym ehlichen leben, umb wilchs willen auch alles tzu leyden unnd tzu thun were, ist, das gott frucht gibt unnd befilht auff tzutzihen tzu gottis dienst, das ist auff erden das aller edlist theurist werck, weylt gott nicht liebers geschehen mag denn seelen erlößenn. Nu wyr denn alle schuldig sind, wo es nott were, tzu sterben, das wyr eyne seele zu gott bringen mochten, ßo sihestu, wie reych der ehlich stand ist von gutten werkenn [...]«. WA 10/II, p. 301,16–21.

how they and their children are to be fed. God makes children; he will surely also feed them«[26].

In the analysis above we have observed the foundational role of Genesis 1:28 for Luther's thought on marriage and the procreative nature of man and woman. Inasmuch as he applies the words of this verse directly (excluding only divine exception) to every man and woman, to their physical members, and their natural desires, Genesis 1:28 comprises both a very powerful polemic against monastic vows and mandated priestly celibacy. It also establishes a natural cornerstone for not only Luther's, but also the developing Wittenberg understanding of marriage. This understanding, though still acquiring its shape within the wider Reformation movement, would ultimately be further articulated throughout the course of the Wittenberg Reformation and then more widely embraced as a central reformatory understanding of marriage and the sexes in 1530 with the *Augsburg Confession*[27].

4.3 Initial Opposition

For the sake of reference, the general attack against Luther's teaching on »Be fruitful and multiply« was generally comprised of three components. To begin with, Luther's opponents interpreted Genesis 1:28 as a limited command lasting only until the earth was filled prior to Christ's coming. This command was viewed as applicable to Adam and Eve, Noah and his sons, and the Israelites. The second counterargument, and support for the first, was the objection that this imperative lacked the support of the ancient church. The main authority cited in this respect was generally Jerome, though occasionally Augustine was referenced as well. The preferred place of virginity and celibacy over marriage was also generally emphasized in the attack against »Be fruitful and multiply«. Finally, comparison was also made between Luther's understanding of Genesis 1:28 and various heretical groups or individuals. Here we note once again the teachings of Jovinian as well as the followers of Hus, the Pickards, and the Waldensians[28].

---

26 LW 45, p. 48, cf. »[…] lasße gott sorgen, wie sie mit yhren kindern erneeret werden. Got macht kinder, der wirt sie auch wol erneeren«. WA 10/II, p. 304,1–2.
27 See BSELK, p. 137 (CA 23, 6). See also Chapter 5.
28 The titles of various heretical groups were freely and liberally applied to Luther and the early evangelical movement. The Waldensians were the followers of one Peter of Waldes who founded a lay-preaching movement from Lyon in the twelfth century which then spread into neighboring regions. See Walter NIGG, Das Buch der Ketzer, Zürich 1949, pp. 208–225. Jan Hus (condemned to death 1415) was the leader of a reformation movement in Bohemia. »Pickards« is often another designation for the followers of Hus – the Bohemian Brethren. For more on the significance of this epithet during the Reformation and Luther's relationship to the Hussites, see Thomas KAUFMANN,

We might also note that, theologically, Genesis 1:28 (and its repetitions in Genesis 8:17, 9:1 and 9:7) tended to be allied closely with corresponding interpretations of Matthew 19 and 1 Corinthians 7 by Luther and colleagues such as Melanchthon, Jonas, and Bugenhagen. In other words, their interpretations of the latter passages depend in large part on their understanding of Genesis. On the Wittenberg side, because of the general and enduring nature of the Edenic imperative, the counsel of St. Paul to the Corinthians, that »it is better to marry than to burn«, (1 Corinthians 7:9) was interpreted in the light of the abiding efficacy of God's word in Genesis. Luther's opposition, however, interpreted Genesis in light of its understanding of Matthew 19 and 1 Corinthians 7. Thus, they recognized no durative command and saw only sinful lust as the compelling force behind the counsel to marry. In the same way, Jesus's list of those exempted from marriage was understood as an exceptional gift and exemption from the norm of Genesis 1, according to Luther. For his opposition, however, it was understood as something which is humanly possible should one rightly seek such a divine gift. Very often, then, comments on Genesis 1:28 are found in tandem with these verses. Along the same lines, these verses often reflected an understanding of Genesis 1:28 even if the latter was not mentioned.

Johann Faber

While it should be clear from the discussion above that Luther's *Vom ehelichen Leben* was not without its own polemical content, particularly as concerns matters such as celibacy and the contemporary disdainful views toward women and marriage present in Luther's day, it does not seem to have been written as a polemical work directed against any particular opponent[29]. Nevertheless, concurrent with the printing of *Vom ehelichen Leben*, the first, or arguably the second[30], outright attack on Luther's interpretation of Genesis 1:28 appeared. The work, in this case, was *Opus adversus nova quaedam et a Christiana religione prorsus aliena dogmata*

Der Anfang der Reformation. Studien zur Kontextualität der Theologie, Publizistik und Inszenierung Luthers und der reformatorischen Bewegung, Tübingen 2012, pp. 30–67.

29 Doubtless, however, Luther would have had in mind the critiques and attacks which had appeared previously from Murner, Emser, and others.

30 As noted previously with Thomas Murner's *An den Großmechtigsten vn[d] Durchlüchtigste[n] adel tütscher nation* (1520), the exact circumstances under which Genesis 1:28 first appeared as a topic of debate vs. Luther – even though Luther had not yet written about Genesis 1:28 – remain a matter of speculation. One possibility for the unprovoked appearance of this verse was to show an association with the seemingly well-known teachings of heretical groups such as Pickards, Waldensians and those in Bohemia, thereby discrediting Luther. In the case of Faber's *Opus adversus nova quaedam [...] Dogmata M. Lutheri*, it is possible that he is attempting to refute various writings of Luther in a collected work organized around Luther's *Von dem Papstum in Rom*. Nevertheless, as with Murner, the origin for Faber's concern with Genesis 1:28 remains elusive.

Martini Lutheri[31]. Its author was Johann Faber, the general vicar of Constance, who had come to Rome in 1521 in the hopes of finding fortune with Pope Leo X. Nevertheless, following the untimely demise of the pontiff, Faber found himself largely shut out of any beneficial association with his predecessor, Adrian[32]. Thus, the work itself was an attempt by Faber to achieve sought-after fortune by proving, with overwhelming use of citations and apparent show of learning, that Luther's teachings were in error[33]. More pertinent to our own topic, although the nearly six-hundred-page work was primarily in answer to Luther's *Von dem Papstum in Rom* (and thus overwhelmingly concerned with teachings about the papacy and church), it dealt more extensively with the topic of priestly marriage than Luther's own treatment of priestly marriage in his original work necessarily warranted[34].

Turning to Faber's arguments against priestly marriage, we find that his attack is generally comprised of a large collection of biblical, classical, and ecclesiastical authorities (even the Quran is included!)[35] and shows a great deal of contempt for marriage and women[36], despite alluding to a high regard for the former[37]. With respect to the command to »Be fruitful and multiply«, it is mentioned three times in the relevant segment of the discussion. The first time, in citing his own praise of marriage, Faber mentions (among other things) that the command to »Be fruitful

---

31 Johann FABRI, IOANNIS FABRI EPISCOPI CONSTANTIENSIS IN SPIRITVALIBVS VICARII OPVS ADVERSVS NOVA QVAEDAM ET A CHRISTIANA RELIGIONE PRORSVS ALIENA DOGMATA MARTINI LVTHERI, Rome 1522, URL: <https://opacplus.bsb-muenchen.de/title/BV001520350> (14 Oct 2021). This work was subsequently republished in Leipzig (1523) and then once again under the title Johann FABRI, Mallevs Ioannis Fabri Doctoris Celeberrimi […] in hæresim Lutheranā, iam denuo uehemētiori studio & labore recognitus, in Tractatus etiam & Paragraphos diuisus, Cologne 1524 (VD16 F 214). See BORNKAMM/BORNKAMM, Luther in Mid-Career, p. 262, fn. 34. For a brief history of this work, both in Rome and Germany, see also Otto CLEMEN, Die Luterisch Strebkatz, in: Archiv für Reformationsgeschichte 2 (1905), pp. 78–93, at p. 85.

32 Karl SCHOTTENLOHER, Johann Fabri in Rom, nach einem Berichte Jakob Zieglers, in: Archiv für Reformationsgeschichte 5 (1907/1908), pp. 31–46, discusses the evidence for Johann Faber's presence in Rome and his hope to attain not merely papal recognition, but also money through the composition of *Opus adversus nova quaedam […]*. According to Schottenloher, Ziegler, a contemporary theologian also in Rome, was rather circumspect both with respect to Faber's motives as well as his scholarly ability. See also KAWERAU, Die Reformation und die Ehe, pp. 21f., for an overview of Faber's defense of celibacy.

33 KAWERAU, Die Reformation und die Ehe, p. 21, notes that Faber's efforts were eventually rewarded in being subsequently awarded the bishopric of Vienna.

34 See BUCKWALTER, Priesterehe, p. 128. Luther's treatment of priestly marriage is found in WA 6, p. 307,26–27. WA 12, p. 82, however, states that Faber's work was largely aimed against *Resolutio super propositione XIII. de potestate Papae*. This work, however, was likewise similarly concerned with the papacy and not with the marriage of priests.

35 FABRI, IOANNIS FABRI EPISCOPI, Qiiir (7/8).

36 See, for example, ibid., Qi^v–ii^v.

37 Ibid., Qii^v.

and multiply« was given by God particularly to Noah and his family following the Flood[38]. He later refers to the Talmudic opinion that this command was given to Noah and his sons after the Flood, though during the Flood the men on the ark kept themselves apart from the women[39]. The final time this imperative is mentioned, Faber acknowledges that some have objected to celibacy based on Genesis's words, »Be fruitful and multiply and fill the earth«, or the Old Testament's malediction of barrenness. To this, however, Faber simply quotes Jerome's statement that marriage was given in order to fill the earth, celibacy to fill heaven. The former purpose was being fulfilled in the multiple wives of Abraham and Jacob. Yet, in accordance with St. Paul's counsel, Faber maintains that New Testament teaching decisively favors celibacy. The time is, after all, short, and Christians are to be concerned with the things of God and not with the things of the world (i. e. pleasing a spouse)[40].

Luther evidently became aware of Faber's writing in the spring of 1523 but had no desire to respond directly to his critic. Kawerau notes that Luther avoided answering Faber, whom he viewed as an »arch fool« (*Erznarren*) and »ass's head« (*Eselskopf*), even though Faber's claims in favor of the celibate life would eventually be met in Luther's writing on *Das siebente Kapitel St. Pauli zu den Korinthern*«[41]. Officially, though, Luther referred the Wittenberg defense to Justus Jonas who had been one of the first priests to marry[42]. Both Luther's and Jonas's writings would appear in print in August 1523 and will be addressed in the next section.

---

38 Ibid., Qii^v.
39 Ibid., Qiii (6/8).
40 »Fuere nonnulli, qui obiecere mihi scriptum in genesi, Crescite, & multiplicamini, & replete terram, & maledicta sterilis, que non parit semen in Israel. Nubebant omnes & nubebantur & derelictis parentibus, fiebant una caro, quibus Iaconismo illo respondeo, matrimonio repleri terrā, celibatu coelū. Inde forte factum est, ut fuerit Abraam trigamus, & Iacob quadrigamus scilicet Lyæ/Rachel/Bale/&Selphe. Tunc enim erat replēda terra, nunc coelum. Vnde Hierony.aduersus Heluidium. Quando uox illa pertonuit, Tempus breuiatum est. Reliquum est, ut qui habent uxores, sic sint, quasi non habeant, adhaerentes dño, unus cum eo efficimur spiritus. Et quare? quia qui sine uxore est, cogitat ea, quæ dei sunt, quomodo placeat deo. Qui autem cum uxore est, sollicitus est quæ sunt huius mundi, quomodo placeat uxori. Et diuisa est mulier & uirgo, quæ non est nupta, cogitat que sunt dei, ut sit sancta spiritu & corpore. Nam quæ nupta est, cogitat quæ sunt mūdi, quomodo placeat uiro«. Ibid., Qiii (7–8/8).
41 Kawerau, Die Reformation und die Ehe, p. 22.
42 Ibid., p. 22.

Thomas Murner

In the final days of 1522, Thomas Murner's work, *Vom großen lutherischen Narren*, was published in Strasbourg[43]. This unique work depicted Luther's »foolishness« in over two hundred pages of rhymed meter with numerous woodcuts. Among the many criticisms, caricatures, attacks, and mockeries of »*lutherisch*« teaching which are to be found in this work, a caricature of Luther's teaching regarding »Be fruitful and multiply« is also present.

The most significant and noticeable of these appears in the middle third of the work in which a running dialogue is staged between Murner and the great fool (*der groß Narr*). In this dialogue, the *Narr* (i. e. Luther) is depicted as having taken off his monks' cowl so as to embrace the world and, especially, women under the guise of Genesis 1:28. Rhymed references to the ordering of creation (*seinen orden fieren*), sowing one's wild oats (*Bůbelieren*), and filling the world with children (*Die welt mit lieben kinden meren*) are intended to mock aspects of Luther's teaching on Genesis 1:28 as expounded by Luther in *Vom ehelichen Leben* and *De votis monasticis*[44].

A second occurrence deserving mention takes place in the penultimate section of the book in which Luther offers his daughter to Murner in marriage – if Murner will agree to become »Lutheran«. Murner stages this scene from the nuptial blessing all the way to the banquet and then the bridal bed. Throughout the scene, the Murner character being offered Luther's daughter is seen to entertain Luther's proposal. Even more, at the wedding banquet, we hear Luther making a speech in which the »*lutherisch*« emphasis on Genesis 1:28 is caricatured[45]. It is then finally in the bridal chamber that the scene culminates and Murner is seen in a woodcut to drive Luther's daughter away and decisively reject Luther's offer. Interestingly, the final

---

43 Thomas MURNER, Uon dem grossen Luthersichen Narren wie in doctor Murner beschworen hat [et]č, Strasbourg 1522 (VD16 M 7088). KAWERAU, Die Reformation und die Ehe, p. 20, mentions the publication date as »in den letzten Tagen des Jahres 1522«.

44 »Es müst sunst seinen orden fieren/So laufft es lieber Bůbelieren/Und hofft es wöl sich bald nit schemen/Zů der ee ein iunckfraw nemen/Die welt mit lieben kinden meren/Wie dan der luther das kan weren […]«. MURNER, Uon dem grossen Luthersichen Narren, Ri^v.

45 Murner's Luther character is seen to say, »Nun lieber murner gůter frindt/Und dochtermā meins lieben kind/Ich wünsch dir glück und selikeit/Got wöl euch behüten alle beid/Vor allem unfal und vor leid/Der behüt euch beid in allen sachen/Das ir vil hübscher kinder machen/Und sehen euwere kinder furt/Lange zeit in die fierd geburt/So du nun auch bist lutherisch worden/Und unserm und eelichen orden«. Ibid., b^{2}ii^r.

For further commentary on Murner's *Von dem Grossen Lutherischen Narren*, see also Barbara KÖNNEKER, Die deutsche Literatur der Reformationszeit. Kommentar zu einer Epoche, München 1975, pp. 116–124, including notes on the possible interpretation of the above-mentioned section as commentary on the social implications of Luther's teachings (p. 120).

section of the pamphlet shows Luther's death and burial in which Murner attempts to help Luther repent from his foolishness, but in vain.

Johann Cochlaeus

Only months after the printing of Faber's *Opus adversus* and Murner's *Vom großen lutherischen Narren*, another critical writing against Luther – also including reference to Genesis 1:28 – appeared. On 23 February 1523, *Glosse und Kommentar auf 154 Artikel*, by Johann Cochlaeus came off the press[46]. While this writing dealt primarily with the nature of the Law, faith, what the Mass is, and whether it is a good work, the topic of »Be fruitful and multiply« (*wachßen und mehren euch*) appears on four occasions. The first two appearances occur in connection with Cochlaeus's response to Luther's view of the history and nature of what the Law is. In these instances, Cochlaeus recounts God's commands, first to Adam and Eve, and then later to Noah. These references to »wachßen und mehren« appear to have little or no polemical purpose, unless they are perhaps to blithely emphasize the command to »Be fruitful and multiply« as something limited to former times[47].

More important references to Genesis 1:28 appear in Cochlaeus's response to Luther's 6th and 154th Articles, respectively. The first reference comes as Cochlaeus argues that the Law has differing applicability for various persons as he attacks Luther's assertion that it applies to all in the same way. Here, in addition to Cochlaeus's frequent criticism of Luther's »Hussite« views, which essentially reduced men and women to the level of cattle, Cochlaeus also levels the charge that Luther merely propagated Grubenheimer teachings and was leading people toward libertinism[48]. Cochlaeus took particular offense to Luther's leveling of the

---

46 The timespan and events surrounding the writing and publication of this writing are somewhat complicated and span from the time following Luther's appearance at Worms up until February, and then September, of 1523. This was further complicated by publishing difficulties. For this, see Adolf LAUBE, Das Gespann Cochlaeus/Dietenberger im Kampf gegen Luther, in: Archiv für Reformationsgeschichte 87 (1996), pp. 119–135, at p. 125. At any rate, we can rest assured that Cochlaeus did not heed the warning issued by Justus Jonas in Worms that he should not publish any polemical writings against Luther. Here see Martin LEHMANN, Justus Jonas, Loyal Reformer, Minneapolis 1963, p. 32. For a more detailed account of the origins of Cochlaeus's *Glosse und Kommentar*, see LAUBE/WEISS, Flugschriften, p. 412.

47 Johannes COCHLAEUS, Glos vñ Cōment Doc. Johānes dobneck Cochleus von Wendelstein, vff CLIIII. Articklen gezogen vß einem Sermon Doc. mar. Luterß von der heiligen meß vñ nüem Testamēt, Strasbourg 1523 (VD16 C 4319), Biii[v], Biiii[v].

48 Ibid., Fi[r], charges that Luther opens the door for men and women to merely end up with *hundzhochzeiten*. A *hundzhochzeit* was a reference to wild and unsanctioned forms of married life. Hans Sachs used the expression in one of his *Fastnachtspiele*: »Es geht wie auff einer Hundshochzeit zu, wenig zu fressen, vil zu lauffen«. – H. SACHS, Fastnachtsspiel, III, CCCXL, 2. Cited from: Hundshochzeit, in: Karl Friedrich Wilhelm WANDER, Deutsches Sprichwörter-Lexikon. Hausschatz

various estates in the name of Baptism, while ridiculing the use of Genesis 1:28 as a sanctimonious cover for the lust of Luther's followers[49]. The latter reference to Genesis 1:28, occurring in response to Luther's 154th Article, essentially repeats the same objections to Luther's teachings[50].

4.4 Martin Luther and the Wittenberg Defense

While there was no direct reaction from Luther to Cochlaeus[51] and there was only limited response by Luther to Faber (and that only after Easter of 1523), 1523 gave rise to what amounted to something of a minor theological controversy amid the greater themes of the early Wittenberg Reformation. Luther and his followers, though not with perfect consistency and regularity, were found to regularly call upon Genesis 1:28 in their attack against monastic celibacy, support for priestly marriage, and in their understanding of marriage and humanity in general. Their opposition, as we have seen, denied the ongoing imperative and ordinance of »Be fruitful and multiply«, advocated the greater spiritual worth of celibacy, and associated Luther's teaching as being in league with any number of heretic and schismatic groups, all while viewing Genesis 1:28 as pious language providing cover for sinful lust.

---

für das deutsche Volk, Leipzig 1870, vol. 2, p. 906. Luther also used this expression, as can be seen in WA 30/II, p. 142,17–18.

49 »Sant Pauls sagt/in einem cörper Christi sein vil glid[er]/nit allein das aug/nit allein dz gehör/sunder es sein teilungē der gnaden/d[er] diensten und d[er] wirckungen/was gauckelstu dan mit deinem hussischen buntschů/dz wir alle gleich seyen/und uf ein weiß leben sollen als die kü? Wan wir dir dz zůliessen (das doch unmüglich ist) so woltstu fileicht darnach gar grůbenheimer uß unß machen/dz wir huntzhochzeit hielten/und alle durch einand[er] gleich gülten/es wer schwester oder dochter/sprechst wir werē alle gleiche Christen/und schwester uñ brüder in Christo uß dē tauff/ züchst herfür die alten wort gottes/wachßen und mehren euch/das wer ein lust deins jungen anhangs«. Cochlaeus, Glos vñ Cōment, Fi[r].

A further jab at Luther with the epitaph of Hussite is made shortly later (Fii[r]) when Cochlaeus once again calls Luther a disciple of Johan Hus for distinguishing between Law and Counsels (*Rät*), including St. Paul's counsel of virginity over marriage.

50 »Nun ist ye einē buntschů vil leidlicher vil sündē, aber vil me vor gesetzē/darū sagt Luther/lassen unß hütē für sünde/aber vil me vor gesetzē. Die and[er] ursach/Luther wil die hussen vertedingē und dē grůbenheimern zů Behem liebkosen/nun achtē die hussen d[er] gesatz vil weniger dā d[er] sünden/ uñ die grůbēheimer mögē in irē grüfften gar kein gesatz leidē/wed[er] götlichs noch menschlichs/dan allein dz Crescite et multiplicamini«. Ibid., O²iiii[r].

51 Even though Luther's and Cochlaeus's paths overlapped on several occasions – most notably at Worms in 1521 –, Luther responded only once to Johann Cochlaeus throughout his career. Earlier in 1523 Luther penned *Adversus armatum virum Cocleum* (WA 11, pp. 292–306).

In any case, 1523 witnessed an increase in debate and treatment over this verse for several reasons. First, there was a need to defend evangelical teachings against the sharp counterattacks which flared up following Luther's broadside against monastic vows[52]. Second, there was a need to strengthen and encourage those who had broken with monastic practice and priestly celibacy as well as those who were wavering or still unnecessarily entrapped by its vows. Thus, due to the plethora of polemical writings which appeared against Luther's position, a strong reinforcement of his teachings appeared in the spring of 1523. In Wittenberg circles alone, Luther treated the verse in sermons, biblical commentary, and in the pamphlet, *Ursach und Antwort, dass Jungfrauen Klöster verlassen mögen*. Justus Jonas and Philipp Melanchthon also produced writings that showcased a similar understanding of Genesis 1:28. At least one more opponent, Johann Dietenberger, attacked the Wittenberg reformer over this teaching in this same year. In parallel manifestations of this controversy, 1523 also marked a general increase in the use of this verse as observed in publications in Germany[53]; additionally, the verse seems to have been particularly debated in the city of Erfurt[54]. That is all to say, although one should not pretend that *crescite et multiplicamini* was somehow the epitome and heart of Reformation teaching, it is fair to say that it did have its own place amongst the many matters of debate and that the contours of the argument were reasonably well defined.

Taking a closer look at the Wittenberg response, we observe that at the end of March and then especially in April of 1523, »Be fruitful and multiply« seemed to be on Luther's mind. In point of fact, it appeared in his sermons on Genesis already on 12 April and then again on 26 April, it is one of the major themes of his sermon for 7 April, and also served as an important theme of *Ursach und Antwort, dass Jungfrauen Klöster verlassen mögen*, which was printed on 10 April[55]. Continuing

---

52 In addition to previously mentioned works, further responses also emerged. One example, Kaspar Schatzgeyer, Scrvtinivm Divinae Scriptvrae, pro conciliatione dissidentium dogmatum circa subscriptas materias […], Augsburg 1522 (VD16 S 2336), was a substantial effort aimed at refuting Luther's *De votis monasticis iudicium* on the basis of Scripture. Genesis 1[:28] is referenced twice in this work (eeii^r–ii^v; zziiii^r–iiii^v).

53 See Klawitter, Forceful and Fruitful, pp. 177–182.

54 See Excursus below, pp. 133ff.

55 We might additionally note that Johann Brießmann also released a rejoinder to Schatzgeyer's attack on *De votis monasticis iudicium* on 12 April of this same year. While this study will not give Brießman's work greater attention, we can note that while he does not directly reference Genesis 1:28, there does seem to be at least one section where he comes remarkably close in his argumentation to calling upon the verse, or perhaps does so in a periphrastic manner. See Joannes Briesmann, IOANNIS BRIESMANNI AD CASPAris Schatzgeyri Minoritae plicas responsio, pro Lutherano libello de uotis monasticis. ITEM M.Lutheri ad Briesmannum Epistola, de eodem. […], Strasbourg 1523 (VD16 B 8280), particularly d4^r–d4^v, where he writes, »Obsecro: nonne miraculum est, si quispiam

into May and the summer of 1523, Luther once again addressed Genesis 1:28 on 17 May and 5 July in his Genesis sermons. Additionally, he used it as his basis for opposing vows of celibacy that same month in *Wider die Verkehrer und Falscher kaiserlichs Mandats*. Then, in August, a second round of attention was given to this primordial blessing as Luther came out with his commentary on 1 Corinthians 7 and, perhaps equally significant, Justus Jonas dealt with marriage matters in *Adversus Johannem Fabrem*. In the following pages we will look more closely at the relevant portions of each of these texts.

The first instance of these writings and sermons to explicitly address Genesis 1:28 arrived with Luther's sermon for the Tuesday after Easter[56]. In this sermon Luther addressed good works, spoke out against the Roman Mass, and then turned his attention to monastic vows and marriage. In speaking on monastic vows and marriage vis-à-vis Genesis 1:28, Luther argued as follows:

> That the priests should contract marriage, would be so that fornication might cease. God has created such that the two should be united. The work of God is not to be resisted. It is not in our power that a man should be a woman. Furthermore, there is also the word of God, »Increase and multiply«. It is therefore not God's doing *for* a woman not to have a man. That the woman bears children is also natural, even as *it is natural* for a tree to bear fruit. Furthermore, where there is a man, marriage should not be hindered. A young nun is not able not to be a woman; therefore she does not have control of herself; as God also says »Increase and multiply.« So also with the man, if God does not give to him a gift, he ought to receive a woman as wife; neither a vow nor parents *ought to* impede, for »I myself, God, create you as a male«, etc. The estate of marriage is not only commanded but also instituted by God. A vow and commands might well be a vow and commands, *yet* the work of God we cannot impede. For He says, »This woman I have created that she should be fruitful, but in fact the vow prevails over My will«. We know that it is not customary for us not to keep the commands of God. He Himself has commanded that we should not commit adultery, we should not steal, etc., thus we should abide in the old faith. If there is someone who fights against this, let him grumble. If you think that you are not exempted, then abide in your vocation. If not, say, »My God and His commandment are above every vow and institution of the papacy«, and do this so that you may have a wife. Further, *do this* that indeed others may take wives[57].

---

contra legem naturæ (quam etiam deu stabiliuit, quando masculum & foeminā creauit, Genesis I.) perpetuo coelebs singulari dei dono uixerit?«.
56 Sermon for 7 April 1523 (WA 11, pp. 92–94). The exact relationship with Luther's sermon preached in Kemberg on that same day (WA 11, pp. 87–91) is difficult to ascertain.
57 »Quod presbyteri contrahant matrimonium, fit, ut scortatio cesset. Deus facit, ut copulentur duo. Operi dei non resistendum, in nostra potestate non est, ut vir sit mulier, tandem eciam opus dei est ›Crescite et multiplicamini‹. Non est igitur in manu dei mulierem virum non habere, quod mulier

While Luther's line of argument does not fundamentally change anything from the teaching expounded upon in *Vom ehelichen Leben,* his distinction between something on the order of a commandment as opposed to the work of God (*opus dei*) clearly demonstrates the force which he understands Genesis 1:28 to contain. Furthermore, Luther's argument is clear: unless God has given unmistakable evidence that a commandment or calling has been lifted, then the old order must abide. In that respect, it is possible to see that apart from a clear word of Scripture, Luther exhorted his hearers to remain unmoved by the many quotations of the philosophers and church fathers which his opponents were in the habit of bringing forward.

Interestingly, this sermon took place three days after twelve nuns escaped from the convent in Nimbschen (with Luther's knowledge and approval) and the very day that nine of them (a number that included Katharina von Bora, Luther's later wife) arrived at Luther's residence in Wittenberg[58]. Thus, it is not too unlikely that these events provided special impetus to once again review for the congregation the reasons why vows could be broken and the monastic life abandoned.

On 10 April, three days after this sermon, Luther made a public report of the events which had transpired in a pamphlet which was dedicated to Leonhard Koppe, the man who had helped smuggle the nuns away from the cloister the previous week. This pamphlet, *Ursach und Antwort, dass Jungfrauen Klöster verlassen mögen,* served several purposes, not least of which was to defend the escaped nuns of wrongdoing and to highlight the unjust plight to which they had been subjected.

For our purposes, this pamphlet once again gave Luther the opportunity to exalt the God-given primacy of marriage over against the claims of any monastic vows which would impinge upon it. Not surprisingly, Genesis 1:28 once again found a place in Luther's argumentation in this writing. After explaining that he did not want the matter to remain hidden and that he wanted to remove suspicion from

---

parit filios, et naturale est ut arbori fructus ferre. Non est impediendum matrimonium, ubi vir est. Monialis non potest non esse mulier, igitur sui non compos est, eciam deus dicit ›Crescite et multiplicamini‹. Ita cum viro, si deus gratiam ei non dat, debet mulierem accipere, neque votum neque parens impedire, quia ›ego deus creo te in virum‹ etc. Eelich stand ist gepoten non solum, sed et eingesetzt. Votum et praecepta sint votum et praecepta, dei opus non possumus impedire, quia dicit ›hanc mulierem creavi, ut esset ferax‹, sed votum plus valet quam mea voluntas. Scimus non esse in consuetudine, quod dei praecepta non servemus, is praecepit, ut non committamus adulterium, furemur etc. darumb sol wir manere in veteri fide. Si aliquis est qui huic renititur, laß in murren. Si sentis te non esse außzogen, mane in vocatione tua. Sin non, dic ›deus meus et eius praeceptum est super omnia vota et Papae instituta‹ et illud fac ut habeas mulierem. Alterum quod quidem alii accipiant uxores«. WA 11, pp. 93,23–94,1.

58 This was a matter that would eventually deplete Luther's resources as he was left to support them and thus led to his chastisement of the Wittenberg congregation for not providing greater assistance (WA 11, pp. 387f.). See also BORNKAMM/BORNKAMM, Luther in Mid-Career, p. 255, fn. 10, and pp. 258f.

the escaped nuns, Luther continued by warning parents against interring their children in the cloisters and by offering a criticism of monastic life over against God's creation, marriage. He writes:

> Fourth, no matter how much one must be ashamed on account of this reason, it is nevertheless the greatest reason why one must abandon cloister and habit. Namely: it is impossible for the gift of chastity to be as common as the cloisters. Consider that a woman's body is not created to be a virgin, but rather to bear children as Genesis 1 *says*. God did not speak solely to Adam, but also to Eve, »Be fruitful and multiply«, as also the various parts of the woman's body – set in place by God for this very purpose! – show. And neither was this simply the case for one or two women. Rather it has been said to all and excluded none, except for those whom God Himself excludes, not through our vow or free will, but through His own counsel and powerful will. Where He does not do such, the woman ought to remain a woman and bear fruit. It is for this purpose that God has created her and she cannot improve on that which He has made.
>
> The same can be said when He [God] cursed Eve, for He took from her neither her womanly body nor her members, neither did He withdraw the blessing which He had pronounced over her, that she should be fruitful. Rather, He confirmed the same and says, »I will create labor for you, when you become pregnant.« This burden is not pronounced over one or two women, rather over all. The words sound as though God is confident, that all women would become pregnant and should bear this difficulty – excepting only those whom He Himself excepts. Against this neither vow nor promise is able to be valid or kept, for it is God's word and power[59].

---

59 »Auffs vierde, Wie wol man sich dißer ursach schier schemen mus, so ists doch fast der grossisten eyne, kloster und kappen ʒu lassen: Nemlich das unmuglich ist, die gabe der keuscheyt so gemeyne sey als die kloster sind. Denn eyn weybs bild ist nicht geschaffen, jungfraw ʒu seyn, sondern kinder zu tragen wie Gen. 1. Gott sprach nicht Alleyne ʒu Adam, sondern auch zu Heva ›seyt fruchtbar und mehret euch‹, wie das auch die leyblichen gelidmas weyblichs leybs, von Gott da ʒu eyngeseʒt, beweyßen. Und solchs ist nicht ʒu eynem weyb noch ʒu ʒweyen, sondern ʒu allen gesagt und keyne ausgeschlossen, Got zihe sie den selber aus nicht durch unser gelubd odder freyen willen, sondern durch seynen eygen radt und willen mechtiglich. Wo er das nicht thutt, soll ein weybs bild ein weyb bleyben, frucht tragen, daʒu es gott geschaffen hat, und nicht besser machen den ers gemacht hatt«.
»Item da er Heva verfluchte, nam er yhr nicht den weyblichen leyb noch weybische gelidmas, Widderrieff auch nicht seynen gesprochen segen uber sie, das sie sollt fruchtbar seyn, sondern bestettigt den selben und spricht ›Ich will dyr viel muhe schaffen, wen du schwanger gehest‹. Dyße plage ist auch nicht uber eyns odder ʒwey weyber gesagt, sondern uber alle, das die wortt lautten, als sey got gewißß, das alle weyber werden schwanger seyn und sollen diße plage tragen, on wilche er selbs aus nympt. Da widder kan yhe keyn gelubt noch bund gelten noch hallten, Denn es ist gottis wort und gemechte«. WA 11, p. 398,1–20.

From the above paragraphs, it is worth noting Luther's emphasis upon the universal applicability (barring particular and mightily proven exceptions) of God's Word spoken in Genesis 1:28. Furthermore, he notes that this blessing and ordinance was not taken away with the fall into sin; rather, it was confirmed by the curse. While no direct opponents were cited by such argumentation, it is clear that this »answer« responds fittingly to the attacks that had been lodged by Luther's opponents, namely, that Genesis 1:28 was formerly for the populating of the earth while celibacy was now for filling heaven.

There is a third instance of Luther's apparent focus upon the role of Genesis 1:28 in the ongoing debates from the spring of 1523 that we will now examine. Beginning on 22 March 1523 and running well into 1524, Luther preached a series of sermons that worked their way through the book of Genesis. While his motivation for preaching through Genesis may not be completely clear, what is clear is that the timing of his treatment of chapters one, eight, and nine – with their textual references to »Be fruitful and multiply« – came at a time when questions of man's nature and God's creative will for humanity were significant items of concern and debate[60]. For the purposes of this study, a brief review of the apparent content of Luther's sermons will be beneficial.

While Luther first broached the topic of Genesis 1:28 on the first Sunday after Easter[61], he had presented some of his theological grounding in the weeks prior to this. For example, in a sermon preached on 22 March, Luther emphasized the fact that the creative Word which had spoken was certainly divine and not itself created. Moreover, the speaking itself effected the creation of all created things[62]. Furthermore, the creative word spoken is not to be understood as a transitory word, but a word which was, is, and will be spoken. That is to say, the utterances of this word constantly reverberate without cessation as long as God wills creation

---

60 Note that Luther's sermons on Genesis 1 took place in late March and early April 1523, while his sermons on Genesis 8 and 9 took place in July (WA 14, p. 95). While it would be speculative to say whether or not the Genesis sermons influenced the sermons and writings dealing with priestly marriage and monastic vows, there is indeed a relative chronological correlation between the pertinent Genesis sermons and the waves of response to the related controversies.

For a detailed overview of Luther's Genesis sermons (i. e. *Declamationes*), their transcription, compilation, and the relative valuing of the various hands, see WA 14, pp. iii–xvii, pp. 92–94. Ibid., pp. 95f. contains a relevant chart for the dating of the sermons. See also HIEBSCH, Figura ecclesiae, esp. pp. 16–25, 31–33. Note that it was a compilation of these sermons that would later become the published Genesis sermons of 1527.

61 12 April 1523 (WA 14, p. 109).

62 WA 14, p. 100,24–25.

to continue[63]. According to Roth's notes, »Therefore we see that the earth is filled through the daily working of God, through daily speaking«[64].

The following week, on Palm Sunday, Luther further emphasized the creative and continuous activity of the Word as he pointed out that »this word through which He created the sun, is that which still sustains the sun in its course so that it abides«[65]. Later in the same sermon, Luther addressed the distinction between the creation and the blessing. Specifically, he considered the blessing to be a special work of creation *added* to the creature. Yet, although it is something added to the creature, the blessing causes it to be implanted in the creature's nature and being[66].

Such discussions in the sermons of 22 and 29 March offer a new level of detail to Luther's understanding of God's creative word which previously had not been demonstrated. Obviously, the direct connection of the creative word to the ongoing sustenance of creation – and, by implication, of mankind – is significant for Luther's understanding of the divine utterance, »Be fruitful and multiply«. Indeed, Luther's understanding of that primordial blessing must be understood in light of these thoughts.

As mentioned previously, it is first on 12 April that Luther finally arrived at Genesis 1:28 in this series of sermons (quite timely when one considers the concurrent events going on in Wittenberg!). For our purposes, this sermon offers perhaps the most expansive exposition of our topic (and its polemical application) that we have yet observed and is to be numbered among the most comprehensive treatments of our topic during this period next to *Vom ehelichen Leben* and Justus Jonas's response to Faber later that same year. Georg Rörer's sermon notes on this passage read as follows:

---

63 WA 14, p. 104,13–15.

64 »Videmus itaque, quod terra plena est durch tegliche wirgkung Gottes, durchs tegliche sprechen«. WA 14, p. 105,24–25.

65 »Hoc verbum per quod creavit solem, illud adhuc sustenat solem in suo cursu, ut maneat«. WA 14, p. 107,6–7 (Rörer).

66 »Hic dat benedictionem quod antea non fecit, hoc est: hanc naturam dedit piscibus et volucribus ut crescent. Primum opus est, ut ex aqua fecit volucres et pisces. Ultra hoc adiecit, ut multiplicarentur, sicut supra item fecit: primum creavit, postea iubet, ut fructum ferat, quod ita multiplicantur, est opus maiestatis divinae«. WA 14, pp. 108,13–109,4 (Rörer).

Alternatively, Luther's thoughts are recorded by Roth, »Hic primum benedicit ›Crescite‹ etc. ›Crescere‹ heist proprie ›fruchtragen‹, ›fruchtbar sein‹, sed in abusum venit. Das ist en eingepfflantzte natur, non potuerunt se movere nec crescere priusquam benedicerentur hic«.

»Primum creat, deinde benedicit, ut videas non otiosum deum, postquam creavit, sed opus esse verbi dei quod creaturae multiplicantur, alioqui solae mansissent«.

»Crescere ergo est opus creatoris creaturarum naturae insitum. Porro quibusdam creaturis dicit, ut sint, persistant et serviant nobis, quibusdam vero insuper, ut crescent, ut fructibus terrae qui semen habeant in semet ipsis, et animantibus quibus praeceptum est, ut crescant«. WA 14, p. 109,17–27.

God divided mankind into man and woman. Just as other works are not in a man's power, so it is not in our hand whether we are a man or a woman (even as the sun was not able to be dark), for that would have been against the word of God, Genesis 2, which says, »Increase and multiply.« It is necessary to take note of these words, which absolve all clergy of vows, for it says, »Increase, etc.« There is nothing greater in man's control [i. e. than this command]. Just as it is necessary for the sun to shine, etc., so it is implanted in the woman and the man that they should increase. What someone takes off[67] is in his power. Now therefore, since it is the blessing and work of God, it is not in my control that I should make a vow against this, unless God should Himself do something miraculous with me. If the sun were to vow not to shine, such a vow would be nothing, because such is not in its power. Therefore, those vows which work against the ordinance of God are foolish. If I were to make such a vow, it is as if I were saying, »I do not want to be a human«. If that happens, unspeakable sins follow. There is nothing more horrible than celibacy, that which the regime of the pope has instituted. It is not for us to change even a hair, *that one should* add a cubit to *his* height, [Matt. 6:27; Luke 12:25] etc. So it is not in our powers to restrain God's creation of flesh. Hitherto we have not attempted to demonstrate this, yet through this I do not condemn virginity. If Adam had remained *without sin*, then no one would have been infertile. But after the fall, it has happened that certain men or women are infertile. These certain ones *He* has furthermore set apart that they might not bear fruit, and such a one, to whom God has given a widow's carriage should give thanks to God. If He does not give this favor, such a person should march along the common road. Now for a long time children of either sex have been enticed to live as celibates. This itself has reinforced the decree of the pope, who decreed that no one was able to live chastely except he who should live as a celibate. Thus matrimony came into contempt. And yet we blind ones do not see that the most holy patriarchs had not one *wife*, but four wives, and the priests of the Old Testament were compelled to live with a wife. Take note of these passages, since they are the words of God (i. e. »He created them,« »Be fruitful,« etc.); if you find yourself guilty, go ahead *and* get married. Indeed, it is necessary that you do so. We therefore now conclude: even today it would be impossible to understand what a man and woman might be, unless it may be by faith. For these are words of God, which are not able to be understood except by a believer[68].

---

67 »auszieht«, such as to take off an item of clothing (WA 14, p. 112,10).

68 »Deus divisit hominem in man et feminam. Sicut alia opera non in sua potestate sunt, Ita non est in manu nostra, quod vir vel mulier sit, sicut sol non potuit obscurus esse, quia contra dei verbum fuisset. 2. quod dicit ›Crescite et multiplicamini‹, notanda hec verba, quae absolvunt omnes clericos a votis, quod dicit ›Crescite‹ etc. non est magis in manu hominis. Sicut sol oportet, ut luceat etc. Ita mulieri et viro implantatum est, ut crescant. Quod aliquot außzieht, est in sua potestate. Nunc igitur cum dei sit benedictio et opus, non est in manu mea, ut contra hoc voveam, nisi deus ageret mecum mirabiliter. Si sol vovere velit non lucere, nihil est, quia in potestate eius non est. Fatua ergo sunt illa vota, quae contra dei ordinationem faciunt. Si vovero, tantum est, si dixero ›homo nolo esse‹. Si fit, sequuntur muta peccata, nits greulicher quam celibatus, Id quod papae regimen

We do well to underscore several points from this text (and the companion transcript from Roth). First, while we observe the usual emphasis on the divinely given purpose and efficaciousness of this primordial blessing for the sake of procreation, Luther uses Genesis 1:26–28 and the presence of two definite and complementary sexes to very clearly and expressly highlight this verse's very powerful polemic against monastic vows and priestly celibacy[69]. According to the Rörer transcript, Luther noted that these words »absolve all ministers from vows«[70]. In the Roth transcript, Luther asserts that these words are a »thunderclap« against all human teachings and the doctrine of demons[71].

A second point of emphasis that deserves note from these passages, one which is also made clear in both transcripts, is that apart from faith, these things cannot be rightly understood. While this teaching has certainly been assumed in previous writings, here Luther places explicit emphasis on the matter. This is made clear once again shortly later, as Roth records, »In summary: There is no misery on earth except that which comes from unbelief. It is unbelief that men do not seek out God's works, but instead distort them, etc.«[72]. Similarly, Rörer records from that same sermon,

---

instituit. Non est nostrum vel pilum mutare, ›cubitum addat ad staturam‹ etc. Ita in viribus nostris non est weren carni suum opus. Hactenus non ausi fuimus hoc probare, per hoc tamen non damno virginitatem. Si mansisset Adam, tum nullus fuisset sterilis, sed post casum factum, ut quidam viri vel mulieres sint steriles. Quosdam eciam hat außgezogen, ut non ferant fructum et hic deo gratias agat, cui deus dedit arcuatum currum. Si non dat hanc gratiam, ille incedat communem viam. Iam longo tempore pueri utriusque sexus ad hoc invitati sunt, ut celibes viverent. Hoc ipsum roboravit papae decretum, qui decrevit neminem posse caste vivere nisi qui vivat celebs. Hinc in contemptum venit matrimonium. Et tamen ceci non vidimus sanctissimos patriarchas non unam, sed 4 uxores habuisse et sacerdotes veteris testamenti cogebantur uxorati vivere. Hos locos observa, quia verba dei sunt ›Creavit eos‹, ›Crescite‹ etc. si invenis te schuldig, fac copuleris alteri, imo oportet ut facias. Concludimus ergo nunc, quod eciam hodie impossibile sit cognoscere, quid vir, quid mulier sit, nisi sit in fide. Hec enim sunt verba dei quae non intelligi possunt nisi a fideli«. WA 14, pp. 112,4–113,14. See also Roth's corresponding notes.

69 This is a very powerful argument for Luther and is repeated frequently both in his Genesis sermons (*Declamationes*) as well as in other polemical works. In fact, it is apparent that for Luther, part of what it is to be human is to be a male or female and to live out one's own corresponding sexuality by following the natural procreative order, though in the God-given framework of marriage. One strikingly clear example is the following in which Luther talks about those who would avoid marriage and its troubles: »Exemplum ergo hic est confirmandi matrimonii etc. Jungker Papst hatt die ehe vorpotten, quia oportuit aliquos venire, qui prohiberent matrimonium. Der Papst hatt gemacht, ne vir esset vir, et ne mulier mulier esset etc.«. WA 14, p. 157,26–28.

70 »hec verba, quae absolvunt omnes clericos a votis […]«. WA 14, p. 112,7–8.

71 »Verbum ›crescite‹ expugnat, schlehet darnider als ein donnerschlag omnes traditiones humanas et doctrinas demoniorum«. WA 14, p. 112,27–28.

72 »Summa summarum: Es ist kein Jammer auff erdtreich den auß dem unglauben, unglaub ists, das man Gottes wergk nicht sucht, sonder verkerett es etc.«. WA 14, p. 114,27–29.

If in faith we would come and be made into the image of God, then all peace and abundance would abound unto us. »And they were very good«, is the observation that all which God desired to do as well as how He began *it*, is also how it shall remain. Not only did it please God that Adam and Eve should be fruitful, even more *it remains the case* wherever man and woman are[73].

Two weeks after this sermon[74], Luther returned to the topic of Genesis 1:28 once again in his treatment of Genesis 2. In speaking of the institution of marriage and how God had presented the woman to Adam, Luther discussed the nature of woman's role as man's helper. According to Roth:

> In summary: The woman has been created, finally, so that she might be a help to the man, not for enjoyment, but rather for the fulfillment of that which was said, »Be fruitful and multiply«. For this reason, therefore, she has been created that she might be fruitful. This is often held to be an insult. Yet, God is able to make from me whatever He desires. I am His clay. If He wants me to serve chastely, it is good. If not, then the work of God and the blessing are not able to be hindered. He gives to some such riches of grace that they are chaste. That which would not have been possible to have occurred before the fall, the saying, »Be fruitful and multiply« would have gone over all and would have had to be fulfilled by all. God has not rescinded this text; it stands fast, etc.[75].

---

73 »Si in fidem veniremus et imago fieremus dei, tum omnia tranquille nobis et abundanter affluerent. ›Et valde errant bona‹, das ansehen est, quod deus hat ein lust dran et quomodo incepit, ita manebit. Non solum placuit deo, ut Adam et Eva crescerent, sed ubi vir et mulier sunt«. WA 14, p. 115,11–14.

74 26 April 1523. WA 14, pp. 95, 121. Note that Luther had been at Wenzel Linck's wedding in Altenburg on 14 and 15 April. This trip of some 120 km required two days' travel in one direction and thus Luther and other guests such as Bugenhagen, Jonas, Melanchthon, and others would have been absent the better part of the week for this symbolic event as Linck was not only the pastor at St. Bartholomaus church there, but also an Augustinian monk who had preceded Luther in Wittenberg. Thus, this event was no mere nuptial celebration; rather, it had the form of an all-out protest against both vows of celibacy as well as the existing church law. Given what we have already observed about the significance of Genesis 1:28 in this period, one might imagine that it likely was mentioned in Luther's wedding sermon or perhaps in the blessing of the marital couple. Regardless, it is fair to note that Linck and his wife were indeed fruitful in that they had ten children. See MOELLER, Lincks Hochzeit. We might also note that in the following year, Linck would offer a written protest against monastic vows which, unsurprisingly, included the increasingly prevalent understanding of Genesis 1:28 we have observed previously. See Wenzeslaus LINK, Dyalogus Der Auszgelauffen Münch. Hie sihestu. 1 Ob die außgetretenen oder bleibenden Ordenßpersonen […], Altenburg 1524 (VD16 L 7327), Diii[v].

75 »Summa Summarum: Mulier creata est finaliter, ut sit adiutorium viro, non ad delectationem, sed ut impleatur dictum ›Crescite et multiplicamini‹. Ad hoc ergo creatus est, ut fructificet. Man helt es nur vor ein schimpff. Deus potest facere ex me quicquid vult, ich bin sein teigk: si vult me servare castum, bonum est, si non, tunc opus dei et benedictio non potest arceri. Ehr gibt etlichen solche reiche gnade, das sie keusch seind. Id quod ante lapsum non potuisset fieri: dehr spruch ›crescite et

There is a second contextual factor important for the discussions of Genesis 1:28, marriage, women, and monastic vows during this time. On 25 April 1523, Johann Faber's work, *Opus adversus*, was reprinted in Leipzig and quickly circulated[76]. While it is difficult to say exactly when Luther might have encountered this book, it is clear that sometime during the Easter season he became aware of it – and the disparaging approach it took toward women, marriage, and the authority of God's word vis-à-vis the papacy[77].

On Exaudi Sunday[78], Luther preached on Genesis 3:8–18. In the context of the fall into sin and the resulting curses, Luther once again took the opportunity to comment on Genesis 1:28 and its abiding nature, now also amid the curses and pains connected with procreation and birth. It should, however, be noted that Luther's emphasis on the continued importance of *crescite et multiplicamini* must be understood in the light of Genesis 3:15 and the promised Seed. Here Luther emphasized that the woman's curse (Genesis 3:16) was understood to be a bodily punishment *instead of* an eternal punishment[79]. The curse itself left the blessing of Genesis 1:28 intact, though suffering was added to it – something that would now be inherent to the woman's postlapsarian experience[80].

Secondly, the very God-given, procreative nature was now the means through which the promised Seed of the woman would eventually arrive (excepting, of course, the virgin birth). This was especially so for the patriarchs and matriarchs of the Old Testament and gave them special reverence for the primordial blessing which had now become a sort of instrument leading to the promised Savior[81].

---

multiplicamini‹ wehr uber alle gegangen, hett in allen mußen erfullet werden. Gott hatt den text nicht auffgehoben, fast ihn wol etc.«. WA 14, pp. 126,33–127,21. Note that Luther also had similar comments about the woman's creation and purpose in his sermons on 1 Peter in the latter part of 1522 (WA 12, p. 346,1–10).

76 WA 12, p. 81.
77 BORNKAMM/BORNKAMM, Luther in Mid-Career, p. 262, have some helpful information on the circumstances surrounding this printing and Luther's response.
78 17 May 1523 (WA 14, pp. 95, 135).
79 Roth notes, »Mulieri quoque dixit ›multiplicabo‹ etc. Sed vide misericordiam et iuditium dei. Absolvit deus a miseria animae et premit miseriis corporis, iustissime quidem, sed bene pro nobis, si libenter amplectamur. Die sehel ist erredt. Iam filii rursum sunt Adam et Eva per fidem. Aeterna poena mutata est hic in temporalem poenam. Das ungluck bezealt ehr leiblich, ehr gibt ihr den fuchsschwantz und nimpt von ihr dy eißern ruthen, tollit mortem et dat vitam«. WA 14, p. 140,32–38.
80 Roth notes, »Nulla foemina est hic excepta, nisi gratia paucissimas excipiat. Non abstulit verbum ›Crescite et multiplicamini‹, sed miseriam addidit, quia peccatum additum erat. Non solum miseria est sive poena, sed et necessitas. Hic vides: sicut non possunt non esse mulieres, sic eciam non absque dolore parere«. WA 14, p. 141,16–19.
81 As for the connection between offspring (the Seed) and the patriarchs, see, for example, WA 14, p. 139,26–30. It is also apparent from Luther's sermon that Adam expected the Savior (Christ) to be born of the woman (WA 14, p. 139,15–21).

Nevertheless, no one rightly conceives of either the curse or the hidden blessing, Luther opines, and instead everyone complains about the curse that God placed upon marriage and procreation[82].

As spring turned to summer, Luther continued with his Genesis sermons. By the Day of the Visitation of Mary[83] he had arrived at Genesis 8. Here, once again, he comments on the word *crescite* (Genesis 8:17), noting especially that this word cannot be changed by any monastic vow[84]. Almost humorously, the following Sunday *crescite et multiplicamini* appeared once again as Luther preached on Genesis 9:1[85]. This time, though, Rörer records Luther as saying, »›Be fruitful and multiply‹ *is* the work of God *as* you have often heard«[86]. Roth, meanwhile, simply summarized Luther's comments by saying, »He repeated his word ›crescite‹ as he had previously spoken«[87]. It is, of course, speculation, but perhaps Luther felt that by now the congregation in Wittenberg was beginning to get the idea.

Around the same time, namely by 11 July 1523, Luther's *Wider die Verkehrer und Falscher kaiserlichs Mandats* appeared[88]. The events leading to its composition date back to the proceedings surrounding the Nuremberg Reichstag of 1522/1523[89]. All things considered, the outcome of the Reichstag was favorable for Electoral Saxony and the cause of the Reformation. Yet, there were also many decisions which were nonetheless unacceptable from the Wittenberg perspective. Chief among these was

---

82 Roth: »Haec nemo hodie vult, ad quae deus nos misericorditer damnavit, ideo vigent scortationes, adulteria, immunditiae etc. Contra deum clamatur, dum matrimonia propter addita onera damnatur. Deus hic sic sensit ›Animas quidem salvabimus, sed corpora gravabimus nullo salutis dispendio‹. Stulti vero et insani homines poenam temporalem sibi rursum mutant in poenam spiritualem. Et dum nolunt subesse sententiae divinae secundum corpus, incidunt in damnationem animae et conscientiae, onus intolerabile. Et eum perversis deus omnia pervertit. Ita fit iusto dei iuditio omnibus, qui verbo dei addunt et quid melius excogitare volunt, quam ipsa aeterna sapientia excogitavit«.
»Wu Gott nit sonderliche gnade gibt, ßo muß ein hehr ein hehr bleiben, ein sie ein sie, das ist das herezeleidt und jammer am leibe, gib dich frey hynein, es wirt nicht anders drauß, wag den leib hynan, wir werden sunst den leib vorßorgen und die sehel vordammen etc.«.
»Mundus non scit, quid vir sit, quid mulier, non intelligit opus dei, nec quid sit matrimonium novit. Si quid adversi nobis in matrimonio obtigerit, hic habet textus etc.«. WA 14, p. 142,18–34.
83 2 July 1523 (WA 14, p. 196).
84 Roth: »›Crescite‹. Instaurat suum verbum, quo securos eos facit de non perdendo, de bona sua in eos voluntate, ne credant omnia iam perdita et se esse novissimos in mundo. Serio agit talia deus, per vota monastica hic nihil immutabis«. WA 14, pp. 199,39–200,23.
85 Interestingly, on this same Sunday, Luther preached in another sermon (without direct reference to Genesis 1:28) that God desires to make marriage fruitful, etc. WA 12, p. 618,13–21.
86 Cf. »›Crescite et multiplicamini‹, opus dei et sepius audistis«. WA 14, p. 202,14–15.
87 Cf. »Repetit suum verbum ›Crescite‹ ut supra dictum«. WA 14, p. 201,24.
88 WA 12, p. 60.
89 WA 12, pp. 58f. See also BRECHT, Martin Luther, pp. 111–116, for an overview of the events surrounding the Reichstag and Luther's tract in response to these events.

the forbiddance of continued polemic publications as well as the edict that married priests, monks, and nuns ought to be handed over to their respective bishops for punishment[90]. Thus, Luther's response to these mandates from the Reichstag offers a conditional and qualified acceptance of the moratorium on publishing, his skepticism over the much-discussed council, and then a section on vows and priestly marriage.

For our purposes, it is most interesting to note that, whereas Luther's chief arguments against vows of celibacy had formerly been based on the freedom of the Gospel and the greatness of the baptismal vow, the chief argument now expressed in *Wider die Verkehrer und Falscher kaiserlichs Mandats* is clearly centered in man's divinely-implanted nature. As we have previously noted, Luther directly connects the impossibility of keeping a vow of celibacy – short of God's direct and exceptional intervention – with the abiding ordinance found in Genesis 1:28[91]. This thus explains man's inherent inability to deny his own sexual nature, particularly when combined with his own fallen and sinful condition[92].

Returning briefly to Luther's preaching on Genesis, a little more than a month later (16 August)[93] Luther revisits Genesis 1:28 and once again strikes at one of the major points of contention in this controversy, that the church fathers (Jerome especially) endorsed and encouraged celibacy and virginity above marriage[94]. Luther's comments also reiterated the complaint made originally in *De votis monasticis iudicium*, where Luther charged that monastic vows were nothing other than to tempt God to make exception to His word and institution on account of a human vow[95].

---

90 Ibid., p. 114.
91 »Hilfcgott von hymel, wills uns denn nicht eyn mal eyngehen, das unmügliche gelübde nicht gelübde noch zu hallten sindt? wer will doch fliegen geloben wie eyn fogel und hallten, es sey denn gottis wunderzeichen da? Nu ists doch ia so viel, wenn eyn mans odder weybs bilde keusscheyt gelobt. Denn es ist yhe nicht zur keusscheyt geschaffen, sondern wie gott sagt: ›wachst und mehirt euch‹, das keusscheyt eyn unmüglich ding ist, wo gott nicht wunder thutt, so gillt yhe das wundergelübde nicht, das ynn meyner gewallt nicht stehet, drumb hab ich nerrisch gethan, und byns nicht schuldig zu hallten, und gott föddert es nicht«. WA 12, p. 66,16–24.
92 WA 12, p. 67,20–32.
93 WA 14, p. 223.
94 See, for example, FABRI, IOANNIS FABRI EPISCOPI CONSTANTIENSIS, Qiii (8/8), where he criticizes Luther's interpretation of Genesis 1:28 with the authority of Jerome.
95 In preaching about Abraham and Sarah's journey into Egypt and the trials endured there, Luther took occasion to speak about the difference between faith and tempting God in the face of trials, particularly with reference to monastic vows. Roth records, »Tentatio a dextris est ›Credo et nolo uti quae deus dedit ad vitam conservandam, ad hoc et illud fatiendum, conservabit et fatiet sine illis‹. Ista est tentatio sine necessitate, quod si necessitas adesset et illa non adessent, iam non tentatio dei esset, sed fides, et deus sine dubio efficeret etc. Sic tentant deum, quibus non data est virginitas: ›Ego claudam me in monasterio et non utar remedio a deo dato, ipse a caelis dabit mihi remedium etc. Ex coelis veniet deus et dicet ›Esto virgo‹. Nam primum mandatum eius, quod efficax sentio in me

Even more interesting than the general correlation between Luther's preaching and the ongoing religious strife is the fact that in mid-August a second wave, or perhaps a continuation of the first, was issued against the attacks of Luther's opponents[96]. This was preceded in mid-July by Johann Apel's *Defensio Iohannis Apelli ad Episcopum Herbipolensem pro suo coniugio*, to which Luther had already written an introduction[97]. The greater impetus for the wave of writings in August, however, seems to have been the end result of Johann Faber's earlier writing, *Opus adversus*. Thus, in addition to Luther's congregational preaching in late summer of 1523, we also witness the printing of Luther's *Das siebente Kapitel S. Pauli zu den Korinthern*[98] as well as Justus Jonas's *Adversum Johannem Fabrem*.

Turning to the latter first, Justus Jonas's response, spurred on at Luther's insistence and printed with an accompanying letter from the same on 10 August, sought to take the reader from the desert world of Faber's endless citations back into a living spiritual world[99] as it dealt with questions of monastic vows, priestly marriage, and the good of marriage and women. Luther had turned to Jonas for this response for a couple of reasons. First, Luther had no desire to answer Faber himself, whose writing he summarized as »nothing but fathers, fathers, fathers, councils, councils, councils«[100]. Second, Jonas's status as a relatively newly-married man, made him all the more fit to respond to Faber's disparagement of marriage and women[101].

›Crescite et multiplicamini‹, iam mihi non placet, aliud placet. Cum illo, quod deus excogitavit non possum esse sanctus, sed cum illo, quod ego excogito, quod probavit Hieronymus's etc. Diabolum tibi dabit etc. Regia igitur et media via est fides recta, quae neque ad sinistram neque ad dexteram inclinat‹«. WA 14, p. 227,19–30.

96 There was no shortage of motivation to revisit the theme of monastic vows in light of the events that had followed Luther's initial rejection of such vows. 1523 was a watershed year with the exit of nuns from cloisters. Luther's opponents, as noted, were attacking his writings. There were any number of now-married former monks. All of these developments brought with them changes and difficulties that required attention. BORNKAMM/BORNKAMM, Luther in Mid-Career, pp. 261–263, offer a helpful overview of the state of these questions and issues in 1523.

97 Johann APEL, DEFENSIO IOHANNIS APELLI AD EPSCOPVM HERBIPOLENSEM PRO SVO CONIVGIO, Wittenberg 1523 (VD16 A 3028). In this treatise Apel laid out a brief defense of his own marriage with the chief argument being his appeal to the higher authority of God's word than any human authority. Interestingly, his appeal included no notable reference to the applicable passages governing marriage, let alone Genesis 1:28. BRECHT, Martin Luther, p. 97, also gives brief mention to this treatise.

98 WA 12, pp. 88–142.

99 WA 12, pp. 82f., quoting from Johann Heierlin Horawitz. See also fn., ibid., p. 83.

100 Cf. »Totus enim Faber nihil est nisi Patres, Patres, Patres, Concilia, Concilia, Concilia […]«. WA 12, p. 85,21–22.

101 WA 12, p. 85,1 (a footnote on the same page observes that Jonas had married in February of 1522). We noted previously that the question of the impossibility of the vow had likely become a matter of real concern for Jonas in the fall of 1521. It is worth noting that the matter of Jonas's marriage was far from academic but was a great source of personal liberation by which he viewed himself to have

Finally, although some have suggested Luther's dissatisfaction with Jonas's writing, we might note that Luther could not have been disappointed with Jonas's treatment of Genesis 1:28. After all, it amounted to one of the clearest and best expressions of Luther's own understanding of this verse to come out of Wittenberg[102]. The relevant section reads as follows with Genesis 1:28 clearly prioritized as Jonas's leading argument (following his introductory salvo against Faber)[103]:

---

been led away from the chains and nets of the devil and the many struggles of the celibate life. His ongoing struggle over the question of marriage emerged a second time in a further letter to Johann Lang dated 8 January 1522, in which he posed the question whether he ought to marry (KAWERAU, Briefwechsel, vol. 1, p. 83; LEHMANN, Justus Jonas, p. 43). It is certainly conceivable that Luther hoped to tap into such personal exuberance over marriage in choosing Jonas to respond to Faber. Furthermore, it is certainly not unthinkable that the arguments expounded by Jonas in *Adversus Iohannem Fabrum* were the exact arguments that had led to Jonas's own marriage and likely also his second marriage in 1543, just five months after the death of his first wife (WA Br 10, pp. 251f., pp. 304–306). Indeed, it seems beyond debate that Jonas thoroughly embraced marriage and family life. Due to the passing of his second wife in 1549 (WA Br 10, p. 304), Jonas mentions in a letter in 1551 that he had married a third time. For this see KAWERAU, Briefwechsel, vol. 2, pp. 308f.; LEHMANN, Justus Jonas, p. 175. Jonas also had at least six children (ibid., p. 162).

102 While there is arguably nothing new in Jonas's presentation of the »Wittenberg« understanding of Genesis 1:28, the clarity of this particular text places it next to Luther's *Vom ehelichen Leben* and Luther's Genesis sermons in terms of significance within the first half of the 1520s. We also will observe Jonas's clear expression of Melanchthon's thought on the natural affections.
Robert KOLB, The Theology of Justus Jonas, in: Irene DINGEL (ed.), Justus Jonas (1493–1555) und seine Bedeutung für die Wittenberger Reformation, Leipzig 2009, pp. 103–120, at p. 120, summarizes his own findings on Justus Jonas with the following: »Justus Jonas was not a creative thinker. He was no independent theologian with his own original insights. His contributions to the Wittenberg Reformation do not include the original development of any aspect of its formulation of biblical teaching. At the level at which he wrote, it is difficult to maintain that he favored Luther or Melanchthon; his writings convey that general Wittenberg core of teaching that they both shared [...] Within a framework of pastoral concern and eschatological expectation Jonas propagated Luther's and Melanchthon's fundamental convictions regarding the doctrines of justification and the church [...]«. To this we might simply add »as well as their teachings on man, woman, procreation, and marriage«.
Ibid., p. 107, fn. 20, notes elsewhere that Luther likely found Jonas's writing to be insufficient and thus wrote his commentary on 1 Corinthians 7. A comparison of the two documents shows that this is likely the case considering that Jonas's treatment of that chapter (the main battle ground for the debate over priestly marriage and vows of celibacy) was perhaps a bit lacking, even if his treatment of Genesis 1 (the underlying divisive presupposition) was most certainly sufficient.

103 JONAS, Adversvs Iohannem Fabrum, B4^v, writes in the preceding paragraph, »Sed ut ad rem ipsam tandem descendam [...]«, and also expresses his disinterest in dealing with Faber's numerous quotes from heathen unbelievers – though also noting that Faber has neglected to include the many favorable quotations *for* marriage to be found amongst these same authors.

But I myself will not play here with sacred matters; rather, I would set the plain witness of the Scriptures before you, against which not even the gates of hell are going to prevail. Moses first discusses man's creation (Genesis 1) when he says: »GOD created man according to His image and likeness, according to the image of God He created him, male and female He created them.« We will examine this verse, Faber, a little more closely where it will become apparent, whether perpetual continence might be so common *and so easy* a matter, as you hypocrites make it. Therefore, bestir yourself here, Faber, from you sleep, and consider carefully the words of majesty, that here it says: »Male and female He created them.« Therefore, man has not only been created male, but also female. Thus the human race has been created, that it should consist of two sexes, male and female, or man and woman. So then, whatever the Most High GOD, Maker of all things, has formed or created you *to be*, whether male or whether female, it is necessary that you be this, that you remain this. For neither are you able by your strength to change, to reprint, or to remold the work of God, nor to bring it about so that from the male suddenly you might make a female or from the female a male, or from a man an angel. Therefore that Creator and that Majesty desires either creature to be honored as good and pleasing to the Creator, so that neither the female despises the male nor the male the female.

From this I believe it is not at all obscure how plainly the philosophers of the Gentiles and the heathen writers attack this sex and this good creature of God with ungodly and Satanic blasphemies such as, »The woman is a necessary evil«, »Nothing *is* more evil than a woman«, and reproaches of that sort. It is remarkable if you still do not see how aptly you have used *their* testimonies and dreadful blasphemies in sacred matters and in theological disputation here. Moreover, when GOD had created male and female, He blessed them and said, »Increase and multiply«. Therefore from that verse of Genesis it is clear that the male and the female are created to be united, to increase, and to multiply. And what is more, these words of God are so powerful and effective that no creature, either on earth or in heaven, could alter this nature.

Consequently, since these two natures have been created and made by God to be united, if you are a male, it has no more been placed in your power to be without a woman than not to be that which you have been created *to be*, namely a male. By the same token, if you are a woman, it has no more been placed in your power to be without a man than not to be a woman. Therefore it is not in our powers to take up or lay down that nuptial impetus and disposition engraved in *our* nature [*naturae insculptum affectum*],[104] by which a woman eagerly desires a man and a man *desires* a woman, but this is how we have been created by God, how we have been made, how we have been fashioned. Therefore, just as fire cannot fail to burn *nor* water fail to be wet, because each one has been created this way,

---

104 Note the context and manner, once again, in which *affectum* is used. This once again supports our thesis that the Wittenberg understanding of Genesis 1:28 parallels Melanchthon's *affectus quosdam naturales* from his *Loci Communes* (1521), as has been previously observed.

so the woman cannot fail eagerly to desire the man, and in turn, the man cannot fail to be moved toward the woman.

For this word »Increase and multiply«, is neither law nor command, but a living and effective word. Indeed, *it is* the work of God, which does not cease to act and to work in nature. There is nothing found in us *which is able* to impede or hinder this work of God any more than we might make ourselves *into* different human beings or *into* angels. Therefore, just as it is not from my strength, but it is mere creation and nature that I am male and *that* I have members of this or of that sex, so it is not from me, but this reproduction (or the inclination and desire toward reproduction) is clearly something inborn and engrained. And just as *our* nature is so created that it is not able to abstain from food or drink or from any other necessary things, it is likewise so created that it is unable not to burn and to be inflamed with desire and ardor to reproduce itself. God has never instructed anyone to be male or female, but has so created *and* has so formed and built them to be by nature male and female, as also He has not taught them to increase and multiply, but implanted and inserted it in their nature and this double sex that they should burn toward each other and by an innate force and drive be brought to increase and reproduce. Therefore, it is not for you to attempt, by the strength of any man or of any created thing, to restrain or hinder this drive or these flames thus implanted in *your* nature itself and innate to *each* sex, unless God should remove it by an extraordinary calling or lofty gift. In Matthew 19, Christ enumerates three types of Eunuchs. Unless you consider yourself to be from the first two types, or *are* with certainty of the third, namely, that you have been more highly called by God, nothing is more prudent than to marry – also because the Holy Spirit was knowing and was thoroughly understanding his creature. In the Holy Scriptures you will prove no such thing, even if you might go through both testaments, such as you teach about celibacy. No such example will you discover of such an extremely broad, general chastity[105].

---

105 »Ego uero hic in re sacra non sic ludam, sed manifesta scripturarum testimonia tibi opponam, quibus ne portæ quidem inferorum praevaliturae sunt. Primum Moses cum de creatio hominis disserit, Geñ.i. ait, Creauit D E V S hominem, ad imaginem & similitudinem suam, ad imaginem dei creauit illum, masculum & feminam creauit eos. Hunc locum Faber ubi paulo accuratius excusserimus, apparebit, num tam uulgate, tam facilis res sit perpetua continentia, quam vos Hypocritæ eam facitis. Expergiscere ergo hic Faber e tuo somno, & perpende uerba maiestatis, qd hic dicatur, Masculum, inquit, & feminam creauit eos. Homo igitur nō solum masculus creatus est, sed & femina. Sic ergo hominum genus creatum est, ut constet duplici hoc sexu, Masculi & feminae, seu uiri & mulieris. Proinde, quicquid D E V S summus ille omnium rerum opifex, te finxit seu creauit, siue masculum, siue feminam, hoc sis, hoc maneas necesse est. Neq₃.n. tuis uiribus mutare, recudere aut refingere potes opus dei, neq₃ efficere, ut ex masculo subito fias foemina, aut ex foemina masculus, aut ex homine angelus. Utranq₃ igitur creaturam, tanquā bonam, & placentem suo creatori. Creator ille, & maiestas illa honorari uult, ut neq₃ foemina contemnat masculum neq₃ masculus foeminam«.

»Ex hoc opinor minime obscurum est, quam impiis plane & Satanicis blasphemiis, ut pote, Mulier est necessariū malum, Muliere nihil peius, & id genus cōuiciis, Philosophi gentiū & ethnici scriptores

Several points deserve brief emphasis with Jonas's explanation of the text and polemic versus Faber concerning Genesis 1:27–28. First, the utter clarity and importance of the male/female division for Luther and his colleagues, as stated in Genesis 1:27, is strikingly clear. Furthermore, as this male/female division and its created nature, dispositions, and drives (also those leading toward procreation) are part of what it means to be human, it is therefore clear that, under normal circumstances, man is denying part of his own created identity should human sexuality, and that to which it ought to lead, be denied or prevented. Thus, desires and impulses are not merely expressions of sinful concupiscence but are themselves (apart from the corruption of sin which is not denied) the good creation of God and reflective of His will. Finally, sexuality and its purposes are not a choice. Rather, they

---

hunc sexum & hanc bonā creaturam dei, incesserint. Quorū testimoniis & horrendis blasphemiis quā apte in re sacra & disputatione hic Theologica usus sis, mirum si adhuc non uideas. Præterea, cum creasset D E V S masculum & foeminam benedixit eis, & ait, Crescite & multiplicamini. Ex illo ergo loco Genesis clarum est, Masculum & foeminam sic creatos, ut cōiungantur, crescent & multiplicentur. Atq3 hæc uerba dei tam potentia & efficatia sunt, ut nulla creatura neq3 in terra, neq3 in coelo, aliam hanc naturam facere possit«.

»Proinde, cum hæ duæ naturæ sic a DEO creatæ sint & factæ, ut cōiungātur, si sis masculus, nihilo magis in tua potestate situm est, ut careas muliere, quā illud est, ut non sis, quod creatus es, nempe masculus. Ediuerso si sis mulier nihilo magis in tua potestate situm est, ut careas uiro, quā hoc est, ut nō sis mulier. Illum ergo genialem impetum, & naturæ insculptum affectum quo mulier concupiscit masculum, & masculus foeminam, nō est nostrarum uirium sumere aut ponere, sed sic creati a DEO, sic ficti, sic conditi sumus. Haud aliter ergo atq3 ignis non potest non calere, aqua non potest non madere, quod utrunq3 sic sit creatum, sic mulier non potest non concupiscere masculum, contra, masculus non potest non affici erga foeminam«.

»Nam hoc uerbum, Crescite, & multiplicamini, non est lex aut præceptum, sed uiuum & efficax uerbum, imo opus dei, quod non definit in natura agere & operari. Hoc opus dei impedire, aut remorari nihilo magis in nobis situm est, quā hoc est, ut nosmetipsos alios homines aut angelos faciamus. Perinde igitur atque ex meis uiribus non est, sed mera creatio & natura est quod sum masculus, & huius uel illius sexus membra habeam, sic non ex me est, sed plane innatum & insculptum quiddam est hæc propagatio, seu propensio & ardor ad propagandum«.

»Et haud aliter atq3 sic creata est natura ut non possit carere cibo aut potu aut aliis necessariis rebus, ita & creata est ut non possit nō æstuare & flagrare desiderio & ardore sese propaganda. Non præcepit unquam deus ulli ut esset masculus aut foemina, sed sic creauit, sic finxit & condidit, ut essent ex natura masculus & foemina, sic & non præcepit ut crescerent & multiplicarentur, sed hoc naturæ & gemino huic sexui inseuit & indidit, ut inter sese mutuo exardescat, & natiua ui atq3 impetu feratur ad crescendum & propagandum. Hunc impetum igitur, has flammas, sic ipsi naturæ insitas, & sexui cognatas, nō est ut ullis humanis, aut ullius creature uiribus cohercere aut reprimere coneris, nisi deus quem peculiari uocatione ac dono sublimiore eximat. Matthei.19. Tria genera Eunuchorum recenset Christus, nisi te sentias ex primis duobus generibus esse, aut certe ex tertio, nempe quod sublimius uocatus sis a deo, nihil tutius est quā nubere. Et quia spiritus sanctus sciebat & penitus cognitam habebat creaturam suam. Nihil tale quicquā, etiam si utrunq3 testamentum percurras, in scripturis sanctis ostendes, quale uos de coelibatu docetis. Nullum tale exemplum proferes tam latissimi uulgatae castitatis«. JONAS, Adversvs Iohannem Fabrum, B4ᵛ–C1ᵛ.

are an innate quality and the very nature of man, and thus cannot be contained or extinguished, except for in those persons who have been excepted by God Himself (Matthew 19).

The discussion that follows this excerpt then moves on to the examples of the patriarchs and matriarchs in Genesis, the question of whether or not Genesis 1:28 has been fulfilled and superseded by virginity and chastity (with the oft-cited quote from Jerome), as well as a discussion of 1 Corinthians 7. Of particular note is the fact that this discussion is brought directly into contact with the question of the Gospel itself and whether Scripture speaks of one and the same Gospel throughout and whether creation is ordered consistently both before and after Christ's coming[106]. The remainder of Jonas's writing, largely dedicated to combating Faber's collection of citations and disparagement of women, lies outside the purview of our investigation, though we might note also there that the procreative purpose and even duty of marriage and human nature is never particularly far out of Jonas's sight[107].

We turn our attention now to Luther's *Das siebente Kapitel S. Pauli zu den Korinthern*, published around the same time as Jonas's writing in August 1523[108]. This writing, though not directly a response to Faber, cannot be separated from Faber with respect to either content or context. In fact, already in the introduction,

---

106 Ibid., C1ʳ–C3ʳ. An especially relevant section dealing with Jerome and his oft-repeated quote appears on C3 as follows: »In eo coniugio fuerunt summi & maximi quiqȝ, tum veteris tum noui testamenti homines, ut ceteros transeam, Abraham, Isaac Iacob, Ioseph, Moses &c. quos (opinor) tam sanctos, tam charos DEO, tam pios & spirituales fuisse dabis, quā sunt qui nunc uiuunt, aut omnibus etiam seculis inde a mundo condito uixerint sacerdotes. Atqȝ hic nihil, quā risu dignum est preclarum tuum commentum, quod forsan, Hieronymo auctore, niteris defendere. Tunc terra (inquis) replenda fuit, nunc coelum, Quasi uero hi tanti homines, tantiqȝ patriarchæ, (quamuis tam clare reuelatum non erat) non idem Euangelium, non eundem Christum habuerint quem nos habemus, non eadem fide, eodem uerbo DEI iustificati sint, quasi uero, iam tum, nō & coelum (ut sic loquar) replendum fuerit. Nihil uides hic, Faber, neqȝ sentis, in malleis opinor animus tibi est & follibus, quibus aptior sane esses quā calamo. Stueteris & noui testamēti discrimen ulla ex parte intelligeres aliter loquereris«.

»Tempore partum Euangelium quidem tam clare reuelatum non erat, at promissiones illas Euangelicas iam tum acceperant patres. Quid ergo ineptis, qui tunc terrā replendam fuisse dicas, nunc coelum. Cedo, num sola castitas aut uirginitas iustificant, an nō una & sola fides est quae iustificat coram deo, coelum replet, & omnes unum reddit in Christo, ut neqȝ uirgo neqȝ coniunx sit aliquid, sed fides, seu obseruatio mandatorum DEI«. Ibid., C3ʳ.

107 »Is demum uerissime Solomonem loquutū satebitur, cū ait, Qui mulierem inuenit, inuenit bonū. Qui.n.firmiter credit, coniugiū institutū esse a deo, masculam et foeminā, ad hanc coniunctionē creatos esse, hoc officiū esse, hanc esse propriā uocationē coniugii, ut liberis procreandis, et educandis opera detur«. Ibid., E1ᵛ.

It is worth noting that Jonas was able to proudly look back on this writing in his correspondence some thirteen years later. See LEHMANN, Justus Jonas, p. 95, and KAWERAU, Briefwechsel, vol. 1, pp. 241f.

108 WA 12, pp. 88f.

Luther addresses Faber[109] and challenges his arguments, particularly with respect to women, in a manner indicative of Luther's underlying understanding of Genesis 1:27–28[110]. Nevertheless, the work itself addresses far more than Faber's isolated work. It deals with *a*, or perhaps *the*, central text in the entire debate, namely, 1 Corinthians 7 and its teachings about virginity and marriage. Nevertheless, as will be seen, important for Luther is whether 1 Corinthians 7 is to be understood in light of Genesis 1:28 or in isolation from it as Jerome and other church fathers had argued[111]. Our analysis will show that the former is clearly Luther's understanding.

Luther's *Das siebente Kapitel* is divided up into an introduction and three main sections. For our purposes the first section and, to a slightly lesser extent, the third section are most significant as they deal with whether or not one ought to marry and the stations of widowhood and virginity, respectively. The second section, as it deals primarily with divorce and the Christian's calling to freedom, is less relevant for our study, and thus we will pass over it only noting that Luther's emphasis on Gospel freedom does not militate against his understanding of God's creative ordering of things. Rather, it frees man for service within and according to his own created nature.

To begin with, then, we simply note that Luther's overall emphasis in this writing is that of a Christian's freedom to live in accordance with that gift – whether marriage or celibacy – which God has given him. In other words, Christians are not beholden to the law of Moses which required every man and woman to be married,

---

109 Luther does mention Faber (in rather strong terms) in his introduction. He writes, »Der artt ist auch itzt der ertznarr Johans Schmid von Costnitz [i. e. Faber], ia der hochberumbt hurntreyber, der eyn groß buch geschrieben hatt, newlich zu Leypßick gdrückt, widder den ehestand, yderman davon zu reytzen, und sagt doch nichts mehr, denn wie viel mühe und erbeyt drynnen sey, gerad als wüste das selb die gantze wellt zuvorhyn nicht, und der eselskopff müstes uns nů allererst leren, das auch keynem bawern auff dorffen unbewůst ist«. WA 12, p. 94,3–8.
110 In the paragraph following Luther's comments on Faber, he continues to comment on the nature of woman, emphasizing that woman is the ongoing work and word of God in the same manner in which he speaks of the ongoing work of procreation as God's word and work: »Es sind buben, nicht alleyn ynn der hautt, sondern auch ym grund yhres hertzen, die nicht werd sind, das man yhn antwortten soll. Und was hůlffes, das alle wellt uber den ehestand klagte? Wyr sehen yhe fur augen, das Gott teglich, nicht eyttel menner, sondern auch weyber schaffet und erhellt ym leben, so ist yhe das gewiß, das er keyn weyb schafft der hurerey zu dienst. Weyl denn *gottis werck und wortt* da ligen fur augen, das weyber entweder zur ehe odder zur hurerey můssen gebraucht werden, so sollten solche heydenische larven yhre lester meuler zů hallten, *Gott seyn wortt und werck* ungetaddelt und unverhyndert gehen lassen, Es were denn, das sie nach yhrer hochberümbten weyßheyt uns leren wollten, Gotte zu widder, alle weyber erwůrgen odder vertreyben. Also můs Gott unser narr seyn, was er macht, das taug nicht, was wyr thun, das ist wol gethan«. WA 12, p. 94,15–26.
111 Jerome's exaltation of, and struggle with, the celibate life is criticized by Luther throughout this work. See WA 12, p. 99,20–34, p. 115,22–31, p. 134,23–29.

particularly for the sake of the promised Seed of Abraham[112]. Accordingly, the Christian's life ought to be ordered based on the inward gift and nature one has. If the inner gift fails, then outward rules and regulations will only entrap and ensnare the Christian[113]. Nevertheless, for Luther, St. Paul clearly understands that the vast majority of men are given to marriage and are not endowed with the extraordinary gift of celibacy. Luther's proof of this is that the apostle writes »*Each* man should have his own wife« and not »*some*«[114].

Returning to this same theme a little later, Luther writes of the free, yet necessary, nature of marriage. He states that although marriage and celibacy are free for the Christian, nevertheless, if someone lacks the necessary grace to live freely outside of marriage, »there marriage is commanded, yes, even more than commanded«[115]. Moreover, such a chaste celibate life must truly be recognized as a divine gift and not something to be attained through human works. Therefore, all vows and efforts to attain that which has not been given prove impossible[116]. Luther then veers away from this general theme to expound upon the spiritual nature of marriage[117], while roundly criticizing those practitioners of the »spiritual life« and opponents of clerical marriage who avoid a truly spiritual life and hinder others from entering into it[118]. It is at this point as Luther approaches 1 Corinthians 7:8–9 with St. Paul's words, »It is better to marry than to burn with passion« (*Es ist besser freyen den brennen*), that Luther lays out his foundation for understanding humanity and marriage, and thus, this entire chapter. Luther writes:

> St. Paul well knew that by his teaching and conduct Christ did not want to obstruct or break any of God's creatures or works. Now man is the creature and work of God, created to be fruitful and multiply according to Gen. 1:28. Through His Gospel, and priesthood He therefore does not want to make of man a stick or a stone nor hinder him in his natural

---

112 WA 12, p. 97,11–20.
113 WA 12, pp. 97,32–99,19.
114 LW 28, pp. 12f., cf. WA 12, p. 101,3–5. Luther introduces the near universality of marriage as the intention for humanity in mentioning, »Und er hatt doch (als der voll des heyligen geysts war) bas die menschliche natur, art und vermůgen erkennet, denn on zweyffel alle Bischoff, die nach yhm komen sind, die solch göttlich ordenung verkeret und gewehret haben, das nu S. Paulus wortt nicht mehr gillt: ›Eyn iglicher habe seyn weby‹, sondern also nu predigen: ›Ettliche mügen weyber haben, ettliche sollen nicht weyber haben‹, machen aus dem ›iglichen‹ ›ettliche‹«. WA 12, pp. 100,33–101,5.
115 LW 28, p. 16, cf. »[…] da ist auch die ehe gepotten, ja mehr den gepotten«. WA 12, p. 104. For the extended reference, see WA 12, p. 104,1–9.
116 WA 12, p. 105,5–16. This argument echoes Luther's original presentation of Genesis 1:28 in *De votis monasticis*.
117 WA 12, pp. 105,17–108,8.
118 WA 12, pp. 108,21–109,9.

function, which God implanted in him. As for forbidding priests to marry, what is that but to say that a man is not to be a man but is to cease being God's creature and work in favor of human presumption and legalism? Only God, who created us, may effect such a transformation through His gifts and power; human law or free will or effort are here all wasted and in vain.[119]

Luther then continues to comment upon 1 Corinthians 7:8–9, pointing out that whatever the benefits of celibacy may be, they are nothing if celibacy itself cannot be maintained. He writes, »This is as much as to say: Necessity orders that you marry«[120], and then continues with a further treatment of Genesis 1:27–28:

Much as chastity is praised, and no matter how noble a gift it is, nevertheless necessity prevails so that few can attain it, for they cannot control themselves. For although we are Christians and have the spirit of God in faith, still we do not cease to be God's creatures, you a woman, and I a man. And the spirit permits the body its ways and natural functions, so that it eats, drinks, sleeps, and eliminates like any other human body.

Therefore mankind is not deprived of its male or female form, members, seed, and fruit, so that the body of a Christian must fructify and multiply just like that of other human beings, birds, and all the animals, as it was created by God to do according to Genesis 1:28. So it is by necessity that the man is attracted to the woman and the woman to the man, except where God performs a miracle by means of a special gift and withholds His creatures from one another. When St. Paul says, »But if they cannot exercise self-control, they should marry«, it is as though he were to say, »Those to whom God has not given a special gift but lets their bodies retain their way and nature, from them it is better, yes, necessary, to marry and not to remain virgin or widow. For it is not God's intention to make this special grace a general one; rather marriage is to be general according to God's original institution and creation in both bodies. He will not cancel and deny His creation in everyone«[121].

---

119 LW 28, p. 25, cf. »Er wuste wol S. Paul, das Christus durch seyn lere und regiment gottis Creatur und werck widder zu brechen noch hyndern wollt. Nů ist eyn man yhe gottis Creatur und werck, sich zu besamen und zumehren geschaffen Genesis 1. Darumb will er durch seyn Evangelion und priesterthum nicht eyn holtz odder steyn aus dem man machen, noch yhm seyn natůrliche werck hyndern, die Gott eyngepflantzt hatt. Denn was ists anders gesagt, wo man priestern die ehe verpeutt, denn das eyn man nicht eyn man sey, und gottis Creatur und werck solle abseyn und auffhören, umb menschliches frevels und gepotts willen? Gott alleyn, der yhn geschaffen hatt, mag auch solchs wandeln durch seyne gaben und wirckung, menschlich gesetz und frey will odder vleys ist hie verloren und umb sonst«. WA 12, p. 113,3–13.

120 LW 28, p. 26, cf. »Das ist also viel gesagt: Nott heysst dich ehlich werden«. WA 12, p. 113,21–22.

121 LW 28, p. 26, cf. »Wie hoch nu die keuscheyt gepreyßet wirt, und wie eddel auch die gabe der keuscheyt ist, so weret doch die Nott, das gar wenig hynan können, denn sie können nicht hallten.

Although Luther continues his discussion of 1 Corinthians 7:9 by addressing the necessity caused by the sinful desires of fallen man[122], the fact remains that for him, the necessity of marriage in the face of »burning« is found not merely in man's sinful nature, but just as fundamentally in God's institution, word, and work, all of which dare not merely be glossed over as »sin«[123].

We now briefly turn our attention to Luther's treatment of virginity in the final section of this writing[124]. Here once again Luther notes that virginity, like marriage, is free and neither is it commanded. Moreover, he does not hesitate to highlight the value and use of virginity where it might be attained. Yet, in concluding his commentary on this chapter, Luther once again returns to emphasize the applicability and necessity of God's created order when chastity is not clearly given. He writes:

> Now we may summarize this chapter thus: It is well not to marry unless it is necessary. It becomes necessary when God has not given us the rare gift of chastity, for no one is created

---

Denn wie wol wyr Christen sind, und den geyst gottis ym glawben haben, so ist da mit doch nicht auffgehaben gottis Creatur, das du eyn weyb, ich eyn man byn. Und lesset dennoch der geyst dem leybe seyne art und naturliche werck, das er isset, trincket, schlefft, dewet, auswirfft, wie eyns andern manschen leyb«.

»Also nymbt er auch nicht von dem menschen weyblisch odder menlich gestalt, gelyd, samen und fruchte, das eyns Christen leyb eben so wol sich mus besamen und mehren und zichtigen als ander menschen, vogel und alle thier, da tzu er denn von Gott geschaffen ist Gene. 1. Also das von nott wegen eyn man sich zum weybe, und eyn weyb zum man halten můs, wo Gott nicht wunder thutt durch eyn besondere gabe und seyn geschepffe auffhelt. Das meynet hie S. Paulus: ›Wer sich nicht halten kann, der freye, als sollt er sagen: Wem Gott nicht die besondere gnade gibt, sondern lesst seynem leybe seyn artt und natur, dem ists besser, ia nott zu freyen, und widder widwe noch jungfraw bleyben. Nů hatts Gott nicht ym synn, solch besondere gnad gemeyn machen, sondern das freyen soll gemeyn seyn, wie ers eyn mal eyngesetzt und geschaffen hat an beyden leyben. Er wirt nicht eym yderman seyn geschepffe auffheben und weren‹«. WA 12, pp. 113,22–114.

122 WA 12, p. 114,6–25. Luther writes further, »Man hatt auch viel mehr ursach zu freyen. Ettlich freyen umb gellt und gutts willen, Eyn groß teyl umb furwitz willen, wollust zu suchen und zu büssen, Ettlich das sie erben zeugen. Aber S. Paulus zeygt diße eynige an, und ich weys auch ym grund keyn sterckere und bessere, nemlich die Nott. Nott heysst es. Die natur will eraus und sich besamen und mehren, und Gott wills ausser der ehe nicht haben, so mus yderman dißer nott halben ynn die ehe tretten, wer anders mit guttem gewissen leben und mit Gott faren will«. WA 12, p. 114,26–33.

123 Luther's discussion of this passage fills the remainder of the first section. One interesting note is Luther's allusion to Moloch in addressing St. Paul's usage of »brennen«. The applicability of Moloch had first come up in Karlstadt's discussion of monastic vows in which he had accused unchaste celibates of »burning« their seed by offering it to Moloch via secret sins. Luther had been critical of Karlstadt's interpretation of that verse and here changes the referent to those youth sacrificed by being confined in the monastic life. See WA 12, p. 116,12–17. See also Luther's comments on Moloch offerings already in 1520 in WA 6, p. 252,19–34.

124 WA 12, p. 133,15ff.

for chastity, but we are all born to beget children and carry the burdens of married life, according to Gen. 1, 2, and 3. Now, if someone should not suffer from this necessity, he would be the exception solely by the grace and the miraculous hand of God, not because of command, vow, or intent. Where God does not effect this, it may be attempted, but it will come to no good end[125].

By way of conclusion, with this writing we have now observed the full polemical power of Genesis 1:28 through its application to the main text utilized to prop up celibacy, most often with the authority of the church father Jerome. That is to say, while our verse initially appeared as a seeming afterthought and peripheral argument in *De votis monasticis iudicium*, Luther has now explicitly interpreted 1 Corinthians 7 in light of his understanding of »Be fruitful and multiply«. Although we have observed this general connection and argument previously, it is only now in this writing that the verse has realized its full polemical force.

Continuing on with our survey, in November 1523, Melanchthon had a brief commentary on the first six chapters of Genesis printed[126]. While Melanchthon does not deal extensively with the topic of »Be fruitful and multiply«, his presentation clearly reflects Luther's understanding (post-1521) of the verse[127]. This is evident when he comments upon Genesis 1:22[128] and then more clearly stated when he reaches 1:28 and its continuing universal applicability. Interestingly, and

---

125 LW 28, p. 55. »So ist nů dis die summa dis Capitels: Gutt ists nicht freyen, es sey denn nott. Nott aber ists, wo Gott die seltzam edle gabe der keuscheyt nicht gibt, denn keyn mensch ist zur keuscheyt geschaffen, sondern allesampt sind wyr geschaffen kinder zu tzeugen, und die mühe des ehlichen lebens zu tragen, Gene. 1. 2. und 3. Soll nů yemand ynn dißer nott nicht seyn, den soll widder gepott, noch gelübd, noch fursatz, sondern alleyn gottis gnade und wunder hand ausnemen. Wo es der nicht thutt, so mags wol angehaben werden, aber es wirtt keyn gutt ende gewynnen«. WA 12, p. 141,23–30.
126 Philipp Melanchthon, In obscuriora aliquot capita Geneseos Phil. Melan. annotationes, Hagenau 1523 (VD16 M 3460).
127 This commentary was largely based on the sermons Luther had preached previously (1519–1521) on the early chapters of Genesis. See MAURER, Der junge Melanchthon, pp. 114ff. Here we must note, whereas Maurer (leaning heavily on H. Sick's earlier work, cf. endnote 100, p. 512) heavily emphasizes the connection between Luther's earlier sermons with Melanchthon's 1523 Genesis commentary, it must be asserted that Melanchthon's understanding of the creative and effective word of God bears greater similarity with Luther's Wartburg developments on this topic, particularly as relates to Genesis 1:28. Thus, while there may be reliance upon the earlier Genesis sermons, the development of thought did not remain stagnant and tied merely to the »state of the question« of that earlier date.
128 Melanchthon, In obscuriora aliquot capita Geneseos, Dii[r].

new to our discussion of this text, Melanchthon connects »Be fruitful and multiply« with the *lex charitatis*[129].

The following month, Luther once again touched on Genesis 1:28 as he preached on Genesis 12 and the promised Descendent of Abraham[130]. Here, although Luther adds nothing fundamentally new, he continues to emphasize his teaching on the relationship between God's word and his works. Rörer records, »The Jews make a greeting out of this blessing, though it is not that. As previously *stated*, ›Be fruitful and multiply‹ are not words, rather they are themselves the substance [*das wesen*]. *God* Himself spoke and they were done, *for* speaking and doing is the same with God«[131].

To the closing days of December 1523 also belongs Luther's letter to the Teutonic Knights[132]. This letter, the culmination of two years of diplomatic and theological discussions, offered counsel regarding reformation to be undertaken in the lands of the Teutonic Knights and, above all, the recommendation that they shed their vows of chastity and become Christian husbands.

The central argument pervading Luther's writing in this letter is the supremacy of God's Word over man's word. Accordingly, the human teaching of monastic vows ought to be set aside and marriage, as taught by God's Word, ought to be embraced. In this tract, Genesis 2 serves as the primary argument for marriage. Nevertheless, Luther does refer to Genesis 1 and its irresistible power also as a basis for marriage and as an argument against the possibility of keeping a vow of perpetual chastity[133].

---

129 »Deinde, q videt bonum opus esse, destinat utilitati creaturarum, ut mutuum obsequium alii aliis præstemus. Item lex charitatis expressa est, cum iubet crescere & multiplicari. Nam cum gignere iubet, certe excolere præcipit quae genuimus. Ita inter se omnes homines necessitudine geniturae cohæremus. Iam in Hebraeis pro crescite est fructificate, quod ad omnia obse quia pertinere videtur«. Ibid., Ei^r.
This connection is perhaps especially noteworthy considering Melanchthon's summarized treatment of natural law in his *Loci Communes* (1521) in which his former handling of matters related to marriage and procreation is seemingly omitted but implicitly included under the law of love (cf. in doing no harm to one's neighbor). See MAURER, Der junge Melanchthon, pp. 291–294. It is also noteworthy that Melanchthon has here ordered procreation under the Law of Love (with regard to natural law) and not as something held in common with the animal world. Here he is consistent with his thinking in his *Loci Communes* as well as his shift away from the stance taken in his *Capita* of 1520.
130 *Predigten über das erste Buch Mose*, 13 December 1523 (WA 14, p. 302).
131 »Iudei faciunt ex hac benedictione ein gruß, sed non. Sicut supra ›Crescite et multiplicamini‹ non sunt verba, sed das wesen selbert. Ipse dixit et facta sunt, loqui et facere idem est deo«. WA 14, p. 306,8–11.
132 *An die herren deutschs Ordens [...]* (December 1523). For dating considerations and the background of this letter see WA 12, pp. 228–230.
133 »Darumb wilcher geystlicher will ehlich werden, der soll gottis wort fur sich nehmen, daselbs sich auff verlassen und ynn des selben namen freyen, unangesehen, ob Concilia fur odder hernach

The final appearance of Genesis 1:28 from this wave of attacks against monastic vows appeared in March 1524 with Luther's accompanying letter to Florentina von Oberweimar's own account of her escape from the Neu-Helfta convent outside of Eisleben[134]. While Oberweimar's retelling of her experiences lacks any allusion to our verse, Luther's introduction does not fail to state what had become one of the most powerful biblical arguments against vows of celibacy, God's command to »Be fruitful and multiply«[135].

---

komen, und soll also sagen: Gott spricht Gene. 1. und 2. Ich sey eyn man und du eyn web, und sollen und müssen zu samen, uns zu mehren, das kann und soll uns niemand weren noch verpieten, und ist nicht unser macht anders geloben. Auff das wort wagen wyrs und thuns, nur zu troʒ und zu widder allen Concilien, kirchen, allen menschen seʒen, allen gelübden, gewonheytten, und was da widder seyn möcht oder yhe gewesen ist. Augen und oren zu, und nur gottis wort yns herʒ gefasset! Und obs uns die Concilia und menschen hynfurt erleubten und zu liessen, so wollen wyr yhr urlaub nicht haben, und umb yhrs zulassens willen nichts widder thun noch lassen«. WA 12, p. 238,15–26. One note of interest is that this tract's entire argument fits the basic pattern of argument which Luther would later employ by means of Aristotle's four causes in such writings as his later commentary on Psalm 127.

134 *Eyn geschicht wie Got eyner Erbarn kloster Jungfrawen ausgeholffen hat. Mit eynem Sendebrieff M. Luthers an die Graffen zu Manßfelt.* (March 1524). For dating of this letter and background information, see WA 15, pp. 79f. For an extended treatment of the history, context, and content of this writing, see Antje RÜTTGARDT, Klosteraustritte in der frühen Reformation. Studien zu Flugschriften der Jahre 1522 bis 1524, Gütersloh 2007, pp. 256–315.

135 As with Luther's writing to the Teutonic Knights, Luther once again frames the debate around the authority of God's Word versus that of human teaching. Moreover, he emphasizes the importance of freely given, and not forced, works that accord with God's will. Along these lines, he poses the question as to why a nun or monk ought to leave the cloister. Answering, Luther emphasizes freedom of conscience and so that God is not tempted through opposition to His own created order. He states, »Ists doch nicht zuthůn umb der schnöden schendlichen lust willen des fleyschs, wilche man doch ynn klöstern nicht lesst, wer sonst nicht frum seyn will, es geschehe auch alleyn odder selb ander. Es ist umb der nott willen zu thůn, das eyn mensch nicht zur keuscheyt, sondern sich zu mehren geschaffen ist, Gen. 1., wilchs werck bey uns nicht stehet widder zuverloben noch zu hyndern. Es sind ettliche fursten und herrn zornig uber diese sache, Und ist nicht wunder: wůsten sie, was ich weys, sie wurden villeicht nicht wissen, wie sie mich drumb genug loben und ehren sollten, und mehr da zu thůn denn ich. Gott wollt E. G. mit seyner barmherʒickeyt erweichen, disem Göttlichen angehabenen werck zu folgen und aller welt eyn gůt exempel geben, die armen gefangen zu erlösen, Amen«. WA 15, p. 88,21–31.

Not included in our analysis, but of relevance to this section is Luther's letter dated 3 August 1524 to three nuns (WA Br 3, pp. 326–328). In this letter Luther includes, next to evangelical freedom, concerns about the flesh as a central reason for embracing marriage. He writes, »Dy ander ursach ist das fleisch. wye wol hyrin das weibervolck sich schemet, solchs zcu bekennen, ßo gibts doch dy schrifft unnd erfarunge, das unter vyl tausent nicht eyne ist, der goth gnade gibt, reyne keuscheith zcu halden, Szonder eyn weip hoth sich selber nicht in der gewalt, Goth hoth yhren leib geschaffen, bey eynem man zcu seyn, kinder tragen und zeihen, wye dy worth klar [lauten] Gen.1.[28] und dy geliedmas des leibs von goth selbs dorzu vor[ordnet] auß weisen. Szo naturlich alz essen und trincken, Schloffen und [wachen] ist von goth alzo geschaffen, Alzo wyl er auch das naturlich,

4.5 Further Opposition to Luther

As we give further consideration to the debate surrounding Genesis 1:28, it is rather surprising that Luther's opponents spent relatively little time and energy attempting to oppose his interpretation of our verse. This is perhaps especially unexpected if we keep in mind the strength of the argument and its underlying importance to the Wittenberg rejection of monastic vows and insistence on priestly marriage. While the following brief survey of oppositional writings is not intended to be complete, it does demonstrate the relative unconcern on the part of Luther's opponents for the *substance* of this particular teaching of his.

Of the responses that appeared in 1523 and 1524 to Luther's underlying emphasis upon Genesis 1:28, Johann Dietenberger issued perhaps the most thorough response to this teaching – particularly with regard to scriptural argumentation and reasoning[136] – in his *Antwort das Junckfrawen die klöster und klösterliche gelübt nümer götlich verlassen mögen*[137]. In this writing, published in September 1523[138], the Dominican professor from Mainz took on Luther's *Ursach und Antwort, dass Jungfrauen Klöster verlassen mögen* in point by point fashion[139]. In the interest of our theme, we will concentrate primarily on Dietenberger's response to Luther's fourth point. Prior to this, however, Dietenberger accused Luther of inciting Christians to break sacred vows[140]. He turned especially to the authority of St. Augustine and 1 Corinthians 7:20 to argue that those who have taken vows ought to remain in the calling in which they find themselves[141]. The Dominican then proceeded to

---

[daß] man und weip beynander ehelich seyn sollen. Dorumb ist dises genugsam und sol sich nymandt des schemen, dozeu yn goth geschaffen und gemacht hoth, wo sichs fuleth, das es dye hohe selczame gabe nicht hoth, eraus zcugehen und thun, wozcu sichs findet geschaffen. Solchs werdet yhr alles reichlich und genugsame lesen und lernen, wen yhr heraus kompt und rechte prediget horen werden«. WA Br 3, p. 327,21–34.

136 LAUBE, Das Gespann Cochlaeus, pp. 128f., points out that Dietenberger sought not merely to argue on the basis of the church fathers as other opponents of Luther did, but to oppose Luther on his own turf – that of biblical exegesis.

137 Johann DIETENBERGER, Antwort das Junckfrawen die klöster vnd klösterliche gelübt nümer götlich verlassen mögen, edited by Johannes COCHLAEUS, Strasbourg 1523 (VD16 L 6886). Perhaps unsurprisingly, the forward to this work was written by Johann Cochlaeus.

138 Based on the date given in the dedication of ibid., Ai^v. For Cochlaeus's role in the publication of Dietenberger's writings as well as the writing timeline, see LAUBE, Das Gespann Cochlaeus, pp. 130–132.

139 KAWERAU, Die Reformation und die Ehe, pp. 25–27, includes a discussion of Dietenberger and his polemical writings against Luther.

140 DIETENBERGER, Antwort das Junckfrawen, Aiii^v–Bi^r.

141 Ibid., Aiiii^v.

defend the spiritual estate against accusations that children were brought in against their will to a place where the Gospel itself was silenced[142].

With that, Dietenberger began to answer Luther's fourth point, namely, that women were not designed to be virgins, but rather, according to Genesis 1, were made to »be fruitful and multiply«[143]. After an initial paragraph of verbal skirmishing, Dietenberger responds that chastity is indeed a common gift[144], even calling on the authority of Sts. Paul (1 Corinthians 7) and James (1) to affirm that those who seek it will receive it[145]. Dietenberger then proceeds more directly to Luther's argument – particularly in criticizing Luther's understanding of the woman as created not for virginity but for bearing children. Of particular note is Dietenberger's argument that the mere endorsement of virginity in Scripture undoes Luther's teaching. Moreover, he asks, how can the Holy Spirit counsel a vocation for which He has not created the woman? Thus, Dietenberger charges Luther with knowing more about women than the Creator and argues that Luther has indeed blasphemed God[146].

Dietenberger then continues to attack Luther's understanding of *crescite et multiplicamini* – that these words were a command of a durative nature – by affirming, as was customary for Luther's opponents, that this command was only for certain people and only at a time when the earth needed to be filled. Otherwise, if women really were created for the sole purpose of bearing children, how could a virgin be saved or virginity be recommended in Scripture by Christ or St. Paul[147]?

142　Ibid., Bi^r–Ci^r.
143　Ibid., Ci^r.
144　»Die erste lügen. Es ist unmüglich/das die gab der keüscheit so gemein sey/alß die klöster seindt. Sagt an du gotßloser münch/wie kā die gab d[er] keüscheit nit also gemein sein alß klöster/so doch gott die selbige sampt andern gaben dem mensche̅ zů seiner sele seligkeit fürderlich zůgesagt unnd verheissen hat/nit allein klöster leüten/sund[er] allen die in darumb anrüffen/ir hoffnūg zů im setzen/nit in sichselbst/od[er] in eygnen krefften getrawen«. Ibid., Ci^v–Cii^r.
145　Ibid., Cii^v.
146　»Die ander lügen. Weibs bild seind nitt geschaffen junckfrawen zů sein/ sunder kind[er] zů tragen. Das diß geloge̅ sey/bezeügt sant Pauls/da er sagt/dz die jhene̅ die junckfrawchafft wöllen behalten/recht unnd wol thůn/die sie aber behalten/und nit zu der ee greiffen/noch vil besser thůn. Werden auch seliger sein/die also junckfrawen bleiben/nach dem rath des heiligen geistes. Wie kan aber nun gott der heilig geist weibs bilden rathen/zů dem er sie nit geschaffen hat? Es můß ye ein unweiser schöpffer sein/dem das ende seines geschöpffs verborge̅ ist/und nit weißt/zů welche̅ ende er sein geschöpff geschaffen hab. Was ist es nun anders gesagt/weibs bild seind nit geschaffen jungfrawen zů sein/sunder zů trage̅/dan sagen/ gott ist ein unweiser schöpffer/d[er] nitt so vil weißheit bey im hat/dz er wissen mög das ende seines geschöpffs. Dañ er wenet/er hab weibs bilder zů kinder tragen gechaffen/so rath er in/dz sie sollen iügkfrawe̅ bleibe̅. Ist aber dz nit ein grosse gotßlesterūg/genůgsamliche ursach zů verwerffen uñ zů vertilgken dise deine unbilliche antwort/mit lügen besudelt/und mit gottes lesterung befestiget«. Ibid., Ciiii^v–Di^r.
147　»Die dritten lügen/wie gott sprach. Es ist doch mer dan klärlichen erlogen/dz got hab gesprochen/ weibs bild seyen geschaffen/nit iungkfrawen zů sein. Es it wol geschribe̅/gott hab gesagt/ in d[er]

The remainder of *Antwort das Junckfrawen* is concerned primarily with 1 Corinthians 7 and Matthew 19. Nevertheless, it is clear from the above that the main argument central to the entire discussion, aside from fundamental questions related to evangelical freedom and the Gospel itself, centered on the proper understanding of Genesis 1:28. Did it have abiding importance for mankind and thus necessitate that other relevant passages such as 1 Corinthians 7 and Matthew 19 should be understood in its light, or was it to be interpreted in the light of the preferred oppositional understanding of these New Testament passages? By this point in the controversy, the answers offered by each side had clearly been firmly drawn.

A second significant work to appear against Luther's *De votis monasticis* was the third volume of Josse Clichtove's *Antilutherus Iudoci Clichtovei Neoportuensis, doctoris theologi, Tres libros complectens*[148]. Here, as might be expected, Clichthove offers criticism to Luther's understanding of *crescite et multiplicamini*. Nevertheless, he takes a different approach than typically taken by Luther's other opponents. Namely, he argues that Luther's understanding of the sinfulness of marriage implied that God is commanding sin with His command that man »Be fruitful and multiply«[149]. In this way, although he does touch on this important verse, he seems to miss the fact that Luther's understanding of »Be fruitful and multiply« is that which actually lies behind his understanding of 1 Corinthians 7 and Matthew 19.

A further example of polemical writing involving monastic vows appeared on 13 August 1524. On that day, the second of two tomes directed against Luther's *De votis monasticis* was published in Cologne by Johann Dietenberger[150]. Although these volumes deal extensively with many of the prominent arguments from his opponent's work, somewhat surprisingly, he offers no obvious attention to the

---

zeit/do noch wenig menschen warē/uñ menschliche geschlecht solt gemeret werdē zů unsern ersten eltern Adā uñ Eua/uñ andern/alß Noe etc. Seyt fruchtbar uñ meret eüch. Hat doch in disen wortē nitt gebottē allen weibern die ym̄er geboren sollen werdē/kind[er] zů tragē/auch nit v[er]bottē zů seine zeitē iūgkfrawē zů bleibē/sunder het Christus nit zů d[er] iūgkfrawschafft gerattē/auch den iūgfrawen den hym̄el nit v[er]heissen. Het auch S. Pauls durch den heiligē geist nit geratē/ iūgfrawschafft zů behaltē/nit gesagt/es sey eerlicher/besser/ zu got behilffliger/uñ seliger auß d[er] ee in d[er] iūgkfrawschafft bleibē«. Ibid., Di^r.

148 KAWERAU, Die Reformation und die Ehe, p. 27.
149 Josse CLICTHOVE, Antilutherus Iudoci Clichtovei Neoportuensis, doctoris theologi, Tres libros complectens, Paris 1524, X.iiii^v–X.v^r, URL: <https://books.google.no/books?id=xVhbAAAAcAAJ&printsec=frontcover&hl=no#v=onepage&q&f=false> (18 Aug 22).
150 Johann DIETENBERGER, Iohan. Dytenbergii Theologi, contra temerarium Martini Luteri de uotis monasticis iudicium, liber [...] : quo singulatim illius rationibus, quas omnes ex ordine passim autor praetexit, ex sacris literis luculentissime respondet [...], Cologne 1524 (VD16 D 1479). KAWERAU, Die Reformation und die Ehe, pp. 25f., writes briefly about this work which Luther paid little or no attention to.

merits or demerits of Genesis 1:28 or the importance of *crescite et multiplicamini* to Luther's argumentation.

Kaspar Schatzgeyer, a name not exactly new to this debate[151], once again joined the fray in 1524 to write against Luther's attack on monastic vows in his *Von dem waren Christlichen Leben*[152]. Schatzgeyer, though he seemingly gives Genesis 1:28 greater significance by singling out Luther's teaching on this verse as »Der xxvi. irrsal«, in the end says little more with this verse than any other opponent. He merely asserts that the verse is no longer binding[153].

Finally, we note that Faber's *Opus adversus* (examined above) was reprinted in Cologne as *Malleus in haeresim Lutheranam* this same year[154]. With that work we noted that Faber merely states that the command *crescite et multiplicamini* was given previously to fill the earth while celibacy now serves to fill heaven. Thus, in this entire line of substantial works appearing in 1524, nothing of true significance is added against the »Lutheran« arguments in the polemical writings aimed directly at Luther and his teachings.

4.6 Traces of Melanchthon's *Affektenlehre* in the Writings of Luther and His Wittenberg Colleagues on Genesis 1:28 (1522–1524)

Proceeding from our working hypothesis that Melanchthon's understanding of *naturales quosdam affectus* comprised a part of Luther's emerging teaching on Genesis 1:28, we might speculate that we would find traces both of relevant terms and their related discussions in the ensuing writings dealing with our topic. In particular, we might expect to find not merely rote statements of Genesis 1:28 as a sort of command but elements of the verse's explication that reflect Melanchthon's ideas of innate drives or urges. We might even expect to find not only *affectus* but the corresponding vocabulary in such discussions, whether terms such as *insitus*, *natura*, *lex naturae*, or their German equivalents.

With this in mind, we will here endeavor a *tour de force* through relevant writings of Luther (and his Wittenberg colleagues) to see if such a correspondence might be found. Thus, we turn our attention once again to Luther's *De votis monasticis*

---

151 See fn. 52 of this chapter.
152 Kaspar SCHATZGEYER, Von dem waren Christlichen Leben, in wem es stee : Vil materi inn lateinischen biechlin von dem klösterlichen leben und gelybten verauß gangen zu samen getragen [...], Augsburg 1524 (VD16 S 2346).
153 »Es irren auch gröslich/die sagēd dz/das gebot d[er] erstē satzung/unsern ersten eltern gegeben (wachsend/uñ werden gemanigfaltiget) auch v[er]bind jederman im newen gesatz/das auß ob angezaygten orten götlicher geschrifft/klar erscheint/das falsch ist«. Ibid., Mi^v.
154 FABRI, Mallevs Ioannis Fabri.

iudicium. Although we have previously set forth contextual and circumstantial arguments that suggest the influence of Melanchthon's teachings regarding the natural affects and natural law, the relevant passage of this work does not offer enough information to establish any firm textual relationship. After all, Luther's inclusion of Genesis 1:28 in arguments based on natural reason[155], as we noted, along with his reference to »that divine commandment of nature«[156] do not have to be understood in light of his colleague's thought, though neither ought such a possibility be excluded. Nevertheless, if Melanchthon's understanding is to be observed here, it remains in the background and not explicitly in the text. A similar conclusion might be reached on the basis of Luther's *Weihnachtpostille*[157], though we see once again Luther's usage of *vorordnet* – certainly conceptually close to *lex naturae*[158].

Moving forward to Luther's *Vom ehelichen Leben*, a general correspondence of thought can be better observed. We note this at two separate points. First, Luther does not shy away from such terminology as *eyngepflantzte natur und artt*, which, he notes, cannot be hindered. Interestingly, although Luther bases the effective power of this in God's creative word, its power to influence man seems little different from that of Melanchthon's high estimation of human affects. A further point, however, which suggests that Luther is interacting with at least some of the same philosophical conversations as Melanchthon, is the fact that he draws a correspondence between the affective nature and the relevant parts of the body[159]. Given that the affects

---

155 WA 8, p. 629,23.
156 LW 44, p. 339; cf. »illud statutum divinum naturae«. WA 8, p. 631,13.
157 WA 10/I/1, p. 615,19–22.
158 While I have left any notion of *ordo* out of the discussion to this point, it should be noted that *ordo* is conceptionally relevant for Melanchthon's later *Affektenlehre* (and perhaps already at this point). See Philipp Melanchthon, Ethicae Doctrinae Elementa et Enarratio Libri quinti Ethicorum, edited by Günter FRANK and Michael BEYER, Stuttgart-Bad Cannstatt 2008, p. 100. Henning LINDSTRÖM, Skapelse och Frälsing i Melanchthons Teologi, Stockholm 1944, pp. 87–122, notes the interplay and interrelatedness between all of nature, *affectus*, *ordo*, and *lex* and their relationship to the divine will. Moreover, it is of note that, for Melanchthon, it is through the affects that the rational and volitional elements of man are bound to the bodily and earthly, and thus to the created, physical ordering of nature (pp. 170, 174, 187, 198).
159 »Denn diß wort, da got spricht: ›Wachsset und mehret euch‹, ist nicht eyn gepot ßondern mehr den eyn gepot, nemlich eyn gottlich werck, das nicht bey uns stehet tzuverhyndern odder noch tzulaßen, ßondern ist eben alßo nott, *alß das ich eyn manß bild sey, und nöttiger denn essen und trinken, fegen und außwerffen, schlaffen und wachen. Es ist eyn eyngepflantzte natur und artt eben ßo wol als die glidmaß, die datzu gehören.* Drumb gleych wie got niemandt gepeut, das er man sey oder weyb, ßondern schaffet, das sie ßo mussen seyn, Alßo gepeutt er auch nicht, sich mehren, ßondern schafft, das sie sich mussen mehren. Und wo man das wil weren, das ists dennoch ungeweret und gehet doch durch hurerey, ehebruch und stummen sund seynen weg, denn es ist natur und nicht wilkore hierynnen«. WA 10/II, p. 276,21–26 (emphasis added).

were understood to have their seat in the organs of the body, most especially in the heart, such mention of the various parts of the body as were acknowledged to have particular drives suggests, at a minimum, that Luther is here taking part in the discourse surrounding the affects.

Skipping over Luther's sermon for the Tuesday after Easter (1523) as well as his writing to Leonhard Koppe[160], we arrive at Luther's sermons on Genesis also in the spring of 1523. Here we see Luther designating the effects of God's blessing in Genesis 1:28 once again as »implanted nature« and »a work of the Creator implanted in creaturely nature«[161]. Somewhat later, Rörer notes Luther as saying that God's word, »Be fruitful!«, has been implanted in the man and the woman, in order that they would increase[162]. Furthermore, he refers to this as an ordinance of God[163]. To be sure, Luther's treatment of Genesis 1:28 in the spring of 1523 does not offer any clear indications of direct reliance or connection with Melanchthon's own teaching. It is not, however, a stretch to note that it does contain a certain amount of the vocabulary and conceptual framework which we have previously traced out with Melanchthon on this topic.

Jumping ahead to the summer of 1523, however, we find a much clearer reflection of Melanchthon's *Naturaffektenlehre* in Justus Jonas's response to Johann Faber, a task which had been assigned to Jonas by Luther and which was also printed with a dedication by Luther. Thus, although we are not dealing first and foremost with a writing of Luther, we are at least dealing within the purview of Luther's knowledge and approval. Here, although the major lines of argumentation brought forth by Jonas reflect Luther's teaching on God's creative word, Jonas is clearly speaking to Melanchthon's *affectus quosdam naturales* when he writes,

> Therefore it is not in our powers to take up or lay down that nuptial impetus and disposition engraved in *our* nature [*naturae insculptum affectum*][164], by which a woman eagerly desires a man and a man *desires* a woman, but this is how we have been created by God, how we have been made, how we have been fashioned. Therefore, just as fire cannot fail to

---

160 See WA 11, pp. 92–94 and p. 398,1–20, respectively. With the former, the line of argumentation is bound almost entirely with Luther's teaching of the effective word and working of God. In addition to this, with the latter, significant attention is given to the purpose of the woman's body.
161 Cf. »eingepflantzte natur« and »opus creatoris creaturarum naturae insitum«. WA 14, p. 109,19 & 24.
162 Cf. »›Crescite et multiplicamini‹ […] Ita mulieri et viro implantatum est, ut crescant«. WA 14, p. 112,7–9.
163 Cf. »Fatua ergo sunt illa vota, quae contra dei ordinationem faciunt«. WA 14, p. 112,13.
164 Note the context and manner, once again, in which *affectum* is used. This supports our thesis that the Wittenberg understanding of Genesis 1:28 parallels Melanchthon's *affectus quosdam naturales* from his *Loci Communes* (1521), as has been previously observed.

burn *nor* water fail to be wet, because each one has been created this way, so the woman cannot fail eagerly to desire the man, and in turn, the man cannot fail to be moved toward the woman[165].

Moreover, as Jonas continues, he perfectly demonstrates our hypothesis that Melanchthon's *Affektenlehre* does indeed take its rightful place in the Wittenberg teaching on Genesis 1:28. Jonas writes,

> For this word »Increase and multiply«, is neither law nor command, but a living and effective word. Indeed, *it is* the work of God, which does not cease to act and to work in nature. There is nothing found in us *which is able* to impede or hinder this work of God any more than we might make ourselves *into* different human beings or *into* angels. Therefore, just as it is not from my strength, but it is mere creation and nature that I am male and *that* I have members of this or of that sex, so it is not from me, but this reproduction (or the inclination and desire toward reproduction) is clearly something inborn and engrained.
> And just as *our* nature is so created that it is not able to abstain from food or drink or from any other necessary things, it is likewise so created that it is unable not to burn and to be inflamed with desire and ardor to reproduce itself. God has never instructed anyone to be male or female, but has so created *and* has so formed and built them to be by nature male and female, as also He has not taught them to increase and multiply, but implanted and inserted it in their nature and this double sex that they should burn toward each other and by an innate force and drive be brought to increase and reproduce. Therefore, it is not for you to attempt, by the strength of any man or of any created thing, to restrain or hinder this drive or these flames thus implanted in *your* nature itself and innate to *each* sex, unless God should remove it by an extraordinary calling or lofty gift. In Matthew 19, Christ enumerates three types of Eunuchs. Unless you consider yourself to be from the first two types, or *are* with certainty of the third, namely, that you have been more highly called by God, nothing is more prudent than to marry – also because the Holy Spirit was knowing and was thoroughly understanding his creature. In the Holy Scriptures you will prove no such thing, even if you might go through both testaments, such as you teach about celibacy. No such example will you discover of such an extremely broad, general chastity[166].

---

165 »Illum ergo genialem impetum, & naturæ insculptum affectum quo mulier concupiscit masculum, & masculus foeminam, nō est nostrarum uirium sumere aut ponere, sed sic creati a DEO, sic ficti, sic conditi sumus. Haud aliter ergo atqʒ ignis non potest non calere, aqua non potest non madere, quod utrunqʒ sic sit creatum, sic mulier non potest non concupiscere masculum, contra, masculus non potest non affici erga foeminam«. Jonas, Adversvs Iohannem Fabrum, Ci[r].

166 »Nam hoc uerbum, Crescite, & multiplicamini, non est lex aut præceptum, sed uiuum & efficax uerbum, imo opus dei, quod non definit in natura agere & operari. Hoc opus dei impedire, aut

That same month, Luther also published his commentary on 1 Corinthians 7. Here, although there is ample referral to Genesis 1:28, we note that Luther largely adheres to his pattern of emphasizing God's creative power and word without significant attention being given to desire. Nevertheless, we do find reference to the body's »ways and natural functions« which are described as *created* by God[167]. Moreover, immediately after referring to God's creative word of Genesis 1:28, Luther writes, »So it is by necessity that the man is attracted to the woman and woman to the man, except where God performs a miracle by means of a special gift [...]«[168]. We also find comparison with the natural functions as previously observed in *Vom ehelichen Leben*[169]. Similar observations might be made regarding the other appearances of Genesis 1:28 in Luther's writings throughout the remainder of 1523–1524.

We can therefore conclude this brief survey with the observation that, with respect to Luther's writings, the emphasis is clearly upon his understanding of the creative and enduring power of God's word. While it cannot be clearly shown that he borrows from our hypothesized understanding of Melanchthon's *affectus quosdam naturales*, we can at the very least demonstrate that there is a great amount of semantic and conceptual overlap. What can, however, unquestionably be demonstrated – vis-à-vis Jonas – is that our hypothesized understanding of Melanchthon's teaching on the natural affects is indeed present in Wittenberg circles. Luther certainly must have

---

remorari nihilo magis in nobis situm est, quā hoc est, ut nosmetipsos alios homines aut angelos faciamus. Perinde igitur atque ex meis uiribus non est, sed mera creatio & natura est quod sum masculus, & huius uel illius sexus membra habeam, sic non ex me est, sed plane innatum & insculptum quiddam est hæc propagatio, seu propensio & ardor ad propagandum«.

»Et haud aliter atqȝ sic creata est natura ut non possit carere cibo aut potu aut aliis necessariis rebus, ita & creata est ut non possit nō æstuare & flagrare desiderio & ardore sese propaganda. Non praecepit unquam deus ulli ut esset masculus aut foemina, sed sic creauit, sic finxit & condidit, ut essent ex natura masculus & foemina, sic & non præcepit ut crescerent & multiplicarentur, sed hoc naturæ & gemino huic sexui inseuit & indidit, ut inter sese mutuo exardescat, & natiua ui atqȝ impetu feratur ad crescendum & propagandum. Hunc impetum igitur, has flammas, sic ipsi naturæ insitas, & sexui cognatas, nō est ut ullis humanis, aut ullius creature uiribus cohercere aut reprimere coneris, nisi deus quem peculiari uocatione ac dono sublimiore eximat. Matthei.19. Tria genera Eunuchorum recenset Christus, nisi te sentias ex primis duobus generibus esse, aut certe ex tertio, nempe quod sublimius uocatus sis a deo, nihil tutius est quā nubere. Et quia spiritus sanctus sciebat & penitus cognitam habebat creaturam suam. Nihil tale quicquā, etiam si utrunqȝ testamentum percurras, in scripturis sanctis ostendes, quale uos de coelibatu docetis. Nullum tale exemplum proferes tam latissimi uulgatae castitatis«. Ibid., Ci$^\mathrm{v}$.

167 LW 28, p. 26, cf. »Und lesset dennoch der geyst dem *leybe seyne art und natůrliche werck* [...]«. WA 12, p. 113,27; emphasis added. Shortly later Luther similarly comments, »Wem Gott nicht die besondere gnade gibt, sondern lesst seynem leybe seyn art und natur [...]«. WA 12, pp. 113,36–114,1.

168 LW 28, p. 26, cf. »Also das von nott wegen eyn man sich zum weybe, und eyn weyb zum man halten můs, wo Gott nicht wunder thutt durch eyn besondere gabe [...]«. WA 12, p. 113,32–34.

169 WA 12, p. 113,27–28.

had knowledge of it, and it is furthermore apparently employed with his approval. This understanding of the relevant aspect of Melanchthon's natural affects teaching and its elevation as the good creation of God will only be heightened as we later proceed with our investigation of this hypothesis.

4.7 Excursus: Controversy in Erfurt Surrounding Genesis 1:28

By way of introduction to this section, the question arises: why focus on Erfurt with respect to our verse and its importance to wider Reformation thought and controversy? Stephen Buckwalter notes several reasons why Erfurt is an important area of study concerning questions of celibacy and priestly marriage. He notes, for example, that in no other location was the participation – by both sides – so intense and personal[170]. Along these lines, one is able to observe not just one side of the argument in Erfurt but both the arguments and counterarguments as they go back and forth. Secondly, Erfurt, with its print industry and importance for trade and education, played an important role in the spread of Reformation teaching[171]. Moreover, Buckwalter notes that the debate which unfolded in Erfurt between 1522–1525 included strong undercurrents of personality, age, and learning. It set forth in both print and oral media intended for erudite and popular consumption alike. Finally, it displayed enough distance from Wittenberg so as to demonstrate its own character but enough connections to find strong continuity with that nexus of Reformation thought[172]. Although perhaps on a more limited scale with respect to our verse and its importance, these same factors also make the strife in Erfurt a noteworthy case study, even as Genesis 1:28 finds its place in the midst of these larger questions.

While the debate over celibacy and priestly marriage in Erfurt was introduced and first experienced via works from the outside world, with the flow of the Reformation, the themes of celibacy and priestly marriage protruded more and more into Erfurt

---

170 BUCKWALTER, Priesterehe, pp. 136f. It should also be noted that, on the personal level, the chief opponent of evangelical views (Arnoldi) had been both Luther's teacher and close friend while the latter lived in Erfurt. See Kenneth A. STRAND, Arnoldi von Usingen's Sermo de Matrimonio Sacerdotum et Monachorum. The Text of a Rare Edition, in: Archiv für Reformationsgeschichte 56 (1965), pp. 145–155, at p. 145. Thus, the division and conflict were, in every way, very personal for both sides.
171 BUCKWALTER, Priesterehe, p. 137.
172 Ibid., pp. 137–140. Concerning the connections between Wittenberg and Erfurt in the larger theological context of the Reformation, see Ulman WEISS, Die frommen Bürger von Erfurt. Die Stadt und ihre Kirche im Spätmittelalter und in der Reformationszeit, Weimar 1988, pp. 112–143, in which he documents not only the growth of Reformation influence in Erfurt, but especially the strong personal Wittenberg connections that nursed its development.

dialogue and debate. Buckwalter notes that in July 1523 these subjects were first treated on their own in Erfurt, and that by none other than the esteemed and erudite Erfurt professor Bartholomäus Arnoldi von Usingen[173], Luther's erstwhile professor. For our purposes, it is with Arnoldi's work, *Sermo de Matrimonio Sacerdotum Ex Monachorum exiticiorum* that our verse officially enters the Erfurt controversy. Yet, before we look at its debut and context, we do well at least to ask, how did it come to be there in the first place?

Buckwalter offers a helpful overview of relevant tracts and writings that were known to have existed or been printed in Erfurt in the early 1520s leading up to Arnoldi's *Sermo de Matrimonio*. What is interesting is that the majority of the texts mentioned do not directly deal with Genesis 1:28[174]. In other words, as noted elsewhere[175], outside of Wittenberg circles early Reformation pamphlets against imposed clerical celibacy largely lacked emphasis on Genesis 1:28. This was something that was particularly true prior to 1523. The question remains, then, if the debate about Genesis 1:28 was not a general feature of discussion prior to 1523, what caused Arnoldi to strike out against the reformation teaching with such explosive force in the summer of 1523 – particularly attacking and caricaturing the »Lutheran« view of »Be fruitful and multiply«?

While our answer must remain somewhat tentative on this point, there are several possibilities that could have given rise to this issue in Erfurt. First, although it is a point that had not yet been addressed in the written sources outlined by Buckwalter[176], Arnoldi's comments point to the reality that Genesis 1:28 was indeed part of the ongoing dialogue of the time. Thus, one can perhaps assume that it was present at least in the spoken sermons of his opponents. Barring this, there exists the possibility that Arnoldi was not actually responding to such sermons, but rather merely trying to caricature and lampoon the broader Wittenberg teaching, particularly through association with sects and heretical groups as had happened elsewhere in the Strasbourg controversy[177]. This possibility is perhaps more plausible when one notes that throughout the entire relevant written corpus of Arnoldi's opponents,

---

173 BUCKWALTER, Priesterehe, p. 148.
174 Buckwalter mentions Karlstadt's *Apologia* (1521) as the initial impetus to the Erfurt debates and then such works as Augustin von Alveldt's *Von dem ehlichen standt* and the anonymously printed *Eyn buchleyn wieder den Sermon Augustini Alveldes*, Erfurt 1522 (VD16 B 9125). Although these works dealt with the themes of monastic vows and the marriage of priests, none of them brought Genesis 1:28 explicitly into the debate. See BUCKWALTER, Priesterehe, pp. 148–152.
175 See KLAWITTER, Forceful and Fruitful, Chapter 5.
176 BUCKWALTER, Priesterehe, p. 139, provides a chart chronicling the central *Flugschriften* in the Erfurt context (1522–1525). Noteworthy is the fact that neither Arnoldi's earlier *Responsio ad confutationem* (1522) nor his opponent, Johann Culsamer's, prior works included any reference to »Be fruitful and multiply«.
177 See BUCKWALTER, Priesterehe, p. 228.

»Be fruitful and multiply« occurs in print only once[178]. Yet, the question remains, how did this theme come to be a part of the discussions in the Erfurt context?

In answer to this question, we can put forth several possibilities. First, although such early significant works on our verse as *De votis monasticis iudicium* and *Vom ehelichen Leben* were not printed in Erfurt, several relevant works were indeed printed there. This, when combined with the continual flow of information and materials between Wittenberg and Erfurt, would have provided adequate opportunity for relevant ideas to arrive and circulate in Erfurt[179]. Second, there were also key personal connections making this much more likely. Perhaps the prime candidate through whom such influence might have flowed would be Justus Jonas. Jonas, a humanist, professor, and preacher in Erfurt, had been an earlier follower of Erasmus. By the time of Luther's trip to Worms in 1521, however, he had decisively proven himself to be a faithful supporter of Luther and the evangelical cause[180]. During the summer of 1521, after receiving a position at the University of Wittenberg, he continued to carry on lively correspondence with his personal friend (and one of the main Erfurt protagonists), Johann Lang. It was through this friendship, in fact, that several of Luther's works arrived in and were published in Erfurt[181]. During this period, Luther had also arranged for Jonas to stay with Lang during a visit to Erfurt[182]. Furthermore, Justus Jonas was not far removed from the main issue in question. He married in 1522, was responsible for the German translation of Luther's *De votis monasticis*[183], and, as noted earlier, penned the Wittenberg response to Faber in August 1523.

---

178 See ibid., p. 139, for a more complete listing of the works of Arnoldi's main opponents. So far as I have found, the sole exception to this claim is the work of Thomas Stör as will be discussed below.
179 A review of Josef BENZING/Helmut CLAUS, Lutherbibliographie. Verzeichnis der gedruckten Schriften Martin Luthers bis zu dessen Tod, Baden-Baden 1989, pp. 141f., shows that the first of Luther's Erfurt-printed writings to emphasize man's procreative disposition was *Wider den falsch genannten geistlichen Stand des Papsts und der Bischöfe* (WA 10/II, p. 156). This work was printed twice in 1522 by Matthes Maler. Significantly also for the Erfurt context, in this writing Luther argued that the ancient deplorable practices associated with Priapus differed only in kind to the Roman church's inclusion of human teaching (WA 10/II, p. 119,1ff.).
Further relevant printings in Erfurt included *Ursach und Antwort* (Maler 1523; Johann Loersfeld 1523), cf. BENZING/CLAUS, Lutherbibliographie, p. 183; *An die Herren des Deutschen Ordens* (Maler 1524), cf. ibid., p. 201; *Ein Geschichte, wie Gott einer Klosterjungfrau ausgeholfen hat* (Maler 1524; Wolfgang Stürmer 1524), cf. ibid., pp. 221f.; *Der 127. Psalm ausgelegt an die Christen zu Riga 1524* (Stürmer 1524), cf. ibid., pp. 228f.
180 LEHMANN, Justus Jonas, pp. 27f. See ibid., pp. 18f., 21f., 41, regarding Jonas and Lang during this time.
181 BUCKWALTER, Priesterehe, p. 141, fn. 22.
182 WA Br 2, p. 595. Letter dated end of August/beginning of September 1522.
183 Martin LUTHER, Uon denn geystlichen und kloster gelubden Martini Luthers urteyll, translated by Justus Jonas, Wittenberg 1522 (VD16 L 7327).

A second human conduit through which impetus and influence concerning Genesis 1:28 might have come is Johann Eberlin. Eberlin, though perhaps better known for his connection with the Reformation in southern Germany and his work in Switzerland, was a student and associate of both Luther and Melanchthon in Wittenberg periodically between the years 1521 and 1523. During this time, he wrote an influential work against monastic and priestly celibacy, *Wie gar gefährlich*[184]. This work, with its emphasis upon Genesis 1:28, enjoyed four separate printings in Erfurt in 1523, both in Latin and German[185]. Furthermore, Buckwalter notes that Eberlin publicly read the Latin translation of this work during his stay in Erfurt[186].

A final human conduit for the flow of these ideas would be Martin Luther himself. After all, Johann Lang and Luther had known each other in Erfurt and continued to maintain correspondence into the 1520s[187]. Along these lines, the *Weimar Ausgabe* offers some fifteen letters between Luther and Lang in the years 1520–1522. Of interest with respect to our own investigation, we can observe that Luther referred Lang to *De votis monasticis* and his thoughts there with respect to the question of widows and their relevance to the monastic vow. Clearly, then, Lang – and thus the reform-minded in Erfurt – had the opportunity to have been aware of Luther's teaching on Genesis 1:28 by April 1522[188]. Lang was, apparently, also already familiar with Karlstadt's *Super coelibatu* by this time[189]. Finally, we note that Luther was following the developments in Erfurt closely enough that he knew of, and was pleased with, Arnoldi's initial outrage against Reformation teaching in Erfurt[190].

---

184 For an indication of the popularity, at least based upon print editions, enjoyed by this work, see Christian PETERS, Johann Eberlin von Günzburg ca. 1465–1533, Gütersloh 1994, pp. 351–353. See also Johann EBERLIN VON GÜNZBURG, Wie gar gfarlich sey. So Ain Priester kain Eeweyb hat. Wye Vnchristlich. vnd schedlich aim gmainen Nutz Die menschen seynd. Welche hindern die Pfaffen Am Eelichen stand, Augsburg 1522 (VD16 E 156).

185 PETERS, Johann Eberlin, pp. 352f.

186 BUCKWALTER, Priesterehe, p. 140. The Latin translation of the work dates to 1523; thus, it seems likely that Eberlin read his writing in Erfurt *after* he began service as a pastor in that city on 1 May 1524. See PETERS, Johann Eberlin, p. 257.

187 WEISS, Die frommen Bürger, pp. 114, 137, notes that Luther also was a longstanding friend of Lang and the two were certainly in contact in the early 1520s. Josef PILVOUSEK, Martin Luther und Erfurt, in: Josef FREITAG (ed.), Luther in Erfurt und die katholische Theologie, Leipzig 2001, pp. 18f., details the friendship between Luther and Lang back into the 1510s where the two were both simultaneously assigned to Wittenberg and, even following Lang's return to Erfurt, continued to remain in touch. In fact, Luther installed Lang as the prior of the Erfurt monastery in May of 1516. Moreover, Luther's Ninety-Five Theses were likely introduced in Erfurt via Lang.

188 WA Br 2, p. 495,12f.

189 WA Br 2, p. 495, fn. 4.

190 WA Br 2, p. 595. See also letters dated 29 May (cf. WA Br 2, pp. 547f.) and 26 June 1522 (WA Br 2, pp. 565–566). Luther's correspondence with Lang throughout this time shows that Luther is well aware of Arnoldi and the developments in Erfurt.

Furthermore, Luther himself, accompanied by Melanchthon, apparently visited Erfurt in October of 1522 and preached several sermons both at the *Michaeliskirche* and at the *Kaufmännerkirche*[191].

Whatever the origin of this debate surrounding Genesis 1:28 in Erfurt, on 13 July 1523, Arnoldi preached a sermon which shortly later was printed as *Sermo de matrimonio*. This sermon, not coincidentally, was preached on the wedding day of another priest, Aegidius Mechler[192]. With this sermon, finally, the divide surrounding the words »Be fruitful and multiply« came to the fore also in this important city.

Looking at the sermon itself, we note that our theme, *crescite et multiplicamini*, appears on three separate occasions and that Arnoldi also repeatedly applies the crude epithet »priapists« toward his opponents, thus mocking their teaching on Genesis 1:28[193]. To begin with, then, Arnoldi first brings up the topic after his introduction and then continues to discuss the necessity of chastity outside of marriage. He even notes that marriage is necessary for most people on the grounds of avoiding fornication (1 Corinthians 7)[194]. Nevertheless, he then proceeds to a second point concerning human nature and the divine will. Namely, regarding the connection between *crescite et multiplicamini* (Genesis 1:28 and 9:1) and the Christian, he states,

> Second is the question, whether in the old law marriage was commanded according to Genesis 1 (which is also repeated in Genesis 9), *namely*, »Increase and multiply and fill the earth«? That *commandment*, however, has been lifted by Christ who has rendered marriage free and, at the same time, rendered chastity free. *This He did* insofar as He gave the counsel, so to speak, that the latter [i. e. chastity] *was* a better good than marriage, when He said *that* [Matthew 19] »there are eunuchs who got themselves castrated for the sake of the kingdom of heaven. He who is able to receive *this* let him receive *it*«. The Apostle Paul gave the same counsel when he said [1 Corinthians 7], »Concerning virgins, I do not have a command of the Lord, but I give counsel as one who has acquired mercy from God that *it* is good for a man to be so, etc.«[195].

---

191 PILVOUSEK, Martin Luther und Erfurt, pp. 22f.
192 BUCKWALTER, Priesterehe, p. 153. Aegidius Mechler would later become one of Arnoldi's primary opponents concerning priestly marriage. See ibid., pp. 139, 165–173, 183–185.
193 Ibid., pp. 153–164, provides a more thorough treatment on the entire contents and argumentation of this sermon than this study will attempt to provide.
194 Bartholomäus ARNOLDI, Sermo de Matrimonio Sacerdotum et Monachorum exiticiorum. F. Bartholomei de Vsingen. Ordinis Eremitani S. Augustini, Erfurt 1523 (VD16 A 3752), A2ʳ.
195 »Secundum est Q̃ si in veteri lege preceptum fuerit matrimonium iuxta illud.gene. I. quod et repetitur.ge. 9. crescite et multiplicamini et replete terram illud tamen sublatū est a christo qui liberum dedit matrimonium et simul liberam dedit castitatem in hoc q̃ illam consuluit tanquā melius ßonum matrimonio cū dixit mat.19. sunt eunuchi qui se castraverunt propter regnum celorū qui potest capere capiat. Idē consuluit apostolus Paulus quando.I.cor.7. dixit de virginibus

Of note here is the fact that Arnoldi clearly regards the primordial command as limited primarily to those first recipients at creation and after the Flood (whether Adam and Eve or Noah and his family). He then argues that this command has been abrogated and become non-binding since the time of Christ. This interpretation is made under the assumption that Christ recommended chastity as the better good and has therefore lifted any imperative associated with marriage and procreation. Implicitly rejected, then, is the claim that the command to »Be fruitful and multiply« constitutes human nature and underlies human drives and dispositions.

As *Sermo de matrimonio* continues, it is interesting to note that Arnoldi recognizes a different verse to actually be the favorite verse of his opponents, namely, Matthew 19:6, where Jesus declares, »What God has joined together let no man put asunder«[196]. Nevertheless, shortly thereafter Arnoldi returns to his attack on *crescite et multiplicamini* as he deals with his opponents' argument about the impossibility of the vow of celibacy[197]. He writes,

> If you do not want to make Christ, or his apostle James, a liar, you have to believe *that it is* possible for you with the help of God to keep the vow of continence just as it was possible for Paul to overcome the thorn in the flesh by the grace of God, which Christ said *would* suffice for him when he repeatedly prayed three times, for that *thorn* might be taken from him (2 Corinthians 12), seeing that grace is stronger than nature; he therefore also says in another place, »I can do all things in Him who strengthens me«. Wherefore *it [grace?]* is stupidly and vainly subsumed *[under nature? by the opponents?]*. But perhaps God wants to give it to me. And where now is the faith of the pistologists, who attribute all things to faith, *and* who, while they disparagingly call others sophists and papists, show that they are priapists? *They do this, namely,* by often repeating in their sermons and impressing upon the people the *verse,* »Increase and multiply and fill the earth«. *Here* they

---

preceptū domini non habeo consiliũ autē do tanquā misericordiā cōsecut⁹ a deo qm̄ Bonũ est homini sic esse etc.«. Ibid., A2ʳ. BUCKWALTER, Priesterehe, p. 155, offers a summary of this section. For questions on the proper reading of the text, I have consulted STRAND, Sermo de Matrimonio Sacerdotum, pp. 148–155, and the 1524 Strasbourg print (VD16 ZV 773), though I have retained the originally printed abbreviations.

196 BUCKWALTER, Priesterehe, pp. 156f. (cf. ARNOLDI, Sermo de Matrimonio, A3ʳ). It is interesting to observe Buckwalter's conclusion on this point with reference to the relative importance of *An den Adel*, which seems to be the main text to emphasize this verse (p. 157).

197 While BUCKWALTER, Priesterehe, p. 161, directs the reader to Luther's *Wider den falsch genannten geistlichen Stand des papstes und der Bischöfe* (1522; cf. WA 10/II, pp. 105–158) as the probable background for Arnoldi's comments in this location, it should be noted that Luther's *De votis monasticis*, though lacking the reference to Priapus, deals extensively with the question of the impossibility of a vow and also uses Genesis 1:28 as a supporting text in that argument. Thus, it is possible that Arnoldi is responding to an amalgamation of Luther's writings or their promulgation through the preaching of his opponents.

say *that* man is not born for virginity and chastity, but for begetting and multiplying. This teaching against the counsel of Christ agrees with the writings of the Waldensians, which *teaching* the Pickards in Bohemia and Moravia, whom they say *are* nearest to receiving the gospel, embrace[198].

Noteworthy in this section are the following: First, the evangelical argument is termed as a lack of faith on the part of the reform-minded. Second, such derisive terms as pistologists (*pistologori*)[199] and priapists are applied to them, the latter seemingly in reference to their supposed lust-inspired teaching regarding multiplication[200]. Third, Arnoldi argues that their teaching about human nature and its ends is against the commandment of Christ and more clearly aligned with such heretical groups as the Pickards and Waldensians[201].

As if Arnoldi had not already sufficiently made his point, in the *additio* of his *Sermo de matrimonio*, he once again takes up the theme and closes his work with a final caricaturization of his opponents as »our priapists«. Here he describes them as

---

198 »Qua propter si non vis Christum ac Apostolum eius Ia. facere mēdacē credere habes possibile ti[bi] cum dei adiutorio votū cōtinētiae [ser]uare sicut possibile fuit. pau. stimulū carnis supare grā dei quā illi christus dixit sufficere dū ter rogaret sibi illū auferri. 2.cor.12. qm̄ gracia fortior est natura ppter quod et alibi.d.Oīa possum in eo qui me cōfortat. Quare stolide et frustra subsumitur. Sed qui scio an dare velit mihi deus. Et ubi nūc ē fides pistologorū, qui oīa fidei tribuūt/qui cū alios de spective vocēt sophistas et papistas/se docēt esse priapistas Eo quod in suis cōcionibus illud frequētent et populo inculcent/crescite et multiplicamini et replete terrā/dicētes hoīm natū nō ad virginitatem et castimoniā/sed ad generationē et [multi]plificationē. Que doctrina cōtra cōsiliū Christi/Waldensiū congruit [s]criptis/quā pighardi in Bohemia et Moravia amplectuntur/q̊s illi dicūt pxime accedere evangelio«. Arnoldi, Sermo de Matrimonio, A4ᵛ.
199 This epithet (in this case) refers to those who study faith (Gk. πιστος) and was intended to mock those who placed such emphasis upon the Reformation teaching of faith alone.
200 This point is clearly portrayed in the following section when Arnoldi writes, »Q autem quibus dā priapistis videtur castitas impossibilis/puerile est ridiculosum/cum etiā ex ethnicis eā multi tenuerint. Nōne virgines vestales votū castitatis fecerūt, et illud βauerūt dee Veste et Diane Nonne philosophi quidē naturales castitatis erāt amici/legiīī quippe apud ILaer: de Xeno: q scortū sibi appositum p noctē nō attigerit/quod se cum statua, nō cum hoīe dorminisse dixit. Nō sunt igiī oēs tā titillo si et adeo ppensi in venerem sicut priapiste q̃les sunt exiticij monachi cum sue farine sacerdotib: Si igitur ethnici naturali v̄tute poterāt castitatē βuare quāto magis fideles quibus auxiliū dei spēciale et gratia eius cooperatur dum illa a Christo desiderant et humiliter petūt Qui Mat. 7. dicit petite et dabitur vobis. Querite et invenietis pulsate et aperietur vobis. Oīs enim qui petit accipit. et qui querit invenit et pulsāti aperietur«. Arnoldi, Sermo de Matrimonio, A4ᵛ–B1ʳ.
We might note that the epithet »priapist« is used some six times in the final pages of *Sermo de matrimonio*. Thus, if the question of *crescite et multiplicamini* was not already front and center in the debate, the three direct references to it and the constant mudslinging of »priapist« – with all of its implications – certainly increased the significance of this verse in the Erfurt context.
201 See also Buckwalter, Priesterehe, p. 161.

those who daily speak of »Be fruitful and multiply and fill the earth« as if the continuance of the world depended on their reproduction in opposition to their vows[202].

Interestingly, with regard to the Erfurt debates, Arnoldi's opponents in Erfurt did not deal with Genesis 1:28 in their publications, at least leading into the year 1524. Considering the force with which Arnoldi made his arguments in *Sermo de matrimonio*, this seems somewhat surprising. Reasons for such quietude on the topic can only be the subject of speculation, but one must assume that Aegidius Mechler and Johann Lang, in particular, did not find the topic to be the best manner in which to promote their cause. After all, in the two works by Mechler which deal with monastic vows and priestly marriage[203] and the one work by Lang[204], no reference to Genesis 1:28 is to be found. The same will hold true in the latter stages of the debate after Arnoldi once again introduces his caricaturization of (or perhaps responds to) the evangelical argument. Even then, no published reference to Genesis 1:28 by Arnoldi's main opponents will be seen[205].

While we might lack any evidence from their pens or sermons, there does at least exist some evidence that Luther's adherents in Erfurt – and not merely Wittenberg – were concerned with the question of Genesis 1:28 and that Arnoldi's continual harping on the subject was an actual response to more widespread teaching. Sometime during 1524, the relatively unknown figure, Thomas Stör, published *Der Ehelich standt von Got mit gebenedeyng auffgesetzt soll umb schwaerheyt wegen der selzamen gaben der Junckfrawschafft yederman frey sein und niemant verboten werden*[206]. The title alone indicates the importance given to the divine blessing found in Genesis 1:28. The title-print of this work makes this implication more than certain

---

[202] »Et in quos hec magis congruūt quā in priapistas nostros qui per oīa illis se conformāt Quibus quotidie in ore est illud crescite et multiplicamini et replete terram quasi mundus conservari non possit sine illorum multiplicatione contra sua vota«. ARNOLDI, Sermo de Matrimonio, B2ᵛ.

[203] Ägidius MECHLER, APOLOGIA. ODER schutzrede Egidy Mechlery pferners tzu Sanct Bartholomeus tzu Erffort. Jn welcher wyrt grund vnd vrsach ertzelt seynes weyb nemens, Erfurt 1523 (VD16 M 1763), and id., Eyn christliche Unterrichtung von guten Werken, Erfurt 1524 (VD16 M 1766).

[204] Johann LANG, Von gehorsam der Weltlichen oberkait, und den außgangen klosterleuten, ain schutzred, an doctor Andreas Frowin, Augsburg 1523 (VD16 L 318).

[205] Unfortunately, the spoken sermons of Culsamer, Mechler, and Lang can no longer be accessed directly. It would most certainly be interesting to note whether or not Genesis 1:28 found a place in them during this time period. In fact, short of some evidence of Genesis 1:28 in their writings and sermons, it is difficult to believe that Arnoldi's continual references to Genesis 1:28 are anything other than a mockery of his opponents and an attempt to merely caricature their teachings so as to win points in a debate.

[206] BUCKWALTER, Priesterehe, pp. 184f., gives brief mention to this work. See also CLASSEN, Der Liebes- und Ehediskurs, pp. 119ff. See also Thomas STÖR, Der Ehelich standt vonn got mit gebenedeyung auffgesetzt/soll vmb schw[ae]rheyt wegen der seltzamen gaben der Junckfrawschafft yederman frey seyn/vnd nyemant verboten werden, Erfurt 1524 (VD16 S 9212).

as it depicts an image of Adam and Eve with the words of Genesis 1 and 9, »Be fruitful and multiply and fill the earth« (*seyt fruchtßar/und meret euch/und erfullet das Erdtrich*), captioning the image.

Stör's work does not itself provide any thorough-going treatment of Genesis 1:28 comparable to such benchmarks as *Vom ehelichen Leben* or Jonas's writing against Faber. It is, however, quite clear that Genesis 1:28 along with Genesis 2 serve as foundational texts in his exposition of marriage and that both of these texts, respectively, constitute God's establishment and institution of the marital estate. Furthermore, it is clear from Stör's writing that these texts have ongoing applicability and are foundational for a proper understanding of man and God's will for him.

Turning our attention now to Stör's text, we note that he did not wait long to introduce this topic. After citing Genesis 1 and 2 in his first page, following a brief dedication to the Saxon Elector, Frederick, Stör writes,

> Whereas now God has created the woman, that she should be near the man, and the man, that he should cleave to his wife, it should satisfy us that God is with us. *We should also maintain the marital estate as a divine and noble work and creature. He Himself has declared that humans should increase and produce offspring, as was said above. He also once again renewed and established this command following the Flood with the selfsame words and blessing, commanding this exact thing to the sons of Noah that the entire world might see this for itself* [...]. The marital estate is God's work, made certain with His holy Word. We are all ordained and created unto this. Whoever would now hinder such a work and keep himself from a wife must certainly become soiled with other types of unchastity[207].

This same applicability of God's created ordering for human life is then assumed throughout the remainder of Stör's tract. For example, after the initial introduction of Genesis 1 and 2, Stör turns to the Apocrypha's account of Tobit and his son as evidence that man's nature compels him toward sexual activity, whether properly in

---

207 »Weil nun Gott das weib geschaffen hat/daß es umb den man soll sein/und den man/daß er seinem weib anhang/soll uns gnůg sein/daß Gott mit unns ist/unnd den Ehelichen standt in Eeren halten/ als ein götlich/edles werck und geschöpff. Er haist sich die mensche meren/uñ besamen/wie oben gesagt ist. Hat auch nachmals nach der Sindtflut/diß gebot/mit gleychformigen worten und gebenedeyung/widerumb vernewert uñ auffgesetzt/Gepewt daselbē den Sünen Noe uñ allerwelt/sich zů bezichtigen [...] Der Ehelich standt/ist Gottes werck/mit seinen hailigen wortē befestiget/ dar zů wir alle verordnet unnd erschaffen seind. Wer nun sölch werck in im hindert/und sich der Eheweiber enthelt/der můß gewißlich mit andern geschlechten der unkeüschait/befleckt werden«. Thomas Stör, Der Ehelich standt von Got mit gebenedeyung auffgesetzt/sollvmb schw[æ]rheyt wegen der seltzamen gaben der Junckfrawschafft/yederman frey sein/vñd niemāt verboten wird~e. [...], Nuremberg 1525 (VD16 S 9213), Aiii[r].

marriage or else sinfully through unchastity (*unkeüschait*)[208]. While Stör acknowledges that both marriage and chastity are free, he also is strongly convinced that celibate chastity is a gift from God which, as such, man has neither the right nor the divine promise to vow[209]. Neither are most men gifted with it. Along these lines, Stör presents several biblical evidences that the apostle Paul, the very one whose counsel recommends unmarried celibacy, was almost certainly married[210].

Underscoring all of this is Stör's view that, in accordance with God's creative intention expressed in Genesis 1 and 2, man's nature is created to further itself through procreation. Man's fall into sin requires that man seek marriage so as to live in this manner rather than in sin[211]. Stör terms it more positively a short while later when he writes:

> A priest is ever a man, a creature and work of God, created to increase and produce fruit as other people (Genesis 1). Therefore, through their devilish command, they will not make out of man either stone or wood, neither will they hinder him in his natural work which God has implanted in him. For how is it different for one to forbid marriage to priests than *to forbid* that a man should be a man? God alone, his Creator, may well change such through His gift and working[212].

In light of the observations made above, we make the following general conclusions: First, inasmuch as Stör may be taken as indicative of the evangelical preaching in Erfurt, we can note that the teaching on Genesis 1:28 and procreation defended by the evangelical pastors hit upon most of the same points as those propagated in Wittenberg circles. This comes as no surprise considering the close connections between several key personalities in Wittenberg and Erfurt. Secondly, Stör's work also gives the indication that those Erfurt pastors who followed after Luther's teachings, at least to some extent, did lean upon and emphasize the normative function of »Be fruitful and multiply« for mankind. To what extent this was present,

---

208 Ibid.
209 Ibid., Ci^r–Ci^v.
210 Ibid., Cii^r–Cii^v.
211 »Wie hoch nun/khegen dieser unrůw der Ehelichen/Junckfrawschafft gepreißet wirdt/und wie edel sy ist/so wäret doch die not/und ist hynderlich/daß ir wenig hyankhoṁen/deṅ wir uns nit an himel vermögen zůhaltē/unser flaisch ist in Adā uṅ Eva verderbt/uṅ voller bösen lust uṅ begir gemacht/davō wütet unnd brent es/will sich der natur nach/besamen und meren. Sölchs will got ausserthalb der ehe nit haben/darumb můß yederman dyser not halbē/in die Ehe tretten«. Ibid., Ci^r.
212 »Ain Priester/ist ye ain man/gottes Creatur und werck/sich zů meren uṅ zůbesamen/wie ander lewt geschaffen. Geṅ.i. Darůb werdē sy durch ire Teüfelisch gebot/auß mannen/nit staine und hölt3er machen/noch im sein naturlich werck hyndern/die im got einpflāt3t hat. deṅ was ist es anders/weṅ man Priestern die Ehe verbewt/deṅ daß ain man kayn man sey. got sein schöpffer allain/mag sölchs durch seine gab und würckung/wol wandeln«. Ibid., Ci^v–Cii^r.

however, can only be speculated upon. Nevertheless, to the extent that Stör's writing might serve as a sort of litmus test, the normative nature of Genesis 1:28 does indeed serve as a substantial foundation of thought regarding both man's nature and the questions of marriage and procreation. In that respect, it is perfectly understandable why Arnoldi attacked this particular argument with such vehemence.

Also printed in 1524, in response to a wave of evangelical preaching on the subjects of priestly marriage and monastic vows[213] and corresponding approximately with the marriage of Johann Lang[214], Arnoldi wrote another work, *Sermo de sancto cruce*. This print once again took occasion to deal with the arguments tied to Genesis 1:28 in the first of the two sections that comprise the printed work[215].

With respect to the first section of this work, we can make the following observations: First, it is noteworthy that Arnoldi continues the frequent use of what seems to be his favorite epithet, »priapists« (*priapistae*), in connection with his evangelical opponents. Indeed, in reading through this section, this is nearly the only title he makes use of! Secondly, in the final portion of the body of the sermon, »on the warlike polecat« (*de marte feline*), Arnoldi addresses the topic of priestly marriage and the imported Wittenberg teaching of Genesis 1:28. He writes,

> The priapists are exiled monks and bedeviled men together with the evangelical preachers who adhere to them. These, since they have nothing and preach the Gospel (as they say), also want to live from the Gospel, on account of which they speak pleasing things to the people, knowing themselves incapable of advancing without their adherence. Therefore, they press to overturn all things in the church, to drive its ministers out, to introduce a new rite, that they might rejoice in its observance. Yet certain of them take wives (and indeed virgins), lest it should be believed *that* they were irregular, that they might increase and multiply and replenish the earth, which would certainly become empty unless they bring help to it. Others *marry* widows and wealthy ones at that, that they might with more hindrance be free from the word of God which they adulterate (I ought to say »preach«),

---

213 BUCKWALTER, Priesterehe, p. 139, diagrams that in late spring/early summer there was a wave of preaching linked to these topics with the initial impetus arising from a sermon preached by Arnoldi on 3 May 1524 to which the evangelical pastors, Culsamer, Mechler, and Lang, responded in force.
214 Ibid., p. 181, esp. fn. 253.
215 Bartholomäus ARNOLDI, Liber Tertivs F. B. de Vsingen ordinis Eremitani S. Augustini : In quo respondet nebulis Culsameri quas comme[n]tus est ille in responsionem ad libellum suum vernaculu[m] quibus seipsum pingit: qualis quantusq[ue] in sacris sit litteris, Erfurt 1524 (VD16 A 3722). This print consists of the sermon itself (Ai^r–Bi^r) followed by animated responses to each of Arnoldi's three evangelical clerical opponents (Bi^r–end). See also BUCKWALTER, Priesterehe, pp. 180–183, for his comments on this sermon.

not that they might replenish the earth but that they might feed and cherish the stomach – their god[216].

Here, once again, we see the attempt by Arnoldi to caricature the »priapists« as merely hiding behind Genesis 1:28 as an excuse for worldliness and for serving their true god, their stomach. Indeed, Arnoldi claims that they seek everything in marriage, whether wealth or pleasure. They do not, however, seek children. Interestingly, Buckwalter notes that this claim was almost certainly leveled against Johann Lang who had married a well-to-do widow[217]. Finally, we note that Arnoldi once again mocks the evangelical preachers for any suggestion that the replenishment of the earth is in any way dependent upon them.

In response to Arnoldi's *Sermo*, the evangelical pastor, Aegidius Mechler, wrote a rebuttal later that same year[218]. In this writing there are no references relating to Genesis 1:28, and there is very little in connection with the topic of clerical marriage[219].

Despite the non-existence of Genesis 1:28 in Mechler's rebuttal and only a mere quotation containing Arnoldi's derisive epithet[220], Arnoldi's response to Mechler, *Libellus in quo respondet*, once again brought up the pertinent themes[221]. As previously observed, Arnoldi's inclusion of the theme seems more to serve the purposes of castigation and guilt by association than theological dispute. Early in the text, for example, Arnoldi's main goals seem to be to associate his opponents with the Hussite and Pickard heresies and to especially include Mechler in that group which is more concerned with the goddess of love under the pretext of »Be fruitful and multiply«[222]. Similarly, near the conclusion of *Libellus in quo respondet*, Arnoldi

---

216 »Priapistæ sunt exiticii mōachi & laruales [=larvati]: cū sibi adherentibus euāgelicis predicatoribus: qui cū nihil habeāt: & euāgeliū (vt dicūt) predicāt: de euāgelio viuere volūt: ͵ppter qd' ͵pplō placētia loquunt: sciētes se nihil ͵pficere posse sine illius adhsiōe. Nituntur ideo oīa in ecclīa euertere: ministros eius ͵ppellere & novū ritū inducere vt illius gaudeāt ͵puisione. Quidā tamē eorum vxores ducunt: & quidē virgines: ne vt credēdū est fīat irregulares: qtūs crescāt & multiplicētur & repleāt terrā: que utiqȝ vacua fieret: nisi suppetias ei ferrēt. Alii viduas & quidē opulētas. vt verbo dei quod adulterāt (predicāt dicere debui) impeditius vacare possint. Nō vt terrā repleāt sed vt ventrē deum suum pascāt & foueant«. Arnoldi, Liber Tertivs F. B. de Vsingen, Bi[r].
217 Buckwalter, Priesterehe, p. 181, fn. 253.
218 Ägidius Mechler, Eyn wyderlegung Egidij Mechlers Pfarners zů/Erffort/zů Sanct [...], Erfurt 1524 (VD16 M 1780).
219 Ibid., Eiii[r]–Eiii[v]. See also Buckwalter, Priesterehe, pp. 183–185.
220 Mechler, Eyn wyderlegung, Di[v].
221 Bartholomäus Arnoldi, Libellus F. Bartholomei de vsingen augustiniani Jn quo respondet confutationi fratris Egidij mechlerij monachi frāciscani sed exiticij laruati et cōiugati. Nitentis tueri errores et p[er]fidiam Culsameri [...] Cōtra Lutheranos, Erfurt 1524 (VD16 A 3719).
222 »quia lucri et questus gratia cū ceteris exiticijs monachis a synceritate fidei catholice ad stercora defecit hussitica et pycardica ex quibus nuper ermersis ecclesia euāgelica omnium hereticorū fex et

once again appropriates the Genesis 1:28 motif as part of a barrage of insinuations and insults heaped upon his collective opponents, charging that the »Lutherans« are merely earthly-minded in their teaching of »Be fruitful and multiply«[223]. It is perhaps worth noting that Genesis 1:28 does not appear in Arnoldi's actual response to the question of priestly marriage and vows of celibacy in this work[224]. That is merely to point out that the function of our verse seems to be merely polemic and not particularly substantive in terms of theology.

Moving ahead into 1525, however, two further writings by Arnoldi were printed. The first of these writings, *Libellus de merito bonorum operum*, was written in response to Aegidius Mechler's *Christliche Unterrichtung von guten Werken* (written prior to the aforementioned *Eyn wyderlegung Egidij Mechlers*) and simultaneously was a response to a sermon Johann Culsamer preached on 16 June 1524[225]. By way of introduction to Arnoldi's general argumentation in this work, we note once again his understanding of his opponents' usage of Genesis 1:28 as a justification for worldliness and a cover for serving the flesh. Early in this work, without direct reference to »Be fruitful and multiply«, he begins to make this case respecting the true motives of the »exiled, bedeviled, and married monks«[226]. This argument can clearly be seen again later in the first portion of Arnoldi's *Libellus de merito* where he seeks to refute Mechler's argument against those who forbid certain days, vestments,

---

amurca in q̃ exiticij et laruati monachi veneri vacant vt crescant̄. multiplicent et repleant terram de quorū nūero noster est egidius qui degere maluit in castris cypriacis quā franciscanis qm̃ sic persuasit illum genius suus«. Ibid., Aii[r]. For the explanation of »cypriacis« as alluding to Aphrodite, the goddess of love, see Buckwalter, Priesterehe, p. 186, fn. 282.

223 »Sed rogo mittas mihi interea quoad colores picture mee concinnaueris et paraueris. duas myrmices nuper de monte carmelo lapsas.que me aliquando suo lotio partier ceperunt perfundere. Culsamerus enim qui se rediturum pollicebatur non comparet. et Langus orator eius qui se oratorem in me acturum promisit mutescit. vos etenim quinq3 magistri estis et porticus. non piscine probatice. sed rhanalis lacune. in qua non lauantur oues immolande deo. sed bulbi salaces et satureia cum erucis vorande *priapistis ut crescant et multiplicentur atq3 repleāt terram*. qui quia de terra sunt de terra loquūtur. nostra aūt cōuersatio vt apostolus ait. debet esse in celis«. Arnoldi, Libellus Jn quo respondet, Tii[v]–Tiii[r]; emphasis added.

224 See, for example, ibid., Qiiii[r] ff.

225 Bartholomäus Arnoldi, Libellus F. Bartholomei de Vsingen Augustiniani de Merito bonorum operum. Jn quo veris argumentis respondet ad instructionem fratris Mechlerij Franciscani de bonis operibus […] Jnsuper respondet ad Euangelium Culsameri […] Contra factionem Lutheranam, Erfurt 1525 (VD16 A 3723). See also Buckwalter, Priesterehe, pp. 139, 188–190.

226 »Quid enim putas potissimum exiticios monachos laruatos et coniugatos quęrere quam vt extra monasteria tuti degere possint in opulentia. et cum vxoribus ductis quieti viuere in voluptaria vita que si illis concesseris facile cederent reliquis«. Arnoldi, Libellus de Merito bonorum operum, Aii[r]. Buckwalter, Priesterehe, p. 189, also refers to this passage.

foods, etc.[227]. Of particular note in this section is the attempt to implicate the evangelical preachers as having adopted a fleshly teaching which might be based on the »Mohamedan teaching«. Such an accusation would not only insult Reformation teaching, but also at some level aligned its teachers with the very enemy which represented an ever-increasing threat for the Holy Roman Empire[228]. Furthermore, Arnoldi accuses his evangelical opponents of constantly twisting the words of Genesis 1:28 and such other passages as Matthew 15 and 1 Timothy 4, which are then used to support the former monastic's demonic practice of taking wives[229].

The latter section of *Libellus de merito*, in response to Culsamer, addresses Genesis 1:28 in a similar manner. That is to say, as we have seen elsewhere in Arnoldi's writings, he finds little more in the »Lutheran« teaching on *crescite et multiplicamini* than a basis for derision and an apparent excuse for what he views as fleshly living. This is made apparent, most egregiously, in the fact that these followers of Luther do not even do what they themselves teach. After all, when one of their pastors has married a rich and supposedly sterile woman, the marriage cannot be said to correspond with the much-touted command to procreate[230].

---

227 Buckwalter bypasses this section of ARNOLDI, Libellus de Merito bonorum operum, Fi[r]–Fii[r], in which Arnoldi clearly interprets Mechler as addressing the theme of priestly marriage and responds accordingly.

228 The extremity of such an epithet at that period in time is noted also in KAUFMANN, Der Anfang der Reformation, p. 32.

229 »Tibi autem dispensatio eo moderamine pergit ne libertas spiritus detur in occasionem carnis. sicut ad Galatas.5.hortatur Apostolus. Secundum quam carnē si vixerimus. morte moriemur. si autem spiritu facta carnis mortificauerimus viuemus. vt idem ad Rhomanos 8. habet Apostolus. Sed tua tuorūq3 doctrina instar doctrine Mahametice eo tendit. vt spiritus carni. non caro spiritui seruiat. ad quod scripturam torquentes semper in ore est vobis. Crescite et multiplicamini et replete terram. Genesis 1. Et illud Mathei 15. Quod per os intrauerit nō coinquinat hominem. ac illud.1.Timotheo 4. Spiritus manifeste dicit. Quia in nouissimis temporibus discedent quidam a fide. attendentes spiritibus erroris. et doctrinis demoniorum in hypocrisi. loquentium mendacium et cauteriatam habentium suam conscientiam. prohibentium nubere. abstinere a cibis quos deus creauit ad percipiēdum cum gratiarum actione etc. hac litera laruales monachi animantur uxores ducere«. ARNOLDI, Libellus de Merito bonorum operum, Fii[r].

230 »Q autem dicis vos bona terrena non curare. vestram ex ponis magnam perfectionem quorum conuersatio in celis est et si ligua transeat in terra virulenta insectatione et diffamatione plena. Certe huius perfectionis exemplum egregium hoc anno dedit vnus tuorum. quando duxit uxorem opulentissimam sterilem et vetulam. et quid is tibi quesiuisse videtur an pulpamentum et aruinam. an pocius vt crescat multiplicetur et repleat terram«. Ibid., Hiiii[r].

As an interesting aside, Luther was aware of Lang's marriage. In a letter dated 6 July 1524 (WA Br 3, pp. 318f.), Luther refers to the fact that Lang no longer must live in want and for that reason he ought to be better able to assist Jonas, who now is experiencing difficulties. A further letter, interestingly, dated 22 February 1525, wishes Lang the gift of offspring just as Melanchthon had recently welcomed a young son into the world (WA Br 3, pp. 445f.). It is difficult to know if any interpretation on these sayings aside from a straight-forward reading is called for. What is

The second of these writings appearing in 1525, *Libellus F. Bartholomei de Vsingen Augustiniani de falsis prophetis [...]*[231], proves itself to deal with the topic of Genesis 1:28 in a more substantial manner. To begin our analysis of this book and the relevant information it contains, we simply note that this book is written in eight chapters which divide up into roughly two main sections. Chapters one through seven form a sort of doctrinal exposition of various controversies between traditional and »Lutheran« teaching (with chapters six and seven addressing priestly marriage, but not directly our topic). Chapter eight is more personal and polemic in nature as it responds to a sermon preached by Johann Lang on the occasion of Johann Culsamer's marriage on 15 January 1525[232]. It also proves to be more apropos to this study's investigation and thus will require more of our attention.

Before addressing Arnoldi's response to Johann Lang's sermon, however, there are a couple more general items of note deserving of brief comment. To begin with, we briefly observe that while the name-calling and harsh polemic is generally absent from this section, Arnoldi does not refrain from the continued employment of his favorite epithet, *priapistae*[233]. Neither does he change his *modus operandi* of maligning his opponents and their teaching through guilt by association – in this case with the heretical teachings of John Wycliffe[234].

A second note requiring our attention is Arnoldi's connection of priestly marriage and celibacy with his understanding of other important topics such as the priestly function[235] and human ability, both generally and with respect to vows of celibacy[236]. While both of these topics are not directly connected to our own topic of »Be fruitful and multiply«, they are helpful in illustrating the intensity of

---

known, though, is that Lang's first wife was markedly older than Lang and that only his second marriage was fruitful. Thus, it certainly is possible that Arnoldi's complaints were not without their own merit.

231 Bartholomäus ARNOLDI, Libellus F. Bartholomei de Vsingen Augustiniani de falsis prophetis tam in persona quā doctrina vitandis a fidelibus. De recta et mūda p̄dicatiōe euāgelij [et] [qui?]bus [con]formiter ill[u]d debeat p̄dicari. De Celibatu sacerdotum [...] Responsio ad Sermonē Langi de Matrimonio sacerdotali quē fecit in Nuptijs Culsameri sacerdotis Cōtra factionē Luttheranā, Erfurt 1525 (VD16 A 3702).

232 For an overview of this work and its place in the larger debate, see BUCKWALTER, Priesterehe, pp. 139, 191–200.

233 In chapters six and seven of ARNOLDI, Libellus F.Bartholomei de Vsingen Augustiniani de falsis prophetis, see Eiiii^r and Fii^r.

234 Wycliffe's teaching on priestly marriage is introduced in ibid., Fii^r, and the constant comparison and accusation of Wycliffian teaching continues throughout the remainder of the work. See also BUCKWALTER, Priesterehe, pp. 193f., for a further discussion of this point.

235 ARNOLDI, Libellus F.Bartholomei de Vsingen Augustiniani de falsis prophetis, Eiii^r–Eiiii^r. BUCKWALTER, Priesterehe, pp. 192f., also includes summary treatment of this point.

236 ARNOLDI, Libellus F.Bartholomei de Vsingen Augustiniani de falsis prophetis, Hiii^r. See also BUCKWALTER, Priesterehe, p. 198.

the fight over matters – including our verse – which otherwise might seem rather innocuous. Yet, because the topics of marriage and procreation do not, and never have, existed in a vacuum, these matters were indeed proverbial powder kegs. Via Arnoldi's mention of priestly celibacy and its significance for the Mass – and thus in an entire religious system – it becomes apparent that the discussion is not simply about the merit of children or of marriage. Much more is at stake. In the same way, any argument denying man's freedom over these matters and the general inability of man (barring the extraordinary gift of God) to maintain celibacy is also, through implication, proposing revolution and rejection of an entire ecclesiastical system and theology. Moreover, here it can clearly be understood that the debate over *crescite et multiplicamini* was in fact an extension of the controversy surrounding man's nature and not merely a discussion of man's sexuality.

For the purposes of this chapter, Arnoldi's response to Johann Lang's sermon proves to trail in significance only behind his earlier *Sermo de matrimonio* and Stör's *Der ehelich standt*. There are two reasons for this. First, Arnoldi's response, written as it is in statement/response fashion, provides us with one of the best pictures of the evangelical teaching on Genesis 1:28 and procreation in this debate – assuming, of course, that Arnoldi is fairly quoting Lang. The second reason for the importance of this work in our study is that, in contrast with Arnoldi's other works, he addresses some of the actual arguments and does not merely caricature and demonize his opponents' teaching. Needless to say, he does, of course, also do that in his response to Lang.

With respect to Arnoldi's chapter eight (or *Sermo Langi de Matri. Sacerd.*)[237], we begin by observing that Arnoldi divides the sermon into seventeen different sections to which he offers responses[238]. While the entirety of this section deals with the topic of priestly marriage, for the purposes of this study, sections I, II, VI, and XVI are of most significance.

Arnoldi's first segment of Lang's sermon immediately introduces the matter of procreation, though with no express mention of Genesis 1:28. Arnoldi quotes Lang as follows:

Lang. In the early church, there were heretics who prohibited marriage as an illicit thing, and their rashness was immediately repressed, since no one of sound mind could understand this example of theirs as not being foolish, since thus, at whatever time the

---

237 ARNOLDI, Libellus F.Bartholomei de Vsingen Augustiniani de falsis prophetis, Gi[r].
238 BUCKWALTER, Priesterehe, p. 197, numbers these as only sixteen sections. A possibility for this numbering is that one of the headings is not left-justified in the text, but is included in a line of Arnoldi's response. See ARNOLDI, Libellus F.Bartholomei de Vsingen Augustiniani de falsis prophetis, Giiii[v].

world and mankind should not be preserved by the procreation of offspring, they would immediately disappear[239].

This quotation shows a certain urgency and necessity in his opponent's understanding of the world with the clear implication that, unless the work of *crescite et multiplicamini* continues, the world will immediately fall into decline. Interestingly, this substantiates Arnoldi's earlier claim that the »Lutherans« seemed to think the world's continuance depended on their own procreation[240].

In responding to Lang's position, Arnoldi focuses on establishing his own views as being in accordance with the same Scripture passages Lang has alluded to and also claims the church fathers, particularly Augustine and Jerome, for himself. Arnoldi, however, does not respond to Lang's final statement regarding the ongoing state of the world's decline at this point. Rather, his response to the matter of procreation he saves for his response to the second section of Lang's sermon in which Lang argues that marriage and celibacy are indeed left free to each person, according to the grace given to each, as also the church fathers maintained[241].

It is in response to this, then, that Arnoldi offers his answer to the question of the ongoing necessity of procreation – of *crescite et multiplicamini*. Arnoldi comments,

> Response: That there was a command in the old law – indeed, before the written law – about the undertaking of marriage, is sufficiently known from Scripture, which says in Genesis 1 and repeats in Genesis 9, »Increase and multiply and fill the earth«, because God, by whom all things have been ordained, did not desire the increase to take place outside of marriage, as the apostle teaches sufficiently (1 Corinthians 7). But I do not find that it was also necessary for all men to keep this commandment after mankind had multiplied, seeing that actually some holy men in the law were without marriage as is known about Elijah, John the Baptizer of Christ. This I rather pass over, while the freedom of the new law is clear enough from the Gospel and the apostle Paul[242].

---

239 »Langus. In nascenti ecclesia non deerant heretici nupcias prohibentes tanquā rem illicitā quorū temeritas statim est repressa. cū nemo sane mentis nō frivolum fuisse hoc eorū documētum potuit intelligere. Cum sic mundus et humanū genus quando prolis procreatione non cōseruaretur statim dificerent«. ARNOLDI, Libellus F. Bartholomei de Vsingen Augustiniani de falsis prophetis, Gi[v].
240 See, for example, id., Sermo de Matrimonio, B2[r].
241 Id., Libellus F. Bartholomei de Vsingen Augustiniani de falsis prophetis, Gii[r].
242 »Responsio. Preceptum fuisse in veteri lege immo ante legem scriptā de ineundo matrimonio satis notū est ex scriptura que dicit. Gene.1. et repetit. Gene.9. Crescite et multiplicamini et replete terram..Quod crescere deus cuius omnia ordinata sunt noluit fieri extra matrimoniū ut satis docet Apostolus.1. Corinthians 7. An autem omnibus multiplicato humano genere hoc preceptum fuierit et seruatu necessarium non in venio cum etiam in lege aliqui fuerāt sine matrimonio sancti viri vt notum est de helia et Joanne Baptista Christi. sed hec transeo at libertas Noue legis satis clara est ex Evangelio et Apostolo Paulo«. Ibid., Gii[r].

After establishing this position that God has left marriage as a matter of freedom and not a necessity for the replenishment of the earth, Arnoldi then continues by asserting that man is free to make the vow of perpetual celibacy and to seek it as a gift from God. Furthermore, he questions the assertion that unless the gift of celibacy has been given to someone, such a vow ought not be made. After all, how can someone ever know if they, in fact, have such a gift? Arnoldi then continues on to assure his reader that those who vow chastity are able to receive this gift with God's help[243]. This line of thought, of course, flies in the face of the Wittenberg contention that to make such a vow was nothing other than to tempt God.

Arnoldi next continues by addressing Lang's arguments respecting fornication, harlotry, and the punishment required by the Law[244]. He then discusses once again the previous topic, the question whether the vow of chastity merely tempts God. This is reintroduced by the sixth excerpt taken from Lang's sermon, which reads:

> Long [sic]. Besides, marriage has not only been instituted for the sake of the procreation of offspring, but even for the avoidance of fornication. For Genesis 2 says, »It is not good *that* the man is alone«. Therefore, if you are unable to restrain *yourself*, you should take a wife. Christ has given you freedom to take or not to take *a wife*. Therefore, embrace whichever option you prefer[245].

Two points naturally emerge from this excerpt. First, one must question whether the apparent misspelling of Lang's name is perhaps intentional (!) and serves as simply another example of Arnoldi's sometimes crude derision of the »Lutheran« teaching, more or less tantamount to his epithet *priapistae*[246]. Secondly, this excerpt clarifies the fact that the argument based upon procreation – *crescite et multiplicamini* – was Lang's first basis for his teaching on marriage. Only at this point does he proceed to a further foundational argument for marriage, namely, that it is not good that the man should be alone (Genesis 2).

The remainder of the excerpt from Lang, as well as Arnoldi's response, indicates that many of the main concerns of this and the following sections revolve around

---

243 Ibid., Gii[v].
244 Ibid., Giiii[r]–Hi[r].
245 »Longus. Preterea matrimoniū non solum prolis procreande gratia institutum est. sed etā vitande fornicationis. qm̄ Gene.2.dicitur. Non esse bonum hominē esse solum. Itaq; si continere nequeas uxorem ducas. Christus dedit tibi libertatem vel ducendi vel non ducendi amplectere ergo alterutrā quam magis velis partem«. Ibid., Hi[r].
246 This is the only example I have discovered of the use of »Longus« instead of »Langus«. Given the context and the fact that this somewhat glaring error (?) is not noted in the corrections listed at the end of the document, it does strongly suggest that this (mis)spelling was, in fact, intentional.

whether vows of chastity ought to be made, can be kept, or should be repaid[247]. As has been shown throughout this study, the answer to these questions depended largely on one's understanding of Genesis 1:28. In any event, in response to the excerpt from Lang, Arnoldi affirms both human freedom and ability by arguing that the good of procreation was only being emphasized because of the circumstances present at the time of creation[248].

The remainder of the text does not directly deal with our topic. Nevertheless, it is of interest to note Arnoldi's repeated personal attack regarding Lang's apparent neglect to practice what he preaches concerning *crescite et multiplicamini*. In the penultimate section of the work, Arnoldi charges Lang once again[249] with the following:

> You say above: That [i. e. marriage] ought nevertheless not be done out of consideration for the fulfillment of lust or in following avarice. In this you speak well, but in this, *namely that you do not do that which you teach, you do not do well*. If for you, lust was not the cause for taking a wife, why have you not remained in your celibacy which you have vowed and sworn? If you have sought after children, why have you taken an old and sterile wife? If likewise you are not following avarice, why have you accepted a rich woman? You therefore rightly proclaim woe upon yourself unless you come to your senses and free yourself from error[250].

In summing up this excursus, there are several points worth mentioning. To begin with, it is important to highlight that, if nothing else, the Reformation developments in Erfurt respecting our verse both corresponded with developments elsewhere and yet played out in their own *entirely unique* manner. Concerning matters of

---

247 Ibid., Hi[r]–Hiiii[r].
248 »Responsio. Verum est matrimoniū institutum esse duplici causa saltem post lapsum hominis. Non tamen ex loco a te citato. Gene.2. habetur q vitande fornicationis gratia sit institutum. Quia mulier formata est ad multiplicationem humani generis que q₂ non poterat esse per solum masculum ideo dixit dominus. Non est bonum hominē esse solum quia tolleretur multiplicationis bonū etc. Consequenter dico Christum dedisse libertatem hanc ad utrumq₃ quam satis etiam confirmat Apostolus.1. Corinthians 7. Sed si quis vovit castitatem privavit se libertate ista et limitavit se ad alte₂. Quia vota reddi iubet lex divina. Necessitatus ergo ad alterum nō remanet liber ad utrumq₃«. Ibid., Hi[r].
249 See also id., Libellus de merito bonorum operum, Hiiii[r].
250 »Insuper dicis. Quod tamen fieri non debet explende libidinis intuitu aut auariciam sequendo in quo bene loqueris. sed in hoc q non facis que doces non bene facis. Si tibi libido non erat causa ducendi uxorem. cur non mansisti in Celibatu tuo quem vouisti et iurasti. Si prolem quesivisti.cur vetulam et sterilem uxorem duxisti. Si etiam nō es secutus auariciam cur opulentam accepisti. Recte ergo ve tibi annuncias nisi re sipueris et te emendaueris«. Id., Libellus F.Bartholomei de Vsingen Augustiniani de falsis prophetis, Kiii[r].

correspondence, we have now observed that the appearance of Genesis 1:28 as a topic of controversy came at roughly the same time as this verse received significant attention from Wittenberg circles. Along these same lines, we noted that the evangelical teaching on Genesis 1:28 invariably originated from, or at least had connections to, Wittenberg. These came both via personal and print sources. Furthermore, we have noted that the contours of thought and debate surrounding this verse – insofar as they can be discerned from Arnoldi's writings and the tract from Thomas Stör – correspond very well with the basic outlines of teaching and controversy we observed in Wittenberg. Finally, the papal response in Erfurt also was formulated along similar lines in Erfurt as we have observed elsewhere. Here we observed a reversion back to the argumentation of such church fathers as Jerome and Augustine and the harsh use of heretical associations and *ad hominem* attacks.

For as many commonalities as we have observed between Erfurt and the Wittenberg situation, however, we have also been confronted with the unquestionable uniqueness of the Erfurt events. Here there can be no question that the exceptional combination of actors, with their personal and even intimate connections (particularly through the university and Augustinian monastery), led to an intensity of animosity and verve that is hardly otherwise to be found. It was also a truly singular situation in that the debate played out on both the academic and popular level, in both Latin and German, and also both in written and oral mediums – all more or less simultaneously. Thus, we see in Erfurt a consistent and yet personalized expression of this particular point of Reformation controversy.

5. Confessing and Conforming to a Verse – The Ongoing Influence of Genesis 1:28

> Secundo, Christus inquit: *Non omnes capiunt verbum hoc,* ubi docet non omnes homines ad coelibatum idoneos esse, quia Deus creavit hominem ad procreationem, Gene. 1. Nec est humanae potestatis sine singulari dono et opera Dei creationem mutare.

> *In the second place, Christ says, »Not everyone can accept this teaching«, where he is teaching that not everyone is fit for celibacy, because God created the human being for procreation (Gen. 1[:28]). It is not humanly possible to change creation without a singular gift and work of God.*

> —*Confessio Augustana*, art. 23

5.1 Genesis 1:28 and Wittenberg Theology

While there can be little doubt that the use and contours of Genesis 1:28 within early Wittenberg teaching are, in large part, to be attributed to Luther himself, we have clearly caught glimpses of the fact that Luther was far from alone respecting his involvement with the initial appearance of this verse, specific aspects of its understanding, the spread of this teaching, and its defense. In fact, as E.G. Schwiebert once noted, the German Reformation must be viewed as a much larger movement, more akin to that of an army, than the workings of a mere man. Thus, the faculty of the University of Wittenberg – particularly Melanchthon, Jonas, Amsdorf, and Bugenhagen – might be viewed as Luther's advisory staff[1]. To be sure, our own findings to this point as well as those to come, will bear out this role played by the reformer's Wittenberg circle.

We have also previously noted that the initial emergence of Genesis 1:28 in Luther's writings occurred particularly at the impetus of Melanchthon and Amsdorf

---

1 E. G. Schwiebert, Luther and His Times. The Reformation from a New Perspective, St. Louis 1950, pp. 2–5. More recently, Dingel, Confessional Transformations, pp. 3f., emphasizes the idea that the descriptive »Wittenberg Theology« (as opposed to »Lutheran theology«) is fitting for the Wittenberg-centered Reformation movement effected by Luther *and* his team of colleagues.

in the context of controversy surrounding monastic vows. Here, it will be recalled, both Melanchthon and Amsdorf pressed Luther in the fall of 1521 to consider the question of the impossibility of keeping any vow of celibacy for the majority of men and women. Moreover, Melanchthon's thoughts on natural affections seem to have played their own role in the development of Luther's understanding of Genesis 1:28 at this point, given Melanchthon's own simultaneous consideration of these affections while composing *Loci Communes* (1521). Bugenhagen also seems to have been keenly aware of, if not distantly involved with, the discussions surrounding this topic already at this point.

From this initial emergence of our verse, the involvement of Luther's Wittenberg colleagues can be readily observed. Although Luther appears to be the primary proponent of the teaching on Genesis 1:28 in the years 1522–1524 (as was observed in Chapter 4), there is no question that others were also involved. Perhaps most telling for our purposes is that the official response to Johann Faber was delegated to Justus Jonas, who, consequently, offered what was the most thorough treatment of Genesis 1:28 to date. Yet, it should be noted that Jonas was, prior to this, also responsible for the 1522 translation of Luther's *De votis monasticis*. Melanchthon's *In Obscuriora Aliquot Capita Geneseos* further contributed to the collective front found already in the first half of the 1520s.

On a slightly wider scale, as observed in Erfurt, we note that the spread of Luther's teachings throughout Reformation Germany, almost always emanated from Wittenberg – be it through personal, university, print, or ecclesial connections[2]. Additionally, corresponding to this development, we note in passing that the leading lights of Wittenberg (Luther, Jonas, Melanchthon, and Bugenhagen) collectively approved of Genesis 1:28 as a proof-text, of sorts, for the teaching of the procreative purpose and work of marriage as early as September 1525[3]. In light of the preceding, as we look at the wider developments of the mid and late 1520s, we do well to keep in mind the status of Genesis 1:28 not merely as Luther's own personal teaching but already as a component of both Wittenberg and, to a certain extent at least, »Lutheran« theological teaching.

---

2 See, once again, the first half of KLAWITTER, Forceful and Fruitful, Chapter 5, for a study of the spread of Luther's thought regarding Genesis 1:28 throughout Reformation Germany (1521–1525).

3 WA Br 3, pp. 568–570. For the relevant approved-of text for this *Gutachten*, see Johann SCHOPPER, Eyn Ratschlag, Den etliche Christenliche Pfarherrn, Prediger Cochlaeus Einem Fürsten, welcher yetzigen stritigen leer halb, auff den abschied, jüngst gehaltens Reichßtags zu Nürnberg, Christlicher warhait vnderricht begert, gemacht haben (etc.), Nuremberg 1525 (VD16 S 3920), p. 76.

The Liturgy, *Haustafel* Literature, and the Three Estates

The employment of *crescite et multiplicamini* in Wittenberg circles was not limited merely to destructive work directed against monastic vows and the forbiddance of priestly marriage. In point of fact, by the latter part of the 1520s, more and more attention was given to such matters as helping to better instruct, order, and strengthen the marital institution.[4] In this sense, Genesis 1:28 was not merely a destructive, polemic force within Reformation teaching. Instead, it also assumed foundational significance to the divine institutions and estates advocated by Wittenberg-related reformers. Here we have in mind particularly *oeconomia* (household) and *politia* (government) as often described in Luther's teaching on the three estates which also emerged during this period[5]. Moreover, we will observe that this verse served a noticeable role within church life both in Wittenberg as well as in wider circles, serving a particularly significant and profound liturgical function in wedding services that would have been most apparent to all.

Perhaps a good place to begin, then, with our discussion of the constructive place of Genesis 1:28, is with the final point: the liturgical place and use of this verse in wedding services. The first record we find of the liturgical use of *crescite et multiplicamini* in Wittenberg circles, can be traced back to the late spring of 1524 with the wedding of Caspar Cruciger to Elisabeth von Meseritz of which Spalatin is said to have left a record[6]. According to Spalatin's record, the brief service began with a reading of Genesis 3, but then concluded with the words of Christ followed by the imperative pronouncement of »Be fruitful and multiply« over the bridal couple[7].

---

4 Walter BEHRENDT, Lehr-, Wehr- und Nährstand: Haustafelliteratur und Dreiständelehre im 16. Jahrhundert, Berlin 2009, p. 94, URL: <https://refubium.fu-berlin.de/bitstream/handle/fub188/10734/Behrendt_Walter_Diss.pdf> (18 Aug 2022), notes that this shift occurred near the end of the 1520s, something which my own research also demonstrates.

5 Christopher VOIGT-GOY, Die gesellschaftlichen Stände, die Schöpfung und der Fall. Zur Ständelehre in Luthers Genesisvorlesung (1535), in: Thomas WAGNER et al. (eds.), Kontexte. Biografische und forschungsgeschichtliche Schnittpunkte der alttestamentlichen Wissenschaft. FS H.J. Boecker, Neukirchen-Vluyn 2008, pp. 65–80, at p. 67.

6 Wie Doctor Martinus Luther Caspar Creutziger und Elisabeth von Meßeritz Dienstag vor Viti vor der Pfarrkirchen zu Wittenberg zusamen gegeben hat, in: Hallisches patriot. Wochenblatt (3 December 1835), pp. 1530f. See also Volker GUMMELT, Elisabeth Cruciger, geb. von Meseritz, in Pommern und Wittenberg. Anmerkungen zu Stationen ihres Lebens, in: Armin KOHNLE/Irene DINGEL (eds.), Die Crucigers. Caspar der Ältere, Caspar der Jüngere und Elisabeth Cruciger in ihrer Bedeutung für die Wittenberger Reformation, Leipzig 2021, p. 292, fn. 6.

7 »Da stecket Doctor Martinus dem Bräutigam und der Braut den Ring an und sprach: ›Quod ergo Deus coniunxit, homo non separet. Was Gott zusammen fügt, soll der Mensch nicht scheiden‹. Gab also den Bräutigam und die Braut mit den Händen zusammen und sagt: ›Crescite et multiplicamini.‹

This account seems to be a reflection of the marriage service which was at that time already used by Bugenhagen and which appeared in print (against his will) that same year[8]. An authorized version appeared the following year, *Wie man die so zu der Ehe greyffent eynleytet zu Wittemberg [...]*[9]. This work included two parts: the first is the wedding liturgy as used by Bugenhagen in Wittenberg while the second part contains simply the seventh chapter of 1 Corinthians. The liturgy itself states the scriptural basis generally as being found in Genesis and then gives more attention to Genesis 2 and 3. In that sense, it initially gives the appearance that Genesis 1:28 is not of central importance within the liturgy. Nevertheless, following the actual solemnization of the bridal couple, the brief service concludes with a benediction. Apparently, the bridal couple in Wittenberg would have heard the following at the conclusion of the wedding service (with the same wording being used in both the 1524 and 1525 versions): »What God has joined together, let man not separate (Matthew 19). God our Father and our Lord Jesus Christ, through the grace of the Holy Spirit, be with you, *make you fruitful so that you would increase the world. Amen*«[10].

Georg Kretschmar notes that such a blessing was not to be found in the liturgical predecessors which would have had any bearing on the practice of Wittenberg. The most important of these sources, he notes, would have been the *Brandenburger Ordnung*[11]. Most interesting in that liturgy is that the conclusion of the service did not include such a blessing. Its blessing, instead, was derived from Tobit and,

---

 Seyd fruchtbar und mehret Euch‹! Damit hätt das Zusammengeben sein Ende«. Wie Doctor Martinus Luther, p. 1531.

8 Johannes BUGENHAGEN, Von der Euangelischen Meß, was die Meß sey, wie un[d] durch wenn, und warumb sy auffgesetzt sey, auch wie man Meß sol hören, un[d] das hochwirdig sacrament empfahe[n], un[d] warumb man es empfecht, Nuremberg 1524 (VD16 B 9461). The wedding service begins on diiii[r]. Otto CLEMEN, Bugenhagensche Trauformulare, in: Archiv für Reformationsgeschichte 3 & 4 (1905–1907), p. 88, fn. 1, notes that Bugenhagen's reaction to this printing was not particularly favorable. See also KRETSCHMAR, Luthers Konzeption, p. 196, for this observation. We might also add that WA 30/3, pp. 49ff. offers a discussion on the importance of Bugenhagen's wedding service as a background and source for Luther's own wedding booklet that accompanied his *Small Catechism* in 1529.

9 Johannes BUGENHAGEN, Wie man die so zu der Ehe greyffent eynleytet zu Wittemberg darin angezeygt wird was die Ehe sey von wem vnd warumb sie auffgesetzt ist, Magdeburg 1525 (VD16 A 837).

10 »Was Gott zusammen gefügt hat/sol der mensch nicht teylen/Math. am 19. Capittel. Gott vnser vater vnd vnser herre Jesus Christus/durch die genad des heyligen Geysts/sey mit euch/*macht euch fruchtbar/auff das yhr die welt meret Amen*«. Ibid., Aii[v] (Aiii[v]); emphasis added. See also CLEMEN, Bugenhagensche Trauformulare, whose article offers further information on the general origin of Bugenhagen's wedding service (though very limited information regarding the inclusion of our verse in this liturgy).

11 KRETSCHMAR, Luthers Konzeption, pp. 195f.

most notably, not a blessing of fertility[12]. Furthermore, immediately prior to that blessing the bridal couple would have been admonished to observe three days of abstinence[13]. Thus, we observe in Bugenhagen's wedding service not merely an emphasis on Genesis 1:28 and its burgeoning importance in the Wittenberg understanding of marriage, but – as Kretschmar notes – also something of an antithesis to the locally inherited medieval nuptial tradition.

We might further note that it would have been *this* service and the words of *this* blessing, that would have been heard on the evening of 13 June 1525 as Bugenhagen conducted the wedding service for Luther and Katharina[14]. This is certainly worth underscoring due to the prominent and, indeed, epitomic importance of Luther's wedding for the Reformation. Even more, the archetypal function of Luther and Katharina's own marriage for the later development of what the *Pfarrhaus* or pastor's family would become, gives further significance to Bugenhagen's wedding service[15].

When Luther wrote a pamphlet only four years later introducing his own design for a wedding service, the format and emphasis on Genesis 1:28 was much the same. In Luther's service, though, following the pronouncement of the bridal couple as man and wife, there follows a series of readings which set forth the scriptural basis of marriage. These include Genesis 2, Ephesians 5, and Genesis 3, all of which is followed by readings from Genesis 1 and Proverbs 18. Here Proverbs 18 seems to have served as an exclamation point for Genesis 1:27–31. The service then concludes with the following prayer in which marital fruitfulness certainly is to be understood as one of the main components:

> Lord God, who have created man and woman and have ordained them for the married estate, have blessed them also with the fruit of the womb, and have therein signified the sacrament of your dear Son Jesus Christ and the church, his bride: We beseech your never-ending goodness that you would not permit this your creation, ordinance, and blessing to be removed or destroyed, but graciously preserve it among us through Jesus Christ our Lord[16].

---

12 Ibid., p. 195, notes that this blessing was based on Raguel's blessing for Tobias and Sara – as associated with Tobit 10:11.
13 Ibid.
14 BRECHT, Martin Luther, p. 197. See also WA 30/III, p. 49, though note the date of the wedding is incorrectly given there as *13 Juli*.
15 The concept of the *evangelischen Pfarrhauses* as well as its origin goes, inevitably, back to Luther's own marriage. Thus, as noted by Tina FRITZSCHE/Nicole PAGELS, Das evangelische Pfarrhaus. Ein Haus zwischen Himmel und Erde, Hamburg 2013, pp. 15–17, the events and activities of this house would go on to influence many subsequent generations.
16 Robert KOLB et al., The Book of Concord. The Confessions of the Evangelical Lutheran Church, Minneapolis 2000, p. 371,17–23, cf. »Herre Gott, der du man und weib geschaffen und zum ehestand verordenet hast, dazu mit früchte des leibs gesegenet, Und das Sacrament deines lieben sons Jhesu

There are a couple of further incidents, which, though occurring somewhat after our period of interest in this chapter, further confirm the inclusion of Genesis 1:28 as a pronounced blessing which was typically included in the wedding service. The first of these occurred in February of 1536 at the wedding of Herzog Philip I of Pomerania and Maria, the daughter of the Saxon Elector John. Apparently, as Luther officiated at this wedding and, following the occurrence of some unexpected happening (perhaps the dropping of one of the rings), he addressed the devil and then immediately the bridal couple: »Listen, devil, this doesn't concern you! Be fruitful and let your seed not pass away«[17].

One final discussion, this one from the late 1530s and early 1540s, deserves mention. Johannes Mathesius records comments made by Luther around September of 1540 questioning whether the marriage of a younger man with an older woman could be regarded as a proper marriage considering that there would be no hope of offspring. To this Luther is supposed to have answered that it could, »Yet I would prefer, that one would leave out the word, ›Be fruitful and multiply‹, during the wedding«[18]. Of course, as has often been noted, Luther's *Tischreden* present a complex set of issues and cannot always be relied upon as accurate accounts of the reformer's words and thoughts[19]. With regard to this subject, however, it is interesting to note that this very topic had been the subject of discussion in previous years. In 1533 Melanchthon had written a letter to Antonius Corvinus, a one-time student in Wittenberg, in which he commented on the topic of the benediction in the wedding and its proper form in the case of an older couple. Melanchthon stated that it is better to simply use the apostle Paul's words in such a ceremony

---

Christi und der kirchen, seiner braut, darinn bezeichnet, Wir bitten deine grundlose güte, du wollest solch dein geschepff, ordenung und segen nicht lassen verrucken noch verderben, sondern gnediglich ynn uns bewaren durch Jhesum Christ unsern Herrn, Amen«. WA 30/III, p. 80, 8–13.

17 »[Hörst du Teufel, es geht dir nicht an: crescite et] semen vestrum non deficiat!«. Roderich SCHMIDT, Das historische Pommern. Personen, Orte, Ereignisse, Köln 2009, p. 320. For Schmidt's complete treatment of this wedding and these events, see pp. 311–328 (esp. 319–326). We should note that there is some discussion as to the actual words spoken by Luther and at least three different versions recorded by different sources. Schmidt concludes that, at the very least, Luther must have at least said »Semen tuum non deficiet« with anything beyond that being the subject of debate (p. 321). The words of Genesis 1:28, however, would have been mentioned in the wedding blessing given that Luther's *Traubüchlein* was used (p. 314). Apparently, Luther's blessing was effective in that the couple brought forth a total of seven sons, though one died in childhood, and three daughters (p. 322). WA 41, p. xxxi, also notes these events and Luther's apparent response.

18 Cf. »Doch wolt ich gern, das man die wort aussen ließ im trawen: Crescite et multiplicamini!«. WA Tr 5, p. 10,15f. (#5212).

19 See, for example, Katharina BÄRENFÄNGER et al., Martin Luthers Tischreden. Neuansätze der Forschung, Tübingen 2011, for several essays addressing the complicated compositional, editorial, and publication history of the so-called »Table Talks« as well as the various issues of reliability arising from this history.

(i. e. »On account of fornication let each one have his own wife«) rather than those of Genesis 1:28[20].

During the second half of the 1520s, we also observe the emergence of catechetical material related to our verse, something which further demonstrates this verse's function in helping to establish and promote the Wittenberg teaching on marriage and its connection to the matter of procreation. Of course, the most important of these catechetical writings, written largely in response to the state of affairs observed during the visitation[21], are to be found with Luther's *Small* and *Large Catechisms* in 1529 as well as both the *Haustafel* (Table of Duties) and marriage booklet which often came to be appended to especially the *Small Catechism*. Nevertheless, we do find evidence of such a catechetical approach to marriage and family already prior to the release of Luther's own catechisms. In 1528, for example, Justus Menius, the former student and close companion of Luther and especially Melanchthon – and at that time pastor and visitor in Thuringia[22] – published *Erynnerung was denen so sich ynn Ehestand begeben zu bedencken sey*[23].

This writing is noteworthy for several reasons. First, its structure and content establish it as a sort of forerunner of the evangelical *Haustafel* literature that would shortly emerge, especially through Menius's own *Oeconomia christiana* the following year. For the purposes of our own study, though, this print proves important as it clearly demonstrates the positive place and function which Genesis 1:28 and procreation had in Menius's teaching on marriage and family. To this end, Menius not only cites Genesis 1:28 as part of the establishment of marriage[24], he then goes on to emphasize God's thoughtfulness in every aspect of creation – to include the creation of mankind as *male* and *female* – as the reason that man ought to adhere to the words of Moses and not to his own wishes and thoughts[25]. With such a basis established, Menius then proceeds to discuss the effective power establishing the sexes (i. e. God's word and power) while at the same time emphasizing the end for

---

20 »De forma initiandi coniuges vetulas, placeret mihi magis uti forma Pauli: ›Propter fornicationem habeat unusquisque uxorem suam‹. Saepe enim et hic vidi, irridere in vetulis formam illam: ›Crescite‹ etc.«. MBW T5 (#1337; 25 Juni 1533); cf. CR 2, col. 657.
21 See Editors' Introduction to the Small Catechism, in: Kolb et al., The Book of Concord, pp. 345–347. Note that the visitation itself was concerned with such topics as marriage (WA 26, p. 225,10–30) under which topic we might certainly imagine that the Biblical foundations of marriage would have been addressed, and these not merely limited to Genesis 2 as is mentioned in Luther's introduction.
22 Behrendt, Lehr-, Wehr- und Nährstand, pp. 92f.
23 Justus Menius, Erynnerung was denen/so sich ynn Ehestand begeben zu bedencken sey. Just. Menius, Wittenberg 1528 (VD16 M 4567).
24 Ibid., Aiii^v.
25 Ibid., Aiiii^r–Aiiii^v.

which they were divinely created: to be fruitful and multiply as men and women[26]. From there, Menius goes on to mock human wisdom which thinks it can know and order things better than the Creator. For example, Menius writes,

> For we are inherently disposed to believe that we do a thing better than God has made it for us. We poor fools also forever allow ourselves to think that we will be more successful than God. Thus we direct our own course, desiring not to be human (i. e. to be men, women, and fruitful), but rather always desiring to propel ourselves higher toward heaven[27].

On this basis, Menius then concludes that there is not much reason for people to give serious consideration to whether or not they ought to marry. After all, they were created to do just that. Furthermore, the normal man and woman will realize from experience that they are driven by nature toward marriage and procreation[28]. Thus, Menius's conclusion for the rank and file of humanity:

> On this basis, it is my view *that* each individual has enough in asking himself, whether or not he belongs in this order of marriage and is accordingly blessed. For it will simply not do that an individual enters into or else exempts himself on the basis of free determination. Rather, one must be the plant he is. Thus summarized: if you are a man (or have been created and blessed by God accordingly unto procreation), you must enter into this ordinance. There is no way out. Otherwise, you would despise God's command and obedience, and find your freedom in the devil's name – to the loss of your own soul's salvation[29].

---

26 Ibid., Aiiii^v, writes, »Wenn du nu also geleret hast von wem/und wie du geschaffen seyest/so lere nu auch weiter/wo zu du also geschaffen seyest/das zeiget dir Moses auch an/da er also sagt/Vnd Gott segnet sie vñ sprach/Seyd fruchbar vnd mehret euch etc. Da sihe/dieser segen ist eben so wehrend so ein mechtig Gottes wort vnd krafft/als das/damit er sonne vnd monde geschaffen uñ an den himel geheftet/da herab vber den gantzen erdboden zu leuchten. Item nichts onmnechtiger vnd krafftloser/deñ der wort yrgend eines/die wir itzund drob gehandelt haben/Darümb ist dirs eben so unmüglich dawidder dich freuelich zu wehren und auff zu halten/als kegen der ytz gehandelten ersten einem«. He then continues by saying that if men and women want to avoid being man, woman, and fruitful in God's name, they will find out that things are only worse under the devil's name; cf. ibid., Aiiii^v–Bi^v.
27 Cf. »Denn wir sind von art also gesynnet/das wir ymerdar vermeinen/ die sachen besser zu machen/ deñ es Gott mit vns gemacht hat/vñ lassen vns allewege bedüncken/wir armen narren/wollens auch wol besser treffen/denn Gott/vnd faren vnser eins teyles zu/wollen nicht menschen/menner/weiber vnd fruchtbar sein/sondern wollen vns selbest ymerdar yhe höher gen himel hinauff schwingen«. Ibid., Bi^r.
28 Ibid., Bi^v–Bii^r.
29 Cf. »Daraus meine ich/habe sich ein iglicher gnugsam zu prüffen/ob er ynn diesen orden des ehestandes gehöre/vnd darein gesegnet sey odder nicht/Denn es will sich nicht thun lassen/das man sich aus freyer wilköre hineyn begebe/oder eraussen bleibe/sondern ist ein kraut/das heisset/Mus dran/Drümb kurtzumb/bistu ein Man odder von Got geschaffen/vnd yn diesen orden dich zu

Thus, in *Erynnerung was denen so sich ynn Ehestand begeben*, we clearly see once again Menius's understanding of both marriage and mankind's created nature as well as the heavy emphasis Genesis 1:28 received in the formulation of its purpose.

As we come to 1529 and Menius's *Oeconomia christiana*, we observe much of the same argumentation. Yet, we should note that in the larger scheme of the Wittenberg Reformation, *Oeconomia christiana* belongs in the category – along with the marital writings of Luther – as one of the most significant texts on marriage and family overall, both on account of its popularity as well as the influence it had upon an entire genre of writing[30]. What is more, it actually superseded the marital writings of Luther throughout the 1530s and was, in fact, quantitatively the leading publication with respect to marriage literature in Germany throughout that decade[31]. Moreover, it further supports our thesis that Luther's teaching on Genesis 1:28 was not merely Luther's but was the collective teaching of the Wittenberg reformers and their cohorts. Such connections and interplay are seen in two areas (aside from the fact that Menius's writing is itself a reflection of Luther's thought). Not only was *Oeconomia christiana*'s author, Menius, a former student and colleague of both Luther and Melanchthon, Luther himself wrote the introduction for Menius's work *and* was perhaps himself influenced to write his own *Haustafel* and catechism by none other than Menius[32]. With respect to *Oeconomia* we might further note that it can be viewed both as belonging to the category of marital literature as well as the broader category of *Haustafel* literature. It is also one of the first writings to reflect Luther's teaching about the three estates (*Stände*) and is thus important for the discussion of that teaching.

Before undertaking a discussion of our verse's relationship with Luther's initial *Haustafel* and the *Stände*, we might first quickly review the place and function of

---

gemehren gesegnet/so mustu hineyn/da wird nicht anders aus/du wollest denn mit verlust deiner seelen selickeit/Gottes gebot und gehorsam verachten/vnd yns teuffels namen davon frey sein«. Ibid., Biii^r. See also Menius's remarks on the wife's role in marriage: »gehorsam sein/vnd kinder geberen [...]«. Ibid., Cii^v.

30 BEHRENDT, Lehr-, Wehr- und Nährstand, pp. 79f., 92. According to ibid., p. 101, by 1556 *Oeconomia Christiana* had been printed no fewer than seventeen times throughout German lands. To this we might also add a Scandinavian presence as noted in C.W. BRUUN (ed.), Den danske Literatur fra Bogtrykkerkunstens Indførelse i Danmark til 1550, Copenhagen 1875, vol. 2, pp. 189–191, where it is observed that a Hans Tausen translation of *Oeconomia Christiania* appeared in Danish as Justi Menij | Oeconomia Chri-|stiana. | Det er, En Christelige hws-|holding, 1538.

31 BEHRENDT, Lehr-, Wehr- und Nährstand, pp. 101–105.

32 Sabine KRÜGER, Zum Verständnis der Oeconomia Konrads von Megenberg. Griechische Ursprünge der spätmittelalterlichen Lehre vom Haus, in: Deutsches Archiv für Erforschung des Mittelalters 20 (1964), pp. 475–561, at p. 534, URL: <https://resolver.sub.uni-goettingen.de/purl?PPN345858735_0020> (18 Aug 2022), argues that Luther depended on Menius for his inspiration to compose his *Haustafel* and catechism and not vice versa.

Genesis 1:28 in Menius's *Oeconomia christiana*. Luther's introduction sets the tone for the work. In it, he expresses concern primarily for matters related to marriage and family. Most notably, he likens marriage to something of an eleventh commandment set in place by God that man and woman dare not seek to avoid of their own reason and accord[33]. While Luther does not explicitly refer to Genesis 1:28, his gloss of Genesis 1 and 2 – along with his glowing endorsement of the contents of Menius's writing – cannot help but include the command to procreate, even if not mentioned explicitly.

With regard to that which is directly applicable to Genesis 1:28 in *Oeconomia*, sections IIII and V are most pertinent[34]. In these, similar to Menius's marriage book of 1528, he once again underscores that God Himself has instituted the estate and work of marriage in Genesis 1 and 2[35]. Likewise, the design and function of man and woman are such that they express and fulfill God's intent for them, that mankind would »Be fruitful and multiply«. Indeed, God declared such design and creation to be nothing less than *seer gut* (very good)[36]. Furthermore, God's intent for the marital estate is two-fold. Thus, secondarily and in light of sin, marriage now serves as an antidote to sinful lust and fornication[37]. Primarily, however, Menius dramatically and powerfully emphasizes the abiding divine word, command, and will for procreation as is expressed in Genesis 1:28[38]. Thus, as previously observed,

---

33 Justus MENIUS, An die hochgeborne Furstin fraw Sibilla Hertzogin zu Sachsen, Oeconomia Christiana: das ist von christlicher Haußhaltung, Wittenberg 1529 (VD16 M 4542), Aii^r–Aii^v.
34 Ibid., Ci^r–Dii^v.
35 Ibid., Ci^r–Cii^r.
36 Ibid., Cii^r.
37 Ibid., Di^r–Dii^r.
38 »Und ist zu mercken/das/wie die schrifft zeuget/Gott den ehestand umb zweyer vrsachen willen geschaffen/eingesatzt vnd gepotten hat/Die erste ist/das man kinder zeuge/wie Gott befolhen hat Gēn.1. Wachset und mehret euch/welchs wort/die weil es eben so wol ein Gottes wort ist/als das/da er saget/Es werde liecht/Item/Es lasse die erde auffgehen gras vnd kraut/das sich besamet/vnd fruchtbare bewine etc. So ists yhe gewis/es mus auch eben so mechtig vnd krefftig sein/ynn seinem werck/als der andern Gottes wort eins/ynn dem seinen«.
»Darumb/so mechtig das wort ynn der Sonnen vnd andern sternen ist/das sie mussen liechter sein vnd scheinen/Item/so mechtig es ist yn kreutern vnd bewmen/das sie mussen wachsen/sich besamen/vnd frucht tragen/vn̄ mag diesem almechtigen Gottes wort ynn seinem werck kein creatur/ widder yn hymel noch auff erden/wehren/also mus auch dis Gottes wort zum menschen geredt/ Wachset vnd mehret euch etc. ynn seinem werck krefftig vnd mechtig sein/vnd seinen furgang/ on aller creaturen hindernis/haben vnd behalten/und wenn sich auch beide hymel vnd erden dawidder sperreten/Da wird nicht anders aus/Es wolt denn Gott etliche ynn sonderheit von solchem werck ausziehen vnd frey behalten/wie ers denn nach seinem gefallen/mit einem sonst/mit dem andern aber so machet/einem diese/dem andern aber ein ander gabe gibt etc.«.
»Weil denn des menschen natur von Gott zu solchem werck/das da wachsen vnd sich mehren sol/ geschaffen ist/vnd solch des almechtigen schepffers wort vnd werck niemand wehren/hindern/noch endern kann/sol yhe billich ein iglicher/nach dem er sich von Gott geschaffen entfindet/Gott seinem

there can be little question that the primordial command to »Be fruitful and multiply« forms the very foundation for Menius's understanding of marriage as well as God's intention for it.

Yet, taking a step back from Menius's explanation of marriage and its scriptural foundations, it is also important for us to note his framing of the topic in *Oeconomia christiana*. Unlike his previous marriage booklet, *Oeconomia christiana* is constructed as a *Haustafel* around the framework of Luther's newly-emergent *Ständelehre*.

Much has been written and debated about this *Drei-Ständelehre*, both with respect to its historic origins and its commencement in Luther's thought and writing[39]. The general consensus seems to be that this theological framework – as is unique to Luther and Lutheran tradition – seems to have first been referred to in Luther's *Bekenntnis* of 1528[40]. It was not until 1529, however, with Luther's own *Haustafel*, that the *Drei-Ständelehre* more clearly emerged in Luther's catechetical instruments and writing. From there it was to be found sporadically throughout the remainder of Luther's career, even if its presence has often been overshadowed by his *Zwei-Reichlehre* and its own prominence is somewhat vague as Luther never systematically developed this teaching. Leaving such debates aside, however, for the purposes of this study, it is enough for us to note the appearance of Luther's *Drei-Ständelehre* contemporaneous to this time. Thus, the adoption and utilization of both it and the two regiments teaching in Menius's *Oeconomia* should be kept in mind.

Now, to be fair, the following is somewhat conjecture. Nevertheless, the relationship between the three estates/two regiments and Genesis 1:28 is a question worthy of our consideration. Officially, both Luther and Menius base the authority

---

schepffer vnd herrn zu ehren vnd gefallen/sich dazu gehorsamlich vnd willig gebrauchen lassen/dazu yhn sein Gott geschaffen hat/vnd haben will/vnd nicht ansehen noch achten/was mühe vnd arbeit yhm damit zugleich auffgelegt werde/sondern viel mehr bedencken vnd achten/was Gottes werck vnd wille sey/vnd gantzlich glewben/Gott/der des wercks ein einiger meister vnd almechtig ist/werde yhm ynn allen den sachen wol raten vnd helffen […]«.

»Aber sihe/wie es yhnen drob gehet/die also widder Gottes wort/werck vnd willen freuelen? Gott schaffet sie/vnd schaffet sie menlin und frewlin/gibt dazu seinen segen vber solch geschepff/vnd sagt/sie sollen wachsen vnd sich mehren/bezeuget weiter/es sey also mit dem menschen/gleich wie auch mit andern creaturen recht wol gemacht/vnd alles seer gut und fein/Ja widderholets zum andern mal/vnd spricht/Es sey nicht gut/das der mensch allein sey/er musse seinen gehülffen haben etc. Damit denn alle welt billich solt gnugsam vnterrichtet und verwarnet sein/sich an Gottes willen genügen zu lassen/ vnd fur solchem schedlichen vnd erschrecklichen freuel zu hüten«. Ibid., Ciii^r–Ciiii^r.

39 See BEHRENDT, Lehr-, Wehr- und Nährstand; Wilhelm MAURER, Luthers Lehre von den drei Hierarchien und ihr mittelalterlicher Hintergrund, München 1970, and VOIGT-GOY, Die gesellschaftlichen Stände, among others.

40 See *Vom Abendmahl Christi, Bekenntnis. 1528* (WA 26, pp. 504,30–505,10).

of the estates and regiments on God's own institution as confirmed in the Ten Commandments and especially the Fourth Commandment. Nevertheless, unofficially, or perhaps tangentially, the case can be made that for Luther – and perhaps Menius also – Genesis 1:28 stands in the background of both earthly estates (or the second regiment as consists of *oeconomia* and *politia*).

The reasons for such a hypothesis are multiple. To begin with, Luther's understanding of the Commandments argues that he is not under the impression that their reception by Moses somehow first established their validity and instituted the precepts contained in them[41]. Rather, for Luther the Commandments were the most perfect synopsis of natural and divine law. In other words, the Commandments merely confirm that which has been otherwise established by and is present in creation.

Menius expresses just this understanding of the actual authority and origin of the Commandments as he argues for and establishes the basis for marriage and authority. While referring to the Commandments, it is clear that he bases their imperative in God's original ordering of creation[42]. Similarly, Luther speaks on occasion of marriage and God's will for procreation as instituted or established by the Fourth and Sixth Commandments. For example, in Luther's *Large Catechism*, in preaching on the Sixth Commandment, he comments,

> However, because this commandment is directed specifically toward marriage as a walk of life and gives occasion to speak of it, you should carefully note, first, how highly God honors and praises this walk of life, endorsing and protecting it by his commandment. He endorsed it above in the Fourth Commandment, »You shall honor father and mother«. But here, as I said, he has secured and protected it. For the following reasons he also wishes us to honor, maintain, and cherish it as a divine and blessed walk of life. He has established it before all others as the first of all institutions, and he created man and woman differently (as is evident) not for indecency but to be true to each other, to be fruitful, to beget children, and to nurture and bring them up to the glory of God[43].

---

41 We might here briefly note that Luther finds the decalogue to be binding upon all mankind, not in the sense that it was given by Moses to the Israelites, but in light of the fact that it corresponds with the natural law. See Heinrich BORNKAMM, Luther und das Alte Testament, Tübingen 1948, pp. 108–116, and HERMANN, Studien zur Theologie Luthers, pp. 101, 108. STÖVE, Natürliches Recht, pp. 11–25, offers a case study in light of the Second Commandment, of the relationship between the Decalogue and natural law in Luther's thought.

42 MENIUS, Oeconomia Christiana, Biii^v.

43 KOLB et al., The Book of Concord, p. 414; cf. »Dieweil aber diss Gebot so eben auff den Ehestand gerichtet ist, und Ursach gibt, davon zu reden, soltu wol fassen und mercken. Zum ersten, wie Gott diesen Stand so herrlich ehret und preiset, damit, das er in durch sein gebot beide bestetiget und bewaret. Befestiget hat er in droben im vierdten Gebot: Du solt Vater und Mutter ehren, hie aber, hat er in (wie gesagt) verwaret und beschützet. Darumb wil er in auch von uns geehret und

Clearly, Luther does not mean that God's will for created life was established with Moses. Rather, Luther understands the Commandments to correspond with the structure of creation.

A further argument, however, contends even more powerfully that, for Luther, not only *oeconomia* but also *politia* are grounded in Genesis 1:28 and simultaneously in the Commandments which correspond to it. Namely, an element of Luther's thought which first emerged late in the summer of 1525 shows that he understood man's rule over creation and earthly authority itself to have been instituted with Genesis 1:28[44]. The first evidence of such argumentation on the basis of Genesis 1:28 appears in Luther's *Predigten über 2. Buch Mose*, and specifically with a sermon based on Exodus 18 preached on 13 August 1525. In this sermon, Luther discusses at length the *zwei Regimente* as well as the realm of human reason in earthly matters. Luther furthermore points out that this realm is not only understood by the heathen, but is, in fact, given by God:

> Thus God would say: O the worldly government I have beautifully made and established. Where? Genesis 1, where it states: »*Be fruitful and multiply and fill the earth and have dominion over the animals, fish, and birds*« etc. Thus, the earth is brought under you. It was at that time that God gave power and all provision, immediately after He had created the man[45].

---

also gehalten und gefüret haben als einen Göttlichen seligen Stand, weil er in erstlich für allen andern eingesetzt hat und darumb unterschiedlich Mann und Weib geschaffen (wie für augen) nicht zur büberey, sondern das sie sich zusamen halten, fruchtbar seien, Kinder zeugen, nehren und auffziehen zu Gottes ehren«. BSELK, p. 1002,7–17. Some years later, during Luther's *Lectures on Genesis* (1535–1545), this idea of the Decalogue's affirmation of the divine will for procreation is quite manifest. For example, Luther says in this regard, »Cavere itaque doctrinas istas daemoniorum decet, et discere, ut reverenter habeamus coniugium, et reverenter loquamur de hoc genere vitae, quod videmus Deum instituisse, quod audimus in Decalogo commendari, ubi dicitur: ›Honora patrem tuum et matrem tuam‹. Cui addita est benedictio: ›Crescite et multiplicamini‹. De quo audimus hic Spiritum sanctum loqui, cuius os castum est [...] Honorifice enim coniugium tractari debet, ex quo omnes nascimur, quod seminarium est non solum politiae, sed etiam Ecclesiae et regni Christi usque ad finem mundi«. WA 42, p. 178,23–28 & 31–33. See also WA 43, p. 113,21–25, p. 203,12–18, p. 345,26–37; WA 44, p. 624,1–10.

44 It is worth noting that the institution of man's rule has received frequent attention throughout the church's history. Thus, Luther is not doing anything novel in giving consideration to man's dominion but simply stands in a long line of Christian biblical interpreters. See COHEN, Be Fertile, pp. 224–231, 235f., 259f., 264, 268f.

45 Cf. »Und wil Gott sagen: O das Weltlich Regiment hab ich schön gemacht und bestellet, wo? Genesis am Ersten, da gesaget ward ›*Wachset und mehret euch und füllet die Erde und herrschet uber Thier, Fische und Vogel*‹ etc. bringet die Erde unter euch. Da hat Gott zum Weltlichen Regiment macht und allen vorrat gegeben, als balde als er nur den Menschen geschaffen hatte«. WA 16, pp. 353,34–354,10; emphasis in original.

Luther writes similarly, though he does not expound in as great of detail, in *De servo arbitrio* late in 1525. Here, although Luther does not directly make the connection between government and Genesis 1:28, per se, he does explain that with the divine command to »have dominion« the foundation for human rule in things below, via human reason, was established – even if this realm was already limited prior to the fall[46].

Skimming forward to a sermon/lecture on John 20:2–10 (dated 12 June 1529), Luther expounds once again upon this rule first given to Adam in Genesis 1:28. After speaking of the purpose of Christ's preaching, that it was not to establish and instruct about earthly and political matters, Luther states, »Christ commanded Adam to exercise worldly rule when He said to the man in Genesis 1, ›Be fruitful and multiply and fill the earth and subdue it and have dominion over the fish of the sea and over the birds of the air, and over all the animals that creep upon the earth‹«[47].

As we wrap up our brief survey of Luther's *Drei-Ständelehre* (to say nothing of the *zwei Reiche*), we are left with the distinct impression, though perhaps it is not always clearly and explicitly stated, that Genesis 1:28 *is* the basis for his – and likely also that of the other reformers – understanding of the origin and purpose not only of marriage, but also of human reason and dominion. Furthermore, with respect to the *Haustafel* literature, which was both undergirded by and expressive of such *Drei-Stände* thought, the place and importance of Genesis 1:28 ought not be underestimated, most especially in any discussion of *oeconomia*.

Further Polemic Usage

Before we advance to the more confessional aspects of our verse's role in the Reformation, we do well to note the continued polemical nature of Genesis 1:28 during the middle and latter years of the 1520s. While the battle lines had been formed already quite clearly in 1522–24 and some of the liveliest salvos were fired in those years, the skirmishing involving our verse certainly continued into the latter half of the 1520s. On the papal side of the debate we find familiar names such as Johann Faber, who was by this time chaplain and confessor to King Ferdinand of Austria

---

46 WA 18, p. 671,33–39.
47 Cf. »Das weltlich Regiment hat er [i. e. Christus] dem Adam befolhen, da er zum menschen sagt Gene. 1. ›Seid fruchtbar und mehret euch und füllet die Erden und macht sie euch unterthan und herrschet uber fissch im Meer und uber vogel unter dem himel und uber alles Thier das auff erden kreucht‹«. WA 28, p. 441,32–36.

and on his way to becoming bishop of Vienna in 1530[48], and Josse Clichtove[49], as well as names newer to our investigation such as Wolfgang Wulffer[50], Konrad Wimpina[51], and Johann Eck[52]. Notably, many of these names – as well as others mentioned previously in this study – will show up once again in the context of the *Confutation of the Augsburg Confession*[53]. We can furthermore note that others, such as Erasmus, were quick to summarize the »Lutherans« as merely caring about wealth and wives[54].

It is thus into such a controverted situation that Genesis 1:28 was often employed by the wider Wittenberg front. We have previously noted our verse's original employment as an argument aimed against monastic vows and priestly celibacy. Throughout the years leading up to the Augsburg Confession, this most certainly continued to be the case. Indeed, though not the only battering ram against vows of celibacy, it was one – if not one of the foremost – of the Wittenberg lines of argumentation. For Luther, such argumentation continued to appear in a variety

---

48 Johann FABRI, Summarium Underricht aus was christenlichen Ursachen D. Johan Fabri bisher der Lutherischen Lere nicht anhängig, Mainz 1526 (VD16 F 238), Liiii^r–Liiii^v. While Genesis 1:28 is not explicitly mentioned in Faber's criticism of Luther's attack on virginity, the argumentation is clearly directed against Luther's understanding of man's created nature and thus, by implication, Genesis 1:28.

49 Josse CLICTHOVE, Propugnaculu[m] Ecclesie, adversus Lutheranos, Cologne 1526 (VD16 C 4207), Giiii^v/CXXI^v, Liii^v/CXXXVII^v. The latter reference once again clearly shows the response of Luther's opponents (referring back to Jerome's writing versus Jovinian) to the Wittenberg assertion that *crescite et multiplicamini* comprised some sort of ongoing imperative for mankind.

50 Wolfgang WULFFER, Epithalamion vnd Braudlied Mertē Luthers/ Deutscher nation Ertzketzers/ erclert durch Wolff Wolfher/Zw Dresden/allen zu gutt/die es gelust zu lesen/vber S. Pauls Capittel. 1 Chorin: 7, Dresden 1525 (VD16 ZV 22408), Aiii^v, Ciii^r–Ciiii^r. Id., Tacianus der ertzketzer in Krichenland/hat verpotten Ehelich zuwerden/Luther der Ertzketzer in Dewtschen land/gepewt Ehelich zuwerden/beydes wider.s.Pauls Text.i.Corin.vij. […], Dresden 1528 (VD16 W 4582), Ai^v, Aiiii^r–Aiiii^v. The latter reference expressly denies the ongoing necessity of Genesis 1:28.

51 Konrad WIMPINA, SECTARVM ERRORVM, HALLVTINAtionū, & Schismatum, ab origine ferme Christianae ecclesiae, ad haec us[que] nostra tempora,concisioris Anacephalaeoseos,Vna cū aliquantis Pigardicarū, Vuiglefticarū, & Lutheranarum haeresum: confutationibus, Librorum partes Tres. […], Frankfurt/Oder 1528 (VD16 K 1533), »De Providentia«, Fol. CV^v.

52 Johannes ECK, Enchiridion locorum communium adversus Lutteranos. ab autore jam quarto recognitum auctum et a mendis emunctum, Ingolstadt 1527 (VD16 E 338), G2^r–G3^r.

53 Robert KOLB/James A. NESTINGEN (eds.), Sources and Contexts of the Book of Concord, Minneapolis 2001, p. 105.

54 John W. MONTGOMERY, The Suicide of Christian Theology, Minneapolis 1970, p. 423, notes Erasmus complaining in a letter to Willibald Pirckheimer, dated 20 March 1528, that the »Lutherans« sought only two things – wealth and wives; cf. »Duo tantum querunt, censum et vxorem«, Percy S. ALLEN, Opvs Epistolarvm Des. Erasmi Roterodami, Clarendon 1928, vol. T. 7. 1527–1528, p. 366,42.

of formats, whether through preaching[55], published tracts[56], or even in personal letters as we have witnessed elsewhere.

It is worth recalling at this point that even when Genesis 1:28 is not explicitly mentioned, it often stands behind those texts which are mentioned at a presuppositional level. This is most frequently the case with 1 Corinthians 7, Matthew 19, and Genesis 2. A good example of this is seen in a letter written to Wolfgang Reissenbusch (written simultaneously for printed purposes)[57]. In this letter Luther pressed a powerful argument against monastic vows on the explicit basis of Genesis 2 (»*Non est bonum homini esse solum [...]*«) Interestingly, although »crescite et multiplicamini« is not explicitly mentioned, Luther's line of argumentation almost certainly understands Genesis 2:18 in light of Genesis 1:28. Indeed, in this passage Luther emphasized the companionship of offspring as much as he did that of the woman. Even more, in connection with his offensive against monastic vows, Luther pressed the point that God's word and work compel man and woman to be together and therefore any sort of vow of celibacy is damnable, as if one vowed to be God's mother or to create a heaven[58].

As previously noted, Luther was not alone in Wittenberg in arguing against vows of celibacy and the monastic institution on the basis of Genesis 1:28. As it turns out, neither was Luther alone in writing (and simultaneously publishing) to Wolfgang Reissenbusch. Later that same year Bugenhagen wrote *De conjugio Episcoporum*

---

55 An example of a sermonic attack against papal teaching appears in Luther's sermon on John 2 (15 Jan. 1525) in which Luther states, »Deus hunc statum creavit, addidit verbum: ›Non est bonum‹. Papa contra: Non est bonum. Paulus: ›doctrinis demoniorum‹, ubi clare papatum, verbieten hurerei, ›habent quidem speciem‹. Et ideo fecit hominem, ut scriptura dicit, ›masculum et feminam‹, ut videmus natura unum ad alterum pertinere, quia ita creavit. Ita dixit ›Crescite et multiplicamini‹«. WA 17/I, p. 9,12–16.

56 Luther's 1527 pamphlet on the martyrdom of Leonhard Kaiser of Bavaria provides a great example of the continued »Wittenberg« application of Genesis 1:28 against vows of celibacy (WA 23, pp. 443ff.). In this case, Luther published a pamphlet including his own dedication followed by a collection of writings from the recently martyred Kaiser. Kaiser, who had studied in Wittenberg under Luther's tutelage for a year and a half beginning in 1525, expressed Luther's sentiment about Genesis 1:28 precisely when he wrote, »Item, ob auch einem Priester uber sein glübd zufreyen gezyme? Antwort: ›ya, das gelübd gethan kann odder mag Gottes wort nicht dempfen, es sei nicht unsers thuens keüscheit zugeloben, Sonder Gottes gnad mus es zuvor geben, dan das wort krefftig dar widder; ›Wachst und mehrt euch‹«. WA 23, p. 456,33–36.

57 Early in 1525 Luther had received a request via Spalatin to offer counsel to Reissenbusch as his order, that of St. Antony, had dissolved its monastery. The letter Luther wrote later that spring contained Luther's advice to marry and be freed from monastic vows with a clear conscience (WA 18, pp. 270f.).

58 WA 18, pp. 275,12–276,19. Note also Luther's emphasis both upon »brünstige, natürliche neigung zum weib« (p. 275,26) and the procreational intent in creating the woman (p. 275,19–26).

et Diaconorum[59] and dedicated it in honor of Reissenbusch's marriage to Anna Herzog of Torgau[60].

In connection with *De conjugio Episcoporum*, it can be noted that Bugenhagen's writing is strongly aimed against monastic vows and any human, demonic teaching, that would encroach upon God's institution of marriage as established in Genesis and reaffirmed by Christ and St. Paul. Bugenhagen particularly takes aim in this writing at the fathers' (i. e. Jerome and Anthony) teachings on virginity and celibacy and opposes them repeatedly with Genesis 1:28 as well as other arguments[61]. Elsewhere in this writing, Bugenhagen clearly reaffirms God's ordinance of marriage – with its procreative intent as based upon Genesis 1:28 – as something that is to be received as a good creation of God and not opposed[62].

We find further support for our understanding of Luther's teaching on Genesis 1:28 as not merely a personal teaching but the united teaching of the Wittenberg movement against vows of perpetual celibacy, with the Licentiate Steffan Klingebeyl's 1528 writing, *Von Priester Ehe*. It is noteworthy that the introduction to this writing was written by Luther[63]. Furthermore, in attacking perpetual vows of celibacy, Klingebeyl bases one of his main arguments, as we might expect by this point, on none other than Genesis 1:28. Here he states that God's word, »Be fruitful and multiply and fill the earth«, was and is »also from nature implanted in us all«[64].

Perhaps somewhat surprisingly, Genesis 1:28's polemical work was not confined to controversies against papal teachings. It also exercised its own role in controversy which arose within the wider Wittenberg-oriented Reformation itself. In December 1527, Dominikus Schleupner, preacher at Nuremberg's St. Sebald Church, remarried following the death of his previous wife. That event gave rise to severe criticism of clerical remarriage (based on 1 Timothy 3:2) and was written in the form of twenty-eight theses. These theses were especially dramatic and problematic due to their assertion, by the anonymous self-acclaimed supporter of the Reformation,

---

59 Johannes Bugenhagen, DE CONIVGIO EPISCOPORVM ET Diaconorum ad uenerandum Doctorem VVolfgangum Reissenbusch monasterij Lichtenbergensis Praeceptorem per Ioannem Bugenhag. Pomeranum, Nuremberg 1525 (VD16 B 9294). This work was also published in Wittenberg (in both Latin as well as a German translation by Stephan Roth) in 1525 and Strasbourg in 1526.
60 Johannes Bugenhagen, Johanns Bugenhagen. Selected Writings, edited and translated by Kurt K. Hendel, Minneapolis 2015, 2 vols., vol. 2, p. 843, fn. 2.
61 Id., DE CONIVGIO EPISCOPORVM, B2^r–B3^r, D2^r–D2^v, H3^r–H5^r.
62 Ibid., H1^r, I1^r.
63 Steffan Klingebeyl, Von Priester Ehe des wirdigen herrñ Licentiaten Steffan Klingebeyl/mit einer Vorrede Mart. Luther, Wittenberg 1528 (VD16 K 1340).
64 »Seyt fruchtbar vnd mehret euch vnd füllet die erden/Welches auch von natur vns allen eingepflantzt [...]«. Ibid., Ciii^v.

that such bigamy was in fact a deadly sin and that those who commit such sin belong on the gallows[65].

In response to these theses, Luther levels several arguments involving both the meaning of 1 Timothy 3:2 as well as the teaching of Scripture. Of importance for our purposes is that Luther, citing St. Paul both as a widow and as one claiming the right to marry (1 Corinthians 7:8; 9:5), shows the apostle's teaching to clearly oppose the twenty-eight theses. Furthermore, according to Luther, St. Paul's approval of the remarriage of clergy stemmed from his understanding of the divine benediction (Genesis 1:28) and noting that it is also scandalous to the papists[66].

Moreover, somewhat later Luther points to the problem that Christ only excluded certain individuals from marriage (Matthew 19) and that not all are able to receive His counsel of singleness. Likewise, St. Paul does not make an exception when he commands that each should have his own wife (1 Corinthians 7:2). Additionally, he notes that the forbiddance of marriage is termed the doctrine of demons, something Luther also understands to be at work in this debate and which is the actual reason why one would not make concession for priestly remarriage. Luther then argues:

[99] Finally, that word, »Be fruitful and multiply«, is generally created within and necessarily imposed upon all who are human.
[100] Against this it is lawful for none to decide or to live, unless by another more certain word, work, or gift of God he is excepted.
[101] For as it is lawful for no one to kill himself or to castrate himself by his own hand, neither is it lawful for anyone to destroy his own sex (unless by God's will) or to restrain it from duty[67].

5.2 The *Confessio Augustana*, the *Confutatio*, and the *Apologia*

Having surveyed the role and significance of Genesis 1:28 during the late 1520s, it is now appropriate to turn our attention toward further events which, on the one hand, do not offer any further significant developments in theological thought, yet which

---

65 WA 26, pp. 510f. The anonymous author later turned out to be none other than the famous humanist Willibald Pirckheimer (p. 511).
66 Luther writes, »Simul constat, Digamiam opus Dei esse, a Paulo probatum et in benedictione Dei Gen. 1. comprehensum. Si vero scandalum est, apud impios Papistas scandalum est, quibus omnia verba et opera Dei nihil nisi scandalum sunt«. WA 26, p. 522,15–18.
67 »[99.] Denique verbum illud ›Crescite et multiplicamini‹ generaliter omnibus, qui homines sunt, accreatum et necessario impositum est, [100.] Contra quod nulli statuere aut vivere licet, nisi alio certiore verbo, facto aut dono Dei excipiatur. [101.] Sicut enim nulli licet seipsum occidere aut manu propria castrare, Ita nulli licet sexum suum (nisi Volente Deo) extinguere aut ab officio cohibere«. WA 26, p. 525,13–18.

were themselves exceedingly significant in securing Genesis 1:28 as an important foundation of not only Luther's teaching on marriage, but of official evangelical – and eventually, Lutheran – teaching, to include its procreative intent and function. Along these lines, a discussion of our verse's presence both explicitly and implicitly in the formative and normative confessions of the emerging Evangelical-Lutheran church is entirely in order.

We begin by noting that, in the various drafts and documents leading up to the Augsburg Confession, although there was no question that priestly marriage and monastic celibacy were to be addressed[68], there was a certain ambiguity as to what points of emphasis were to be employed. For example, although Genesis 1:28 played a decisive role, both explicitly and also on a presuppositional level in the Wittenberg polemic against enforced priestly celibacy and monastic vows, we note that the creational arguments are somewhat minimized or greatly abbreviated in, for example, the *Schwabach Articles* (1529)[69]. Indeed, the driving explicit concern expressed in this document – relating to the marriage of priests and monastic vows – concerns itself more with matters of conscience and the pursuit of salvation, and somewhat less with creational arguments (to include the impossibility of vows of celibacy) and not at all with Genesis 1:28[70]. Beyond this, following the January 1530 summons of Emperor Charles V to the Protestant rulers and proceeding to early May, it is difficult to say with any certainty what manner of presentation the questions of priestly marriage and monastic vows took and what possible changes the Torgau discussions of March 1530 contributed to their general form[71].

---

68 It must be kept in mind that the marriage of priests was one of the foremost issues of concern in the years leading up to the Augsburg Reichstag. KELLER, Zölibat und Priesterehe, p. 155, notes that the debate surrounding the marriage of priests had expressed itself pointedly at the Speyer Reichstag of 1526 and was part of the reason for its mildly stated compromise expressed along the lines of conscience.

69 The *Schwabach Articles* were composed in late summer of 1529 and presented in October that same year. They served as a direct source text first for the Marburg Colloquy and then later for the *CA*. See Wilhelm MAURER, Historischer Kommentar zur Confessio. Einleitung und Ordnungsfragen, Gütersloh 1976, vol. 1, pp. 16, 20, and KOLB/NESTINGEN, Sources and Contexts, p. 83.

70 Schwabach Article 15 affirms that celibacy and the monastic life in pursuit of grace and salvation (as had previously occurred) are to be condemned as a doctrine of the devil. Here there is to be found no mention of either Genesis 1:28 let alone any argument from creation. See BSELK. Quellen und Materialien, with the assistance of team of eleven colleagues. Göttingen 2014, vol. 1, p. 41.

71 Regarding the problematic nature of the so-called »Torgau Articles«, Volker Leppin summarizes the situation as follows: »Die genaue Textgeschichte und -gestalt der Torgauer Artikel konnte bislang nicht rekonstruiert werden; wahrscheinlich handelt es sich gar nicht um einen fest umreißbaren Textbestand, sondern um eine Anzahl unterschiedlicher Stellungnahmen zu einzelnen Sachproblemen. Die Diskussion um die ›spänigen Artikel‹ XXI–XXVIII der späteren Confessio Augustana zog sich jedenfalls noch bis kurz vor deren Überreichung hin«. BSELK, p. 56. See also Gunther WENZ, Theologie der Bekenntnisschriften der evangelisch-lutherische Kirche, Berlin 1996, vol. 1,

By the beginning of May, however, the situation begins to increase in clarity. To begin with, within two days of the Saxon party's arrival in Augsburg, Johann Eck's *404 Articles* were circulating in the Imperial City[72]. These articles almost immediately put the evangelical cities and princes on the defensive on a wide variety of topics, including, as is pertinent to our discussion, articles related to Jerome and Jovinian (esp. 133 and 134), evangelical counsels and commandments (173–176), marriage and divorce (280–293), and finally celibacy and vows (294–313). While none of the above-mentioned articles expressly addressed Genesis 1:28 and the corresponding Wittenberg understanding of marriage and man's sexual nature, many of them did implicitly strike at precisely these matters. This is especially to be observed in the articles dealing with Jerome and Jovinian (133, 134 and 306)[73], certain Wittenberg teachings on marital matters (287–290)[74], and man's created nature (305)[75].

---

pp. 423–429. It should be noted, nevertheless, that if something more definitively could be stated, the so-called »draft E« – with its general emphasis on creation, albeit Genesis 2 and 3 – would very much be of interest. Here see Karl Eduard FÖRSTEMANN, Urkundenbuch zu der Geschichte des Reichstages zu Augsburg im Jahre 1530. Von dem Ausgange des kaiserlichen Ausschreibens bis zu der Uebergabe der Augsburgischen Confession, Halle 1833, vol. 1, p. 94.

72 KOLB/NESTINGEN, Sources and Contexts, p. 31.

73 Numbered according to ibid., pp. 49,70. The numbering of the original runs ahead beginning with the 166th thesis as the original skips 165 in transitioning from Ci^r to Ci^v.

»133 Hieronymus contra Iouinianum superstitiosæ extollit virginitatem: hoc genus multa sunt apud Hieronymum, superstitiosa potius quam pia. Melanchthon«.

»134 Hieronymus non digne scripsit in Iouinianum: plus torquet eū autoritate quam eruditioñ: & locos sacræ scripturæ torquet, ne dicam deprauat: quis scit si Hieronymus vnus illoℝ suerit, de quibus dicitur in Ezechiele, propheta cum errauerit & mendatium locutus fuerit, ego dominus qui decepi prophetam illum. Lutther«. Johannes ECK, Svb Domini Ihesv Et Mariae Patrocinio. Articulos 404. partim ad disputationes Lipsicam Baden[sem] et Bernen[sem] attinentes, partim vero ex scriptis pacem ecclesiae perturbantium extractos, Ingolstadt 1530 (VD16 E 270), Biiii^r.

»307 Status virginitatis est infra statum coniugalem quo non est melior super terram. Lutther. S. Hieronymus nouisset matrimonium vnum esse de septem ecclesiæ sacramentis partis, extulisset virginitatem: ac reuerentius locutus fuisset de matrimonio qnidam«. Ibid., Dii^r.

74 These articles cite especially Luther's controversial teachings regarding divorce in the case of impotence (or the permissibility of secret marriages in such cases), the preferability of bigamy to divorce, and the permissibility of divorce when a spouse refuses to render the conjugal duty. See KOLB/NESTINGEN, Sources and Contexts, p. 67, and ECK, Articulos 404, Di^v. In each case, the condemned teaching goes back to Luther's *Vom ehelichen Leben*, which, as we have previously observed, was built around the skeletal structure of Genesis 1:28.

75 »306 Continere est homini impossibile: sed sicut necessarium est homini comedere & bibere, dormire 7č. ita etiam commisceri: qa nullus vir potest esse sine muliere, & nulla mulier sine viro. Lutther«. ECK, Articulos 404, Dii^r. Once again, this line of argumentation is taken from such writings as *Vom ehelichen Leben* and *De votis monasticis iudicium* (KOLB/NESTINGEN, Sources and Contexts, p. 69, fn. 413) and, although not expressly mentioned, centers precisely around Luther's interpretation of Genesis 1:28.

Moreover, in addition to the appearance of Eck's *404 Articles*, the Protestant hope and expectation that the emperor had called the Reichstag in an effort to resolve the existing religious controversy, had by mid-May dissipated[76]. It had become clear that the emperor would not deal with the evangelical princes and cities as a neutral official. Thus, the increasingly hostile situation not only caused the evangelical rulers to come together in common cause, but now there was added reason to unite behind a common confession[77]. Whereas upon initially arriving at the Reichstag there had been any number of provincial expressions of faith, the political pressure experienced in Augsburg caused the evangelical princes to unite behind the efforts and confession authored by the Saxon party. Those cities who would not subscribe to the Saxon confession later united behind what became known as the *Tetrapolitan Confession*[78].

At any rate, it would appear that Eck's attack and the growing pressure upon the evangelical princes (and their theologians) forced them to reformulate, clarify, and strengthen their apology and particular articles within it[79]. Thus, in the German translation of an early Latin draft of the Augsburg Confession (late May/early June 1530), it is possible to observe that significant changes had occurred with respect to the discussion of the marriage of priests[80]. In fact, the article on priestly marriage now demonstrated a decisive and enduring shift towards the inclusion of Genesis 1[81]. Along with this, the article on monastic vows now also expressed concern for the impossibility of monastic chastity and the normativity of God's

---

76 See Charles P. ARAND et al., The Lutheran Confessions. History and Theology of The Book of Concord, Minneapolis 2012, p. 98, regarding the change in the emperor's disposition towards the protestant princes.
77 D. [Heinrich] DRESCHER, Der Reichstag zu Augsburg 1530 und das Augsburgische Glaubensbekenntnis, Kaiserslautern 1930, pp. 23f. For an indication of this change in tenor, see Melanchthon's 11 May letter to Luther (WA Br 5, pp. 314f.).
78 These cities were Strasbourg, Constance, Lindau, and Memmingen. See BSELK, p. 69.
79 Luther's own *Vermahnung an die Geistlichen, versammelt auf dem Reichstag zu Augsburg* (WA 30/II, pp. 237ff.) is of negligible import to the developments of the *CA*'s treatment of the marriage of priests and monastic vows given its late release date (7 June). Additionally, even though this writing does address the celibate estate (pp. 323–345), its argumentation is not expressly grounded in creational arguments. Thus, in reviewing the correspondence, it seems that the changed argumentation was implemented by Melanchthon and those with him in Augsburg without further input from Luther.
80 A brief history of this text (Na) may be found in BSELK. Quellen und Materialien, vol. 1, p. 47, and is translated from the Latin version of 30 May (MAURER, Historischer Kommentar, p. 42). Na was then sent to Nuremberg on 3 June (BSELK, pp. 67f.; cf. CR 2, nr. 95, col. 83).
81 In the article »[20] *Von der priester ee*«, after mentioning the deplorable moral situation found amongst clergy and citing St. Paul concerning the necessity for marriage, the text reads, »Item als Christus spricht: ›Sy faßen diß wort nit alle‹, damit er zuversteen gibt, das sy nit alle zu der keuscheit geschickt sein, dann Got hat den menschen sich zu meren erschaffen, Genesis 1. Solche beschaffung Gottes kan kein mensch an sondere gab und wirckung Gottes endern. Wer nun keuschheit zuhaltten

command and ordering[82]. Nevertheless, even though Genesis 1 had now become a permanent fixture of all subsequent articles dealing with the marriage of priests, a question of proper emphasis of expression remained.

Here we find an emerging divergence as to whether sex (Genesis 1:27) or the divine procreative will (Genesis 1:28) should be highlighted. Along these lines, it is to be observed that, whereas the developments of the first Nuremberg draft and the later Spalatin copy find their subsequent home in the Latin version of the *CA*, Melanchthon's further adjustments and alterations to the confession would eventuate in a text with a slightly different emphasis in what would become the official German version[83].

With respect to these developments which eventuated in the German text, we find that, although argumentation based upon Genesis 1 remains constant, the emphasis is switched away from the procreative emphasis of Genesis 1:28 and toward humanity's creation as two sexes as is evidenced by the creation of man and woman (Genesis 1:27)[84]. This new formulation is thus largely retained to comprise that of the presumed German text read on 25 June 1530[85]. While it can only be speculated, we might perhaps deduce that this change – although not representing any sort of difference in theology – does represent an attempt to offer what was perhaps the most amenable presentation of Wittenberg teaching possible. Given the attacks and polemics surrounding Genesis 1:28 and oft-cited claims that the »Lutheran« teaching merely repristinated Jovinian's heretical teaching, such a move likely sought to sidestep an otherwise loaded topic in the genuine pursuit of unity or, perhaps more likely, a somewhat fairer hearing.

Having now offered at least an overview of the place of our verse and its corresponding teaching in developments leading up to the Augsburg Confession, we can now offer some observations as to the *CA* itself, both to its relevant content and its significance. To begin with, it should be observed that whatever version was

---

untuglich ist, der soll eelich werden. Dann Gottes ordnung und gebott kann kein menschlich satzung noch gelubd aufheben«. BSELK. Quellen und Materialien, vol. 1, p. 59,17–23.

[82] Ibid., pp. 63–65. Spalatin's draft copy of mid-June is substantially the same in its treatment of the marriage of priests, both in flow of argumentation and its understanding of man's procreative purpose, though without parenthetic citation of Genesis 1:28 (p. 76).

[83] Here, the so-called *Ansbacher Exemplar* (Nü2) is of significance. According to ibid., p. 94, Nü2 takes us very near to the text which was then read on 25 June, though the editorial process had not yet been entirely completed. The article concerning the marriage of priests appears in ibid., pp. 97–101, and FÖRSTEMANN, Urkundenbuch, pp. 401–406.

[84] FÖRSTEMANN, Urkundenbuch, p. 402.

[85] Leppin notes, »Diejenigen Exemplare des deutschen und lateinischen Textes, die an eben dem 25. Juni, an welchem der kursächsische Kanzler Christian Beyer das Bekenntnis verlas […], übergeben wurden, existieren nicht mehr. Entsprechend lässt sich die reichsrechtlich eigentlich relevante Fassung nicht eindeutig greifen und auch nicht klar rekonstruieren«. BSELK, p. 69.

originally read and handed over to Emperor Charles V no longer exists[86]. There were any number of early (unauthorized) print editions that sought to reproduce the confession for the wider public, but the official edition, the so-called *editio princeps*, was first printed in 1531 in Latin and German, respectively[87].

Leaving discussion of the subsequent printings and *variata* of the *CA* aside[88], what should be noted with the presentation of the Augsburg Confession is that an important shift had now taken place. Whereas previously the teaching of Luther and the Wittenberg theologians had been something of a *de facto* official teaching of the evangelical princes and their respective territories, with the presentation of the Augsburg Confession, this understanding on procreation and sex – based largely upon Genesis 1:28 – was adopted as the *official* teaching of these territories and cities[89].

As concerns the official German edition of the *CA*, the teaching on Genesis 1:28 is implicit but undeniable. This is clearly apparent in the reference to Genesis 1:27 in *CA* 23:

---

[86] Ibid.
[87] Ibid., p. 70. For further discussion of the various editions which appeared throughout the 1530s and 40s and until the *Book of Concord* in 1580, see pp. 71–83.
[88] This question is of some importance in the time following our study given that Melanchthon's *Variata* of 1540 has substantially changed wording which seems to lend itself to a more ambiguous and even differing theological interpretation in favor of celibacy. See FRANZEN, Zölibat und Priesterehe, pp. 36f.
[89] This initially included Electoral Saxony, Brandenburg, Lüneburg, Hessia, Ducal Saxony, Anhalt, and also the free cities of Reutlingen and Nuremberg (BSELK, pp. 222–224). By the mid-1530s the *CA* was the confessional document binding members of the Schmalkaldic League. Furthermore, the signatories of the *Book of Concord* (1580) offer an indication as to the normative extent of this confession near the end of the sixteenth century (see KOLB et al., The Book of Concord, pp. 15–17). In addition to this, it must be remembered that entire lands (e. g. Denmark-Norway) adhered to the *CA* and, nevertheless, did not undersign the *Book of Concord*.
Regarding the initial status of the *CA*, scholars have rightly offered the important reminder that its nature as a *political* document preclude an understanding of it as merely a theological confession. As a political-theological document, it offered cursory presentations of the catholicity of the teachings espoused by the Wittenberg reformers. Only with time did it acquire its full import as a theological norm of Lutheran lands and then of Lutheran churches. For more on this, see Bernd MOELLER, Das Reich und die Kirche in der frühen Reformationszeit, in: Bernhard LOHSE/Otto Hermann PESCH (eds.), Das Augsburger Bekenntnis von 1530 damals und heute, München 1980, pp. 28–30, and also Matthias KROEGER, Das Augsburger Bekenntnis in seiner Sozial- und Wirkungsgeschichte, in: Ibid., pp. 99–124. Nevertheless, it must also be noted that the *CA* was simultaneously *theological*. ARAND et al., The Book of Concord, pp. 3f., point to this with the observation that Melanchthon's usage of the theologically-loaded term, *confessio*, was unprecedented and undeniably shows the document to be a confession and expression of faith.

> When Christ says, in Matthew 19[:11], »Not everyone can accept this teaching«, he shows that he knew human nature quite well, namely, that few people have the gift to live a celibate life. For »God created humankind […] male and female« (Gen. 1[:27]). Experience has made it all too clear whether human power and ability can improve or change the creation of God, the supreme Majesty, through their own intentions or vows without a special gift or grace of God. What good, honorable, chaste life, what Christian, honest, or upright existence has resulted for many? For it is clear – as many have confessed about their own lives – how much abominable, terrifying disturbance and torment of conscience they experienced at the time of their death. Therefore, because God's word and command cannot be changed by any human vow or law, priests and other clergy have taken wives for themselves for these and other reasons and causes[90].

Here, as we have repeatedly observed throughout our study, we once again find the impossibility of vows to be connected with God's creative word spoken in Genesis 1. Moreover, similar argumentation based on the working of God's word, though alluding to Genesis 2, appears in *CA* 27 and thus further evidences the creational theology we have become accustomed to[91]. The Latin version of the *CA*, of course, states explicitly what is implicit in the German version when it states in Article 23,

> In the second place, Christ says [Mattias 19:11], »Not everyone can accept this teaching«, where he is teaching that not everyone is fit for celibacy, because God created the human being for procreation (Genesis 1[:28]). It is not humanly possible to change creation without a singular gift and work of God[92].

---

90 Kolb et al., The Book of Concord, p. 62,5–9; cf. »Und nach dem Christus sagt Matt. xix.: ›Sie fassen nicht alle das wort‹, da zeiget Christus an (welcher wol gewust hat, was am menschen sey), das wenig leute die gabe, keusch zu leben, haben. ›Denn Gott hat den menschen menlin und freulin geschaffen‹, Genesis am ersten. Ob es nu inn menschlicher macht odder gelübde, Gottes der hohen Maiestet geschepffe besser zu machen odder zuendern, hat die erfarung alzu klar geben. Denn was guts, was erbar, züchtiges leben, was Christlichs, ehrlichs oder redlichs wandels an vielen daraus erfolget, wie greulich, schrecklich unruhe und quall ihrer gewissen viel an ihrem letzten ende derhalb gehabt, ist am tag, und ihr viel haben es selb bekennet. So denn Gottes wort und gepot durch kein menschlich gelübd odder gesetz mag geendert werden, haben aus dieser und anderen ursachen und gründen die Priester und ander geistliche eheweiber genomen«. BSELK, pp. 134,25–136,12.
91 Interestingly, we find the compelling, creative power of God's word cited also in *CA* 27, though in reference to Genesis 2. For this, see BSELK, pp. 169,24–171,14, though this should be compared with pp. 164,11–166,3, in which text Genesis 2 is not cited. Regardless of the differences, there is no compelling reason to assume that the underlying theology differs, given that they both stand in relation to *CA* 23. Regarding the textual difficulties with *CA* 27, note ibid., p. 74.
92 Kolb et al., The Book of Concord, p. 63,5–7, cf. »Secundo, Christus inquit: *Non omnes capiunt verbum hoc*, ubi docet non omnes homines ad coelibatum idoneos esse, quia Deus creavit hominem ad procreationem, Gene. 1. Nec est humanae potestatis sine singulari dono et opera Dei creationem mutare«. BSELK, p. 137,2–5.

In light of the above considerations and varying manner in which the different articles and versions of the *CA* present and allude to our verse, we do well to reiterate that these texts were not intended to offer the definitive detailed statement of the evangelical understanding of our verse – or any other topic, for that matter. Even if and even though these statements truly comprised the confession of the evangelical princes, they were, nonetheless, statements in shorthand. This reality, as corresponds with our own verse and topic, is perhaps best illustrated by the ensuing events following the reading of the *CA*.

Turning our attention, therefore, to the Catholic response, we can note that by 26 June it was already clear that the theologians of the majority party, those loyal to the pope, would not offer their own confession. Rather, they would prepare a response to – including a critique and even repudiation of – the evangelical confession[93]. In the days that followed, this situation only crystallized through the maneuverings of Charles V's theological advisors as well as the papal legate Campeggio[94]. Thus, on 12 July the initial response of the papal theologians (led by Johann Faber), was delivered to Campeggio and then subsequently to the emperor. This response, however, fell far short of the emperor's expectations in that it was a general criticism of evangelical teachings – with its many »heretical« tenets – and not a direct response to the newly presented confession[95]. Consequently, as deliberations continued, the form and content of the desired confutation was drastically changed. Clearly, the ultimate product was still decidedly against the evangelical confession of faith. Nevertheless, the resulting confutation was considerably moderated and focused more directly on the content of the Augsburg Confession rather than the entire spectrum of the writings of the various reformers[96]. Thus, after considerable negotiations between the various Catholic parties and extensive editing on the part of the theologians, the finalized *Confutatio* was presented on the afternoon of 3 August[97].

With respect to our own topic, it is of more than passing interest to observe that the chief authors of the *Confutatio* were not in any way new to the entire debate. To read through their names is in some ways akin to a review of the names we have already seen in this study. After all, the theologians were led by Johann Faber and their ranks included Johann Eck, Johann Cochlaeus, Bartholomäus Arnoldi von

---

93 Herbert IMMENKÖTTER, Die Confutatio der Confessio Augustana vom 3. August 1530, Münster 1979, p. 25.
94 Ibid., p. 33.
95 Ibid., pp. 37f.
96 Ibid., pp. 39f.
97 Ibid., pp. 41–47.

Usingen, and Johann Dietenberger[98]. As we have previously observed, none of these men were reluctant to condemn the »Lutheran« understanding of Genesis 1:28. Neither were they reticent about associating it with the charge of Jovinianism along with other heresies.

A second note of significance is the relative importance given to the topic of the marriage of priests, especially following the reading of the Augsburg Confession. In ongoing discussions held between Melanchthon and Campeggio (amongst others)[99], in what can appear to be almost desperate attempts toward unity and reconciliation on the part of the former[100], one of the »minimal demands« – next to Communion in two kinds and changes to the Mass – was the retention of priestly marriage in Protestant territories[101]. While Campeggio was himself somewhat sympathetic to Melanchthon's propositions, from the perspective of the Roman Curia, the marriage of priests could not even be considered[102]. Thus, it became quite clear both that the evangelicals would not give ground on this practice and that Rome could not make exception for it.

Given the participants involved in the writing of the *Confutatio* and the circumstances surrounding its composition, we should not expect anything novel in the material presented in it. Such is indeed the case. With respect to Genesis 1:28, the *Confutatio* limits itself to the oft-presented condemnation of the evangelical understanding on the basis of Jerome's claim that this verse is no longer applicable

---

98 For a list of the theologians involved in the *Confutatio*, see ibid., pp. 17–23. Of particular interest is the pay scale for the various theologians, of which Faber and Eck were the most highly paid (p. 23). See also WENZ, Theologie der Bekenntnisschriften, pp. 401–404.

99 For a helpful overview of Melanchthon's various negotiations in the month following the presentation of the *CA*, see Beate KOBLER, Die Entstehung des negativen Melanchthonbildes. Protestantische Melanchthonkritik bis 1560, Tübingen 2014, pp. 141–154.

100 These negotiation attempts were, both then and later, viewed by some evangelicals with disdain and/or as betrayal of Reformation teaching. It was especially Melanchthon's letter to Campeggio on 4 July that would come to cast a shadow upon Melanchthon in the years that followed and especially during the Adiaphorist Controversy. See ibid., pp. 211–215, 218–220.

101 IMMENKÖTTER, Die Confutatio der Confessio Augustana, p. 27. This corresponds also with the *Gutachten* prepared by Justus Jonas and others for the use of the evangelical princes. Jonas informed Luther of this in a letter sent on/about 30 June 1530 (see WA Br 5, pp. 426–429) to which he appended a summarized form of the articles over which the evangelical rulers were not prepared to compromise or give way. With respect to the marriage of priests, it states, »Hie kann unser gnädiger Herr gar nicht bewilligen, daß die Priester, wie vorhin, ahn Ehe leben sollten. Denn da stehet starke Schrift, daß Gott hat geschaffen Mann und Weib, daß sie sich mehren sollen, Gen. 2 et 3«. WA Br 5, p. 431,20–22. See also KELLER, Zölibat und Priesterehe, pp. 161–163, for the role that the marriage of priests had in the ongoing discussions surrounding and succeeding the presentation of the Augsburg Confession. FRANZEN, Zölibat und Priesterehe, p. 36, also offers brief discussion to clerical marriage as one of the »minimal« evangelical demands.

102 IMMENKÖTTER, Die Confutatio der Confessio Augustana, pp. 28–30.

to all people as well as the condemnation of Luther's teaching on priestly marriage as a *de facto* repristination of Jovinian's teachings.[103] It is noteworthy, however, to also observe that the *Confutatio* concerned itself with the ritual purity and functioning of priests in the Mass as we note the ongoing systemic relationship between these topics[104].

Throughout the time of the *Confutatio*'s composition, although private negotiations did continue, the evangelicals grew increasingly cognizant of the reality that the imperial response would not be favorable toward them. Thus, already by the end of July, there were quiet talks amongst the evangelicals to offer a further response, or apology, for their confession[105]. By early August, at the time of the reading of the *Confutatio*, Melanchthon and others were already working privately on a defense of the *CA*. It was, no doubt, partly in sensing such a response, and because the imperial side wanted to prevent precisely this, that copies of the *Confutatio* were not distributed to the evangelical party following its presentation on 3 August. Rather, they were left with only what their own recorders had been able to copy as a basis against which they might compose the defense of their own confession[106]. Melanchthon's compositional efforts, aided by the other Saxon theologians, continued off and on throughout August and into September. On 22 September, when Charles V refused

---

103 With respect to the association of Jovinianism, see ibid., pp. 150, 153. In connection with Genesis 1:28, the *Confutatio* states the following:

»Demnach als weitter ist furbracht, das diß ein ordnung und gebott von Got sei, so hat diß der hailig Jheronimus vor tausent jaren mit disen worten verantwurt, das von // noten sey gewesen, von ersten zu pflanzen den wald, das er darnach wachsen und man daraus nachvolgendts holz hauen möchte. Darumb sey gepoten derselbigen zeit, das man wachsen und meren solt, damit erfult wurde das erdreich; so nun aber das erdtrich erfult ist, also das von menige wegen der volcker ainer den andern drucket, so ist es yetzt nit mer ain gebot denjhenen, so rainigkait halten wellen. Und darumb so beruemen sy sich vergebenlich, so sy sagen, das sy fur sich haben Gottes gebot. Dann sy an kainem ort finden noch zaigen werden, das Got geboten hab den priestern, das sy weyber nehmen sollten [...]« Ibid., p. 152.

»Praetera cum praetendatur hanc esse ordinationem et praeceptum dei, Gen, 1, respondit ante mille annos in haec verba Hieronimus: *Necesse fuit prius plantare sylvam et crescere, ut esset, quod postea posset excidi.* Praeceptum tunc erat de procreatione prolis, ut repleretur terra, qua modo repleta et adeo quidem, ut sit pressura gentium, non est a modo praeceptum valentibus continere. Vane praeterea iactant mandatum dei. Ostendant, si possunt, ubi deus praeceperit sacerdotibus, ut ducant uxores«. Ibid., p. 153.

104 KOLB/NESTINGEN, Sources and Contexts, pp. 123f.
105 KOLB et al., The Book of Concord, p. 107, note that the term *apology* was first born out of Melanchthon's use of the term *antapologeisthai* in a letter dating near the end of July.
106 Ibid.

the evangelicals the opportunity to present their apology, the conclusion of the imperial diet was finally at hand[107].

Melanchthon, however, continued his efforts to edit and improve an apology throughout the remainder of the fall and throughout the winter, spurred on especially by receipt of the actual text of the *Confutatio* in October[108]. By the following spring, around the end of April or beginning of May, the first (quarto) edition of the *Apologia*, printed together with the *CA*, appeared in Wittenberg. Further improvements and editing – with the help of such theologians as Martin Bucer, John Agricola, John Brenz, and especially Luther – followed throughout the summer and resulted in the second (octavo) edition of the *Apologia*. This appeared in Wittenberg in September. It also subsequently became the basis for Justus Jonas's German translation as well as that which was signed by the theologians gathered at Schmalkald in 1537[109].

With respect to our own topic, we have previously noted the non-negotiable nature of priestly marriage for the evangelical faction. It is therefore not surprising to find a more thorough defense of that practice in Melanchthon's *Apologia*, along with such presupposed arguments as were derived from Genesis 1:28. Furthermore, given the *Confutatio*'s clear association of priestly marriage with Jovinianism and its explicit rejection of the *CA*'s usage of Genesis 1, a more substantial reformation defense of priestly marriage and its presuppositional/creational basis was only to be expected.

It is precisely this that we thus witness already in an early draft of Melanchthon's *Apologia*. This draft was recorded by Spalatin and dates to approximately 11 August 1530[110], though it also contains many marginal corrections and improvements by Melanchthon which were added later that month[111]. Here we can note that the *Apologia*'s treatment of priestly marriage already includes most of the points made in its final versions. For example, it distances itself from Jovinianism and defends the good *gift* of virginity – for those who have it.[112] Nevertheless, it disputes that many have this gift and then goes on to emphasize that those who nonetheless do not have this gift and attempt it are only tempting God and going against His

---

107 Ibid., p. 108.
108 Ibid. Christian PETERS, Apologia Confessionis Augustanae. Untersuchungen zur Textgeschichte einer lutherischen Bekenntnisschrift (1530–1584), Stuttgart 1997, p. 126, observes that Melanchthon received a copy of the *Confutatio* at the latest in early November. The possession of the *Confutatio*, however, remained a well-kept secret even within Wittenberg.
109 KOLB et al., The Book of Concord, p. 108.
110 BSELK. Quellen und Materialien, vol. 1, pp. 256–258.
111 Ibid., pp. 257f.
112 Ibid., p. 271,19–25.

ordinance when they ought rather to receive His creative gifts with thanksgiving[113]. Then, continuing, we find the basic arguments involving Genesis 1:28. Namely, Melanchthon rejects the idea that Genesis 1:28 was a command given for only a limited time. Even as the other words of creation are still in force (e. g. that the earth should bring forth green plants), so also do the words »Be fruitful and multiply« continue as a command while also effecting the ongoing creation of nature which man cannot alter. Thus, without a special work of God, one may not expect to be exempted from common nature[114].

While much editing took place throughout the latter part of August and into September (prior to the attempted presentation of this apology on 22 September), we find that almost nothing is altered with respect to our own topic in the likely record of this document, the *Dresdner Handschrift* (*Codex Chytraenus*)[115]. A further early German translation dating to 25 October, *Codex Casselanus*, shows also essentially the same argumentation and content[116]. Of note, however, is that the German translation does clarify one important point. Whereas the Latin less than clearly depicts what it means with »*a conditione illa communi naturae exemptae essent*«, and the reader would not necessarily realize that here is likely already an allusion to a discussion of the natural affects, the German »*dann dieweil sie von der angebornen, naturlichen aigenschafft gefreiet sein*« comes much closer to the point[117]. This, of course, would later be further clarified and become much more explicit. Nevertheless, we can note that the seed for the inclusion of this argument is already visible in the fall of 1530.

From the fall of 1530 to the printing of the quarto edition of the *Apologia* in April 1531, it is readily apparent that Melanchthon's treatment of priestly marriage

---

113 Ibid., p. 271,30–38.
114 »Ridiculum autem est, quod inquiunt hanc vocem Dei: *Crescite et multiplicamini*, tantum ad illud tempus, cum essent pauci homines, pertinere, non ad nostrum tempus«.
»Nos sic sentimus, quod illa verba creent et ordinent naturam, qualem postea existere necesse est*. Sicut alia similia verba: *Germinet terra herbam virentem*. Haec vox vestit agros, quotannis creat fruges, parit victum omnibus animantibus. Ita haec sententia: *Crescite* etc. non solum mandatum, sed etiam naturae conditionem continet, quam mutare non est nostrum, sed Dei opus. Nec fecerunt virgines, siquae vere conservaverunt virginitatem, contra mandatum Dei, quia cum a conditione illa communi naturae exemptae essent, mandato etiam solutae erant, quod ad illam communem conditionem naturae pertinet. Exemit enim istas peculiare donum et opus Dei«. Ibid., p. 272,1–12.
* Here Melanchthon added the marginal note, »nec se refingere ipsa potest« (ibid., p. 272, fn. b), which is then included in the text of the *Dresdner Hanschrift* (p. 308,5).
115 Ibid., p. 289, argues that the *Dresdner Handschrift* gives every indication of being the text which the evangelicals attempted to present to Charles V on 22 September. The difference in the relevant section of the documents has been noted above.
116 Ibid., pp. 350f. For a history of this codex, see pp. 344f.
117 Ibid., p. 351,15f.

received thorough attention. While the general framework of this article had been established already in the fall, Melanchthon reported to Justus Jonas first on 7 April 1531 that he had completed the section on the marriage of priests[118]. While it is not here our aim to establish a more detailed account of the changes that took place during these months, the results are clearly obvious[119].

Here we observe the general extent of the changes. Whereas the evangelical refutation of the *Confutatio*'s understanding of Genesis 1:28 is maintained in a similar form and length – along with the reformation appeal to Genesis 1:11 (and implicitly the entirety of Genesis 1 as inherently proving the theological point that Genesis 1:28 must also still be in force) – significant shifts have now taken place in the manner with which Melanchthon expresses his arguments from nature. Moreover, while in the earlier editions Melanchthon expressed the fact that virginity, when not divinely given, militates against both the command of God as well as mankind's shared nature, now Melanchthon inverts the argument by stating the positive will of God – alluding specifically and approvingly to natural law as consistent with the teachings of Scripture – for marriage and greatly emphasizes the elements of human nature (i. e. natural affections) which attest to this creation and will.

In concluding our brief treatment of the *Apologia*, we do well to add several points. To begin with, it is worth noting that while the *Apologia* was significantly Melanchthon's own work, he did not work alone. As noted previously, such theologians as Brenz, Bucer, Spalatin, Jonas, and – not least of all – Luther, were involved at varying stages of its development. Furthermore, given Luther's editorial involvement both prior to the April quarto edition and leading up to the September octavo edition, it must be conceded once again that Luther collaborated with and approved of Melanchthon's theological writing[120]. Thus, we have in the *Apologia* a document that speaks not just for Melanchthon, but once again offers a collective representation of Wittenberg theology – to include its understanding of Genesis 1:28, procreative/sexual urges, and natural law. Even more importantly, the *Apologia* offers an early and, what must be taken to be, authoritative explanation

---

118 PETERS, Apologia Confessionis Augustanae, p. 123; cf. CR 2, col. 493; MBW T5, pp. 91f.
119 For the sake of comparison, Appendix 2 includes a comparison between the *Spalatinische Handschrift* from Aug. 1530, the version contained in both the quarto/octavo editions, and the Jonas translation.
120 See PETERS, Apologia Confessionis Augustanae, pp. 421ff., for more detailed investigation of Luther's contribution to the *Apologia*. In cursory fashion, though, we might note that Luther, Jonas, and Melanchthon all worked together on a committee aimed at producing a print edition of the *Apologia* beginning already in October 1530 (pp. 421f.). Of much more significance is that Luther offered editorial comments while the quarto version was being prepared for its second edition (octavo). Sometimes these were accepted by Melanchthon (pp. 438f.); oftentimes they did not perceptibly impact the octavo edition. With respect to Article 23, it does not appear that Luther's comments had any perceptible impact. Nevertheless, neither would have Luther's comments substantially altered Melanchthon's argumentation (see pp. 439f.).

of the teachings contained in the *CA*. Thus, whereas the shorthand sketches of the evangelical teaching on marriage and procreation might be misunderstood and misinterpreted based on the limited text of the *CA*, the *Apologia* makes it quite clear exactly *what* understanding of these topics the evangelicals wished to confess.

It is also important to note, however, that this document, like the original *CA*, did not simply express the views of a group of theologians. In point of fact, both the *CA* and the *Apologia* comprised the confessional basis of the Schmalkaldic League[121]. Thus, it was a foregone conclusion that the theologians gathered at Schmalkald in February 1537 would undersign the *Apologia* along with the *CA*, as indeed they did[122]. In addition to all of this, the incorporation of the *Apologia* into the *Book of Concord* (1580) has further increased its lasting status as a confessional norm (to varying degrees) for Lutherans even today.

5.3 Melanchthon and the Debut of στοργαὶ φυσικαί

As has already been alluded to, reference to the natural affects – now under the designation στοργαὶ φυσικαί – finds an important place in the discussion of priestly marriage within Melanchthon's *Apologia*. This represents something of a new development in Melanchthon's thought and, as will be seen, comprises something of a new *terminus technicus* which will be increasingly used by the Wittenberg cohort in discussions of created human relations. In the following paragraphs we will offer a brief account of Melanchthon's introduction of such Aristotelian terminology and its inclusion in Lutheran confessional writings.

In Ethica Aristotelis Commentarius Philipp. Meanchtho. (1529)

We have previously mentioned the likely connection and dispute between Melanchthon's understanding of *affectus quosdam naturales* and Aristotle's writings in *Nicomachean Ethics*. What might also be noted at this point is that Aristotle's *Ethics* had for generations – and particularly following the fall of Constantinople in 1453 – served as the basic text for university instruction of ethics, something

---

[121] For this, see Johann Michael Reu, The Augsburg Confession. A Collection of Sources with a Historical Introduction, Chicago 1930, pp. 141f., who notes that this took place in the spring of 1532 at the meeting in Schweinfurt.

[122] BSELK, p. 233, notes that already in the fall of 1531 the members of the Schmalkaldic League had adopted both the *CA* and its *Apologia* as their commonly held teaching basis. See also Kolb et al., The Book of Concord, p. 296, for a note on the gathering of the theologians of the Schmalkaldic League in February 1537 and ibid., p. 344, for a list of the signatories at this gathering.

that was certainly also the case in Wittenberg[123]. Although Melanchthon's favor of Aristotle is notably negative in the late 1510s and through the mid-1520s, it is unclear what exactly his view of the Stagirite's ethical and political works was[124]. It is, however, clear that by the mid-1520s Aristotle was enjoying something of a rebound in Melanchthon's eyes, even if and even though *Nicomachean Ethics* was officially eliminated from the Wittenberg University curriculum in 1526[125]. Whether or not Melanchthon actually gave any lectures on Aristotle's *Ethics* during this period remains uncertain. It can, however, be demonstrated that Melanchthon was significantly involved with study and reflection on this work. His efforts eventuated in a commentary on *Ethics* (*In Ethica Aristotelis commentaries Philipp. Melanchtho.*)[126], subsequently published in 1529[127].

For the purposes of this study, Melanchthon's *In Ethica Aristotelis* represents a significant development in – or perhaps expression of – his thought on the place of God's creative work with respect to human affects. Skipping over the commentary on book one, we note that with book two, Melanchthon's concern is primarily directed toward virtue and its causes. After initially discussing virtue and its efficient cause, he shifts his focus to the secondary causes of virtue. These, he says, are in the human soul, and he identifies them with *affectus*, *potentia* (power; potential), and *habitus* (disposition)[128]. A treatment of the affects then follows, one that is especially relevant for the understanding of Melanchthon's thought on natural affects and their relationship with our topic.

Melanchthon begins this section with a definition of the affects. He defines them as brief or lasting movements of the soul which affect the heart or other organs in which they arise. External stimuli move these affects which, in turn, stir the body (particularly the heart, but also other members) to certain actions[129]. Shortly later, Melanchthon goes on to note the difference of opinion between Aristotle and the Stoics on the affects. He points out that the Stoics disapproved of all the affects while Aristotle could not disapprove of the affects in that he understood them to be innate. Melanchthon then approvingly states, »He therefore perceives certain

---

123 Günter FRANK, Einleitung, in: Melanchthon, Ethicae Doctrinae Elementa, pp. XXIIIff.
124 Ibid., p. XXX.
125 KUROPKA, Philip Melanchthon and Aristotle, p. 21.
126 Philipp Melanchthon, In Ethica Aristotelis Commentarivs Philipp. Melanchthon, Wittenberg 1529 (VD16 ZV 10667).
127 FRANK, Einleitung, pp. XXX–XXXI.
128 Melanchthon, In Ethica Aristotelis Commentarivs, D3^r.
129 Ibid.

affects of nature to be beneficial because they are instruments of urging[…]«[130] and offers a couple of examples of such useful affects.

Turning his criticism then toward the Stoics (including Augustine), Melanchthon praises the fact that their thoughts have now come into question and that, thus, their abhorrence of nature is now evident[131]. He then presses the unreasonableness of such a position by pointing out that nature itself must include such affects as hunger and thirst, the very things that the Stoics would root out. Even more, Melanchthon indicates that such attitudes are themselves unchristian. Continuing, then, he writes,

> In man there are two kinds of affects, some entirely at odds with reason, such as ambition, hatred, and the like. That these are full of vice, there is no doubt. Now *these affects* arise from original sin, which causes us to strive for or desire nothing except for our own advantage or pleasure. Other affects are consistent with reason, such as the love of parents for children, of children for parents, of spouses for one another, love for the well-deserving and *for* friends. These affects are called στοργαὶ φυσικαί. They do not arise from original sin but are rather creatures of God like the eyes *and* ears[132].

Notably, Melanchthon then seeks to affirm this understanding of these lower affects by appealing to Romans 1:31 and the apostle Paul's condemnation of those who are devoid of such created affections, the ἀστόργοι[133]. It is nevertheless clear from Melanchthon's comments which follow that these στοργαὶ φυσικαί have been affected by sin, chiefly in that they have been overcome by other, base passions. Nevertheless, in further attacking the views of the Stoics and the church fathers, Melanchthon contends for the God-given affects by pointing out that they are, in fact, gifts of God[134]. Continuing shortly thereafter he makes this point again, stating that the Holy Spirit does not free man from his affective nature, but rather plants new affects[135]. Here Melanchthon also includes a renewing of the natural affects.

---

130 »Sentit igitur affectus quædam naturæ beneficia esse, quia sint instrumenta agenda […]«. Ibid., D3ᵛ. One cannot help but note the corresponding terminology here with *affectus quaedam naturae* and that of Melanchthon's *Loci Communes*.
131 Ibid.
132 »In homine sunt duplices affectus, Quidam omnino a ratione dißentiunt ut ambitio, invidia, & similes. Hos esse vitiosos non est dubium. Oriuntur autem a peccato originis, quod efficit ut nihil quæramus seu adpetamus nisi nostræ utilitatis aut voluptatis caussa. Alij sunt affectus rationi convenientes, ut amor parentum erga liberos liberorum erga parentes, coniugum inter se, amor erga benemeritos & amicos. Hi affectus dicuntur στοργαὶ φυσικαί. Nec oriuntur a peccato originis, sed sunt creaturæ dei, sicut oculi, aures«. Ibid., D4ʳ.
133 »Itaq̃ & Paulus tanquam monstrosos argui homines ἀστόργος Rom. .I.«. Ibid.
134 »[…] tales impetus vere sunt singularia dei dona«. Ibid., D4ᵛ.
135 »Nam spiritus sanctus non liberat nos affectibus sed novos affectus inserit«. Ibid.

For the purposes of our investigation, we can now make several important observations. First, through this writing, Melanchthon has brought further clarity to his understanding of the affects and what, if any, positive nature they might have. Connecting them with Romans 1 and leaning somewhat on Aristotle, Melanchthon attacks the Stoic rejection of the affects as both unchristian and unnatural. While he does not in any way view all affects as positive, those that were created by God and which serve such important functions as the preservation of natural life and society, he places under the term στοργαὶ φυσικαί. These natural affections include those natural stirrings of the heart between parents and children, friends, and – most significantly for us – also between husband and wife. As thoroughly good as Melanchthon understands these to be, however, he also sees a need for their renewal through the Holy Spirit's working.

We should further note, although it would be anachronistic to read Melanchthon's 1529 discussion of στοργαὶ φυσικαί back into his discussion of *affectus quosdam naturales* in 1521, that the overall context, whether the background of Aristotle's *Nicomachean Ethics* or his contemplations of Romans, does remain rather consistent. That is to say, although we cannot offer conclusive proof that Melanchthon's 1521 understanding of *affectus quosdam naturales* is that shown forth in his *In Ethica Aristotelis* of 1529, there is indeed a certain plausibility to this line of thought.

Apologia Confessionis Augustanae (1531)

As we have already observed, the events which transpired between the writing of Melanchthon's *In Ethica Aristotelis* (1529) and the *Apologia* were momentous. Nevertheless, the developments which first emerged in the former can also be observed in the latter, namely in Melanchthon's response to the *Confutatio*'s objection to CA 23/27[136].

To begin with, it is important to note the relative infrequency with which *affectus* appears in Melanchthon's *Apologia*. That being the case, we observe that Melanchthon's general treatment of the affects continues to convey his understanding of their deeply corrupted and sinful state[137]. Thus, Article 23's treatment of the natural affects – as also was the case with Melanchthon's *Loci Communes* (1521) – is noteworthy in its *positive* emphasis upon a portion of man's affective nature.

---

136 Kolb et al., The Book of Concord, p. 108, note that the first draft of the *Apologia* can be dated to 1530 as the Wittenberg contingent made its way back to Wittenberg. After undergoing subsequent editing and revision by Melanchthon, it was first printed in 1531.
137 See, for example, BSELK, p. 321,2 (Ap. 4,130), p. 327,2 (Ap. 4,169), p. 337,24 (Ap. 4,171), p. 539,22f. (Ap. 15,47), p. 551,14 (Ap. 18,5).

Turning to paragraph seven of Article 23[138], Melanchthon begins by attempting to distinguish natural affection (στοργὴν φυσικήν) from the inseparable dross of concupiscence. He writes, »First, Genesis [1:28] teaches that human beings were created to be fruitful and that one sex should desire the other sex in a proper way. Now we are not speaking about concupiscence, which is sin, but about that desire which was to have been in our uncorrupted nature, which they call natural affection [στοργὴν φυσικήν]«[139].

Melanchthon then continues by highlighting the fact that this στοργή or natural affection is itself an ordinance of God that, apart from an exceptional work of God, cannot be lifted or abrogated, either by human statute or vow. Furthermore, although the reformers' opponents ridicule the »Lutheran« teaching on Genesis 1:28, Melanchthon nevertheless reasserts the fact that human nature (obviously including and perhaps referring especially to στοργὴν φυσικήν) has been formed by *that* word of God (*illo verbo Dei*)[140]. In other words, once again we see here the fusion of Luther's teaching on God's creative word with the positive aspects of Melanchthon's teaching on the natural affects.

Shortly later, in a discussion of natural law, Melanchthon once again affirms the enduring applicability of God's ordinance as seen in human nature and affections, this time appealing to the obviousness of sexual differentiation and the innateness of attraction[141]. Important, however, is not confusing God's creative work (στοργὴν φυσικήν) with sinful desire (*concupiscentia*). Melanchthon writes:

---

138 Ap. 23,1–6, acts as an introduction and emphasizes the shameful situation created from opposition to the marriage of priests, the tragedy that (en)forced celibacy had been (and continued to be), and the experiential (and not merely theological) obviousness concerning this point of contention. See ibid., pp. 587–591.

139 Kolb et al., The Book of Concord, p. 249, cf. »Primum. Genesis docet homines conditos esse, ut sint foecundi, et sexus recta ratione sexum appetat. Loquimur enim non de concupiscentia, quae peccatum est, sed de illo appetitu, qui in integra natura futurus erat, quem vocant στοργὴν φυσικήν«. BSELK, p. 593,1–4 (Ap. 23,7).

140 »Haec cavillantur adversarii, dicunt initio fuisse mandatum, ut repleretur terra, nunc repleta terra non esse mandatum coniugium. Videte, quam prudenter iudicent. Natura hominum formatur illo verbo Dei, ut sit fecunda non solum initio creationis, sed tantisper dum haec corporum natura existet. Sicut hoc verbo terra fit fecunda: *Germinet terra herbam virentem.* Propter hanc ordinationem non solum initio coepit terra producere gramina, sed quotannis vestiuntur agri, donec existet haec natura. Sicut igitur legibus humanis non potest natura terrae mutari, ita neque votis neque lege humana potest natura hominis mutari sine speciali opere Dei«. BSELK, p. 593,7–15 (Ap. 23,8); underscoring added.

141 In light of our discussion in Chapter 2, it bears mention that the discussion of natural law taking place in the wider context of this paragraph of Ap. 23 – rather uncharacteristically for Melanchthon (and also Luther, for that matter) – allows for the Ulpianic understanding of natural law commonly used by the jurists and which derived natural precepts from the supposed natural ordering of creation (to include urges and appetites). The paragraph reads as follows: »Secundo. Et quia haec creatio seu ordinatio divina in homine est Ius naturale, ideo sapienter et recte dixerunt Iurisconsulti

However, because this right cannot be changed without an extraordinary act of God, the right to contract marriages must of necessity remain, for the natural desire of one sex for the other sex is an ordinance of God in nature. For this reason it is right; otherwise why would both sexes have been created? As we said above, we are speaking not about concupiscence (which is sin), but about that desire which they call natural affection [στορ-γὴν φυσικήν] and which concupiscence has not removed from nature. Concupiscence inflames it so that now it rather needs an antidote. Marriage is necessary not only for the sake of procreation but also as a remedy. These things are so clear and well established that they can in no way be refuted[142].

As we have commented elsewhere on other significant aspects of this text, further comment on this point is unnecessary. We can, however, finally conclude that by 1531 there is to be no question that Melachthon's *Affektenlehre* has now unquestionably become *eyngepflantzt* (implanted!) in the evangelical – and later Lutheran – teaching on marriage and sexuality, not to mention its understanding of human nature and procreation.

---

coniunctionem maris et feminae esse Iuris naturalis. Cum autem Ius naturale sit immutabile, necesse est semper manere Ius contrahendi coniugii. Nam ubi natura non mutatur, necesse est et illam ordinationem manere, quam Deus indidit naturae, nec potest legibus humanis tolli. Ridiculum igitur est, quod adversarii nugantur initio fuisse mandatum coniugium, nunc non esse. Hoc perinde est, ac si dicerent: Olim nascentes homines secum attulerunt sexum, nunc non afferunt. Olim secum attulerunt Ius naturale nascentes, nunc non afferunt. Nullus Faber fabrilius cogitare quidquam posset, quam hae ineptiae excogitatae sunt ad eludendum Ius naturae.
Maneat igitur hoc in causa, quod et Scriptura docet et Iurisconsultus sapienter dixit coniunctionem maris et feminae esse Iuris naturalis. Porro Ius naturale vere est Ius divinum, quia est ordinatio divinitus impressa naturae. Quia autem hoc Ius mutari non potest sine singulari opere Dei, necesse est manere Ius contrahendi coniugii, quia ille naturalis appetitus est ordinatio Dei in natura sexus ad sexum et propterea Ius est; alioqui quare uterque sexus conderetur? Et loquimur, ut supra dictum est, non de concupiscentia, quae peccatum est, sed de illo appetitu, quem vocant στοργὴν φυσικήν; quem concupiscentia non sustulit ex natura, sed accendit, ut nunc remedio magis opus habeat et coniugium non solum procreationis causa necessarium sit, sed etiam remedii causa. Haec sunt perspicua et adeo firma, ut nullo modo labefactari queant«. Ibid., pp. 593,16–595,14 (Ap. 23,9–13).
142 Kolb et al., The Book of Concord, pp. 249f., cf. latter part of citation from previous footnote, BSELK, p. 595,4–14 (Ap. 23,12f.).

6. The Future of a Verse and Concluding Thoughts

> Gud som sade mannenom ey gott wara alleen,
> han skapte honom ena hielp uthaff hans sidobeen,
> och gaff them så welsignilse mʒ thenna orden,
> wexer til foröker idher och upfyller i orden, Gudi wari loff.

> *God spoke now to the man He made, Thou shallt not be alone;*
> *He crafted thus a help for him, formed out of his rib bone;*
> *And gave them thus His blessing with this word He did assert:*
> *Be fruitful now and multiply and fill up all the earth. Hallelujah.*

> —Olaus Petri, *Swenska Psalmboken af 1536*

As we now draw near to the conclusion of this study, we do well both to look ahead to that which still lay in wait for our verse and to look back, once more, over the ground previously traversed. Our method for accomplishing these tasks will be as follows: In looking forward, we will venture briefly into the 1530s and 40s toward the close of Luther's career. Here we will seek to gain a glimpse of a time which was, in many respects, the high-water mark of our verse's career. Our attention here will be given, amongst a few other observations, to Luther's concern for Genesis 1:28 and its conceptual derivative, *procreation*, in his *Lectures on Genesis* (1535–1545). We will furthermore offer some notes on the ongoing place of Genesis 1:28, to include its limitations, in wider Reformation activities. Brief attention to the spread of our verse, as well as the continued presence of the natural affects in the work of our verse, will also be included prior to offering a concluding overview of our findings.

6.1 A Glance Ahead: The Prowess and Limitations of a Verse

Given the structure and presentation of this study, it might be easy to believe that Genesis 1:28 had achieved its crowning moment with its inclusion in the *CA* and then in Melanchthon's *Apologia*. In many ways, however, our verse was merely hitting its stride as we move beyond 1530–1531. A cursory glance over Luther's usage of Genesis 1:28 beyond these years shows that, following the presentation of the Augsburg Confession, the importance of this verse easily kept pace with, if not outshadowed, its significance in the years to which we have previously dedicated our attention.

This is perhaps especially the case if we look to Luther's *Lectures on Genesis* (1535–1545), where Genesis 1:28 and its conceptualization as procreation (*generatio*) receive attention to an extent that almost verges upon excessive[1]. In fact, Luther's development of the working and power of God's creative word throughout the course of these lectures easily outpaces that which we have thus far encountered. In this respect, we observe the reformer once more reiterating the variegated layers of meaning he understands our verse to contain and purvey, even as he can and does speak of procreation (and those things pertaining to it) in such categories as God's divine will[2], word[3], command[4], work[5], blessing[6], creature[7], and gift[8]. Moreover, the connection between Genesis 1:28 and Genesis 3:15 (with its promise of the Blessed Seed) in many ways functions as the hermeneutical key for understanding Luther's interpretation of the book of Genesis[9].

---

1 While multiple authors have given at least brief attention to Luther's comments on procreation and closely related topics in his *Lectures on Genesis*, to my knowledge, no focused study has given thorough attention to this deserving topic. For cursory and related treatments, see CORTRIGHT, Poor Maggot-Sack, pp. 116–133; John A. MAXFIELD, Luther's Lectures on Genesis and the Formation of Evangelical Identity, Kirksville, MO 2008, pp. 117–119; Johannes SCHWANKE, Creatio ex nihilo. Luthers Lehre von der Schöpfung in der Grossen Genesisvorlesung aus dem Nichts (1535–1545), Berlin et al. 2004, pp. 178–181; David LÖFGREN, Die Theologie der Schöpfung bei Luther, Göttingen 1960, pp. 41–44; Ute GAUSE, Reformation und Körperlichkeit am Beispiel von Luthers Genesisvorlesung, in: Evang. Theol. 78, no. 1 (2018), pp. 44–47; YEGERLEHNER, »Be Fruitful«, pp. 160–172; Ulrich ASENDORF, Lectura in Biblia. Luthers Genesisvorlesung (1535–1545), Göttingen 1998, pp. 238, 241, 324f., 339, 360f., 373, etc.; MATTOX, Defender of the Most Holy Matriarchs; WITT, Reformation der Ehe, pp. 305–319.
2 In this and the following footnotes we offer merely several examples: WA 42, p. 91,11–14 & 19–21; WA 43, p. 203,14–18, p. 344,3–6, 10–20, p. 354,10–12, p. 560,26–33.
3 WA 43, p. 138,36–40, p. 139,5–8, p. 141,4–24.
4 WA 42, p. 53,31f. (*mandatum Dei*), p. 354,13 (*praecepto*), p. 362,18f. (*quod iubet Deus*).
5 WA 42, pp. 63,39–64, 26, p. 94,29–32, p. 95,5–10, 12–17, 25–34.
6 WA 42, pp. 39,26–40,2, p. 40,13–18, p. 64,20–21; WA 43, p. 247,22–32.
7 WA 42, p. 343,38–39; WA 43, p. 302,20–28.
8 WA 42, p. 54,35f., p. 88,1–3, p. 354,31–37.
9 GALLUS, »Der Nachkomme der Frau«, pp. 87–115, and ASENDORF, Lectura in Biblia, pp. 68ff. – among others – give attention to the place and importance of the Seed of the woman in Luther's Genesis Lectures. It should, however, be noted that on account of this promise, procreation cannot be separated from the hope of salvation in Luther's reading of the lives of the patriarchs and matriarchs. When tabulating the most frequently cited Scripture passages throughout the entirety of Luther's *Lectures on Genesis* (based on combining the entries of the collected indexes of the volumes of *Luther's Works*), the following results offer an indication toward at least some of the significant themes of the lectures: Genesis 3:15 = 26, Psalm 27:14 = 22, Matthew 16:18 = 21, Genesis 1:28 = 20, Isaiah 42:3 = 20, Romans 15:4 = 20.

Here it must also be recalled that Luther's instruction did not merely serve the purpose of confessing this verse. Rather, he was actively impressing this teaching upon the next generation through such classroom lectures. Through the transcription, editing, and publication of these lectures, the reach of Luther's »mature« thought (as it has sometimes been referred to) would only be exponentially magnified throughout the coming generations[10].

Of course, Luther's teaching about this verse was not isolated merely to his classroom lectures. Genesis 1:28 appears again and again in diverse works[11], sermons[12], collected remarks[13], or in his own correspondence[14]. Wherever it appeared, though, whether in the context of human sexuality, discussions of marriage (barring special exemption), attacks against monastic vows, in discussions of the Sacraments, references to dominion, or simply as one of the highlighted verses in the *Lutherbibel*[15], it was expressive of the unconquerable power of God's word, working, and ordering of creation.

In fact, if we were to make a general observation regarding developments in Luther's use of Genesis 1:28 in the years following the presentation of the Augsburg Confession, it would simply be to note that whereas Luther's earlier usages were largely, though not completely, devoted to the topics of marriage, celibacy, and related themes, his later usage grew in scope. In this manner, while still a mainstay of his thought regarding earlier topics, Genesis 1:28 also became emblematic for the efficacious power of God's Word in Luther's later thought. This can be observed in many different topics, be they Luther's discussion of procreative urges and human

---

It should furthermore be noted that this is far from including the many references to Genesis 1:28 via its conceptualization as »procreation/*generatio*«. Simply stated, there is an overwhelming richness of material related to Genesis 1:28 and procreation that simply awaits further treatment.

10 See, for example, Robert Kolb, Models of the Christian Life in Luther's Genesis Sermons and Lectures, in: Lutherjahrbuch 76 (2009), pp. 193–220, and Maxfield, Luther's Lectures on Genesis.
11 WA 39/II, pp. 386f. (here being discussed with Luther in a disputation concerning traducianism); WA 40/III, p. 221,12, p. 255,14 (*In XV Psalmos graduum*/Psalm 127), p. 277,1 (*In XV Psalmos graduum*/Psalm 128), pp. 519f. (*Enarratio Psalmi XC*); WA 54, p. 76 (*Von den letzten Worten Davids*); WA 60, p. 153 (*Die »Dialectica«*).
12 WA 34/I, p. 59,13–21; WA 36, pp. 412–415; WA 37, p. 242,10–16; WA 47, pp. 322,21–323,13; WA 49, p. 174,31, pp. 797,26–798,30.
13 WA Tr 1, pp. 163f. (#374), pp. 560f. (#1133); WA Tr 2, p. 527 (#2569); WA Tr 3, pp. 25f. (#2847a/b), pp. 300f. (#3390a/b); WA Tr 5, p. 10 (#5212).
14 WA Br 5, p. 574,89; WA Br 7, p. 249,5 (here in jest).
15 Genesis 1:27f. reads as follows: »VND GOTT SCHUFF DEN MENSCHEN JM ZUM BILDE/ZUM BILDE GOTTES SCHUFF ER JN/VND SCHUFF SIE EIN MENLIN VND FREWLIN. Vnd Gott segenet sie/vnd sprach zu jnen/SEID FRUCHTBAR VND MEHRET EUCH VND FÜLLET DIE ERDEN/vnd macht sie euch vnterthan. Vnd herrschet vber Fisch im Meer/vnd vber Vogel vnter dem Himel/vnd vber alles Thier das auff Erden kreucht«. Martin Luther, Die gantze Heilige Schrifft Deudsch [Wittenberg 1545], Darmstadt 1973, vol. 1, p. 26 [C.I.].

generation[16], the power of Christ's word of institution and the efficaciousness of the Sacraments[17], the effective death-working word of God's judgment over sin[18], or the power of God's word to accomplish the resurrection[19].

Returning to the connection between Genesis 1:28 and Luther's later marital thought, however, as we glance ahead it is necessary to underscore the fact that our verse gives no indication of letting up in its intensity; neither does it offer any hints that it was letting go of Luther's mind and attention. The same can be said regarding the further use of Genesis 1:28 in other Reformation writings originating out of near proximity to Wittenberg circles. Wenzeslaus Link's 1543 commentary on Genesis demonstrates the same connection between »Be fruitful and multiply« and the effective working of God's word that we have otherwise so frequently observed in our study[20]. Similarly, Johann Spangenberg's *Des Ehelichen Ordens Spiegel und Regel* (1544) clearly resonates with Luther's teaching on Genesis 1:28[21]. To this brief list we

---

16 The following two quotations are offered as examples: »Et videtur hoc voluisse docere et testari Deus, sibi mirabiliter gratam esse generationem prolis, ut sentiamus eum tueri et defendere verbum suum, CRESCITE. Non est inimicus proli, sicut nos, quorum multi non quaerunt prolem. Sed Deus adeo urget suum verbum, ut aliquando det prolem etiam iis, qui non expetunt, imo oderunt: nisi quod aliquibus interdum vehementer expetentibus tentandi causa non dat. Et quod magis est, ita videtur urgere generationem, ut etiam adulteris et scortatoribus nascantur filii contra voluntatem ipsorum«. WA 43, p. 354,10–17.
A further comparable statement (including a reference to natural affects!) is found in Luther's discussion of Jacob and his wives where he remarks, »Nam et hoc considerandum est, fuisse eo tempore foecunditatem pro eximia benedictione et singulari dono Dei habitam. Sicut ex Deuteronomio apparet, Ubi Moses numerat inter benedictiones foecunditatem. ›Non erit, inquit, apud te sterilis‹. Nos non tanti facimus hodie. In pecudibus quidem amamus et expetimus. Sed in genere humano pauci sunt, qui ducant foecunditatem muliebrem pro benedictione. Imo plures sunt, qui aversentur, et pro singulari felicitate habeant sterilitatem. Quod sane etiam contra naturam est: multo minus pium et sanctum. Haec enim στοργή divinitus naturae humanae est indita, ut optet augmentum et multiplicationem sui. Itaque inhumanum et impium est, fastidire sobolem. Sicut nuper quidem uxorem suam saepius parientem scropham dixit, Homo nihili et impurus. Sic nequaquam adfecti fuerunt sancti patres. Agnoscebant enim singularem Dei benedictionem: mulierem foecundam, et econtra sterilitatem pro maledictione habebant. Atque id iudicium manavit ex verbo Dei Genes[is 1.: ›Crescite et multiplicamini‹. Inde intellexerunt prolem esse donum Dei«. WA 43, pp. 652,36–653,11. See also WA 42, pp. 57,20–58,10, pp. 95,35–96,4; WA 43, p. 138,36–40, p. 139,5–8, p. 354,10–17.
17 WA 37, p. 349,5–9; WA 46, p. 155,3–22.
18 WA 40/III, pp. 519f.
19 WA 49, pp. 434–437.
20 Wenzeslaus LINK, Das erst teyl des alten Testaments. Annotation in die Fünff Bücher Mosi. Eyn schöne Vorred, Martini Lutheri (etc.), Strasbourg 1543 (VD16 L 1790), Bii[v]–Biii[r].
21 Johann SPANGENBERG, Des Ehelichen Ordens Spiegel vnd Regel ynn zehen Capittel geteilt/Darinne man siehet wer den Ehestandt gestifft/was er sey/vnnd wie man sich darinne halten sol/durch Johann. Spangenberg/Der Keiserlichen Stadt Northausen Prediger, Magdeburg 1544 (VD16 S 7782), Aiii[v]–Aiiii[r], Biii[v]–Biiii[r]. Gerhard BODE, Instruction of the Christian Faith by Lutherans, in: Robert KOLB (ed.), Lutheran Ecclesiastical Culture. 1550–1675, Leiden et al. 2008, p. 171, notes that Span-

may easily add such now familiar names as Melanchthon and Jonas (see below), as well as such other Wittenberg associates as Caspar Cruciger[22] or Erasmus Alberus[23].

genberg and Luther had been friends since their time together in Erfurt. That Spangenberg had Wittenberg connections is further demonstrated both by the fact that Luther had sent a letter of recommendation to him in November 1539 regarding a pastor who was being sent to Nordhausen, see WA Br 8, pp. 611f. Moreover, Robert KOLB, Spangenberg, Johann and Cyriacus, in: Timothy J. WENGERT et al. (eds.), Dictionary of Luther and the Lutheran Traditions, Grand Rapids, MI 2017, pp. 1059–1060, at 1059, URL: <https://books.google.no/books?id=i9HlDQAAQBAJ> (19 July 2019), notes that Johann Spangenberg's son, Cyriacus, also lived with the Luther family during his initial studies in Wittenberg. Furthermore, Thomas KAUFMANN, Spangenberg, Johann, in: Neue Deutsche Biographie 24 (2010), pp. 622f., URL: <https://www.deutsche-biographie.de/pnd123624878.html#ndbcontent> (19 Jul 2019), notes that in 1546 Luther also recommended Johann Spangenberg to be the general inspector for the Count of Mansfeld. Finally, we note that Justus Jonas wrote the forward to Spangenberg's earlier work on Luther's Catechism (first published in 1541). That work, incidentally, though lacking an obvious citation of Genesis 1:28, displays clear evidence of Luther's understanding of our verse. Here see Johann SPANGENBERG, Der Gros Catechismus vnd Kinder Lere D.Mart.Luth. Fuer die jungen Christen inn Fragestuecke verfasset Durch M.IOHAN.SPANGENBERG, der Keyserlichen Statt Northausen Prediger, Frankfurt/Main 1543 (VD16 L 4360), 38^v.

22 See Caspar CRUCIGER, Herrn Doctor Caspar Creutzigers auslegung/vber Sanct Paulus spruch zum Thimotheo/wie die Eheweiber selig werden/nicht allein allen Eheweibern/sondern auch allen Christen seer nuetzlich vñ trœstlich durch M. Georgium Spalatinum verdeudscht, Erfurt 1538 (VD16 C 5853). While this work does not quote, verbatim, Genesis 1:28, and instead merely assumes its presence and force in referring to God's creation and ordinance, it does make a point of emphasizing that God's creation of marriage – to include *die Ehelichzusammengattung* (when used modestly) – as God's good work (ibid., Aviii^r–Aviii^v). Furthermore, Cruciger places clear emphasis not only on St. Paul's statement in 1 Timothy 2:15 (i. e. that a woman will be saved in childbearing), but also goes on to drive home the point that *kinder geberen und zeugen* is, in fact, the woman's speacial *ampt* as well as her *Gottesdienst*, as instituted, ordered, and commanded by God (ibid., Biiii^r–Biiii^v). Clearly, it is difficult to imagine Genesis 1:28 being in any sense separated from this discussion.

23 In Erasmus ALBERUS/Francesco BARBARO, Eyn gŭt bŭch von der Ehe was die Ehe sei was sie gŭts mit sich bringe Wie eyn weib geschickt sein soll die eyner zu d[er] Ehe nehmen will wie alt waß sie dem Mañ zubringen solle Vom kosten vnnd gebreng der hochzeit Von dreien Tugendē des weibs […] Wie mann Kinder ziehen solle. weiland zu Latin gemacht durch den Wolgelerten Franciscum Barbarum Rathern zu Venedig Nun aber verdeutscht durch Erasmum Alberum, Hagenau 1536 (VD16 B 357), Alberus offers a translation (with some additions of his own; see Bii^v!) to the work of Barbaro. This work notes the definition of marriage, the emphasis upon its primary purpose of procreation, the corresponding natural desires shared with the beasts, and that also the heathen recognized the importance of the procreation of descendents (ibid., Aiii^r–Aiiii^v).

More interesting for our purposes, however, is Erasmus ALBERUS, Das Ehbüchlin Ein gesprech zweyer weiber, mit namen Agatha vnd Barbara, vnd sunst mancherley vom Ehestand, Eheleuten, vnnd jederman nützlich zulesen, An die Durchleuchtige Hochgeborne Fürstin, Fraw Catharina geborne Hertzogin von Braunschweig, Marggraeffin zu Brandenburg [et]c., Frankfurt/Main 1539 (VD16 A 1487). After a lengthy introductory dialogue, Alberus begins *Das Erst Capitel* by pointing out the natural desire toward pairing and care of children existing in man – but also in common with the animals (Di^r). Then, after something of a repetition of elements of the previously-noted text,

This is not even to mention such non-German proponents of Wittenberg thought who brought Luther's, or perhaps Melanchthon's, teaching on Genesis 1:28 home with them or acquired it through their continued association with Wittenberg writings and personalities once back home. Here we might mention Olaus Petri of Sweden[24] or the translational efforts of Hans Tausen in Denmark[25].

Along these same lines, our verse can also be witnessed in the realm of high-profile international ecclesiastical debates. In the aftermath of Henry VIII's 1539 prohibition of priestly marriage[26], Melanchthon penned *Defensio Coniugii Sacerdotum*[27]. This work, we might note, was not without a certain geographical and linguistic reach, given that it was subsequently translated both into English as *A very godly defense [...] defending the marriage of priestes* (1541)[28] and also into German

---

Alberus continues with God's institution and blessing of marriage (Dii^v–Diii^r). Most interesting, though, is Alberus's topic in *Das Vierdt Capitel/Das ein Weib ihre Kinder selbst seugen sol* (Fiii^r–Fiiii^v). Here, he addresses the question of nursing by applying argumentation which we have often seen elsewhere. In particular, he notes that for a woman to *choose* not to nurse her own child is to sin against the law of nature. After all, the unreasonable animals nurse their own offspring and are not so hard toward their own offspring as a woman in such cases. Furthermore, God has therefore given the woman breast and milk for just this purpose. For a brief commentary on these and related writings, see CLASSEN, Der Liebes- und Ehediskurs, pp. 128–133.

24 Olaus/Olavus Petri studied in Germany beginning in Leipzig in 1516. Sometime thereafter he transferred to Wittenberg where he studied until the fall of 1518, returning at that time to Sweden with his master's degree. See Anna Katharina DÖMLING et al. (eds.), Olavus Petri und die Reformation in Schweden. Schriften aus den Jahren 1528–1531, Zug 2002, p. 9. Like many of our other writers, Wittenberg teachings also led him to embrace marriage (1525), something that is not easily separated from his defense of the same. Judging by the content of his subsequent writings on marriage and vows, it is clear that he stayed abreast of Wittenberg developments given that at least two of his 1528 writings reflect such an understanding of our verse. For example, in *Een liten boock om Sacramenten*, Petri condemns the idea that marriage is a sacrament but then points out that marriage was given by God for multiplication (ibid., pp. 49f.). In *Een liten underuisning om Echteskapet*, however, the tone and influence of Genesis 1:28 is even stronger. See especially ibid., pp. 106–108, 110f., 116. It should be further observed that Petri's appropriation of our verse makes for one of the strongest presentations observed in this study. We might further note that he also goes on to attack the Roman concern of ritual purity for celebrating the Mass as connected with the requirement for clerical celibacy (pp. 119ff.).

25 As previously noted, BRUUN (ed.), Den danske Literatur, pp. 189–191, notes that a Hans Tausen translation of *Oeconomia Christiania* appeared in Danish as *Justi Menij | Oeconomia Chri-|stiana. | Det er, En Christelige hws-|holding* (1538).

26 A[rthur] G[eoffrey] DICKENS, The English Reformation, London ²1989, p. 143. For an account of the many twists and turns involving the negotiations with the Wittenberg theologians, see SCHOFIELD, Philipp Melanchthon and the English Reformation.

27 Philipp Melanchthon, Defensio Conivgii Sacerdotvm Pia & erudita missa ad Regem Angliae, Strasbourg 1540 (VD16 M 2915).

28 Helen L. PARISH, Clerical Marriage and the English Reformation. Precedent Policy and Practice, New York 2017, p. 30.

(1541) in a slightly different format by none other than Justus Jonas[29]. This writing, though, not only furthers our observation on the relationship between Wittenberg theology and our verse, it also allows us the opportunity to note the continuance of two items of concern throughout our study. To begin with, we observe the ongoing significance and power of Genesis 1:28 in Melanchthon's argumentation. Indeed, in connection with the wider scope of this polemical exchange, Helen Parish observes the remark of a certain Robert Smith, himself an opponent of the marriage of priests during this era. According to Smith, the main argument for priestly marriage came down to nothing other than »*Crescite (inquit Deus), multiplicamini & replete terram*«[30].

The second item of significance, Melanchthon's concern for the role of *affectus naturales*, demonstrates the reformers' – or at the very least Melanchthon's – attempts to discern the limits of their own teaching on the relationship between created desire and sinful desire. Thus, beginning in the second section of this text, Melanchthon's concern for God-given appetites (*appetitiones*), affects (στοργαί), and inclinations (*inclinationes*) becomes readily apparent. In particular, Melanchthon notes that human nature was created to be fruitful (*foecunda*), as Genesis 1 states. Yet, before proceeding to *crescite etc.*, Melanchthon pauses at Genesis 1:27 to note the significance of God creating mankind as male and

---

29 Philipp Melanchthon, Eine Schrifft Philip. Melanth. newlich latinisch gestellet widder den unreinen Bapsts Celibat, und verbot der Priesterehe, translated by Justus Jonas, Wittenberg 1541 (VD16 M 2920).
30 Parish, Clerical Marriage and the English Reformation, pp. 82f. We might note that, on the surface, such a claim seems unobserved in much of the literature. Schofield, Philipp Melanchthon and the English Reformation, pp. 103–112, makes note of what he terms the »concession argument«, though he does not seem to notice the weighty presence of Genesis 1:28 in the background of the immediate texts preceding many of these events. Nevertheless, if it is recalled that the negotiations involving possible membership in the Schmalkaldic League are part of this scene *and* that both the *Confessio Augustana* and Melanchthon's *Apologia* were subscribed to by this league, then – if for no other reason – it becomes clear that Genesis 1:28 is indeed in the background and Robert Smith's comment is better accounted for and understood. Furthermore, Parish, Clerical Marriage and the English Reformation, p. 30, observes that Luther's first appearance in the English language came in the form of a translation of his commentary on 1 Corinthians 7 in 1529. This writing, as we have previously noted, was undergirded by his understanding of Genesis 1:28. Thus, there is no reason to doubt that our verse could have exercised a significant presence surrounding this debate in the English context. For the correspondence of August 1538 between the Wittenberg delegation and Henry VIII, see Gilbert Burnet, The History of the Reformation of the Church of England. A Collection of Records, Letters, and Original Papers, with Other Instruments Referred to in the First [and Second] Part[s] […] [Appendices] Concerning Some of the Errors and Falsehoods in Sanders' Book of the English Schism, edited by Nicholas Pocock, Oxford 1865, vol. 4, pp. 365–372, 384–391, URL: <https://books.google.no/books?id=yS-67fDUVYcC&printsec=frontcover&hl=no#v=onepage&q=false> (18 Aug 2022).

female, pointing out the presence of their *appetitionem* for one another even in the beginning in nature's perfect state (*natura integra*)[31]. Nevertheless, God-given as these desires certainly were, since the fall they roam without order, thereby only increasing the importance of marriage[32]. In other words, the twofold nature – i.e. its God-implanted origin and its sin-corrupted disorder – leave man and woman no choice other than to seek one another in marriage. As Melanchthon writes,

> There remains the inclination towards the *opposite* sex, which is a natural affect [στοργή φυσική] implanted by God in men's nature, but which now roams without order. Therefore, seeing that because of this there is a greater need for marriage, Paul has said: »For the avoidance of fornication, let each one have his own wife«[33].

Thus, once again, Melanchthon defends the goodness of God's creation while acknowledging the sad and all-encompassing reality of sin. Nevertheless, God-given desires also find their answer and at least partial restoration through faith, as Melanchthon also later notes[34]. In this manner, it becomes possible to see clearly what Melanchthon has attempted to highlight, going likely back to 1521 and his original use of *affectus quosdam naturales*. Namely, the affects dare not be categorized as sinful *in toto*. That which is good (i. e. God-given) in them must be acknowledged and distinguished from that which has no redemptive value[35].

---

31 »Masculum & foeminam creauit eos. id est, indidit utriq3 sexui mutuam coniunctionis appetitionem, quæ quidem in natura integra fuisset sine uitio«. Melanchthon, Defensio Conivgii Sacerdotvm, Av^r/10.

32 »Nunc non est sublata naturalis inclinatio, sed uagatur sine ordine, eoq3 magis opus est coniugio, ut coherceatur, sicut omnes doctors scribunt, coniugio pos lapsum primorum parentum nō tantum procreationis causa utendum esse, sed etiam ut sit remedium errantium appetitionū«. Ibid., Av^r/10–11.

33 Cf. »Manet inclinatio ad sexum, quæ est στοργή φυσική a Deo indita naturæ hominum, sed nunc sine ordine uagatur. Cū igitur eo magis opus sit coniugio, dixit Paulus: Vitādę scortationis causa, unusquisq3 uxorem suam habeat«. Ibid., Av^r/11. Note that Melanchthon repeats this line of argumentation again later (Bi^v–Bii^v/18–20).

34 »Fuisset hæc στοργή in natura integra ardentior, sed purior, & Deum intuens, prędicasset ipsius beneficia: Nunc nō prorsus extincta est, et pij regere eam fide debent«. Ibid., Ci^r/33.

35 While further discussion regarding the limits of Melanchthon's teaching and distinctions regarding the natural affects in the 1530s and 1540s would take us beyond the scope of our present chapter, it is worth noting that Melanchthon was concerned about both proper terminology and distinctions throughout these years. This can be witnessed also in id., Disputationes theologicae in schola propositae et fideliter explicatae a Philippo Melanthone, ab anno Christi XXIII usque ad annum XLV, Wittenberg 1550, Online Resource from The Digital Library of Classic Protestant Texts (Alexander Street Press), URL: <https://search.alexanderstreet.com/preview/work/bibliographic_entity%7Cbibliographic_details%7C5002283> (18 Aug 22); cf. CR 12, col. 439–441, and Melanchthon, Commentarius De Anima. Here see esp. pp. 178–201, 233–235.

There is a further exploration of the limits of our verse which occurred in the years following the central focus of our study. Namely, with the marital struggles of Philip of Hesse and his overactive sex drive, we find something of a real-world *argumentum ad absurdum* to the theological logic presented by the Wittenberg reformers[36]. Indeed, although Genesis 1:28 was not directly involved in this controversy, the argumentation often aided by its presence was. In perhaps the foremost attempt at defending the Landgrave's bigamy, Hulderichum Neobulum (a.k.a. Johannes Lening) set forth a wide array of arguments in an attempt, theologically and legally, to justify the actions of Landgrave Philip. Noteworthy for our purposes is the presence of both arguments from nature and arguments related to the divinely-implanted inclination and drive of a man for a woman, both of which are reminiscent of arguments we have previously seen derived from Genesis 1:28. In other words, some of the same logic and argumentation as had been used to defend the marriage of priests and the abandonment of monastic vows was now being consciously/conspicuously applied in defense of a heretofore nearly unquestionable taboo. Moreover, Luther and his Wittenberg circle, both in terms of their previous argumentation as well as through their own personal involvement in the matter, were at pains to distance themselves from the Landgrave's actions. We should, however, note that in an unpublished writing, Luther strongly condemned *Dialogus*'s anonymous author of a wide array of errors, to include the misuse of Genesis 1 and Matthew 19[37]. Nevertheless, it is easy to understand how Reformation argumentation could easily be abused – and also made an object of mockery[38].

---

36 Ute Gause notes exactly this point in Ute GAUSE, Durchsetzung neuer Männlichkeit. Ehe und Reformation, in: Evang. Theol. 73, no. 5 (2013), pp. 326–338, URL: <https://doi.org/10.14315/evth-2013-73-5-326> (18 Aug 2022). Gause's essay is of particular interest for our own investigation given that she takes the exceptional instance of Philip of Hesse's bigamy as a sort of case study for what Reformation theology actually did and meant for male sexuality, in this case as she probes the limits and extremes of Reformation teaching. See also Marjorie Elizabeth PLUMMER, »The Much Married Michael Kramer«. Evangelical Clergy and Bigamy in Ernestine Saxony, 1522–1542, in: Ead./Robin B. BARNES (eds.), Ideas and Cultural Margins in Early Modern Germany. Essays in Honor of H.C. Erik Midelfort, Aldershot, Hambleton 2009, pp. 99–115, URL: <https://digitalcommons.wku.edu/cgi/viewcontent.cgi?article=1023&context=history_fac_pubs> (19 Jul 2019), for an overview of Reformation developments in connection with digamy, bigamy, and remarriage.

37 WA 53, p. 194,6.

38 We might note that there is ample other evidence of the continued caricaturization of the evangelical teaching on Genesis 1:28. In a noteworthy rebuttal to the Augsburg Confession, Petrus RAUCH, ANTITHESIS Der Lutherischen Bekenthniß odder Beicht/ßo sie tzu Augspurgk vor K[ae]yserlicher Maiestat/vnd dē Heyligen R[oe]mischen Reich Jm Dreyssigsten jar/angegeben. Dar ynnē du frommer leser erkennen magst/mit was warheyt sye yhren glawben bekanth. Durch Petrum Anspach. […], Frankfurt/Oder ca. 1531 (VD16 R 385), Kii^v–Kiii^v, in responding to *CA XXII* [*XXIII*], seems to show a special interest in *dem Crescere* as well as the abuses he alleges are related to it. Similarly, Johann HASENBERG, Lvdus Lvdentem Lvderum Lvdens quo Ioannes Hasenbergius Bohemus in Bacchanalib.

In many ways, the events of the early 1540s and the debacle created by Philip of Hesse's bigamy highlighted something of a traditional concern over what had perhaps always been latent in the Reformation teaching regarding Genesis 1:28. As early as 1520, Luther's opponents had been concerned that his teachings were, in fact, an attack upon free will and a cover for immorality[39]. In a response to Melanchthon's *Apologia*, Bartholomaeus Arnoldi von Usingen expressed precisely the former concern, namely, that the »Lutheran« teaching on »Be fruitful and multiply« which linked the human affective nature (to include sexual desire) with the unassailable might of God's creative word, turned man into a creature of compulsions which lacked all human freedom and dignity[40]. In other words, as we hinted at with the problem of Philip of Hesse, the answer to the question of where – and how – the limits of natural affections and inclinations were to be rightly drawn were in some ways rather elusive. Moreover, what did the Wittenberg teaching on Genesis 1:28 imply in the realm of ethics and what did it mean for man's status as a morally responsible being? Indeed, can a creature implanted with procreative urges by

---

Lypsiae, omnes ludificantem Ludionem, omnibus ludendum exhibuit. Anno M.D.XXX, Lypsiae 1530 (VD16 H 714), Bii^r–Bii^v, in his biting satirical work manages to strike the varying chords of this same refrain (whether *crescite et multiplicamini* or Luther's associations with the teachings of the heretics), even as Luther's supposed errors are made manifest in the form of Katharina's »pious« questions (e. g. »Es tu magister in Israel, & ignores hoc preaceptum tum datum fuisse, quando primo tres hoīes in mūndo, deinde octo in arca Noe fuere?«). Another example of the mocking association of the »Lutherans« with *crescite et multiplicamini* is recorded in Anne Lake Prescott, Musical Strains. Marot's Double Role as Psalmist and Courtier, in: Marie-Rose Logan et al., Contending Kingdoms. Historical, Psychological, and Feminist Approaches to the Literature of Sixteenth-Century England and France, Detroit 1991, pp. 42–68, here pp. 61f., where, in recounting the life of a certain Clément Morot (d. 1544), at one point makes mention of his association with Lutheranism – and the associations associated with that movement, namely, a reported predilection for meeting under cover of darkness so that they might *crescite et multiplicamini*. Similarly, in Denmark, following the evangelical reformer Hans Tausen's marriage, it was reportedly said of him: »omnium priapistarum in Dania primus«. J.S.B. Suhr (ed.), Tausens levnet. Samt nogle praedikener, Ribe 1836, p. XVII, fn. 3 (cited from »Chronico Schibbyensi 583 8«).

39 Murner, An den Großmechtigsten vñ Durchlüchtigstē adel tütscher nation, Hii^r (cited in Chapter 3, fn. 52). See also Chapter 3, fn. 53.

40 Bartholomaei Arnoldi de Usingen O.S.A., Responsio Contra Apologiam Philippi Melanchthonis, edited by Primoz Simoniti, Würzburg 1978, pp. 511–515. Perhaps most pointedly, Arnoldi writes, »Coniunctio maris et feminae iuris naturalis dicitur ratione appetitus, quia ille est naturalis. At quia contractio matrimonii libere fit, non sequitur, quod tu vis«.

»Ius autem contrahendi coniugii mutabile est secundum imperium liberi arbitrii, licet appetitus coniugii sit naturalis et immutabilis«.

»Verum igitur est, quod ubi natura non mutator, illic ordinationem manere, quam Deus indidit naturae, nec potest legibus humanis tolli; sed Deus indidit appetitum et reliquit hominem liberum, an sequi vellet appetitum illum per coniugii contractionem, ratione cuius mandavit primis parentibus crescere et multiplicari«. Ibid., p. 513,286–297.

God's word (not to mention sinful lust on account of man's own sin) be expected to withstand the assaults of temptation? Clearly, the answer was »yes«, yet the exact justification of that answer was perhaps somewhat less clear, at least for some.

Leaving such questions aside for the present, we can note that they are at least helpful in bringing into focus some of the deeper concerns circulating around our verse. Indeed, if we were to ask the questions, »What was all the fuss about«? and »What was everyone fighting, often quite passionately, about«? we would quickly discover that nothing other than human freedom was at stake. On the evangelical side of things, there was no losing sight of the bonds of vowed and required celibacy that had stretched beyond human ability and which had tortured both the body and soul of many a priest and monastic. Liberated from such captivity, married former celibates rejoiced in the companionship of their God-given helpmates, the divine word of creation which confirmed their way of life, and the divine work of salvation which released them from their past chains of guilt. In this sense, *crescite et multiplicamini* was something of a banner of freedom in which and under which many of the central figures of the Lutheran movement lived. It is therefore no surprise whatsoever that the marriage of priests was one article of teaching and practice about which the evangelicals were in no way willing to compromise as they entered Augsburg[41]!

6.2 Concluding Summary

We began our study inquiring as to what role and significance Genesis 1:28 had for Luther's thought and for the Wittenberg Reformation. In the pages of this study we have thus attempted to account both for the place and importance of our verse in these overlapping and interconnected categories spanning the time frame from our verse's initial polemic appearance in 1521 up through its striking inclusion in Melanchthon's *Apologia* in 1531. In so doing, we now offer the following summary synopsis of our investigation.

To begin with, in Chapter 2 we identified several relevant conversations which existed in the background surrounding our verse. First, we noted ancient debate and potential latent theological ambiguity that formed much of the significant ecclesiastical context of our verse. Regarding ancient debate, we gave attention to discussions surrounding clerical celibacy involving Jerome and Jovinian, noting especially the defeat of the latter. Especially significant in this respect was the

---

[41] Concerning the importance of liberation *unto* marriage for former monks and celibate priests MATTHIAS, Das Verhältnis von Ehe und Sexualität bei Luther, pp. 20, 22, offers a small indication as do the many and various pamphlets of the era written in defense of the now married clergy (not to mention former nuns).

historic association of a more forceful application of Genesis 1:28 with the tag of heresy. In addition to this, we noted the preeminence awarded to the celibate life, a *de facto* hegemony enjoyed up until the eve of the Reformation. In connection with potentially latent theological ambiguity, we observed possible theological tensions involving understandings of Genesis 1 as were present both in the writings of Augustine and Chrysostom, whose writings were certainly also familiar to Luther and other reformers.

Somewhat adjacent to this discussion, we offered discussion of a further point of ambiguity and ambivalence flowing out of the early church, namely, liturgical practice. Here, we noted the presence of Genesis 1:28 in nuptial rites which originated out of early church practice and – somewhat surprisingly – persisted throughout the Middle Ages, even up to the threshold of the Reformation.

We next gave attention both to the natural law and natural philosophical ideological context of our verse. With respect to natural law, we noted the two historic strains of natural law thought which emerged out of classical times. The first strain might be described as those moral precepts deduced from such general precepts as the Golden Rule, the Ten Commandments, or other such general maxims from which reason is able to make moral judgments. The second strain, one historically more associated with the Stoics, Cicero, and the legal thought of Ulpian, might be described as precepts derived from the teachings of nature. That is to say, this strain sought to recognize the ordering of nature and to derive moral conclusions from this ordering. For the purposes of our study, we gave particular attention to the latter strain due to its concern for man's natural inclinations and drives. We thus observed that the mere presence of the Ulpianic tradition, as, for example, was found in Gratian's *Decretum*, was capable of supporting dissenting views in a church otherwise given to marital celibacy. Moreover, although the Ulpianic, civil law understanding of natural law generally fell into neglect amongst the theologians of the Scholastic era prior to the Reformation, we noted that it was precisely this strain of natural law thought that was then somewhat revived by the reformers, even if and even though it was not consistently found under the title of natural law.

With respect to natural philosophy, we particularly noted the important and universal position it enjoyed in the late medieval and early modern university setting. In so doing, we acknowledged that the major actors involved in the academic and theological discourse of our focus-era would have shared in a rather similar background, particularly as concerns the natural philosophical writings of Aristotle. We then pointed out the relative significance of teleological thinking for theology and our study with respect to the human body and its respective members and components, noting especially the roots of such thinking in the philosophical and anatomical discussion of the ancients. Finally, we noted the interconnectedness and general unity of thought within the academy, and that such topics as natural philosophy, in many respects, were minor branches of theology and that they, therefore, are an important part of the thought context of our study.

Chapter 3 then led us into an investigation in which we sought to ascertain not merely the appearance of Genesis 1:28 in Luther's writings but especially the circumstances and significance surrounding its advent. In general, we noted its relative absence and insignificance in the initial discussions surrounding priestly marriage and monastic vows, even if and even though Thomas Murner charged Luther with relying on this verse *even prior to* any polemical application by Luther which we were able to discover! We then discovered our verse's initial polemical debut, first in the writings of Karlstadt in the summer of 1521 and then with Luther later in the fall of 1521. Luther's incorporation of Genesis 1:28 seemed to arise in answer not merely to the debates surrounding priestly marriage and monastic vows, but especially in response to the concerns of Luther's colleagues regarding whether the *impossibility* of maintaining a vow of chastity could be grounds for breaking with such a vow. While Luther initially downplayed such manner of argumentation, in *De votis monasticis* (November 1521) he seemed to find a grounding for such impossibility in the effective divine utterance of »Be fruitful and multiply«. Here, on the basis of Melanchthon's concurrent discussion of natural law and *affectus quosdam naturales* (related to procreation) in his *Loci Communes* (1521), we argued for the likelihood that not only was Luther influenced by his colleague, but that he consequently came to view God's creative word as the effectual power of man's natural affective life, to include his sexual/procreative drive, as we subsequently explored in later sections throughout this work.

Notably, then, if one considers the permissible span of views commonly held at Luther's time – whether as to the significance of Genesis 1:28, the relationship of the natural affects to man's will and reason, or the question of drives and urges as regards natural law – not only do we see that Luther's new understanding of Genesis 1:28 emerged from various strains within these conversations, we also see that Luther, in a very decisive manner, took a clear and perhaps even unprecedented position on each of these questions as he set forth his arguments concerning »Be fruitful and multiply«. Indeed, in witnessing Genesis 1:28 as understood as the ongoing and efficacious creative word of God which is then simultaneously cloaked with the weighty affective language and understanding of the reformers, a more forceful combination of concepts is scarcely imaginable nor historically conceivable!

Furthermore, it seems that without Luther's revolutionary interpretation of Genesis 1:28, a complete break with the celibate tradition *in favor of marriage* would have been difficult, if not unthinkable. After all, it is one thing to say that vows militate against the Gospel, Baptism, or God's Word. It is quite another thing to say all of that and then to draw the conclusion that one ought therefore *to marry*, as opposed to perhaps honoring one's vows in an evangelical manner. Clearly, the compulsion to break vows in favor of marriage was heavily dependent upon

Luther's new understanding of »Be fruitful and multiply« with its corresponding anthropological implications.

In Chapter 4 we then progressed into a variety of writings which showcased the polemic and disputed nature of Genesis 1:28. To begin with, Luther's *Vom ehelichen Leben* received careful attention, given that it established something of a baseline for Luther's thought regarding our verse. Here especially we were introduced to the power and effect which Luther understood this verse to embody, even as it not only commands men and women to reproduce but also forms them – with their members and desires – to do just that. We furthermore observed that Genesis 1:28's presence can be traced as a sort of scaffolding underlying the entirety of *Vom ehelichen Leben*.

We then proceeded to note oppositional voices arising from the likes of Johann Faber, Thomas Murner, and Johann Cochlaeus. Here especially we noted their use of the church fathers, especially Jerome, in arguing against any abiding relevance for Genesis 1:28. Moreover, we observed their insinuations of heresy and mocking caricaturizations of the Lutheran teaching. We furthermore noted something of a general ambivalence and reluctance to engage the actual arguments and thought brought forward by Luther.

Proceeding into 1523, we traced something of a watershed year with respect to the attention given to this verse. In this year alone, such works as Luther's *Declamationes* on the book of Genesis appeared, not to mention a commentary on 1 Corinthians 7, a defense of runaway nuns (*Ursach und Antwort*), and several other occasional writings, all of which further emphasized and expounded upon the importance of Genesis 1:28. Concurrent with this, we observed the important contribution of Justus Jonas with *Adversum Ioannem Fabrum* and Melanchthon's own brief commentary on the initial chapters of Genesis. Jonas's *Adversum* particularly highlighted and expounded upon the importance of Genesis 1:28 for Wittenberg thinking, even as it provides us with what must be considered as a textbook example of the early union of the natural affects with our verse. We furthermore argued that, although in many respects 1 Corinthians 7 (along with Matthew 19) was the central battleground text related to the marriage of priests and the discussion of vows of celibacy, the reality was that, at the presuppositional level, the battle lines over 1 Corinthians were drawn over and originated out of Genesis 1:28. That is to say, however significant Luther's breakthrough exegesis involving 1 Corinthians 7 might have been, such a conclusion seems rather unlikely apart from his foundational development in understanding our own verse.

In rounding out the section, we offered a summary overview of the continued place of Genesis 1:28 in anti-Lutheran writings stemming from the likes of Johannes Dietenberger, Kaspar Schatzgeyer, and Josse Clichtove, though we noted that the contours of their argumentation leave the impression that they failed to engage Luther and his Wittenberg colleagues in substantial argumentation regarding this verse. Their oppositional efforts, as we observed, seem more directed at disarming their Lutheran opponents through the invocation of church fathers and blatant association with heretical teachings. One unresolved question regarding this phenomenon is *why* Luther's opponents did not seek to seriously challenge the reformer in a more substantial manner.

By way of an excursus, we then turned our attention to the role of our verse in the lively debate which took place in Erfurt surrounding the marriage of priests, observing a situation in which a unique blend of factors led to a highly charged polemical atmosphere. Noteworthy, amongst a plethora of other themes and topics, Genesis 1:28 also received significant attention. Somewhat surprisingly, amongst the primary Lutheran participants in the Erfurt debates, we found little direct evidence for the actual employment of Genesis 1:28. Their antagonist, Bartholomäus Arnoldi von Usingen, however, consistently charged his opponents with preaching and teaching nothing other than Genesis 1:28. The exact origin of his accusations remains something of a curiosity, though there is no question that Genesis 1:28 was indeed in the air in Erfurt. This can be deduced from several different sources, whether through Luther's personal connections in Erfurt, the presence of his writings in that city, other original Erfurt writings (e. g. Thomas Stör) which made use of our verse, or the occasional indirect citation attributed to Luther's Erfurt friends and followers. Whatever the case might have been, the controversy was bitter and the attacks, at times, particularly crude and personal. This was especially the case as we recall some of Arnoldi's very personal attacks and the malignment of his Lutheran opponents over, as he claimed, their dependence upon Genesis 1:28 as a cover for their own lust.

Chapter 5 finally took us forward into the latter half of the 1520s toward the *Confessio Augustana* and its *Apologia*. Here we gave attention particularly to three separate roles served by our verse during this time. To begin with, we observed the formative and positive role played by our verse: namely, we witnessed our verse's role as comprising one of the major biblical supports for Lutheran marital teaching, not to mention in establishing two of the three estates. As respects our verse's importance for Lutheran marital teaching, this was traceable throughout a variety of sources, whether liturgical, catechetical (to include the emergence of *Haustafel* literature), or various other tracts and writings. As observed elsewhere in our study, it was also clearly to be observed that Luther's teaching on Genesis 1:28 is not merely to be reduced to Luther as *solus reformator*. Rather, also in this positive development we observed Luther as something of the leader of an otherwise very capable Wittenberg cohort, the members of which embraced the reformer's teaching on our verse as their own and worked in its defense and toward its promotion. This was clearly discernable with such figures as Menius, Melanchthon, and Bugenhagen.

We then noted the continued polemic function carried out by Genesis 1:28 in debate both between Wittenberg adherents and their opponents as well as amongst adherents of the Evangelical movement (e. g. the question of digamy). In many respects, this was merely a continuation of the former debate with no real developments of significance being added to our verse's role.

Finally, we arrived at the *Confessio Augustana* and Melanchthon's *Apologia*. Of note here is that our verse was tied to an issue (the marriage of priests) about which the evangelical princes and theologians were not prepared to compromise. Indeed, our verse served as one of the foundational texts supporting their argument, a reality which became even clearer in Melanchthon's defense of priestly marriage in the *Apologia*. Moreover, the inclusion of our verse in this, and these, confessional writings marked the final and official transition of our verse from the personal teaching of a notable reformer and his colleagues to a component of the collective confession of one strain of the Evangelical movement. Moreover, as we came to Melanchthon's *Apologia*, we observed our theorized conjunction of Genesis 1:28 and the natural affects as these two elements appeared jointly in a manner that was nothing other than unmistakable. Furthermore, as concerns our previous discussion of natural law, the presence of the Ulpianic tradition of natural law in connection with our verse was also witnessed in the argumentation of Melanchthon's *Apologia*.

Appendix

1. *Apologia Confessionis Augustanae* Art. 23 Comparison Table

Codex Guelferbytanus[1]	Oktavausgabe[2]	Jonas Translation[3]
<u>Ridiculum autem est, quod inquiunt hanc vocem Dei: **Crescite et multiplicamini**, tantum ad illud tempus, cum essent pauci homines, pertinere, non ad nostrum tempus.</u> Nos sic sentimus, quod illa verba creent et ordinent naturam, qualem postea existere necesse est. Sicut alia similia verba: **Germinet terra herbam virentem.** Haec vox vestit agros, quotannis creat fruges, parit victum omnibus animantibus. Ita haec sententia: Crescite etc. non solum mandatum, sed etiam naturae conditionem continent, quam mutare non est nostrum, sed Dei opus. Nec fecerunt virgines, siquae vere conservaverunt virginitatem, contra mandatum Dei, quia cum a conditione illa communi naturae exemptae essent, mandato etiam solutae errant, quoad ad illam commune conditionem naturae pertinent. Exemit enim istas peculiar donum et opus Dei.	Primum. Genesis docet homines conditos esse, ut sint foecundi, et sexus recta ratione sexum appetat. Loquimur enim non de concupiscentia, quae peccatum est, sed de illo appetitu, qui in integra natura futurus erat, quem vocant στοργὴν φυσικήν. Et haec στοργὴ est vere ordinatio divina sexus ad sexum. Cum autem haec ordinatio Dei sine singulari opere Dei tolli non possit, Sequitur Ius contrahendi matrimonii non posse tolli statutis aut votis. <u>Haec cavillantur adversarii, dicunt initio fuisse mandatum, ut repleretur terra, nunc repleta terra non esse mandatum coniugium.</u> Videte, quam prudenter iudicent. Natura hominum formatur illo verbo Dei, ut sit fecunda non solum initio creationis, sed tantisper, dum haec corporum natura existet. Sicut hoc verbo terra fit fecunda: **Germinet terra herbam virentem.** Propter hanc ordinationem non solum initio coepit terra produ-	Erstlich ist geschrieben Genesis am i., Das man und weib also geschaffen von Gott sein, das sie sollen fruchtbar sein, kinder zeugen etc., das weib geneigt sey zum man, der man widder zum weibe. Und wir reden hie nicht von der unordenlichen brunst, die nach Adams fal gefolget ist, sondern von natürlicher neigung zwischen man und weib, welche auch gewesen were inn der natur, wenn sie rein blieben were. Und das ist Gottes geschepff und ordnung, das der man zum weib geneigt sey, das weib zum man. So nu die Göttliche ordnung und die angeschaffne art niemands endern mag noch sol denn Gott selbst, so folgt, das der ehestand durch kein menschlich statut odder gelübde mag abgethan werden. Widder diesen starcken grund spielen die widdersacher mit worten, sagen, Im anfang der schepffung habe das wort noch stadgehabt: »Wachset und mehret euch und erfüllet die erden«, Nu aber, so die erde erfüllet ist, sey die ehe nicht gebotten. Sehet aber, wie weise leute sein da die widdersacher! durch dis Göttliche wort: »Wachset und mehret euch«, wilchs noch immer gehet und nicht auffhöret, ist man und weib also geschaffen, das sie sollen fruchtbar sein, nicht allein die zeit des anfangs, sondern solang diese natur weret. Denn gleich wie durch das wort Genesis am i., Da Gott sprach: »Es lasse die erde auffgehen gras und kraut« etc., die erde also geschaffen ist, das sie nicht allein

---

1 Dates to ca. 11 August 1530. See BSELK. Quellen und Materialien, vol. 1, pp. 256–259. The cited text of *De coniugio sacerdotum* is found on p. 272,1–12. Boldening and underlining added to show correspondence.

2 BSELK, pp. 593,1–595,14. Boldening and underlining added to show correspondence.

3 Ibid., pp. 592,1–594,20. Boldening and underlining added to show correspondence.

cere gramina, sed quotannis vestiuntur agri, donec existet haec natura. Sicut igitur legibus humanis non potest natura terrae mutari, Ita neque votis neque lege humana potest natura hominis mutari sine speciali opere Dei.

Secundo. Et quia haec creatio seu ordinatio divina in homine est Ius naturale, ideo sapienter et recte dixerunt Iurisconsulti coniunctionem maris et feminae esse iuris naturalis. Cum autem Ius naturale sit immutabile, necesse est semper manere Ius contrahendi coniugii. Nam ubi natura non mutatur, necesse est et illam ordinationem manere, quam Deus indidit naturae, nec potest legibus humanis tolli. Ridiculum igitur est, quod adversarii nugantur, initio fuisse mandatum coniugium, nunc non esse. Hoc perinde est, ac si dicerent: Olim nascentes homines secum attulerunt sexum, nunc non afferunt. Nullus Faber fabrilius cogitare quidquam posset, quam hae ineptiae excogitatae sunt ad eludendum ius naturae.

Maneat igitur hoc in causa, quod et scriptura docet et Iurisconsultus sapienter dixit: coniunctionem maris et feminae esse Iuris naturalis. Porro Ius naturale vere est Ius divinum, quia est ordinatio divinitus impressa naturae. Quia autem hoc Ius mutari non potest sine singulari opere Dei, necesse est manere Ius contrahendi coniugii, quia ille naturalis appetitus est ordinatio Dei in natura sexus ad sexum, et propterea Ius est alioqui quare uterque sexus conderetur? Et loquimur, ut supra dictum est, non de concupiscentia, quae peccatum est, sed de illo appetitu, quem vocant στοργὴν φυσικὴν; quem concupiscentia non sustulit ex natura, sec accendit, ut nunc remedio magis opus habeat, et coniugium non solum procreationis causa necessarium sit, sed etiam remedii causa. Haec sunt perspicua et adeo firma, ut nullo modo labefactari queant.

im anfang frucht bracht, sondern das sie alle jar gras, kreutter und ander gewechs brecht, solang diese natur weret, Also ist auch man und weib geschaffen, fruchtbar zu sein, solang diese natur weret, Also ist auch man und weib geschaffen, fruchtbar zu sein, solang diese natur weret; wie nu das menschengebot und -gesetz nicht endern kann, das die erde nicht solt grüne werden etc., Also kan auch kein Klostergelübde, kein menschengebot die menschlich natur endern, das ein weib nicht solt eins mans begeren, ein man eins weibs, one ein sonderlich Gotteswerck.

Zum andern, dieweil das Göttliche geschepff und Gottes ordnung natürlich recht und gesetz ist, so haben die Iurisconsulti recht gesagt, das des mans und weibs beinandersein und zusamengehören ist natürlich recht. So aber das natürlich recht niemands verendern kan, so mus jhe einem jdern die ehe frey sein. Denn wo Gott die natur nicht verendert, da mus auch die art bleiben, die Gott der natur eingepflantzt hat, und sie kann mit menschengesetzen nicht verendert werden. Derhalben ist es gantz kindisch, das die widdersacher sagen, Im anfang, da der mensch geschaffen, sey die ehe geboten, nu aber nicht. Denn es ist gleich, als wenn sie sprechen: etwan zu Adams und der Patriarchen zeitten, wenn ein man geborn ward, hatte er mannes art an sich, wenn ein weib geborn ward, hatt sie weibs art an sich, jtzund aber ists anders; vorzeitten bracht ein kind aus mutterleib natürlich art mit sich, nu aber nicht.

So bleiben wir nu billich bey dem spruch, wie die Iurisconsulti weislich und recht gesagt haben, das man und weib beieinandersein ist natürlich recht. Ists nu natürlich recht, so ist es Gottes ordnung, also inn der natur gepflantzt, und ist also auch Göttlich recht. Dieweil aber das Göttlich und natürlich recht niemands zu endern hat denn Gott allein, so mus der Ehestand jderman frey sein, denn die natürlich angeborn neigung des weibs gegen dem man, des mans gegen das weib ist Gottes geschepff und ordnung. Darümb ists recht und hat kein Engel noch mensch zu endern. Gott, der Herr, hat nicht Adam allein geschaffen, sondern auch Evam, nicht allein ein man, sondern auch ein weib und sie gesegnet, das sie fruchtbar seien. Und wir reden, wie ich gesagt habe, nicht von der unordentlichen brunst, die da sundlich ist, sondern von der natürlichen neigung, die zwischen man und weib auch gewesen were, so die natur rein blieben were; die böse lust nach dem fahl hat solche neigung noch stercker gemacht, das wir nu des ehestands viel mehr dürffen, nicht allein kinder zu zeugen, sondern auch erger sund zu verhüten. Dis ist so klarer grund, das es miemans wird umbstossen, sondern der Teuffel und alle welt wird es müssen bleiben lassen.

2. Works Cited

2.1 Primary Sources

Alberus, Erasmus, Das Ehbüchlin Ein gesprech zweyer weiber, mit namen Agatha vnd Barbara, vnd sunst mancherley vom Ehestand, Eheleuten, vnnd jederman nützlich zulesen, An die Durchleuchtige Hochgeborne Fürstin, Fraw Catharina geborne Hertzogin von Braunschweig, Marggraeffin zu Brandenburg [et]c., Frankfurt/Main (Egenolff d.Ä.) 1539; VD16 A 1487.

Alberus, Erasmus/Francesco Barbaro, Eyn gůt bůch von der Ehe was die Ehe sei was sie gůts mit sich bringe Wie eyn weib geschickt sein soll die eyner zu d[er] Ehe nehmen will wie alt waß sie dem Mañ zubringen solle Vom kosten vnnd gebreng der hochzeit Von dreien Tugendē des weibs Cochlaeus Wie mann Kinder ziehen solle. weiland zu Latin gemacht durch den Wolgelerten Franciscum Barbarum Rathern zu Venedig Nun aber verdeutscht durch Erasmum Alberum, Hagenau (Valentin Kobian) 1536; VD16 B 357.

Alveldt, Augustin von, Von dem ehelichen Stand wider Brudern Martin Luther, Leipzig (Martin Landsberg) 1521; VD16 A 2108.

Apel, Johann, DEFENSIO IOHANNIS APELLI AD EPSCOPVM HERBIPOLENSEM PRO SVO CONIVGIO, Wittenberg (Johann Rhau-Grunenberg) 1523; VD16 A 3028.

Arnoldi, Bartholomäus, Libellus F. Bartholomei de Vsingen Augustiniani de Merito bonorum operum. Jn quo veris argumentis respondet ad instructionem fratris Mechlerij Franciscani de bonis operibus Cochlaeus Jnsuper respondet ad Euangelium Culsameri Cochlaeus Contra factionem Lutheranam, Erfurt (Matthes Maler) 1525; VD16 A 3723.

Arnoldi, Bartholomäus, Libellus F. Bartholomei de vsingen augustiniani Jn quo respondet confutationi fratris Egidij mechlerij monachi frāciscani sed exiticij laruati et cõiugati. Nitentis tueri errores et p[er]fidiam Culsameri Cochlaeus Cōtra Lutheranos, Erfurt (Matthes Maler) 1524; VD16 A 3719.

Arnoldi, Bartholomäus, Libellus F. Bartholomei de Vsingen Augustiniani de falsis prophetis tam in persona quā doctrina vitandis a fidelibus. De recta et mūda p̄dicatiōe euāgelij [et] [qui?]bus [con]formiter ill[u]d debeat p̄dicari. De Celibatu sacerdotum Cochlaeus Responsio ad Sermonē Langi de Matrimonio sacerdotali quē fecit in Nuptijs Culsameri sacerdotis Cōtra factionē Luttheranā, Erfurt (Matthes Maler) 1525; VD16 A 3702.

Arnoldi, Bartholomäus, Liber Tertivs F.B. de Vsingen ordinis Eremitani S. Augustini : In quo respondet nebulis Culsameri quas comme[n]tus est ille in responsionem ad libellum suum vernaculu[m] quibus seipsum pingit: qualis quantusq[ue] in sacris sit litteris, Erfurt (Johann Loersfeld) 1524; VD16 A 3722.

Arnoldi, Bartholomäus, Sermo de Matrimonio Sacerdotum Et Monachorum exiticiorum. F. Bartholomei de Vsingen. Ordinis Eremitani S. Augustini, Erfurt (Hans Knappe d.Ä.) 1523; VD16 A 3752.

BOSSLER, Ulrich, Ain schoner Dialogus oder gesprech des Appostolicums Angelica vñ anderer Specerey der Apotecken Antreffen Doctor Marti. Lutthers leer vnd sein anhang, Augsburg (Erhard [Erben] Oeglin) 1521; VD16 B 6782.

BRIESMANN, Joannes, IOANNIS BRIESMANNI AD CASPAris Schatzgeyri Minoritae plicas responsio, pro Lutherano libello de uotis monasticis. ITEM M.Lutheri ad Briesmannum Epistola, de eodem. Cochlaeus, Strasbourg (Johann Werwagen d.Ä.) 1523; VD16 B 8280.

BUCER, Martin, Ain schoener dialog[us] Vñ gespresch zwischen aim Pfarrer vnd aim Schulthayß betreffend allen übel Stand der gaystlichen. Vnd boeß handlüg der weltlichen. Alles mit geytzigkayt beladen. [et]c., Augsburg (Melchior Ramminger) 1521; VD16 B 8911.

BUGENHAGEN, Johannes, DE CONIVGIO EPISCOPORVM ET Diaconorum ad uenerandum Doctorem VVolfgangum Reissenbusch monasterij Lichtenbergensis Praeceptorem per Ioannem Bugenhag. Pomeranum, Nuremberg (Johann Petreius) 1525; VD16 B 9294.

BUGENHAGEN, Johannes, Von der Euangelischen Meß, was die Meß sey, wie un[d] durch wenn, und warumb sy auffgesetzt sey, auch wie man Meß sol hören, un[d] das hochwirdig sacrament empfahe[n], un[d] warumb man es empfecht, Nuremberg (Jobst Gutknecht) 1524; VD16 B 9461.

BUGENHAGEN, Johannes, Wie man die so zu der Ehe greyffent eynleytet zu Wittemberg darin angezeygt wird was die Ehe sey von wem vnd warumb sie auffgesetzt ist, Magdeburg (Hans Knappe d.J.) 1525; VD16 A 837.

CICERO, Marcus Tullius/Philipp Melanchthon, OFFICIA CIERONIS, CVM SCHOLIIS PHIL.MELAN. QVAE possint esse uice prolixi commentarij. Nam pleriq; loci quos hactenus nemo attigit, hic enarrantur, Hagenau (Johann Setzer) 1525; VD16 C 3180.

CLICTHOVE, Josse, Antilutherus Iudoci Clichtovei Neoportuensis, doctoris theologi, Tres libros complectens, Paris 1524, URL: <https://books.google.no/books?id=xVhbAAAA-cAAJ&printsec=frontcover&hl=no#v=onepage&q&f=false> (18 Aug 22).

CLICTHOVE, Josse, Propugnaculu[m] Ecclesie, adversus Lutheranos, Cologne (Peter Quentel) 1526; VD16 C 4207.

COCHLAEUS, Johannes, Glos vñ Cōment Doc. Johānes dobneck Cochleus von Wendelstein, vff CLIIII. Articklen gezogen vß einem Sermon Doc. mar. Luterß von der heiligen meß vñ nüem Testamēt, Strasbourg (Johann Grüninger) 1523; VD16 C 4319.

CRUCIGER, Caspar, Herrn Doctor Caspar Creutzigers auslegung/vber Sanct Paulus spruch zum Thimotheo/wie die Eheweiber selig werden/nicht allein allen Eheweibern/sondern auch allen Christen seer nuetzlich vñ trœstlich durch M. Georgium Spalatinum verdeudscht, Erfurt (Christoffel Golthammer) 1538; VD16 C 5853.

DIETENBERGER, Johann, Antwort das Junckfrawen die klöster vnd klösterliche gelübt nümer götlich verlassen mögen, edited by Johannes COCHLAEUS, Strasbourg (Johann Grüninger) 1523; VD16 L 6886.

DIETENBERGER, Johann, Iohan. Dytenbergii Theologi, contra temerarium Martini Luteri de uotis monasticis iudicium, liber Cochlaeus : quo singulatim illius rationibus, quas omnes ex ordine passim autor praetexit, ex sacris literis luculentissime respondet Cochlaeus, Cologne (Eucharius Cervicornus) 1524; VD16 D 1479.

Eberlin von Günzburg, Johann, Ein vermanung aller christe[n] das sie sich erbarme[n] vber die klosterfrawe[n] [...]; Der. III. bu[n]dtgnosz, Basel (Pamphilus Gengenbach) 1521; VD16 E 100.

Eberlin von Günzburg, Johann, Wie gar gfarlich sey. So Ain Priester kain Eeweyb hat. Wye Vnchristlich. vnd schedlich aim gmainen Nutz Die menschen seynd. Welche hindern die Pfaffen Am Eelichen stand, Augsburg (Melchior Ramminger) 1522; VD16 E 156.

Eck, Johannes, Enchiridion locorum communium adversus Lutteranos. ab autore jam quarto recognitum auctum et a mendis emunctum, Ingolstadt (Peter Apian; George Apian) 1527; VD16 E 338.

Eck, Johannes, Svb Domini Ihesv Et Mariae Patrocinio. Articulos 404. partim ad disputationes Lipsicam Baden[sem] et Bernen[sem] attinentes, partim vero ex scriptis pacem ecclesiae perturbantium extractos, Ingolstadt (Peter Apian; Georg Apian) 1530; VD16 E 270.

Emser, Hieronymus, WId[er] das vnchristenliche buch Martini Luters Augustiners, an den Tewtschen Adel außgangen, Leipzig (Martin Landsberg) 1521; VD16 E 1137.

Erasmus, Desiderius, Encomium Matrimonii, Strasbourg (Matthias Schürer) 1518; VD16 E 2813.

<Eyb>, Albrecht von, Ob ainem sey zu nemen ain Eelich weib, Augsburg (Silvan Otmar; Johann Rynmann) 1517; VD16 E 4743.

<Eyb>, Albrecht von, Von dem Eelichen Standt : Ain schöne leer wie sich ain Eeman halten, un[d] sein Eefrauwen underweisen unnd zyehen soll. Auch widerumb die fraw gegen irem mann. Dardurch sy hye erlang[e]n gut und eer und ewyge fröd, Augsburg (Johann Schönsperger d.J.) ca. 1520; VD16 V 2464.

Fabri, Johann, IOANNIS FABRI EPISCOPI CONSTANTIENSIS IN SPIRITVALIBVS VICARII OPVS ADVERSVS NOVA QVAEDAM ET A CHRISTIANA RELIGIONE PRORSVS ALIENA DOGMATA MARTINI LVTHERI, Rome 1522, URL: <https://opacplus.bsb-muenchen.de/title/BV001520350> (14 Oct 2021).

Fabri, Johann, Mallevs Ioannis Fabri Doctoris Celeberrimi Cochlaeus in hæresim Lutheranā, iam denuo uehemētiori studio & labore recognitus, in Tractatus etiam & Paragraphos diuisus, Cologne (Peter Quentel; Johann Soter) 1524; VD16 F 214.

Fabri, Johann, Summarium Underricht aus was christenlichen Ursachen D. Johan Fabri bisher der Lutherischen Lere nicht anhängig, Mainz (Johann Schöffer) 1526; VD16 F 238.

Hasenberg, Johann, Lvdus Lvdentem Lvderum Lvdens quo Ioannes Hasenbergius Bohemus in Bacchanalib. Lypsiae, omnes ludificantem Ludionem, omnibus ludendum exhibuit. Anno M.D.XXX Lypsiae, Leipzig (Michael Blum) 1530; VD16 H 714.

Hutten, Ulrich von, Gespräch büchlin. Feber das erst. Feber das Ander. Wadiscus oder die Römische dreyfaltigkeit (etc.), Strasbourg (Johan Schott) 1521; VD16 H 6342.

Jonas, Justus, Adversvs Iohannem Fabrum Constantien[sem] Vicarium, scortationis patronum, pro coniugio sacerdotali, Iusti Ionae defensio, Wittenberg (Melchior Lotter d.J.) 1523; VD16 J 871.

Karlstadt, Andreas, Contra Papisticas leges sacerdotibus prohibentes matrimonium apologia pastoris Cemergensis Cochlaeus, Basel (Adam Petri) 1521; VD16 B 6100.
Karlstadt, Andreas, An Maidenbergers etrzbischof. herforderung uber Eelichs stantzhandel aines ersamen pristers Bernhardj leyppfarres Kemberger kirche[n] enschuldigung und antwurt, Colmar (Amandus Farckall) 1521[?]; VD16 ZV 2155.
Karlstadt, Andreas, Super Coelibatu, Monachatu Et Viduitate Axiomata Perpensa Wittembergae, Wittenberg (Nickel Schirlentz) 1521; VD16 B 6126.
Karlstadt, Andreas, Super Coelibatu, Monachatu Et Viduitate Axiomata Perpensa Wittembergae, Wittenberg (Johann Rhau-Grunenberg) 1521; VD16 B 6125.
Karlstadt, Andreas, Von gelubden vnterrichtung Andres Bo. von Carolstadt Doctor : Außlegung, des xxx. capitel Numeri, wilches von gelubden redet Cochlaeus, Wittenberg (Nickel Schirlentz) 1521; VD16 B 6245.
Klingebeyl, Steffan, Von Priester Ehe des wirdigen herrñ Licentiaten Steffan Klingebeyl/mit einer Vorrede Mart. Luther, Wittenberg (Nickel Schirlentz) 1528; VD16 K 1340.
Lang, Johann, Von gehorsam der Weltlichen oberkait, und den außgangen klosterleuten, ain schutzred, an doctor Andreas Frowin, Augsburg (Sigmund Grimm) 1523; VD16 L 318.
Link, Wenzeslaus, Das erst teyl des alten Testaments. Annotation in die Fünff Bücher Mosi. Eyn schöne Vorred, Martini Lutheri (etc.), Strasbourg (Balthasar Beck) 1543; VD16 L 1790.
Link, Wenzeslaus, Dyalogus Der Auszgelauffen Münch. Hie sihestu. 1 Ob die außgetretenen oder bleibenden Ordenßpersonen Cochlaeus, Altenburg (Gabriel Kantz) 1524; VD16 L 1804.
Luther, Martin, Uon denn geystlichen und kloster gelubden Martini Luthers urteyll, translated by Justus Jonas, Wittenberg (Nickel Schirlentz) 1522; VD16 L 7327.
Luther, Martin, et al., Lutheri, Melanch., Carolostadii etc. propositiones, Wittembergae viva voce tractatae, in hocque, pleraeque, aeditae ab auctoribus, ut vel nos absentes cum ipsius agamus, vel certe ut veritatis, et seductionum admoneantur boni Cochlaeus, Basil (Adam Petri) 1522; VD16 L 7642.
Mechler, Ägidius, APOLOGIA. ODER schutzrede Egidy Mechlery pfarners tzu Sanct Bartholomeus tzu Erffort. Jn welcher wyrt grund vnd vrsach ertzelt seynes weyb nemens, Erfurt (Wolfgang Stürmer) 1523; VD16 M 1763.
Mechler, Ägidius, Eyn christliche Unterrichtung von guten Werken, Erfurt (Wolfgang Stürmer) 1524; VD16 M 1766.
Mechler, Ägidius, Eyn wyderlegung Egidij Mechlers Pfarners zů/Erffort/zů Sanct […], Erfurt (Wolfgang Stürmer) 1524; VD16 M 1780.
Melanchthon, Philipp, Commentarius De Anima, Wittenberg (Peter Seitz d.Ä.) 1540; VD16 M 2749.
Melanchthon, Philipp, Defensio Conivgii Sacerdotvm Pia & erudita missa ad Regem Angliae, Strasbourg (Kraft Müller) 1540; VD16 M 2915.
Melanchthon, Philipp, Disputationes theologicae in schola propositae et fideliter explicatae a Philippo Melanthone, ab anno Christi XXIII usque ad annum XLV, Wittenberg

(Iohannem Lufft) 1550; Online Resource from The Digital Library of Classic Protestant Texts (Alexander Street Press), URL: <https://search.alexanderstreet.com/preview/work/bibliographic_entity%7Cbibliographic_details%7C5002283> (18 Aug 22).

Melanchthon, Philipp, Eine Schrifft Philip. Melanth. newlich latinisch gestellet widder den unreinen Bapsts Celibat, und verbot der Priesterehe, translated by Justus Jonas, Wittenberg (Joseph Klug) 1541; VD16 M 2920.

Melanchthon, Philipp, In Ethica Aristotelis Commentarivs Philipp. Melanchtho., Wittenberg (Josef Klug) 1529; VD16 ZV 10667.

Melanchthon, Philipp, In obscuriora aliquot capita Geneseos Phil. Melan. annotationes, Hagenau (Johann Setzer) 1523; VD16 M 3460.

Melanchthon, Philipp, Loci Commvnes Rervm Theologicarvm Sev Hypotyposes Theologicae, Wittenberg (Melchior Lotter d.J.) 1521; VD16 M 3585.

Menius, Justus, An die hochgeborne Furstin fraw Sibilla Hertzogin zu Sachsen, Oeconomia Christiana: das ist von christlicher Haußhaltung, Wittenberg (Hans Lufft) 1529; VD16 M 4542.

Menius, Justus, Erynnerung was denen/so sich ynn Ehestand begeben zu bedencken sey. Just. Menius, Wittenberg (Nickel Schirlentz) 1528; VD16 M 4567.

Murner, Thomas, An den Großmechtigsten vñ Durchlüchtigstē adel tütscher nation das sye den christlichen glauben beschirmen/wyder den zerst[oe]rer des glaubēs christi/ Martinū luther einē [v]fierer der einfeltigē christē, Strasbourg (Johann Grüninger) 1520; VD16 M 7020.

Murner, Thomas, Uon dem grossen Luthersichen Narren wie in doctor Murner beschworen hat [et]c̄., Strasbourg (Johann Grüninger) 1522; VD16 M 7088.

N.N., Eyn buchleyn wieder den Sermon Augustini Alueldes vom ehlichen stande den er wieder Martinum Lutther gemacht/Darinnen auch angezeygt ab es auß goetlicher heyliger schrieft gegruendet das Priester mœchten ehlich weyber habenn. […], Erfurt (Matthes Maler) 1522; VD16 B 9125.

Rauch, Petrus, ANTITHESIS Der Lutherischen Bekenthniß odder Beicht/ßo sie tzu Augspurgk vor K[ae]yserlicher Maiestat/vnd dē Heyligen R[oe]mischen Reich Jm Dreyssigsten jar/angegeben. Dar ynnē du frommer leser erkennen magst/mit was warheyt sye yhren glawben bekanth. Durch Petrum Anspach. Cochlaeus, Frankfurt/Oder (Johannes Hanau d.Ä.) ca. 1531; VD16 R 385.

Roemer, Johann, Eyn schöner Dialogus von den vier grösten bechwernüß eins jeglichen Pfarrers, Strasbourg (Matthias Schürer) 1521; VD16 R 2783.

Rupertus, Opus originale Ruperti abbatis Tuiciensis de Victoria verbi dei in tredecim libros diuisum, Augsburg 1487; BSB-Ink R-286 – GW M39213.

Schatzgeyer, Kaspar, Scrvtinivm Divinae Scriptvrae, pro conciliatione dissidentium dogmatum circa subscriptas materias : De Gratia & libero arbitrio, Fide & operibus, Peccato in bono opere, Exordio uerae poenitentiae, Meritorio actu liberi arbitrii, Sacrificio noui testamenti, Sacerdotio nouae legis, Communione sub utraq[ue] spetie, Baptismo & libertate

Christiana, Votis & statu monasticorum, Augsburg (Sigmund Grimm; Marx Wirsung) 1522; VD16 S 2336.

SCHATZGEYER, Kaspar, Von dem waren Christlichen Leben, in wem es stee : Vil materi inn lateinischen biechlin von dem klösterlichen leben und gelybten vorauß gangen zu samen getragen Cochlaeus, Augsburg (Simprecht Ruff) 1524; VD16 S 2346.

SCHOPPER, Johann, Eyn Ratschlag, Den etliche Christenliche Pfarherrn, Prediger Cochlaeus Einem Fürsten, welcher yetzigen stritigen leer halb, auff den abschied, jüngst gehaltens Reichßtags zu Nürnberg, Christlicher warhait vnderricht begert, gemacht haben (etc.), Nuremberg (Jobst Gutknecht) 1525; VD16 S 3920.

SCHWALB, Hans, Beclagung aines Leyens, genant Hanns schwalb über vil mißbreüch Christliches lebens vnd darin[n] begriffen kürtzlich von Johannes Hußsen: Im Jar MDXXI, Augsburg (Melchior Ramminger) 1521; VD16 S 4582.

SPANGENBERG, Johann, Der Gros Catechismus vnd Kinder Lere D.Mart.Luth. Fuer die jungen Christen inn Fragestuecke verfasset Durch M.IOHAN.SPANGENBERG, der Keyserlichen Statt Northausen Prediger, Frankfurt/Main (Cyriacus Jacob) 1543; VD16 L 4360.

SPANGENBERG, Johann, Des Ehelichen Ordens Spiegel vnd Regel ynn zehen Capitel geteilt/ Darinne man siehet wer den Ehestandt gestifft/was er sey/vnnd wie man sich darinne halten sol/durch Johann. Spangenberg/Der Keiserlichen Stadt Northausen Prediger, Magdeburg (Michael Lotter) 1544; VD16 S 7782.

STÖR, Thomas, Der Ehelich standt vonn got mit gebenedeyung auffgesetzt/soll vmb schw[ae]rheyt wegen der seltzamen gaben der Junckfrawschafft yederman frey seyn/ vnd nyemant verboten werden, Erfurt (Wolfgang Stürmer) 1524; VD16 S 9212.

STÖR, Thomas, Der Ehelich standt von Got mit gebenedeyung auffgesetzt/sollvmb schw[æ]rheyt wegen der seltzamen gaben der Junckfrawschafft/yederman frey sein/vñd niemāt verboten wird~e. [...], Nuremberg (Hieronymus Höltzel) 1525; VD16 S 9213.

WIMPINA, Konrad, SECTARVM ERRORVM, HALLVTINAtionū, & Schismatum, ab origine ferme Christianae ecclesiae, ad haec us[que] nostra tempora, concisioris Anacephalaeoseos,Vna cū aliquantis Pigardicarū, Vuiglefticarū, & Lutheranarum haeresum: confutationibus, Librorum partes Tres. Cochlaeus, Frankfurt/Oder (Johannes Hanau d.Ä.) 1528; VD16 K 1533.

WULFFER, Wolfgang, Epithalamion vnd Braudlied Mertē Luthers/Deutscher nation Ertzketzers/erclert durch Wolff Wolfher/Zw Dresden/allen zu gutt/die es gelust zu lesen/vber S. Pauls Capitel. 1 Chorin: 7., Dresden (Emserpresse) 1525; VD16 ZV 22408.

WULFFER, Wolfgang, Tacianus der ertzketzer in Krichenland/hat verpotten Ehelich zuwerden/Luther der Ertzketzer in Dewtschen land/gepewt Ehelich zuwerden/ beydes wider.s.Pauls Text.i.Corin.vij. Cochlaeus, Dresden (Wolfgang Stöckel) 1528; VD16 W 4582.

2.2 Edited Primary Sources

ALLEN, Percy S. (ed.), Opvs Epistolarvm Des. Erasmi Roterodami, Clarendon 1928, vol. T. 7: 1527–1528.
ARISTOTLE, Generation of Animals, translated by A.L. Peck, Harvard et al. 1979 (Aristotle in Twenty-Three Volumes 13).
ARISTOTLE, On the Soul, translated by W.S. Hett, Cambridge et al. 1975 (Aristotle in Twenty-Three Volumes 8).
ARISTOTLE, Parts of Animals, translated by A.L. Peck, Cambridge et al. 1983 (Aristotle in Twenty-Three Volumes 12).
ARNOLDI DE USINGEN, Bartholomaei, O.S.A. Responsio Contra Apologiam Philippi Melanchthonis, edited by Primoz SIMONITI, Würzburg 1978.
BIEL, Gabriel, Collectorium circa quattuor libros Sententiarum: 4/2 (dist. 14–22), edited by Hans RÜCKERT and Wilfridus WERBECK, Tübingen 1977.
BUGENHAGEN, Johannes, Johanns Bugenhagen. Selected Writings, edited and translated by Kurt K. HENDEL, Minneapolis 2015, 2 vols.
CHRYSOSTOM, John, Homilies on Genesis 1–17, translated by Robert C. Hill, Washington, D.C. 1986.
CHRYSOSTOM, John, Homilies on Genesis 18–45, translated by Robert C. Hill, Washington, D.C. 1990.
CICERO, Marcus Tullius, De Finibus Bonorum et Malorum, translated by H. Rackham, Cambridge et al. 1971, (Cicero in Twenty-Eight Volumes 17).
CICERO, Marcus Tullius, De Officiis, translated by Walter Miller, Cambridge et al. 1975, (Cicero in Twenty-Eight Volumes 21).
CLEMEN, Otto (ed.), Supplementa Melanchthoniana. Werke Philipp Melanchthons die im Corpus Reformatorum vermisst werden, Leipzig 1926, Abt. 6/1.
Corpus scriptorium ecclesiasticorum latinorum, Vienna 1866–.
DINGEL, Irene (ed.), Die Bekenntnisschriften der evangelisch-lutherischen Kirche, Göttingen 2014.
DINGEL, Irene (ed.), Die Bekenntnisschriften der evangelisch-lutherischen Kirche. Quellen und Materialen, Göttingen 2014, vol. 1: Von den altkirchlichen Symbolen bis zu den Katechismen Martin Luthers.
DÖMLING, Anna Katharina et al. (eds.), Olavus Petri und die Reformation in Schweden. Schriften aus den Jahren 1528–1531, translated by Hans Ulrich Bächtold and Hans-Peter Naumann, Zug 2002.
FÖRSTEMANN, Karl Eduard, Urkundenbuch zu der Geschichte des Reichstages zu Augsburg im Jahre 1530. Von dem Ausgange des kaiserlichen Ausschreibens bis zu der Uebergabe der Augsburgischen Confession, Halle 1833, vol. 1, URL: <https://books.google.no/books?id=oBZBAAAAcAAJ> (15 Jan 2019).
KAWERAU, Gustav, Der Briefwechsel des Justus Jonas, Hildesheim 1964, 2 vols.

KOLB, Robert/James A. NESTINGEN (eds.), Sources and Contexts of the Book of Concord, Minneapolis 2001.

KOLB, Robert et al., The Book of Concord. The Confessions of the Evangelical Lutheran Church, Minneapolis 2000.

LAUBE, Adolf/Ulman WEISS, Flugschriften gegen die Reformation (1518–1524), Berlin 1997.

LUTHER, Martin, Die gantze Heilige Schrifft Deudsch, [Wittenberg 1545] Darmstadt 1973, vol. 1.

LUTHER, Martin, Luther's Works, St. Louis et al. 1958–86, 2008–.

LUTHER, Martin, D. Martin Luthers Werke. Kritische Gesamtausgabe [Briefwechsel], Weimar 1906–61, 18 vols.

LUTHER, Martin, Luthers Werke. Kritische Gesamtausgabe [Schriften], Weimar 1883–1993, 65 vols.

LUTHER, Martin, Luthers Werke. Kritische Gesamtausgabe [Tischreden], Weimar 1912–21, 6 vols.

MANSI, J.D. et al. (eds.), Sacrorum Conciliorum Nova et Amplissima Collectio, Florence et al. 1759–1798, URL: <http://patristica.net/mansi> (3 June 2020).

Melanchthon, Philip, Commonplaces. Loci Communes 1521, translated by Christian Preus, Saint Louis 2014.

Melanchthon, Philip, Corpus Reformatorum. Opera quae supersunt omnia, edited by C.G. BRETSCHNEIDER and H.E. BINDSEIL, Halle 1834–60.

Melanchthon, Philipp, Ethicae Doctrinae Elementa et Enarratio Libri quinti Ethicorum, edited by Günter FRANK and Michael BEYER, Stuttgart-Bad Cannstatt 2008.

MIGNE, J.-P. (ed.), Patrologia Graeca, Paris 1857–1886, 162 vols.

MIGNE, J.-P. (ed.), Patrologiae Latina, Paris 1844–1864, 271 vols.

PETRI, L./O. PETRI (eds.), Swenska Psalmboken af 1536. Å nyo utgifwen, Stockholm 1862, URL: <https://books.google.no/books?id=qFBVAAAAcAAJ> (16 Jul 2019).

PLINY (the Elder), Natural History in Ten Volumes, translated by H. Rackham, Cambridge et al. 1969, 10 vols., vol. 2.

PÖHLMANN, Horst Georg (ed./tr.), LOCI COMMUNES 1521. Lateinisch und Deutsch, Gütersloh 1993.

SCHAFF, Philip (ed.), A Select Library of the Christian Church. Nicene and Post-Nicene Fathers, Grand Rapids, MI 1986–1989.

SCHEIBLE, Heinz (ed.), Melanchthons Briefwechsel, Stuttgart-Bad Cannstatt 1977–.

SCHÖNFELDER, Albert, Sammlung gottesdienstlicher Bücher aus dem deutschen Mittelalter, Paderborn 1904, vol. 1.

STONE, Rachel/Charles WEST, The Divorce of King Lothar and Queen Theutberga. Hincmar of Rheims's De Divortio, Manchester 2016.

STRAND, Kenneth A., Arnoldi von Usingen's Sermo de Matrimonio Sacerdotum et Monachorum. The Text of a Rare Edition, in: Archiv für Reformationsgeschichte 56 (1965), pp. 145–155.

2.3 Secondary Sources

ALFSVÅG, Knut, Natural Theology and Natural Law in Martin Luther, in: Oxford Research Encyclopedia of Religion (2016), URL: <https://doi.org/10.1093/acrefore/9780199340378.013.368> (18 Aug 2022).

ALTHAUS, Paul, Luthers Wort von der Ehe, in: Luther 24 (1953), pp. 49–58.

ARAND, Charles P. et al., The Lutheran Confessions. History and Theology of The Book of Concord, Minneapolis 2012.

ARNOLD, Franz Xaver, Zur Frage des Naturrechts bei Martin Luther, München 1936.

ASENDORF, Ulrich, Lectura in Biblia. Luthers Genesisvorlesung (1535–1545). Forschungen zur systematischen und ökumenischen Theologie, Göttingen 1998.

BAADER, Gerhard, Die Antikerezeption in der Entwicklung der medizinischen Wissenschaft während der Renaissance, in: Rudolf SCHMITZ/Gundolf KEIL (eds.), Humanismus und Medizin, Weinheim 1984, pp. 51–66.

BARANOWSKI, Siegmund, Luthers Lehre von der Ehe, Münster 1913.

BÄRENFÄNGER, Katharina et al., Martin Luthers Tischreden. Neuansätze der Forschung, Tübingen 2011.

BAUER, Clemens, Melanchthons Naturrechtslehre, in: Archiv für Reformationsgeschichte 42 (1951), pp. 64–91.

BEHRENDT, Walter, Lehr-, Wehr- und Nährstand. Haustafelliteratur und Dreiständelehre im 16. Jahrhundert, Berlin 2009, URL: <https://refubium.fu-berlin.de/bitstream/handle/fub188/10734/Behrendt_Walter_Diss.pdf> (18 Aug 2022).

BENZING, Josef/Helmut CLAUS, Lutherbibliographie. Verzeichnis der gedruckten Schriften Martin Luthers bis zu dessen Tod, Baden-Baden 1989.

BERGDOLT, Klaus, Das Gewissen der Medizin. Ärztliche Moral von der Antike bis heute, München 2004.

BERMAN, Harold, Law and Revolution. The Formation of the Western Legal Tradition, Cambridge et al. 1983.

BEUTEL, Albrecht, In dem Anfang war das Wort. Studien zu Luthers Sprachverständnis, Tübingen 1991.

BEYER, Hermann Wolfgang, Luther und das Recht, München 1935.

BEYER, Michael, Luthers Ehelehre bis 1525, in: Martin TREU (ed.), Katharina von Bora. Die Lutherin. Aufsätze anlässlich ihres 500. Geburtstags, Wittenberg 1999, pp. 59–82.

BIHLMAIER, Sandra, Anthropologie, in: Günter FRANK (ed.), Philipp Melanchthon. Der Reformator zwischen Glauben und Wissen. Ein Handbuch, Göttingen 2017, pp. 483–494.

BIHLMAIER, Sandra, Naturphilosophie, in: Günter FRANK (ed.), Philipp Melanchthon. Der Reformator zwischen Glauben und Wissen. Ein Handbuch, Göttingen 2017, pp. 469–482.

BODE, Gerhard, Lutheran Ecclesiastical Culture. 1550–1675, edited by Robert KOLB, Leiden et al. 2008.

BOEHMER, Julius, Luthers Ehebuch. Was Martin Luther Ehelosen, Eheleuten und Eltern zu sagen hat, Zwickau 1935.

BOER, Sander Wopke de, The Science of the Soul. The Commentary Tradition on Aristotle's De Anima, c. 1260 –c. 1360, Leuven 2013.

BORNKAMM, Heinrich, Luther und das Alte Testament, Tübingen 1948.

BORNKAMM, Heinrich/Karin BORNKAMM, Luther in Mid-Career, 1521–1530, Philadelphia 1983.

BRAUN, Wilhelm, Die Bedeutung der Concupiscenz in Luthers Leben und Lehre, Berlin 1908.

BRAUNER, Sigrid/Robert H. BROWN, Fearless Wives and Frightened Shrews. The Construction of the Witch in Early Modern Germany, Amherst 1995.

BRECHT, Martin, Martin Luther. Ordnung und Abgrenzung der Reformation 1521–1532, Berlin 1981, vol. 2.

BROWN, Peter, The Body and Society. Men, Women and Sexual Renunciation in Early Christianity, New York 1988.

BRUNDAGE, James A., Law, Sex, and Christian Society in Medieval Europe, Chicago 1987.

BRUNDAGE, James A., The Medieval Origins of the Legal Profession. Canonists, Civilians, and Courts, Chicago et al. 2008.

BRUUN, C.W., Den danske Literatur fra Bogtrykkerkunstens Indførelse i Danmark til 1550, Copenhagen 1875, vol. 2, URL: <https://books.google.de/books?id=uywNkB0IMAIC> (Jul 2019).

BUBENHEIMER, Ulrich, Streit um das Bischofsamt in der Wittenberger Reformation 1521/1522, in: Zeitschrift der Savigny-Stiftung für Rechtsgeschichte (1987), pp. 155–209.

BUCKWALTER, Stephen E., Die Priesterehe in Flugschriften der frühen Reformation, Gütersloh 1998.

BURNET, Gilbert, The History of the Reformation of the Church of England. A Collection of Records, Letters, and Original Papers, with Other Instruments Referred to in the First [and Second] Part[s] […] [Appendices] Concerning Some of the Errors and Falsehoods in Sanders' Book of the English Schism, edited by Nicholas POCOCK, Oxford 1865, vol. 4, URL: <https://books.google.no/books?id=yS-67fDUVYcC&printsec=frontcover&hl=no#v=onepage&q&f=false> (18 Aug 2022).

CAPPELLI, Adriano, The Elements of Abbreviation in Medieval Latin Paleography, Lawrence, KS 1982, URL: <https://kuscholarworks.ku.edu/bitstream/handle/1808/1821/47cappelli.pdf> (18 Jul 2019).

CARLSON, Allan C., A Prophetic Witness to Creation, in: Todd AGLIALORO/Stephen PHELAN (eds.), Inseparable. Five Perspectives on Sex, Life, and Love in Defense of Humanae Vitae, El Cajon, CA 2018, pp. 149–178.

CELLAMARE, Davide, Anatomy and the Body in Renaissance Protestant Psychology, in: Early Science and Medicine 19, 4 (2014), pp. 341–364, URL: <https://doi.org/10.1163/15733823-00194p03> (18 Aug 2022).

CLASSEN, Albrecht, Der Liebes- und Ehediskurs vom hohen Mittelalter bis zum frühen 17. Jahrhundert, Münster 2005, URL: <https://books.google.no/books?id=GTG3KnBDfQC> (19 Jul 2019).

CLEMEN, Otto, Bugenhagensche Trauformulare, in: Archiv für Reformationsgeschichte 3 & 4 (1905-1907), pp. 84-88.

CLEMEN, Otto, Die Luterisch Strebkatz, in: Archiv für Reformationsgeschichte 2 (1905), pp. 78-93.

COCKAYNE, Oswald (ed.), Leechdoms, Wortcunning, and Starcraft of Early England, London 1864, vol. 1.

COHEN, Jeremy, »Be Fertile and Increase, Fill the Earth and Master It«. The Ancient and Medieval Career of a Biblical Text, Ithaca 1989.

CORTRIGHT, Charles Lloyd, »Poor Maggot-Sack That I Am«. The Human Body in the Theology of Martin Luther, Marquette University 2009, URL: <https://epublications.marquette.edu/dissertations_mu/102> (18 Aug 2022).

CROWE, Michael Bertram, The Changing Profile of the Natural Law, The Hague 1977.

CROWTHER, Kathleen M., Adam and Eve in the Protestant Reformation, New York 2010.

CUNNINGHAM, Andrew, The Anatomical Renaissance. The Resurrection of the Anatomical Projects of the Ancients, London et al. 1997, URL: <https://books.google.no/books?id=sBqoDQAAQBAJ&printsec=frontcover&hl=no#v=onepage&q&f=false> (18 Aug 2022).

CZAIKA, Otfried, A Vast and Unfamiliar Field. Swedish Hymnals and Hymnal-Printing in the 16th Century, in: Maria SCHOILDT et al. (eds.), Celebrating Lutheran Music. Scholarly Perspectives at the Quincentenary, Uppsala 2019, pp. 125-138.

DARYL, Charles J., Protestants and Natural Law, in: First Things (Dec 2006), pp. 33-38, URL: <https://www.proquest.com/openview/60fd7bd86fb8eba72ae01b750345ea75/1?pq-origsite=gscholar&cbl=45949> (23 Aug 2022).

DICKENS, A[rthur] G[eoffrey], The English Reformation, London ²1989.

DINGEL, Irene, Confessional Transformations from the Wittenberg Reformation to Lutheranism, in: Lutheran Quarterly 33, 1 (2019), pp. 1-25.

DRAGSETH, Jennifer Hockenbery, Martin Luther's Views on the Body, Desire, and Sexuality, in: Oxford Research Encyclopedia of Religion (Oct 2016), URL: <https://doi.org/10.1093/acrefore/9780199340378.013.354> (18 Aug 2022).

DRESCHER, D. [Heinrich], Der Reichstag zu Augsburg 1530 und das Augsburgische Glaubensbekenntnis, Kaiserslautern 1930.

ECKART, Wolfgang U., Philipp Melanchthon und die Medizin, in: Stefan RHEIN/Günter FRANK (eds.), Melanchthon und die Naturwissenschaften seiner Zeit, Sigmaringen 1998.

EIB, Maja, Der Humanismus und sein Einfluss auf das Eheverständnis im 15. Jahrhundert. Eine philosophisch-moraltheologische Untersuchung unter besonderer Berücksichtigung des frühhumanistischen Gedankenguts Albrechts von Eyb, Münster 2001.

ELERT, Werner, Morphologie des Luthertums, München 1932, vol. 2.

ERNST, Wilhelm, Gott und Mensch am Vorabend der Reformation, Leipzig 1972.

ETZKORN, Girard J., Ockham's View of the Human Passions in the Light of his Philosophical Anthropology, in: Wilhelm VOSSENKUHL/Rolf SCHÖNBERGER (eds.), Die Gegenwart Ockhams, Weinheim 1990, pp. 265-287.

EUSTERSCHULTE, Anne, Zur Rezeption von »de officiis« bei Philipp Melanchthon und im Kreis seiner Schüler, in: Anne EUSTERSCHULTE/Günter FRANK (eds.), Cicero in der frühen Neuzeit, Stuttgart-Bad Cannstatt 2018, pp. 323–362.

FARTHING, John, Thomas Aquinas and Gabriel Biel. Interpretations of St. Thomas Aquinas in German Nominalism on the Eve of the Reformation, Durham 1988.

FISCH, Thomas/David G. HUNTER, Echoes of the Early Roman Nuptial Blessing. Ambrosiaster, De Peccato Adæ Et Evæ, in: Ecclesia Orans 11, 2 (1994), pp. 225–244, URL: <http://search.ebscohost.com/login.aspx?direct=true&db=lsdah&AN=ATLAiBCA170327000129&site=ehost-live> (11 Oct 2021).

FLÜCHTER, Antje, Der Zölibat zwischen Devianz und Norm. Kirchenpolitik und Gemeindealltag in den Herzogtümern Jülich und Berg im 16. und 17. Jahrhundert, Köln et al. 2006.

FLÜCKIGER, Felix, Geschichte des Naturrechtes, Zürich 1954, vol. 1.

FORELL, George W., Luther's Conception of Natural Orders, in: Word and World Supplement Series 2 (1994), pp. 66–82.

FRANK, Günter, Einleitung, in: Philipp Melanchthon, Ethicae Doctrinae Elementa, edited by Günter FRANK and Michael BEYER, Stuttgart-Bad Cannstatt 2008.

FRANK, Günter (ed.), Philipp Melanchthon. Der Reformator zwischen Glauben und Wissen. Ein Handbuch, Göttingen 2017.

FRANZEN, August, Zölibat und Priesterehe in der Auseinandersetzung der Reformationszeit und der katholischen Reform des 16. Jahrhunderts, Münster 1971.

FRAUENKNECHT, Erwin, Die Verteidigung der Priesterehe in der Reformzeit, Hannover 1997.

FRENCH, Roger, Medicine Before Science. The Rational and Learned Doctor from the Middle Ages to the Enlightenment, Cambridge 2003.

FRITZSCHE, Tina/Nicole PAGELS, Das evangelische Pfarrhaus. Ein Haus zwischen Himmel und Erde, Hamburg 2013, URL: <https://books.google.no/books?id=6Z13jBtVmcIC> (19 Jul 2019).

FUDGE, Thomas A., Incest and Lust in Luther's Marriage. Theology and Morality in Reformation Polemics, in: Sixteenth Century Journal 34, 2 (Summer 2003), pp. 319–345, URL: <https://www.jstor.org/stable/20061412> (7 May 2019).

GALLUS, Tibor, »Der Nachkomme der Frau« (Gen 3,15) in der Altlutheranischen Schriftauslegung, Klagenfurt 1964.

GAUSE, Ute, Durchsetzung neuer Männlichkeit. Ehe und Reformation, in: Evang. Theol. 73, 5 (2013), pp. 326–338, URL: <https://doi.org/10.14315/evth-2013-73-5-326> (18 Aug 2022).

GAUSE, Ute, Reformation und Körperlichkeit am Beispiel von Luthers Genesisvorlesung, in: Evang. Theol. 78, 1 (2018), pp. 41–48, URL: <http://ejournals.ebsco.com/Article.asp?ContributionID=44876818> (18 Aug 2022).

GRANE, Leif, Contra Gabrielem. Luthers Auseinandersetzung mit Gabriel Biel in der Disputatio Contra Scholasticam Theologiam 1517, Gyldendal 1962.

GRANE, Leif, Lutherforschung und Geistesgeschichte. Auseinandersetzung mit Heiko A. Oberman, in: Archiv für Reformationsgeschichte 68 (1977), pp. 302–315.

GRANT, Edward, The Nature of Natural Philosophy in the Late Middle Ages, Washington, D.C. 2010, URL: <https://doi.org/10.2307/j.ctt284vbb> (23 Aug 2022).

GREENE, Robert, Instinct of Nature. Natural Law, Synderesis, and the Moral Sense, in: Journal of the History of Ideas 58, 2 (1997), pp. 173–198, URL: <https://doi:10.1353/jhi.1997.0014> (11 Oct 2021).

GRELL, Ole Peter, Medicine and Religion in Sixteenth-Century Europe, in: Peter ELMER (ed.), The Healing Arts. Health, Disease and Society in Europe 1500–1800, Manchester 2004, pp. 84–107.

GRIMM, Robert, Luther et l'experience sexuelle. Sexe, célibat, mariage chez le réformateur, Genève 1999.

GROBIEN, Gifford, A Lutheran Understanding of Natural Law in the Three Estates, in: Concordia Theological Quarterly 73 (2009), pp. 211–229, URL: <http://www.ctsfw.net/media/pdfs/GrobienALutheranUnderstandingOfNaturalLaw.pdf> (18 Aug 2022).

GUMMELT, Volker, Elisabeth Cruciger, geb. von Meseritz, in Pommern und Wittenberg. Anmerkungen zu Stationen ihres Lebens, in: Armin KOHNLE/Irene DINGEL (eds.), Die Crucigers. Caspar der Ältere, Caspar der Jüngere und Elisabeth Cruciger in ihrer Bedeutung für die Wittenberger Reformation, Leipzig 2021, pp. 291–302.

GÜNTHER, Hartmut O., Die Entwicklung der Willenslehre Melanchthons in der Auseinandersetzung mit Luther und Erasmus, Erlangen 1963, URL: <https://books.google.no/books?id=j_5NAQAAIAAJ&printsec=frontcover&hl=no#v=onepage&q&f=false> (18 Aug 2022).

HÄGGLUND, Bengt, De Homine. Människouppfattningen i Äldre Luthersk Tradition, Lund 1959.

HAMM, Berndt, The Early Luther. Stages in a Reformation Reorientation, translated by Martin J. Lohrmann, Grand Rapids 2014.

HANKINSON, R.J., Galen's Anatomy of the Soul, in: Phronesis 36, 2 (1991), pp. 197–233, URL: <https://www.jstor.org/stable/4182386> (5 Dec 2018).

HARRINGTON, Joel F., Reordering Marriage and Society in Reformation Germany, Cambridge et al. 1995.

HATTENHAUER, Hans, Luthers Bedeutung für die Ehe und Familie, in: Hartmut LÖWE/Claus-Jürgen ROEPFE (eds.), Luther und die Folgen. Beiträge zur sozial-geschichtlichen Bedeutung der lutherischen Reformation, München 1983, pp. 86–109.

HAUSTEIN, Jörg, Martin Luthers Stellung zum Zauber- und Hexenwesen, Stuttgart et al. 1990.

HECKEL, Johannes, Lex Charitatis. Eine juristische Untersuchung über das Recht in der Theologie Martin Luthers, edited by Martin HECKEL, Köln 1973.

HEINRICHS, Erik A., Plague, Print, and the Reformation. The German Reform of Healing, 1473–1573, London 2018.

HEINSOHN, Gunnar/Otto STEIGER, Die Vernichtung der Weisen Frauen. Beiträge zur Theorie und Geschichte von Bevölkerung und Kindheit, Herbstein ⁴1985.

HELM, Jürgen, Die »Spiritus« in der medizinischen Tradition und in Melanchthons »Liber de anima«, in: Stefan RHEIN/Günter FRANK (eds.), Melanchthon und die Naturwissenschaften seiner Zeit, Sigmaringen 1998, pp. 219–237.

HELM, Jürgen, Galen-Rezeption im 16. Jahrhundert am Beispiel Philipp Melanchthons, in: Europäische Geschichte Online (EGO) (2010), published by the Leibniz Institute of European History (IEG), URL: <http://www.ieg-ego.eu/helmj-2010-de> (17 Dec 2018).

HELM, Jürgen, Medizin, in: Günter FRANK (ed.), Philipp Melanchthon. Der Reformator zwischen Glauben und Wissen. Ein Handbuch, Göttingen 2017, pp. 507–513.

HELM, Jürgen, Religion and Medicine. Anatomical Education at Wittenberg and Ingolstadt, in: Jürgen HELM/Annette WINKELMANN (eds.), Religious Confessions and the Sciences in the Sixteenth Century, Leiden 2001, pp. 51–68.

HENDRIX, Scott, Luther on Marriage, in: Timothy J. WENGERT (ed.), Harvesting Martin Luther's Reflections on Theology, Ethics, and the Church, Grand Rapids 2004, pp. 169–184.

HENDRIX, Scott H., Masculinity and Patriarchy in Reformation Germany, in: Scott HENDRIX (ed.), Masculinity in the Reformation Era, Kirksville, MO 2008, pp. 71–91.

HENLICKY, Paul R., The Redemption of the Body. Luther on Marriage, in: Paul R. HENLICKY (ed.), Luther and the Beloved Community. A Path for Christian Theology after Christendom, Grand Rapids 2010, pp. 179–218.

HEPPE, Heinrich, Ursprung und Geschichte der Bezeichnungen »reformirte« und »lutherische« Kirche, Gotha 1859.

HERMANN, Rudolf, Studien zur Theologie Luthers und des Luthertums. Gesammelte und nachgelassene Werke, edited by Horst BEINTKER, Göttingen 1981, vol. 2.

HIEBSCH, Sabine, Figura ecclesiae. Lea und Rachel in Luthers Genesispredigten, Münster 2002.

HILLER, Joseph Anthony, Albrecht von Eyb, Medieval Moralist, Washington, D.C. 1939.

HIMES, Norman E., Medical History of Contraception, New York 1970.

HOFHEINZ, Ralf-Dieter, Philipp Melanchthon und die Medizin im Spiegel seiner akademischen Reden, Herbolzheim 2001.

HUNTER, David G., Helvidius, Jovinian, and the Virginity of Mary in Late Fourth-Century Rome, in: Journal of Early Christian Studies 1, 1 (Spring 1993), pp. 47–71.

HUNTER, David G., Marriage, Celibacy, and Heresy in Ancient Christianity. The Jovinianist Controversy, in: Oxford Scholarship Online (May 2007), URL: <https://doi.org/10.1093/acprof:oso/9780199279784.001.0001> (18 Aug 2022).

HUNTER, David G. (ed./tr.), Marriage in the Early Church, Eugene, OR 2001.

HUNTER, David G., »On the Sin of Adam and Eve«. A Little-Known Defense of Marriage and Childbearing by Ambrosiaster, in: The Harvard Theological Review 82, 3 (1989), pp. 283–299, URL: <http://www.jstor.org/stable/1510079> (21 May 2021).

HYMA, Albert, Erasmus and the Sacrament of Marriage, in: Archiv für Reformatorischegeschichte 48 (1957), pp. 145–164.

IMMENKÖTTER, Herbert, Die Confutatio der Confessio Augustana vom 3. August 1530, Münster 1979.

JANZ, Denis R., Luther on Thomas Aquinas. The Angelic Doctor in the Thought of the Reformer, Stuttgart 1989.

JUNTUNEN, Sammeli, Sex, in: Olli-Pekka VAINIO (ed.), Engaging Luther. A New Theological Assessment, Eugene, OR 2010, URL: <https://books.google.no/books?id=H4BJAwAAQBAJ> (19 July 2019).

JÜTTE, Robert, Die Persistenz des Verhütungswissens in der Volkskultur. Sozial- und medizinhistorische Anmerkungen zur These von der »Vernichtung der weisen Frauen«, in: Medizinhistorisches Journal 24, 3/4 (1989), pp. 214–231, URL: <https://www.jstor.org/stable/25803986> (18 Aug 2022).

JÜTTE, Robert, Lust ohne Last. Geschichte der Empfängnisverhütung von der Antike bis zur Gegenwart, Munich 2003.

KARANT-NUNN, Susan C./Merry E. WIESNER-HANKS, Luther on Women. A Sourcebook, Cambridge 2003.

KAUFMANN, Thomas, An den christlichen Adel deutscher Nation von des christlichen Standes Besserung. Kommentare zu Schriften Luthers, Tübingen 2014.

KAUFMANN, Thomas. Der Anfang der Reformation. Studien zur Kontextualität der Theologie, Publizistik und Inszenierung Luthers und der reformatorischen Bewegung, Tübingen 2012.

KAUFMANN, Thomas, Ehetheologie im Kontext der frühen Wittenberger Reformation, in: Ines WEBER/Andreas HOLZEM (eds.), Ehe – Familie – Verwandtschaft. Vergesellschaftung in Religion und sozialer Lebenswelt, München 2008, pp. 285–299.

KAUFMANN, Thomas, Spangenberg, Johann, in: Neue Deutsche Biographie 24 (2010), pp. 622f., URL: <https://www.deutsche-biographie.de/pnd123624878.html#ndbcontent> (19 Jul 2019).

KAWERAU, Waldemar, Die Reformation und die Ehe. Ein Beitrag zur Kulturgeschichte des sechzehnten Jahrhunderts, Halle 1892.

KELLER, Walter, Zölibat und Priesterehe als reformatorische Anliegen auf dem Reichstag zu Augsburg 1530, in: Würzburger Diözesangeschichtsblätter 58 (1996), pp. 153–170.

KINDER, Ernst, Luthers Auffassung von der Ehe, in: Ernst SOMMERLATH/Ernst-Heinz AMBERG (eds.), Bekenntnis zur Kirche. Festgabe für Ernst Sommerlath, Berlin 1960, pp. 325–334.

KLAWITTER, Brandt, A Forceful and Fruitful Verse. Textual and Contextual Studies on Genesis 1:28 in Luther and the Wittenberg Reformation (1521–1531), Oslo 2019.

KLAWITTER, Brandt, Where Laws, Sexes, and Bodies Converge. Discussions of Sex and Gender in Church and Natural Law (ca. 1140–1234), in: Zeitschrift für Kirchengeschichte 132, 1 (2021), pp. 16–32.

KLINNERT, Lars, »Verheißung und Verantwortung. Die Entwicklung der Naturrechtslehre Philipp Melanchthons zwischen 1521 und 1535, in: Kerygma u. Dogma 50 (2004), pp. 25–56.

KLUXEN, Wolfgang, Lex naturalis bei Thomas von Aquin, Wiesbaden 2001.

KOBLER, Beate, Die Entstehung des negativen Melanchthonbildes. Protestantische Melanchthonkritik bis 1560, Tübingen 2014.

KOCH, Hans-Theodor, Melanchthon und die Vesal-Rezeption in Wittenberg, in: Stefan RHEIN/Günter FRANK, Melanchthon und die Naturwissenschaften seiner Zeit, Sigmaringen 1998.

KOHLMEYER, D. Ernst, Die Entstehung der Schrift Luthers An den christlichen Adel deutscher Nation, Gütersloh 1922.

KOLB, Robert, Models of the Christian Life in Luther's Genesis Sermons and Lectures, in: Lutherjahrbuch 76 (2009), pp. 193–220.

KOLB, Robert, Spangenberg, Johann and Cyriacus, in: Timothy J. WENGERT et al., Dictionary of Luther and the Lutheran Traditions, Grand Rapids, MI 2017, pp. 1059–1060, URL: <https://books.google.no/books?id=i9HlDQAAQBAJ> (19 July 2019).

KOLB, Robert, The Theology of Justus Jonas, in: Irene DINGEL (ed.), Justus Jonas (1493–1555) und seine Bedeutung für die Wittenberger Reformation, Leipzig 2009, pp. 103–120.

KÖNNEKER, Barbara, Die deutsche Literatur der Reformationszeit. Kommentar zu einer Epoche, München 1975.

KRETSCHMAR, Georg, Luthers Konzeption von der Ehe. Die Liebe im Spannungsfeld von Eros und Agape, in: Peter MANNS (ed.), Martin Luther »Reformator und Vater im Glauben«, Stuttgart 1985, pp. 187–207.

KROEGER, Matthias, Das Augsburger Bekenntnis in seiner Sozial- und Wirkungsgeschichte, in: Bernhard LOHSE/Otto Hermann PESCH (eds.), Das Augsburger Bekenntnis von 1530 damals und heute, München 1980, pp. 99–124.

KRÜGER, Sabine, Zum Verständnis der Oeconomia Konrads von Megenberg. Griechische Ursprünge der spätmittelalterlichen Lehre vom Haus, in: Deutsches Archiv für Erforschung des Mittelalters 20 (1964), pp. 475–561, URL: <https://resolver.sub.uni-goettingen.de/purl?PPN345858735_0020> (18 Aug 2022).

KUROPKA, Nicole, Philip Melanchthon and Aristotle, in: Irene DINGEL et al. (eds.), Philip Melanchthon. Theologian in Classroom, Confession, and Controversy, Göttingen 2012, pp. 19–28.

KUSUKAWA, Sachiko, The Medical Renaissance of the Sixteenth Century. Vesalius, Medical Humanism and Bloodletting, in: Peter ELMER (ed.), The Healing Arts. Health, Disease and Society in Europe 1500–1800, Manchester 2004, pp. 58–83.

KUSUKAWA, Sachiko, Medicine in Western Europe in 1500, in: Peter ELMER (ed.), The Healing Arts. Health, Disease and Society in Europe 1500–1800, Manchester 2004, pp. 1–26.

KUSUKAWA, Sachiko, The Natural Philosophy of Melanchthon and His Followers, in: École Française de Rome (ed.), Sciences et religions de Copernic à Galilée, (1540–1610), Rome 1999, pp. 443–453, URL: <http://digital.casalini.it/10.1400/36916> (18 Aug 2022).

KUSUKAWA, Sachiko, The Transformation of Natural Philosophy, Cambridge 1995.

KUSUKAWA, Sachiko, A Wittenberg University Library Catalogue of 1536, Cambridge 1995.

KUTTNER, Stephan, Gratian and the Schools of Law, 1140–1234, London et al. ²2018, Vital-Source Bookshelf, URL: <https://doi.org/10.4324/9781351058957> (18 Aug 2022).

LÄHTEENMÄKI, Olavi, Sexus und Ehe bei Luther, Turku 1955.

LANDAU, Peter, Gratian and the Decretum Gratiani, in: William HARTMANN/Kenneth PENNINGTON (eds.), The History of Medieval Canon Law in the Classical Period, 1140–1234. From Gratian to the Decretals of Pope Gregory IX, Washington, D.C. 2008, pp. 22–54, URL: <http://search.ebscohost.com/login.aspx?direct=true&db=nlebk&AN=360295&site=ehost-live> (23 Apr 2020).

LAU, Franz, »Äußerliche Ordnung« und »Weltlich Ding« in Luthers Theologie, Göttingen 1933.

LAUBE, Adolf, Das Gespann Cochlaeus/Dietenberger im Kampf gegen Luther, in: Archiv für Reformationsgeschichte (1996), pp. 119–135.

LEHMANN, Martin, Justus Jonas, Loyal Reformer, Minneapolis 1963.

LEUNISSEN, Mariska, Explanation and Teleology in Aristotle's Science of Nature, Cambridge 2010, URL: <https://doi.org/10.1017/CBO9780511762499> (18 Aug 2022).

LEUNISSEN, Mariska/Allan GOTTHELF, »What's Teleology Got To Do With It?« A Reinterpretation of Aristotle's »Generation of Animals« V, in: Phronesis 55, 4 (2010), pp. 325–356, URL: <https://www.jstor.org/stable/41057449> (5 Dec 2018).

LINDSTRÖM, Henning, Skapelse och Frälsing i Melanchthons Teologi, Stockholm 1944.

LÖFGREN, David, Die Theologie der Schöpfung bei Luther, Göttingen 1960.

LOHSE, Bernhard, Luthers Kritik am Mönchtum, in: Evang. Theol. 20 (1960), pp. 413–432.

LOHSE, Bernhard, Mönchtum und Reformation, Göttingen 1963.

MATTHIAS, Markus, Das Verhältnis von Ehe und Sexualität bei Luther und in der lutherischen Orthodoxie, in: Wolfgang BREUEL/Christian SOBOTH (eds.), »Der Herr wird seine Herrlichkeit an uns offenbaren«. Liebe, Ehe und Sexualität im Pietismus, Wiesbaden 2011, pp. 19–50.

MATTOX, Mickey Leland, Defender of the Most Holy Matriarchs. Martin Luther's Interpretation of the Women of Genesis in the Enarrationes in Genesin, 1535–45, Leiden et al. 2003.

MAURER, Wilhelm, Der junge Melanchthon zwischen Humanismus und Reformation, Göttingen 1967, 2 vols., vol. 2.

MAURER, Wilhelm, Historischer Kommentar zur Confessio. Einleitung und Ordnungsfragen, Gütersloh 1976, 2 vols., vol. 1.

MAURER, Wilhelm, Luthers Lehre von den drei Hierarchien und ihr mittelalterlicher Hintergrund, München 1970.

MAXFIELD, John A., Luther's Lectures on Genesis and the Formation of Evangelical Identity, Kirksville, MO 2008.

MCEWAN, Dorothea, Das Wirken des Vorarlberger Reformators Bartholomäus Bernhardi, Dornbirn 1986.

MCKEOWN, John, God's Babies. Natalism and Bible Interpretation in Modern America, Cambridge 2014, URL: <http://dx.doi.org/10.11647/OBP.0048> (19 July 2019).

McLaren, Angus, A History of Contraception. From Antiquity to the Present Day, Oxford et al. 1992.

McNeill, John T., Natural Law in the Thought of Luther, in: Church History 10, 3 (1941), pp. 211–227, URL: <https://doi.org/10.2307/3160251> (23 Aug 2022).

Messing, Michael, Fatal Discord. Erasmus, Luther, and the Fight for the Western Mind, New York 2018, Kindle edition.

Mikkola, Sini, »In Our Body the Scripture Becomes Fulfilled«. Gendered Bodiliness and the Making of the Gender System in Martin Luther's Anthropology (1520–1530), Helsinki 2017, URL: <https://helda.helsinki.fi/handle/10138/228638> (11 Oct 2021).

Moeller, Bernd, Das Reich und die Kirche in der frühen Reformationszeit, in: Bernhard Lohse/Otto Hermann Pesch (eds.), Das Augsburger Bekenntnis von 1530 damals und heute, München 1980, pp. 17–31.

Moeller, Bernd, Wenzel Lincks Hochzeit. Über Sexualität, Keuschheit und Ehe in der frühen Reformation, in: Zeitschrift für Theologie und Kirche 97, 3 (2000), pp. 317–342, URL: <http://www.jstor.org/stable/23585758> (23 Aug 2022).

Molin, Jean-Baptiste/Protais Mutembe, Le ritual du mariage en France du XIIe au XVIe siècle, Paris 1974.

Montgomery, John W., The Suicide of Christian Theology, Minneapolis 1970.

Mühlen, Karl-Heinz zur, Melanchthons Auffassung vom Affekt in den »Loci communes« von 1521, in: Karl-Heinz zur Mühlen, Reformatorische Prägungen. Studien zur Theologie Martin Luthers und zur Reformationszeit, edited by Athina Lexutt and Volkmar Ortmann, Göttingen 2011, pp. 84–95.

Mühlpfordt, Günter, Das Natürliche bei Martin Luther, in: Wolfram Kaiser/Arina Völker (eds.), Medizin und Naturwissenschaften in der Wittenberger Reformationsära, Bernburg 1982, pp. 203–240.

N.N., Wie Doctor Martinus Luther Caspar Creutziger und Elisabeth von Meßeritz Dienstag vor Viti vor der Pfarrkirchen zu Wittenberg zusamen gegeben hat, in: Hallisches patriot. Wochenblatt (3. December 1835), pp. 1530f., URL: <https://books.google.no/books?id=Lr9DAAAAYAAJ> (17 Apr 2018).

Nielsen, Karen M., The Private Parts of Animals. Aristotle on the Teleology of Sexual Difference, in: Phronesis 53, 4/5 (2008), pp. 373–405, URL: <https://www.jstor.org/stable/40387968> (3 Dec 2018).

Nigg, Walter, Das Buch der Ketzer, Zürich 1949.

Nürnberger, Richard, Die lex naturae als Problem der vita christiana bei Luther, in: Archiv für Reformationsgeschichte 37, 1 (1938), pp. 1–12.

Nutton, Vivian, Wittenberg Anatomy, in: Ole Peter Grell/Andrew Cunningham (eds.), Medicine and the Reformation, New York 2001, pp. 11–32, URL: <https://books.google.no/books?id=9sN5133IBjYC&printsec=frontcover&hl=no#v=onepage&q=f=false> (18 Aug 2022).

O'Connor, D.J., Aquinas and Natural Law, London 1969.

OBERMAN, Heiko, The Harvest of Medieval Theology. Gabriel Biel and Late Medieval Nominalism, Cambridge 1963.

OBERMAN, Heiko, Reformation. Epoche oder Episode, in: Archiv für Reformationsgeschichte 68 (1977), pp. 56–109.

OLSSON, Herbert, Schöpfung, Vernunft und Gesetz in Luthers Theologie, Uppsala 1971.

OVERFIELD, James H., Humanism and Scholasticism in Late Medieval Germany, Princeton 1984.

PARISH, Helen L., Clerical Celibacy in the West, c. 1100–1700, Ashgate 2010.

PARISH, Helen L., Clerical Marriage and the English Reformation. Precedent Policy and Practice, New York 2017, URL: <https://books.google.no/books?id=UkUrDwAAQBAJ> (24 Feb 2019).

PARSONS, Michael, Reformation Marriage, Eugene, OR 2005.

PAUL VI (Pope), Über die Geburtenregelung. Rundschreiben »Humanae vitae« »Vom menschlichen Leben«, Leutesdorf am Rhein 1968.

PEARSON, Thomas D., Luther's Pragmatic Appropriation of the Natural Law Tradition, in: Roland Cap EHLKE/Robert C. BAKER (eds.), Natural Law. A Lutheran Reappraisal, St. Louis 2011, pp. 39–64.

PEASE, Arthur Stanley, Caeli Enarrant, in: Harvard Theological Review 34, 3 (1941), pp. 163–200, URL: <https://doi.org/10.1017/S0017816000022537> (23 Aug 2022).

PENNINGTON, Kenneth, The Decretalists 1190 to 1234, in: William HARTMANN/Kenneth PENNINGTON (eds.), The History of Medieval Canon Law in the Classical Period, 1140-1234. From Gratian to the Decretals of Pope Gregory IX, Washington, D.C. 2008, pp. 211–245, URL: <http://search.ebscohost.com/login.aspx?direct=true&db=nlebk&AN=360295&site=ehost-live> (23 April 2020).

PENNINGTON, Kenneth/Wolfgang P. MÜLLER, The Decretists. The Italian School, in: William HARTMANN/Kenneth PENNINGTON (eds.), The History of Medieval Canon Law in the Classical Period, 1140-1234. From Gratian to the Decretals of Pope Gregory IX, Washington, D.C. 2008, pp. 121–173, URL: <http://search.ebscohost.com/login.aspx?direct=true&db=nlebk&AN=360295&site=ehost-live> (23 April 2020).

PETERS, Christian, Apologia Confessionis Augustanae. Untersuchungen zur Textgeschichte einer lutherischen Bekenntnisschrift (1530–1584), Stuttgart 1997.

PETERS, Christian, Johann Eberlin von Günzburg ca. 1465–1533. Franziskanischer Reformer, Humanist und konservativer Reformator, Gütersloh 1994.

PETTEGREE, Andrew, The Legion of the Lost. Recovering the Lost Books of Early Modern Europe, in: Flavia BRUNI/Andrew PETTEGREE (eds.), Lost Books. Reconstructing the Print World of Pre-industrial Europe, Leiden 2016, pp. 1–27.

PILVOUSEK, Josef, Martin Luther und Erfurt, in: Josef FREITAG (ed.), Luther in Erfurt und die katholische Theologie, Leipzig 2001, pp. 13–27.

PLUMMER, Marjorie Elizabeth, From Priest's Whore to Pastor's Wife. Clerical Marriage and the Process of Reform in the Early German Reformation, Farnham, England et al. 2012.

PLUMMER, Marjorie Elizabeth, The Much Married Michael Kramer. Evangelical Clergy and Bigamy in Ernestine Saxony, 1522–1542, in: Marjorie E. PLUMMER/Robin B. BARNES (eds.), Ideas and Cultural Margins in Early Modern Germany. Essays in Honor of H.C. Erik Midelfort, Aldershot, Hambleton 2009, URL: <https://digitalcommons.wku.edu/cgi/viewcontent.cgi?article=1023&context=history_fac_pubs> (19 Jul 2019).

PLUMMER, Marjorie Elizabeth, Reforming the Family. Marriage, Gender and the Lutheran Household in Early Modern Germany, 1500–1620, Charlottesville, University of Virginia 1996.

PORTER, Jean, Natural & Divine Law. Reclaiming the Tradition for Christian Ethics, Grand Rapids 1999.

PORTER, Jean, Natural Law as a Scriptural Concept. Theological Reflections on a Medieval Theme, in: Theology Today (Jan 2002), pp. 226–243, URL: <https://doi.org/10.1177/004057360205900205> (23 Aug 2022).

PRESCOTT, Anne Lake, Musical Strains. Marot's Double Role as Psalmist and Courtier, in: Marie-Rose LOGAN/Peter L. RUDNYTSKY (eds.), Contending Kingdoms. Historical, Psychological, and Feminist Approaches to the Literature of Sixteenth-Century England and France, Detroit 1991, pp. 42–68.

RAATH, A[ndries], Moral-Jural Reflections on the Right to Marital Dignity and the »Nursery of Human Society«. Interpreting Luther's Views on Conjugal Rights and Benevolent Love, in: Koers – Bulletin for Christian Scholarship 73, 3 (2008), pp. 411–443, URL: <https://doi.org/10.4102/koers.v73i3.168> (18 Aug 2022).

RADDING, Charles/Francis NEWTON, Theology, Rhetoric, and Politics in the Eucharistic Controversy, 1078–1079. Alberic of Monte Cassino Against Berengar of Tours, New York 2003, URL: <https://books.google.no/books?id=Oxpiji7UovcC> (4 Jul 2019).

RAUNIO, Antti, Divine and Natural Law in Luther and Melanchthon, in: Virpi MÄKINEN (ed.), Lutheran Reformation and the Law, Boston 2006.

RAUNIO, Antti, Summe des christlichen Lebens, Mainz 2001.

RENNIE, Kriston R., Medieval Canon Law, Leeds 2018, Digital Edition, URL: <https://doi.org/10.1515/9781942401698> (23 Aug 2022).

REU, Johann Michael, The Augsburg Confession. A Collection of Sources with a Historical Introduction, Chicago 1930.

REYNOLDS, Philip L., How Marriage Became One of the Sacraments. The Sacramental Theology of Marriage from Its Medieval Origins to the Council of Trent, Cambridge 2016.

REYNOLDS, Philip Lyndon, Marriage in the Western Church. The Christianization of Marriage during the Patristic and Early Medieval Periods, Leiden et al. 1994.

RICŒUR, Paul, What Is a Text? Explanation and Understanding, in: John B. THOMPSON (ed.), Hermeneutics and the Human Sciences. Essays on Language, Action, and Interpretation, Cambridge et al. 1981, pp. 145–164.

RIDDLE, John M., Contraception and Abortion from the Ancient World to the Renaissance, Cambridge 1992.

Ritzer, Korbinian, Formen, Riten und religiöses Brauchtum der Eheschliessung in den christlichen Kirchen des ersten Jahrtausends, Münster ²1981.

Roper, Lyndal, Oedipus & the Devil. Witchcraft, Sexuality and Religion in Early Modern Europe, London et al. 2013.

Rüttgardt, Antje, Klosteraustritte in der frühen Reformation. Studien zu Flugschriften der Jahre 1522 bis 1524, Gütersloh 2007.

Salatowsky, Sascha, Die aristotelische Psychologie bei Luther und Melanchthon. De Anima. Rezeption der aristotelischen Psychologie im 16. und 17. Jahrhundert, Amsterdam 2006, URL: <https://books.google.no/books?id=EY06AAAAQBAJ&printsec=frontcover#v=onepage&q&f=false> (23 Aug 2022).

Scattola, Merio, Das Naturrecht vor dem Naturrecht. Zur Geschichte des »ius naturae« im 16. Jahrhundert, Tübingen 1999.

Scheel, Otto (ed.), Luthers Werke, Ergänzungsbände, Berlin 1905, 2 vols., vol. 1.

Scherz, Luis Tomás, Das Naturgesetz bei Thomas von Aquin und die tentatio stoicorum. Heutige Auffassungen eines umstrittenen Begriffs, Tübingen 2006.

Schiefsky, Mark J., Galen's Teleology and Functional Explanation, edited by D. Sedley, Oxford 2007, URL: <http://nrs.harvard.edu/urn-3:HUL.InstRepos:3708554> (11 Dec 2018).

Schloemann, Martin, Natürliches und gepredigtes Gesetz bei Luther, Berlin 1961.

Schmidt, Roderich, Das historische Pommern. Personen, Orte, Ereignisse, Köln 2009.

Schofield, John, Philipp Melanchthon and the English Reformation, Burlington 2006.

Schottenloher, Karl, Johann Fabri in Rom, nach einem Berichte Jakob Zieglers, in: Archiv für Reformationsgeschichte 5 (1907/08), pp. 31–47.

Schulz, Klaus Detlev, Two Kinds of Righteousness and Moral Philosophy. Confessio Augustana XVIII, Philipp Melanchthon, and Martin Luther, in: Concordia Theological Quarterly 73 (2009), pp. 17–40, URL: <http://www.ctsfw.net/media/pdfs/SchulzTwoKindsofRighteosnessAndMoralPhilosophy.pdf> (18 Aug 2022).

Schwanke, Johannes, Creatio ex nihilo. Luthers Lehre von der Schöpfung in der Großen Genesisvorlesung aus dem Nichts (1535–1545), Berlin et al. 2004.

Schwiebert, E.G., Luther and His Times. The Reformation from a New Perspective, St. Louis 1950.

Seeberg, Reinhold, Luthers Anschauung von dem Geschlechtsleben und der Ehe und ihre geschichtliche Stellung, in: Lutherjahrbuch 7 (1925), pp. 77–122.

Simpson, Gary, »Written on their Hearts«. Thinking with Luther about Scripture, Natural Law, and the Moral Life, in: Word and World 30, 4 (2010), pp. 419–428, URL: <https://wordandworld.luthersem.edu/content/pdfs/30-4_Paul/30-4_simpson.pdf> (18 Aug 2022).

Sjöholm, Josef, Luthers Åskådning i Kampen Mot Klosterlifvet, Lund 1908 (reprinted 2012).

Skinner, Quentin, Meaning and Understanding in the History of Ideas, in: History and Theory 8, 1 (1969), pp. 3–53, URL: <https://www.jstor.org/stable/2504188> (18 Apr 19).

Sperl, Adolf, Melanchthon zwischen Humanismus und Reformation, München 1959.

SPRINGER, Carl P.E., Cicero in Heaven. The Roman Rhetor and Luther's Reformation, Leiden 2018.

STAMM, Heinz-Meinolf, Luthers Stellung zum Ordensleben, Wiesbaden 1980.

STEGMANN, Andreas, Bibliographie zur Ethik Martin Luthers, in: Lutherjahrbuch 79 (2012), pp. 305–342.

STEGMANN, Andreas, Luthers Auffassung vom christlichen Leben. Beiträge zur historischen Theologie, Tübingen 2014.

STEVENSON, Kenneth, Nuptial Blessing. A Study of Christian Marriage Rites, New York 1983.

STÖVE, Eckehart, Natürliches Recht und Heilige Schrift. Zu einem vergessenen Aspekt in Martin Luthers Hermeneutik, in: Irene DINGEL et al. (eds.), Reformation und Recht, FS G. Seebaß, Gütersloh 2002, pp. 11–25.

STRATENWERTH, Günter, Die Naturrechtslehre des Johannes Duns Scotus, Göttingen 1951.

STROHL, Jane, Luther's New View on Marriage, Sexuality and the Family, in: Lutherjahrbuch 76 (2009), pp. 159–192.

SUHR, J.S.B. (ed.), Tausens levnet. Samt nogle praedikener, Ribe 1836, URL: <https://books.google.de/books?id=-kE6AAAAcAAJ> (26 June 2019).

SUPPAN, Klaus, Die Ehelehre Martin Luthers. Theologische und rechtshistorische Aspekte des reformatorischen Eheverständnisses, Salzburg 1971.

TILLMANN, Walter, Unkeuschheit und Werk der Liebe. Diskurse über Sexualität am Beginn der Neuzeit in Deutschland, Berlin 1998.

TOELLNER, Richard, Die medizinischen Fakultäten unter dem Einfluß der Reformation, in: August BUCK (ed.), Renaissance – Reformation. Gegensätze und Gemeinsamkeiten, Wiesbaden 1984, pp. 287–297.

VETULANI, Adam, Gratien et le Droit Romain, in: Revue Historique de Droit Français et étranger Quatrième Série 24 (1946), pp. 11–48, URL: <www.jstor.org/stable/43844212> (25 May 2020).

VIDAL, Fernando, The Sciences of the Soul. The Early Modern Origins of Psychology, Chicago 2011, URL: <https://books.google.no/books?id=4SS0fcbm3xMC&printsec=frontcover#v=onepage&q&f=false> (23 Aug 2022).

VOGELSANG, Erich, Das Deutsche in Luthers Christentum, in: Lutherjahrbuch 16 (1934), pp. 92ff.

VOIGT-GOY, Christopher, Die gesellschaftlichen Stände, die Schöpfung und der Fall. Zur Ständelehre in Luthers Genesisvorlesung (1535), in: Thomas WAGNER et al. (eds.), Kontexte. Biografische und forschungsgeschichtliche Schnittpunkte der alttestamentlichen Wissenschaft. FS H.J. Boecker, Neukirchen-Vluyn 2008, pp. 65–80.

VOLZ, Carl A., The Medieval Church. From the Dawn of the Middle Ages to the Eve of the Reformation, Nashville 1997.

Vos, Antonie, The Scotian Notion of Natural Law, in: Vivarium 38, 2 (2000), pp. 197–221, URL: <https://doi.org/10.1163/156853400753621725> (23 Aug 2022).

WANDER, Karl Friedrich Wilhelm, Deutsches Sprichwörter-Lexikon. Hausschatz für das deutsche Volk, Leipzig 1870, vol. 2, URL: <https://books.google.no/books?id=fJOVDZ8_BaMC> (19 July 2019).

WEIGAND, Rudolf, Die Naturrechtslehre der Legisten und Dekretisten von Irnerius bis Accursius und von Gratian bis Johannes Teutonicus, München 1967.

WEIGAND, Rudolf, Zur Problematik des Naturrechts. Inhalt, Erkennbarkeit, Veränderlichkeit, Dispensierbarkeit, in: Rudolf WEIGAND, Liebe und Ehe im Mittelalter, Goldbach 1998, pp. 217*–241*.

WEISS, Ulman, Die frommen Bürger von Erfurt. Die Stadt und ihre Kirche im Spätmittelalter und in der Reformationszeit, Weimar 1988.

WELS, Volkhard, Melanchthons Anthropologie zwischen Theologie, Medizin und Astrologie, in: Kaspar von GREYERZ et al. (eds.), Religion und Naturwissenschaften im 16. und 17. Jahrhundert, Gütersloh 2010, pp. 51–85.

WENGERT, Timothy J. et al., Dictionary of Luther and the Lutheran Traditions, Grand Rapids, MI 2017, pp. 1059–1060, URL: <https://books.google.no/books?id=i9HlDQAAQBAJ> (19 July 2019).

WENZ, Gunther, Theologie der Bekenntnisschriften der evangelisch-lutherische Kirche, Berlin 1996, vol. 1.

WETZEL, Richard, Melanchthon und Karlstadt im Spiegel von Melanchthons Briefwechsel, in: Sigrid LOOSS/Markus MATTHIAS (eds.), Andreas Bodenstein von Karlstadt (1486–1541). Ein Theologe der frühen Reformation, Wittenberg 1998, pp. 159–222.

WIESNER-HANKS, Merry E., Christianity and Sexuality in the Early Modern World. Regulating Desire, Reforming Practice, New York 2000.

WIESNER-HANKS, Merry E., Martin Luther on Marriage and the Family, in: Oxford Research Encyclopedia of Religion (2016), URL: <https://doi.org/10.1093/acrefore/9780199340378.013.365> (18 Aug 2022).

WIESNER-HANKS, Merry E., Women and Gender in Early Modern Europe, New York 2008.

WITT, Christian Volkmar, Martin Luthers Reformation der Ehe, Tübingen 2017.

YEGERLEHNER, David Anthony, »Be Fruitful and Multiply, and Fill the Earth…«. A History of the Interpretation of Genesis 1:28a and Related Texts in Selected Periods, Boston 1975.

3. Abbreviations

Ap. Apologia Confessionis Augustanae
BHS Biblia Hebraica Stuttgartensia, Stuttgart ⁵1997.
BSELK Irene Dingel (ed.), Die Bekenntnisschriften der evangelisch-lutherischen Kirche, Göttingen 2014.
CA Confessio Augustana
CCSL Corpus Christianorum, series Latina, Steenbrugge 1954; also with a medieval continuation.
CIC(L) Corpus iuris civilis, Ed. Lipsiensis.
CR Melanchthon, Philip. Corpus Reformatorum. Opera quae supersunt omnia, in: Carolus Gottlieb Bretschneider/Heinrich Ernst Bindseil (eds.), Halle and Braunschweig 1834–1860.
CSEL Corpus scriptorium ecclesiasticorum latinorum, Vienna 1866.
LW Martin Luther, Luther's Works. American Edition, St. Louis/Philadelphia 1958–86.
Mansi J.D. Mansi et al. (eds.), Sacrorum Conciliorum Nova et Amplissima Collectio, Florence et al. 1759–1798.
MBW Heinz Scheible (ed.), Melanchthons Briefwechsel, Stuttgart-Bad Cannstatt 1977.
NKJV The Holy Bible. The New King James Version, Nashville 1988.
NPNF Philip Schaff (ed.), A Select Library of the Christian Church. Nicene and Post-Nicene Fathers, Grand Rapids, MI 1986–1989.
PG J.-P. Migne (ed.), Patrologia Graeca, Paris 1857–1886, 162 vols.
PL J.-P. Migne (ed.), Patrologiae Latina, Paris 1844–1864, 271 vols.
VD16 Verzeichnis der im deutschen Sprachbereich erschienenen Drucke des 16. Jahrhunderts, URL: <https://www.bsb-muenchen.de/sammlungen/historische-drucke/recherche/vd-16/>.
WA Martin Luther, Luthers Werke. Kritische Gesamtausgabe, Schriften, Weimar 1883–1993, 65 vols.
WA Br Martin Luther, Luthers Werke. Kritische Gesamtausgabe, Briefwechsel, Weimar 1906–1961, 18 vols.
WA Tr Martin Luther, Luthers Werke. Kritische Gesamtausgabe, Tischreden, Weimar 1912–1921, 6 vols.

4. Glossary

affectus (lat.)	*n.* passion or desire; movement or emotion arising from the heart (or other bodily organ)
Affektenlehre (ger.)	*n.* teaching about the affects
ἄστοργοι (grk.)	*adj.* lacking natural love or affection
crescite et multiplicamini (lat.)	Vulgate rendering of Genesis 1:28; »increase and multiply«
eyngepflantzt (ger.)	*adj.* implanted, innate
Flugschriften (ger.)	*n.* printed pamphlets
Gutachten (ger.)	*n.* theological opinion offered by an individual or faculty
ius naturale (lat.)	*n.* natural right or law
Kirchenordnung (ger.)	*n.* church ordinance
lex charitatis (lat.)	*n.* law of love
lex naturae (lat.)	*n.* law of nature; natural law
naturales affectus (lat.)	*n.* natural affects, natural love
Naturrecht (ger.)	*n.* natural law
seid fruchtbar und mehret euch (ger.)	German rendering of Genesis 1:28; »increase and multiply«
στοργαὶ φυσικαί (grk.)	*n.* natural affections

5. Index

5.1 Index of Names

A

Abraham   86, 141, 156, 162, 164, 168
Adam   39, 44, 45, 138, 143, 148, 151–154, 183, 186, 212
Adrian VI (pope)   140
Agricola, John   226
Alberic of Monte Cassino   39
Albertus Magnus   41
Alberus, Erasmus   239, 240
Albrecht of Mainz (archbishop)   100
Althamar, Andreas   22
Ambrose/Ambrosius   33, 35, 36, 53, 130
Ambrosiaster   36, 42, 43
Anna (countess of Torgau)   215
Anna (mother of Mary)   97
Anthony (church father)   215
Apel, Johann   157
Aquinas, Thomas   40, 41, 48, 53, 62–66, 78, 118
Aristotle   33, 51, 63, 68–74, 76, 77, 124, 169, 229, 230, 232, 246
Arnoldi von Usingen, Bartholomäus   178–185, 188–197, 224, 244, 249
Augustine, Aurelius   22, 26, 28, 33, 37, 39, 41, 42, 53, 108, 113, 130, 131, 138, 194, 197, 231, 246
Azo, Portius   53

B

Barbaro, Francesco   239
Basil of Caesarea   42
Bernhardi, Batholomäus   95, 99
Beyer, Christian   220
Biel, Gabriel   63, 65, 66
Brenz, John   226, 228
Brießmann, Johann   145
Bucer, Martin   226, 228

Bugenhagen, Johannes   22, 45, 112, 139, 153, 199, 200, 202, 203, 214, 215, 249
Burchard of Worms   54
Burckhard, Peter   74

C

Cajetan, Thomas (cardinal)   63
Calvin, John   22, 63
Campeggio, Lorenzo   223, 224
Charles V (emperor)   94, 217, 221, 223, 225, 227
Chaucer, Geoffrey   45
Chrysostom, John   28, 33, 38–42, 94, 118, 246
Cicero, Marcus Tullius   47, 48, 50–52, 69, 70, 77, 124, 246
Clement of Alexandria   34, 42, 52
Clichtove, Josse   172, 213, 248
Cochlaeus, Johann   129, 143, 144, 170, 223, 248
Corvinus, Antonius   204
Cruciger, Caspar   201, 239
Culsamer, Johann   179, 185, 188, 190–192
Cyprian (bishop of Carthage)   34

D

Dietenberger, Johann   129, 145, 170–172, 224, 248

E

Eberlin von Günzberg, Johann   94, 181
Eck, Johann   213, 218, 219, 223, 224
Elijah   194
Elisabeth von Meseritz   201
Emser, Hieronymus   90, 139
Erasistratus   71
Erasmus, Desiderius   82, 180, 213

Index

Eusebius (of Ceasarea) 34, 35
Eve 39, 44, 138, 143, 148, 153, 183, 186

F

Faber, Johann 129, 139–141, 143, 144, 150, 154, 157–163, 173, 175, 180, 186, 200, 212, 213, 223, 224, 234, 248
Ferdinand, King of Austria 212
Florentina von Oberweimar 169
Frederick the Wise (elector) 103, 186
Fuchs, Heinrich 95

G

Galen 33, 69–74, 76, 77
Gerbel, Nic 112
Gratian (canon lawyer) 55–58, 60, 246
Gregory IX (pope) 56
Gregory of Nazianzus 42

H

Helvidius 42
Henry VIII, King of England 240, 241
Herod (the Great) 119
Hincmar of Reims 44, 45
Hippocrates 74
Homer 108
Hugo of St. Victor 57
Huguccio 59, 60
Hus(s), Jan 138

I

Irenaeus of Lyon 34
Isadore of Seville 44, 57
Ivo of Chartres 54

J

Jacob 141, 238
James 171, 183
Jeremiah 135

Jerome 28, 33, 35–38, 41–43, 130, 138, 141, 156, 162, 163, 167, 194, 197, 213, 215, 218, 224, 245, 248
Jesus Christ 28, 35, 37, 45, 78, 87, 89, 91, 93, 98, 105, 107, 110, 111, 113, 114, 118, 119, 129, 131, 133, 135, 138, 139, 154, 160–162, 164, 165, 171, 172, 176, 177, 182–184, 194, 195, 199, 201–204, 212, 215, 216, 219, 222, 238
John (elector of Saxony) 204
John the Baptizer 97, 194
Jonas, Justus 29, 75, 100, 109, 139, 141, 143, 145, 146, 150, 153, 157, 158, 161, 162, 175–177, 180, 186, 191, 199, 200, 224, 226, 228, 239, 241, 248
Jovinian(us) 28, 33–37, 41, 42, 114, 138, 213, 218, 220, 225, 245

K

Kaiser, Leonhard 214
Karlstadt, Andreas (Bodenstein von) 63, 94–100, 104–107, 109, 111, 114, 117, 120, 121, 166, 179, 181, 247
Klingebeyl, Steffan 22, 215
Koppe, Leonhard 147, 175

L

Lang, Johann 109, 158, 180, 181, 185, 188, 189, 191–196
Lening, Johannes 243
Leo X (pope) 140
Linck, Wenzel 16
Lothar II 44
Luther, Martin 13–32, 38, 40, 41, 45–50, 52, 63, 66, 67, 70, 72–82, 84–96, 102–123, 127, 129–150, 152–158, 161–175, 177–183, 185, 187, 191, 199–205, 207–219, 221, 224–226, 228, 233, 235–241, 243–249

M

Maler, Matthes   180
Manasseh   108
Maria, daughter of John of Saxony   204
Mary (mother of Jesus)   37, 155
Mathesius, Johannes   204
Mechler, Aegidius   182, 185, 188–191
Melanchthon, Philipp   28–30, 47, 50, 63, 66, 67, 70, 72–76, 80, 88, 94, 100–109, 111, 112, 114, 115, 117, 121–128, 133, 139, 145, 153, 158, 159, 167, 168, 173–178, 181, 182, 191, 199, 200, 204, 205, 207, 218–221, 224–235, 239–242, 244, 245, 247–250
Menius, Justus   29, 205–210, 249
Mohamed   191
More, Thomas   22
Morot, Clèment   244
Moses   111, 159, 160, 162, 163, 205, 206, 210, 211, 238
Murner, Thomas   87–90, 94, 129, 139, 142, 143, 247, 248

N

Nicholas I (pope)   44
Noah   39, 92, 93, 138, 141, 143, 183, 186

O

Odo of Dover   59
Oldendorp, John   47
Onan   32, 76, 105
Origen   34, 35

P

Paul (apostle)   97, 98, 100, 105–108, 110, 114–117, 139, 141, 144, 164–166, 171, 172, 182, 183, 187, 194, 204, 205, 213–216, 219, 231, 239, 242
Peter (apostle)   115, 116, 154
Peter of Waldes   138
Petri, Olaus   235, 240

Philip I, Herzog of Pomerania   204
Philip of Hesse   243, 244
Pirckheimer, Willibald   213, 216
Placentinus   58
Plato   69–72
Plinius/Pliny   70, 73
Plotin   53

R

Rachel   97, 141
Radbert(us), Pascase   39
Raguel   203
Ratramnus   39
Raymond de Peñafort   56
Rebecca/Rebecka   97
Reissenbusch, Wolfgang   214, 215
Rhau-Grunenberg, Johann   120, 121
Rörer, Georg   150, 152, 155, 168, 175
Roth, Stephan   150, 152–156, 215
Rufinus   57

S

Sachs, Hans   143
Sara (wife of Tobias)   203
Sarah/Sara   97, 156
Schatzgeyer, Kaspar   145, 173, 248
Schleupner, Dominikus   215
Scotus, Duns   63–65
Simon of Bisignano   57, 59
Siricius (pope)   36
Smith, Robert   241
Spalatin, Georg   74, 103, 104, 106, 112, 201, 214, 220, 226, 228, 239
Spangenberg, Cyriacus   239
Spangenberg, Johann   238, 239
Stör, Thomas   180, 185–188, 193, 197, 249
Swaven, Peter   112

T

Tausen, Hans   207, 240, 244
Tertullian of Carthage   34, 42

Teutonicus, Johannes   56
Theutberga   44
Tobit/Tobias   43, 44, 186, 202, 203
Tuitensis, Rupertus   92, 94

U
Ülin, Oswald   107
Ulpian(us), Domitius   47, 48, 52, 53, 56–62, 64, 246

V
Virgil   108
von Alveldt, Augustin   179
von Amsdorf, Nicholaus   29, 109–111, 114, 117, 127, 199, 200

von Bora, Katherina   21, 147
von Eyb, Albrecht   83, 84
von Staupitz, Johann   68

W
William of Occam   63, 65
Wimpina, Konrad   213
Wulffer, Wolfgang   213
Wycliffe, John   192

Z
Zeiger, Balthasar   95
Ziegler, Jakob   140

5.2 Index of Places

A
Altenburg   153
Anhalt   221
Antioch   38
Augsburg   83, 84, 92, 217–219, 245

B
Bethlehem   119
Bithynia   115
Bohemia   138, 139, 184
Brandenburg   221, 239

C
Cologne   82, 172, 173
Constance   140, 219
Constantinople   229

D
Denmark   221, 240, 244
Ducal Saxony   221

E
Eisenach   103
Eisleben   169
Electoral Saxony   155, 221
England/Anglia   22, 45
Erfurt   29, 31, 73, 145, 178–182, 184, 185, 187, 196, 197, 200, 239, 249

G
Germany   140, 145, 181, 200, 207, 240

H
Hessia   221

K
Kemberg   146

L
Leipzig   140, 154, 240
Lindau   219
Lüneburg   221
Lyon   34, 45, 138

M
Mainz   100, 170
Mansfeld   239
Marburg   217
Meissen   45
Memmingen   219
Moravia   184

N
Neu-Helfta   169
Nimbschen   147
Norway   221
Nuremberg   155, 215, 219–221

R
Reutlingen   221
Rome   36, 37, 42, 86, 90, 115, 116, 140, 224

S
Scandinavia   207
Schmalkald   226, 229
Speyer   217
Strasbourg   82, 142, 179, 215, 219
Sweden   240
Switzerland   181

T
Thuringia   103, 205
Torgau   215, 217

V
Vienna   140, 213

W

Wartburg 88, 94, 95, 103, 104, 130, 167
Wittenberg 14, 15, 23, 24, 27–29, 31, 45, 47, 53, 67, 68, 70, 72–74, 81, 82, 84, 85, 94–96, 99, 100, 103, 104, 107–109, 111, 112, 114, 117, 120–123, 128, 129, 138, 139, 141, 144, 145, 147, 150, 153, 155, 158, 159, 170, 173, 175–181, 185, 187, 188, 195, 197, 199–205, 207, 213–215, 217, 218, 220, 221, 226, 228–230, 232, 238–241, 243–245, 248, 249
Worms 54, 94, 103, 143, 144, 180

5.3 Index of Scripture References

Gen 1   19, 117–120, 137, 139, 148, 159, 167–169, 171, 182, 186, 187, 194, 203, 208, 211, 212, 216, 219, 220, 222, 226, 228, 241, 243, 246
Gen 1,11   228
Gen 1,22   40, 43, 88, 90, 167
Gen 1,26–28   131, 152
Gen 1,27   21, 132, 161, 220, 221, 241
Gen 1,27–28   92, 132, 161, 163, 165, 237
Gen 1,27–31   203
Gen 1,28   13–29, 31–46, 52, 62, 66, 67, 75, 76, 79–82, 84–87, 90, 92–97, 99, 100, 102, 103, 105, 111, 114–118, 120–123, 127–133, 135–139, 142–147, 149, 150, 153–159, 162–165, 167–170, 172–179, 181–183, 185–193, 196, 197, 199–205, 207–218, 220, 221, 224, 226–228, 233, 235–241, 243–250
Gen 1,28a   13, 15
Gen 1,31   132, 136
Gen 1–2   19
Gen 1–3   24
Gen 2   21, 66, 151, 153, 167, 168, 186, 187, 195, 196, 202, 203, 208, 214, 222, 224
Gen 2,18   136, 214
Gen 3   66, 167, 201–203, 224
Gen 3,8–18 154
Gen 3,15   92, 101, 102, 125, 154, 236
Gen 3,16   154
Gen 8   149, 155
Gen 8,17 139, 155
Gen 9   149, 182, 186, 194
Gen 9,1 155, 182
Gen 9,18 39
Gen 12   168
Gen 38   96, 111

Ex 18   211

Lev 18   105
Lev 20   96

Num 30   98, 111

Ps 27,14   236
Ps 33   118
Ps 33,6   118
Ps 37,25   137
Ps 104   118
Ps 127   169, 237
Ps 128   237

Prov 18   203
Prov 18,22   136

Isa 42,3   236

Ez   218

Tob 9,10–12   43

Mt 2,1–12   119
Mt 6,25   137
Mt 6,33   137
Mt 15   191
Mt 16,18   236
Mt 19   19, 89, 133, 139, 160, 162, 172, 176, 182, 202, 214, 216, 243, 248
Mt 19,6   86, 91, 183
Mt 19,11   222

Lk 12,25   151

John 1   118
John 1,1–14   118
John 1,3   118
John 2   44, 214
John 20,2–10   212

Rom 1   232
Rom 1,31   123, 237
Rom 2   100
Rom 7,19   117
Rom 15,4   236

1 Cor   18, 202, 248
1 Cor 7   19, 22, 44, 97, 105, 107, 136, 139, 146, 158, 162, 163, 167, 171, 172, 177, 182, 194, 196, 214, 241, 248
1 Cor 7,2   216
1 Cor 7,8   216
1 Cor 7,8–9   164, 165
1 Cor 7,9   139, 176
1 Cor 7,20   170
1 Cor 9,5   216

2 Cor 11,29   108
2 Cor 12   183, 184

Gal 5,17   117

Eph 5   19, 44, 203

1 Tim 2,15   239
1 Tim 3,2   87, 215, 216
1 Tim 4   191
1 Tim 4,1–3   86, 87, 104
1 Tim 5   96, 98, 105–108, 111
1 Tim 5,9   104
1 Tim 5,11   104

Tit 1,6   87

Heb 1,2–3   118
Heb 1,3   40, 118